聞いて覚えるコーパス単熟語

キクタン
英検 準1級

一杉武史 編著

英語は聞いて覚える！
アルク・キクタンシリーズ

「読む」だけでは、言葉は決して身につきません。私たちが日本語を習得できたのは、赤ちゃんのころから日本語を繰り返し「聞いて」きたから──『キクタン』シリーズは、この「当たり前のこと」にこだわり抜いた単語集・熟語集です。「読んでは忘れ、忘れては読む」──そんな悪循環とはもうサヨナラです。「聞いて覚える」、そして「読んで理解する」、さらに「使って磨く」──英語習得の「新しい1歩」が、この1冊から必ず始まります！

Preface
英検準1級合格に必要な単語と熟語がこの1冊で完ぺきに身につきます！

過去問題を徹底分析！話題の「コーパス」が見出し語の実用性をバックアップ！

本書は、英検準1級合格に必要な単語と熟語、計1120を10週間で効率的に身につけるための語彙集です。見出し語の選定にあたっては、2004年リニューアル以降の英検準1級の全過去問題を徹底的に分析しました。そこでリストアップされた約5500の単語と熟語を、「頻出＝出る」順に1120まで絞り込んだのが本書です。

「出る」順の絞り込みに際しては、過去問題での頻出度はもちろんのこと、膨大な数の話し言葉・書き言葉を集めたデータベース、「コーパス」も参考にしています。単に英検合格に必要なだけでなく、広く日常生活で使われる単語・熟語が覚えられる――。「必要性」に加え、この「実用性」も本書の特長の1つです。

「完全にマスターする」ための仕掛けが満載！「出合いの数」が語彙習得のカギ！

こうして得られた1120の単語と熟語ですが、従来のように1回「目を通す」だけではなかなか身につきません。語彙習得のためには、「目（＝読む）」だけでなく、「耳（＝聞く）」「口（＝音読する）」も総動員した学習が不可欠です。この学習を無理・無駄なく可能にしているのが、付属の「チャンツCD」です。

本書では、1つの見出しにつき「定義」→「フレーズ」→「センテンス」での3回に加え、CD内でも3回、計6回の「出合い」が用意されています。それも1日16の見出しを最短2分で押さえられます。この「読む・聞く」に、「音読する」学習も取り入れて、英検合格だけでなく、「使える英語の習得」を目指しましょう！

Contents

**1日16単語・熟語×10週間で
英検準1級合格の1120単語・熟語をマスター！**

Chapter 1

名詞：超頻出176
Page 13 ▶ 59

- Day 1 【名詞1】
- Day 2 【名詞2】
- Day 3 【名詞3】
- Day 4 【名詞4】
- Day 5 【名詞5】
- Day 6 【名詞6】
- Day 7 【名詞7】
- Day 8 【名詞8】
- Day 9 【名詞9】
- Day 10 【名詞10】
- Day 11 【名詞11】

Chapter 2

動詞：超頻出112
Page 61 ▶ 91

- Day 12 【動詞1】
- Day 13 【動詞2】
- Day 14 【動詞3】
- Day 15 【動詞4】
- Day 16 【動詞5】
- Day 17 【動詞6】
- Day 18 【動詞7】

Chapter 3

形容詞：超頻出112
Page 93 ▶ 123

- Day 19 【形容詞1】
- Day 20 【形容詞2】
- Day 21 【形容詞3】
- Day 22 【形容詞4】
- Day 23 【形容詞5】
- Day 24 【形容詞6】
- Day 25 【形容詞7】

Chapter 4

名詞：頻出176
Page 125 ▶ 171

| Day 26 【名詞12】
| Day 27 【名詞13】
| Day 28 【名詞14】
| Day 29 【名詞15】
| Day 30 【名詞16】
| Day 31 【名詞17】
| Day 32 【名詞18】
| Day 33 【名詞19】
| Day 34 【名詞20】
| Day 35 【名詞21】
| Day 36 【名詞22】

Chapter 5

動詞：頻出112
Page 173 ▶ 203

| Day 37 【動詞8】
| Day 38 【動詞9】
| Day 39 【動詞10】
| Day 40 【動詞11】
| Day 41 【動詞12】
| Day 42 【動詞13】
| Day 43 【動詞14】

Chapter 6

形容詞：頻出112
Page 205 ▶ 235

| Day 44 【形容詞8】
| Day 45 【形容詞9】
| Day 46 【形容詞10】
| Day 47 【形容詞11】
| Day 48 【形容詞12】
| Day 49 【形容詞13】
| Day 50 【形容詞14】

Chapter 7

副詞：頻出32
Page 237 ▶ 247

| Day 51 【副詞1】
| Day 52 【副詞2】

Contents

Chapter 8

動詞句：頻出240
Page 249 ▶ 311

Day 53 【動詞句1】「動詞＋副詞［前置詞］」型1
Day 54 【動詞句2】「動詞＋副詞［前置詞］」型2
Day 55 【動詞句3】「動詞＋副詞［前置詞］」型3
Day 56 【動詞句4】「動詞＋副詞［前置詞］」型4
Day 57 【動詞句5】「動詞＋副詞［前置詞］」型5
Day 58 【動詞句6】「動詞＋副詞［前置詞］」型6
Day 59 【動詞句7】「動詞＋副詞［前置詞］」型7
Day 60 【動詞句8】「動詞＋副詞［前置詞］」型8
Day 61 【動詞句9】「動詞＋A＋前置詞＋B」型1
Day 62 【動詞句10】「動詞＋A＋前置詞＋B」型2
Day 63 【動詞句11】「動詞＋to do」「動詞＋A＋to do」型
Day 64 【動詞句12】「be動詞＋形容詞＋前置詞」型1
Day 65 【動詞句13】「be動詞＋形容詞＋前置詞」型2
Day 66 【動詞句14】「be動詞＋形容詞＋to do」型
Day 67 【動詞句15】その他

Chapter 9

形容詞句・副詞句：頻出32
Page 313 ▶ 323

| Day 68【形容詞句・副詞句1】
| Day 69【形容詞句・副詞句2】

Chapter 10

群前置詞：頻出16
Page 325 ▶ 331

| Day 70【群前置詞】

Preface
Page 3

本書の4大特長
Page 8 ▶ 9

本書とCDの利用法
Page 10 ▶ 11

Index
Page 333 ▶ 361

【記号説明】
・CD-A1：「CD-Aのトラック1を呼び出してください」という意味です。
・見出し中の［　］：言い換え可能を表します。
・見出し中の（　）：省略可能を表します。
・見出し中のA、B：語句（主に名詞・代名詞）が入ることを表します。
・見出し中のbe：be動詞が入ることを表します。be動詞は主語の人称・時制によって変化します。
・見出し中のdo：動詞が入ることを表します。
・見出し中のdoing：動名詞が入ることを表します。
・見出し中のone's：名詞・代名詞の所有格が入ることを表します。
・定義中の（　）：補足を表します。
・定義中の［　］：言い換えを表します。
・❶：発音、アクセントに注意すべき単語についています。
・❶：補足説明を表します。
・≒：同意・類義語［熟語］を表します。
・⇔：反意・反対語［熟語］を表します。

だから「ゼッタイに覚えられる」!
本書の4大特長

1
英検準1級の過去問題と コーパスデータを 徹底分析！

英検準1級に出る！ 日常生活で使える！

英検準1級のための単語・熟語集である限り、「英検準1級に出る」のは当然――。本書の目標は、そこから「実用英語」に対応できる単語・熟語力をいかに身につけてもらうかにあります。見出し語・熟語の選定にあたっては、2004年のリニューアル以降の英検準1級全過去問題に加え、最新の語彙研究から生まれたコーパス*のデータを徹底的に分析。英検準1級に合格するだけでなく、将来英語を使って世界で活躍するための土台となる単語・熟語が選ばれています。

*コーパス：実際に話されたり書かれたりした言葉を大量に収集した「言語テキスト・データベース」のこと。コーパスを分析すると、どんな単語・熟語がどのくらいの頻度で使われるのか、といったことを客観的に調べられるので、辞書の編さんの際などに活用されている。

2
「目」だけでなく 「耳」と「口」までも フル活用して覚える！

「聞く単（キクタン）」！ しっかり身につく！

「読む」だけでは、言葉は決して身につきません。私たちが日本語を習得できたのは、小さいころから日本語を繰り返し「聞いて・口に出して」きたから――この「当たり前のこと」を忘れてはいけません。本書では、音楽のリズムに乗りながら単語・熟語の学習ができる「チャンツCD」を2枚用意。「目」と「耳」から同時に単語・熟語をインプットし、さらに「口」に出していきますので、「覚えられない」不安を一発解消。読解・聴解力もダブルアップします。

『キクタン英検準1級』では、2004年のリニューアル以降の英検準1級全過去問題と、最新の語彙研究の成果であるコーパスを基に収録単語・熟語を厳選していますので、「英検準1級に出る」「日常生活で使える」ものばかりです。その上で「いかに効率的に単語・熟語を定着させるか」──このことを本書は最も重視しました。ここでは、なぜ「出る・使える」のか、そしてなぜ「覚えられる」のかに関して、本書の特長をご紹介します。

3
1日16見出し×10週間、10のチャプターの「スケジュール学習」！

ムリなくマスターできる！

「継続は力なり」、とは分かっていても、続けるのは大変なことです。では、なぜ「大変」なのか？ それは、覚えきれないほどの量の単語や熟語をムリに詰め込もうとするからです。本書では、「ゼッタイに覚える」ことを前提に、1日の学習量をあえて16見出しに抑えています。さらに、単語は品詞ごとに「頻出順」に、熟語は「表現型別」に、計10のチャプターに分けていますので、効率的・効果的に学習単語・熟語をマスターできます。

4
1日最短2分、最長でも6分の3つの「モード学習」！

挫折することなく最後まで続けられる！

今まで単語集や熟語集を手にしたときに、「1日でどこからどこまでやればいいのだろう？」と思ったことはありませんか？ 見出し語・熟語、フレーズ、例文……1度に目を通すのは、忙しいときには難しいものです。本書は、Check 1（単語・熟語＋定義）→ Check 2（フレーズ）→ Check 3（センテンス）と、3つのポイントごとに学習できる「モード学習」を用意。生活スタイルやその日の忙しさに合わせて学習量を調整できます。

生活スタイルに合わせて選べる
Check 1▶2▶3の「モード学習」
本書とCDの利用法

Check 1

該当のCDトラックを呼び出して、「英語→日本語→英語」の順に収録されている「チャンツ音楽」で見出し語・熟語とその意味をチェック。時間に余裕がある人は、太字以外の定義も押さえておきましょう。

Check 2

Check 1で「見出し語・熟語→定義」を押さえたら、その単語・熟語が含まれているフレーズをチェック。フレーズレベルで使用例を確認することで、単語・熟語の定着度が高まります。

Check 3

Check 2のフレーズレベルから、Check 3ではセンテンスレベルへとさらに実践的な例に触れていきます。ここまで学習すると、「音」と「文字」で最低6回は学習単語・熟語に触れるので、定着度は格段にアップします。

見出し語・熟語

1日の学習単語・熟語数は16です。見開きの左側に単語・熟語が掲載されています。チャンツでは上から順に単語・熟語が登場します。最初の8つが流れたら、ページをめくって次の8つに進みましょう。

チェックシート

本書に付属のチェックシートは復習用に活用してください。Check 1では見出し語・熟語の定義が身についているか、Check 2と3では訳を参照しながらチェックシートで隠されている単語・熟語がすぐに浮かんでくるかを確認しましょう。

定義

見出し語・熟語の定義が掲載されています。単語・熟語によっては複数の意味があるので、第1義以外の定義もなるべく覚えるようにしましょう。

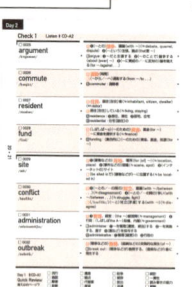

Quick Review

前日に学習した単語・熟語のチェックリストです。左ページに日本語、右ページに英語が掲載されています。時間に余裕があるときは、該当のCDトラックでチャンツも聞いておきましょう。

1日の学習量は4ページ、学習単語・熟語数は16となっています。1つの見出し語・熟語につき、定義を学ぶ「Check 1」、フレーズ中で単語・熟語を学ぶ「Check 2」、センテンス中で学ぶ「Check 3」の3つの「モード学習」が用意されています。まずは、該当のCDトラックを呼び出して、「チャンツ音楽」のリズムに乗りながら見出し語・熟語と定義を「耳」と「目」で押さえましょう。時間に余裕がある人は、Check 2とCheck 3にもトライ！

こんなアナタにオススメ！
3つの「学習モード」

> 忙しいけど
> マイペースなAさんには！

聞くだけモード
Check 1

学習時間の目安：1日2分

とにかく忙しくて、できれば単語・熟語学習は短時間で済ませたい人にオススメなのが、Check 1だけの「聞くだけモード」。該当のCDトラックで「チャンツ音楽」を聞き流すだけでもOK。でも、時間があるときはCheck 2とCheck 3で復習も忘れずに！

> おしゃれも勉強も、
> 前向きに欲張りなBさんには！

しっかりモード
Check 1 ▶ Check 2

学習時間の目安：1日4分

そこそこ英語はできるけど、さらなる英語力アップが必要だと感じている人にオススメなのが、Check 1とCheck 2を学習する「しっかりモード」。声に出してフレーズを「音読」すれば、定着度もさらにアップするはず。

> 自他ともに認める
> 完ぺき主義のCさんには！

かんぺきモード
Check 1 ▶ Check 2 ▶ Check 3

学習時間の目安：1日6分

やるからには完ぺきにしなければ気が済まない人には「かんぺきモード」がオススメ。ここまでやっても学習時間の目安はたったの6分。できればみんな「かんぺきモード」でパーフェクトを目指そう！

＊学習時間はあくまでも目安です。時間に余裕があるときは、チャンツ音楽を繰り返し聞いたり、フレーズやセンテンスの音読を重ねたりして、なるべく多く学習単語・熟語に触れるように心がけましょう。

＊CDには見出し語・熟語と定義のみが収録されています。

モバイルツールでも「キクタン英検」が学習できます。

[ダウンロード音声版]
「キクタン英検準1級:例文音声」

本書のCDには収録されていない、例文〈Check 3 : Sentence〉の音声を収録したダウンロードコンテンツです。iPodやWalkmanなどのMP3プレーヤーがあれば、例文の音声を使った発展学習で確実に単語が覚えられます。

詳しくは、以下にアクセス！
(http://www.alc.co.jp/book/onsei-dl/)

音声ダウンロードコンテンツを使った学習の
仕方をご案内しています。

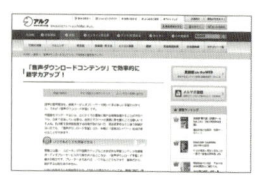

＊iTunes Store、amisoft、mora、楽天、Amazon.co.jpなど、お好きなダウンロードサイトよりお求めください。
＊各ダウンロードサイトにより、音声の形式、再生可能なプレーヤーが異なりますので、事前にご確認ください。
＊本サービスの内容は、予告なく変更する場合がございます。あらかじめご了承ください。

[iPhone・iPod touch 専用アプリ]
「キク★英検」シリーズ好評発売中！

書籍の内容をまるごと収録し、アプリならではの自動めくり機能や、
聞くだけ学習もサポート。通勤通学のお伴にも最適です。
「準2級」「2級」「準1級」「1級」発売中。

＊iTunes Store内AppStoreよりお求めください。

付属CDについて
- 弊社制作の音声CDは、CDプレーヤーでの再生を保証する規格品です。
- パソコンでご使用になる場合、CD-ROMドライブとの相性により、ディスクを再生できない場合がございます。ご了承ください。
- パソコンでタイトル・トラック情報を表示させたい場合は、iTunesをご利用ください。iTunesでは、弊社がCDのタイトル・トラック情報を登録しているGracenote社のCDDB（データベース）からインターネットを介してトラック情報を取得することができます。
- CDとして正常に音声が再生できるディスクからパソコンやMP3プレーヤー等への取り込み時にトラブルが生じた際は、まず、そのアプリケーション（ソフト）、プレーヤーの製作元へご相談ください。

CHAPTER 1

名詞：超頻出176

Chapter 1のスタートです！このChapterでは、英検準1級で「超頻出」の名詞176をマスターしていきます。先はまだまだ長いけれど、焦らず急がず学習を進めていきましょう。

Day 1 【名詞1】
▶ 14
Day 2 【名詞2】
▶ 18
Day 3 【名詞3】
▶ 22
Day 4 【名詞4】
▶ 26
Day 5 【名詞5】
▶ 30
Day 6 【名詞6】
▶ 34
Day 7 【名詞7】
▶ 38
Day 8 【名詞8】
▶ 42
Day 9 【名詞9】
▶ 46
Day 10 【名詞10】
▶ 50
Day 11 【名詞11】
▶ 54
Chapter 1 Review
▶ 58

 こんなの出たよ！

The government announced a budget ( ) of almost $25 billion for the year. Tax revenues were not adequate to cover increased spending on defense. (2009年度第1回)

1 rite　　2 deficit
3 circuit　4 slant

▼
答えはDay 9でチェック！

CHAPTER 1
CHAPTER 2
CHAPTER 3
CHAPTER 4
CHAPTER 5
CHAPTER 6
CHAPTER 7
CHAPTER 8
CHAPTER 9
CHAPTER 10

Day 1　名詞1

Check 1　Listen 》CD-A1

□ 0001
epidemic
/èpədémik/

名❶(病気などの)**流行**、蔓延(≒outbreak)　❷伝染病(≒infection, contagion, plague)　❶endemicは「風土病」、pandemicは「全国[世界]的流行病」
形(病気が)流行[伝染]性の

□ 0002
facility
/fəsíləti/

名(しばしば~ies)**施設**、設備、機関(≒institution, organization)
動facilitate:〜を促進[助成]する;〜を容易にする

□ 0003
obstacle
/ábstəkl/

名(〜に対する)**障害**(物)、邪魔(to 〜)　❶比喩的にも用いる(≒barrier, hurdle, hindrance)

□ 0004
diagnosis
/dàiəgnóusis/
❶発音注意

名**診断**　❶複数形はdiagnoses
動diagnose: (diagnose A with [as] Bで)AをBと診断する
形diagnostic: 診断(上)の

□ 0005
heritage
/héritidʒ/

名(文化的)**遺産**、伝統(≒tradition, inheritance)

□ 0006
perspective
/pərspéktiv/

名❶(〜についての)**観点**、視点(on 〜)(≒point of view, viewpoint, standpoint)　❷総括的な見方　❸遠近法

□ 0007
alternative
/ɔːltɚːrnətiv/
❶アクセント注意

名(〜の)**代替案**[手段]、代わりとなるもの(to 〜)(≒option, choice)
形代わりの;二者択一の
形alternate: ❶交互の　❷代わりの
動alternate: ❶交互に起こる　❷〜を交互にする

□ 0008
resource
/ríːsɔːrs/

名(通例〜s)**資源**;資産(≒property, fortune, asset, capital)
形resourceful: ❶臨機の才のある、機知に富んだ　❷資源に富んだ

continued
▼

いよいよDay 1のスタート！ 今日から11日間は「超頻出」の名詞176をチェック。まずはCDでチャンツを聞いてみよう！

□ 聞くだけモード　Check 1
□ しっかりモード　Check 1 ▶ 2
□ かんぺきモード　Check 1 ▶ 2 ▶ 3

CHAPTER 1

Check 2　　Phrase

□ a flu epidemic（インフルエンザの流行）
□ prevention of an epidemic（伝染病の予防）

□ a leisure facility（レジャー施設）
□ banking facilities（金融機関）

□ an obstacle to progress（進歩の妨げ）
□ overcome obstacles（障害を克服する）

□ diagnosis of breast cancer（乳がんの診断）
□ an incorrect diagnosis（誤診）

□ a World Heritage Site（世界遺産）

□ from a historical perspective（歴史的観点から）
□ keep the issue in perspective（その問題を総体的にとらえる）

□ a viable alternative（実行可能な代案）
□ have no alternative but to do ～（～するより仕方がない）

□ mineral resources（鉱物資源）
□ financial resources（金融資産）

Check 3　　Sentence

□ The AIDS epidemic began in the 1980s.（エイズの流行は1980年代に始まった）

□ There are many military facilities in this state.（この州には多くの軍事施設がある）

□ A lack of business experience is often a major obstacle to finding a job.（実務経験の不足は職探しの大きな障害になることが多い）

□ Early diagnosis is crucial for appropriate treatment.（早期の診断は適切な治療に欠かせない）

□ The city is famous for its rich cultural heritage.（その都市は豊かな文化遺産で有名だ）

□ We need to see the situation from a different perspective.（私たちは状況を別の観点から見る必要がある）

□ One alternative to raising taxes is cutting unnecessary spending.（増税に対する1つの代替案は不必要な支出を削減することだ）

□ The country is poor in natural resources.（その国は天然資源が乏しい）

CHAPTER 2
CHAPTER 3
CHAPTER 4
CHAPTER 5
CHAPTER 6
CHAPTER 7
CHAPTER 8
CHAPTER 9
CHAPTER 10

continued
▼

Day 1

Check 1 Listen)) CD-A1

☐ 0009 **dispute** /dispjúːt/
- 名 (〜間の／…についての)**紛争**；論争(between 〜/over [about] …)(≒ conflict, debate, argument, controversy)
- 動 ❶〜に反論[反対]する ❷(〜と／…について)論争[口論]する(with 〜/about [on, over] …)

☐ 0010 **tribute** /tríbjuːt/
- 名 (〜への)**賛辞**、尊敬[感謝、称賛]の印、贈り物(to 〜)(≒ praise, commendation)

☐ 0011 **emission** /imíʃən/
- 名 (熱・光・ガスなどの)**放出**、放射(≒ discharge, release)
- 動 emit：(熱・光・ガスなど)を放出[放射]する、放つ

☐ 0012 **circulation** /sèːrkjəléiʃən/
- 名 ❶(貨幣などの)**流通**(≒ distribution) ❷発行部数(≒ issue) ❸(血液の)循環
- 動 circulate：❶循環する ❷〜を循環させる ❸(うわさなどが)広がる ❹(うわさなど)を広める

☐ 0013 **statistics** /stətístiks/
- 名 **統計**
- 名 statistician：統計学者
- 形 statistical：統計(上)の

☐ 0014 **consistency** /kənsístənsi/
- 名 ❶(主義・言動などの)**一貫性**(in 〜)(⇔ inconsistency) ❷(液体などの)濃度(≒ thickness)
- 形 consistent：❶(言動などが)首尾一貫した(in 〜) ❷(成長などが)堅実な、安定した ❸(be consistent with で)(言動などが)〜と一致[調和、両立]している

☐ 0015 **literacy** /lítərəsi/
- 名 ❶**読み書きの能力**、識字能力(⇔ illiteracy) ❷(コンピューターなどの)使用能力；(特定の分野の)知識、能力
- 形 literate：❶読み書きができる ❷(特定分野の)知識[技能]がある

☐ 0016 **strategy** /strǽtədʒi/
- 名 (〜の／…するための)**戦略**、戦術(for 〜/to do)(≒ tactics)
- 名 strategist：戦略家
- 形 strategic：戦略(上)の；戦略的な
- 副 strategically：戦略上

Check 2　Phrase

- ☐ a labor dispute（労使紛争）
- ☐ be in dispute with ～（～と論争中である）

- ☐ pay tribute to ～（～に賛辞を贈る、～を称賛する）
- ☐ floral tributes（献花）

- ☐ emissions of greenhouse gases（温室効果ガスの放出）

- ☐ in circulation（流通して、出回って）
- ☐ have a daily circulation of ～（1日の発行部数が～である）

- ☐ reliable [latest] statistics（信頼できる[最新の]統計）
- ☐ release statistics（統計を発表する）

- ☐ maintain consistency（一貫性を維持する）
- ☐ the right consistency（適切な濃度）

- ☐ the literacy rate（識字率）
- ☐ computer literacy（コンピューターの使用能力）

- ☐ a sales strategy for the new product（新製品の販売戦略）
- ☐ devise a strategy（戦略を考え出す）

Check 3　Sentence

- ☐ The border dispute between the two countries is a very sensitive matter.（両国間の国境紛争は非常にデリケートな問題だ）

- ☐ The governor paid tribute to the firefighters' bravery.（知事は消防士たちの勇気ある行動に賛辞を贈った）

- ☐ Many nations are trying to reduce emissions of carbon dioxide.（多くの国が二酸化炭素の放出の削減に努めている）

- ☐ It is said that there are a lot of fake US banknotes in circulation in that country.（その国では多くの偽造米国紙幣が流通していると言われている）

- ☐ Statistics show that the domestic economy is recovering from recession.（統計によると、国内経済は景気後退から回復しつつある）

- ☐ The prime minister's foreign policy lacks consistency.（首相の外交政策は一貫性を欠いている）

- ☐ The program aims to develop literacy among pre-school children.（その計画は就学前の子どもたちの読み書きの能力を養うことを目指している）

- ☐ The government should adopt more effective strategies to prevent drug abuse.（政府は薬物乱用を防止するためのより効果的な戦略を採用すべきだ）

Day 2　名詞2

Check 1　Listen 》CD-A2

0017
disorder
/disɔ́:rdər/

名 ❶(心身機能の)**障害**、不調、病気(≒disease, illness, sickness)　❷(社会的)無秩序、混乱(≒unrest, disturbance)　❸乱雑(≒untidiness, confusion)
形 disordered：❶乱雑な、乱れた　❷病気の、不調な
形 disorderly：❶無法な、乱暴な　❷無秩序の、混乱した

0018
compensation
/kὰmpənséiʃən/

名 (〜に対する)**補償**[賠償]**金**(for 〜)(≒recompense)
動 compensate：❶(compensate forで)(損失など)の埋め合わせをする、〜を償う、補う　❷(compensate A for Bで)AにB(損害など)の賠償[補償]をする

0019
ban
/bǽn/

名 (法による)(〜の)**禁止**(on 〜)(≒prohibition)
動 ❶〜を(法的に)禁止する(≒forbid, prohibit)(⇔allow, permit)　❷(ban A from doingで)Aが〜するのを禁止する(≒forbid A to do [from doing], prohibit A from doing)

0020
petition
/pətíʃən/

名 (〜を求める／…に反対する)**請願**[嘆願]**書**(for 〜/against . . .)(≒appeal, plea, request)
動 (〜を求めて／…するよう)請願する(for 〜/to do)(≒ask, appeal, request)

0021
estimate
/éstəmət/
❶アクセント注意

名 **見積もり**、概算(≒approximation)
動 (/éstəmèit/)❶〜を見積もる　❷〜を評価する
名 estimation：❶評価、判断　❷見積もり
形 estimated：見積もりの、概算の

0022
species
/spí:ʃi:z/
❶発音注意

名 (生物の)**種**(しゅ)(≒kind, sort)　➕単複同形

0023
infrastructure
/ínfrəstrὰktʃər/
❶アクセント注意

名 **インフラ**(ストラクチャー)、基幹施設　➕道路・鉄道・通信施設・下水道・公共施設などの社会的基盤の総称

0024
congestion
/kəndʒéstʃən/

名 ❶(交通の)**渋滞**、混雑(≒jam)　❷うっ血
形 congested：❶混雑した　❷鼻が詰まった

continued ▼

チャンツを聞く際には、「英語→日本語→英語」の2回目の「英語」の部分で声に出して読んでみよう。定着度が倍増するはず！

☐ 聞くだけモード　Check 1
☐ しっかりモード　Check 1 ▶ 2
☐ かんぺきモード　Check 1 ▶ 2 ▶ 3

Check 2　Phrase

☐ eating [learning] disorder(摂食[学習]障害)
☐ throw ~ into disorder(~を混乱に陥らせる)

☐ receive $1 million in compensation for ~(~の補償金として100万ドルを受け取る)
☐ seek compensation(補償を求める)

☐ a total ban on cigarette advertising(たばこ広告の全面禁止)

☐ a petition for a new hospital(新しい病院を求める請願書)
☐ draw up a petition(請願書を作成する)

☐ a conservative [rough] estimate(控えめな[大ざっぱな]見積もり)

☐ an extinct species(絶滅種)

☐ build [develop] infrastructure(インフラを構築[整備]する)

☐ traffic congestion(交通渋滞)
☐ nasal congestion(鼻詰まり)

Check 3　Sentence

☐ The patient is suffering from a mental disorder.(その患者は精神障害を患っている)

☐ He was awarded $50,000 compensation for unfair dismissal.(彼は不当解雇に対して5万ドルの補償金を与えられた)

☐ Many people support the ban on smoking in public places.(多くの人が公共の場所での喫煙の禁止を支持している)

☐ More than 500 residents signed a petition against the construction of the dam.(500人を超える住民がそのダムの建設に反対する請願書に署名した)

☐ The cost estimate of the project is $90 million.(そのプロジェクトの経費見積もりは9000万ドルだ)

☐ The giant panda is an endangered species.(ジャイアントパンダは絶滅危惧種だ)

☐ The earthquake damaged local infrastructure.(その地震は地元のインフラに損害を与えた)

☐ Bangkok is notorious for its serious traffic congestion.(バンコクは深刻な交通渋滞で悪名高い)

continued ▼

Day 2

Check 1　Listen))) CD-A2

0025 argument
/ɑ́ːrɡjumənt/

名❶(〜との)**論争**、議論(with 〜)(≒debate, quarrel, dispute) ❷(〜という)主張、論点(that節 〜)
動argue：❶〜だと主張する ❷(〜のことで)論争する(about [over] 〜) ❸(〜に賛成の／…に反対の)論を唱える(for 〜/against . . .)

0026 commute
/kəmjúːt/

名**通勤**(時間)
動(〜から／…へ)通勤する(from 〜/to . . .)
名commuter：通勤者

0027 resident
/rézədənt/

名**住民**、居住[在住]者(≒inhabitant, citizen, dweller)(⇔visitor)
形居住[在住]している(≒living, staying)
名residence：❶居住、滞在 ❷邸宅、住宅
形residential：住宅[居住]の

0028 fund
/fʌ́nd/

名(しばしば〜s)(〜のための)**資金**、基金(for 〜)
動〜に資金を提供する(≒finance)
名funding：(集合的に)(〜のための)資金、基金、財源(for 〜)

0029 site
/sáit/

名❶(建物などの)**用地**、場所(for [of] 〜)(≒location, place) ❷(事件などの)現場(≒scene, spot) ❸(インターネットの)サイト
動(be sited inで)(建物などが)〜に位置する(≒be located in)

0030 conflict
/kánflikt/

名❶(〜との／…の間の)**対立**、葛藤(with 〜/between . . .)(≒disagreement) ❷(〜との／…の間の)争い(with 〜/between . . .)(≒struggle, fight)
動(/kənflíkt/)(〜と)対立[矛盾]する(with 〜)(≒disagree)

0031 administration
/ædmìnəstréiʃən/

名❶**管理**、経営；(the 〜)経営陣(≒management) ❷行政；(しばしばthe A〜)政権、内閣(≒government)
動administer：❶〜を管理[運営、統治]する ❷〜を実施する、施す ❸(薬など)を投与する
形administrative：❶管理[経営]の ❷行政の

0032 outbreak
/áutbrèik/

名(戦争などの)**勃発**、(疫病などの)突発的な発生(of 〜)
動break out：(戦争などが)勃発する、(疫病などが)急に発生する

Day 1　))) CD-A1
Quick Review
答えは右ページ下

☐ 流行　☐ 遺産　☐ 紛争　☐ 統計
☐ 施設　☐ 観点　☐ 賛辞　☐ 一貫性
☐ 障害　☐ 代替案　☐ 放出　☐ 読み書きの能力
☐ 診断　☐ 資源　☐ 流通　☐ 戦略

Check 2　Phrase

- □ have an argument with ~(~と論争する)
- □ an argument against smoking(喫煙への反対論)

- □ a one-hour commute to work(職場への1時間の通勤)

- □ local residents(地元住民)
- □ a resident of Germany(ドイツ在住者)

- □ public funds(公的資金)
- □ a pension fund(年金基金)

- □ a site for a new stadium(新しいスタジアムの用地)
- □ a construction site(建設現場)

- □ conflict between parents and children(親子間の対立)
- □ armed conflict(武力紛争)

- □ business administration(企業経営)
- □ the Democratic administration(民主党政権)

- □ the outbreak of civil war(内戦の勃発)
- □ an outbreak of flu(インフルエンザの突発的発生)

Check 3　Sentence

- □ They had a heated argument over the issue.(彼らはその問題をめぐって激しい論争をした)

- □ My morning commute takes about 50 minutes.(私の朝の通勤は50分ほどかかる)

- □ Local residents have rejected plans to build a new mall.(地元住民たちは新しいショッピングモールを建設する計画を拒絶している)

- □ Obama raised his campaign funds through millions of small donations.(オバマは数百万もの小口献金を通して選挙資金を調達した)

- □ The company is looking for a site for a new factory.(その会社は新しい工場の用地を探している)

- □ Conflict between generations is a common theme in literature.(世代間の対立は文学でよく用いられるテーマだ)

- □ She works in the sales administration department.(彼女は販売管理部で働いている)

- □ The rise of nationalism, imperialism, and militarism led to the outbreak of World War I.(国家主義、帝国主義、そして軍国主義の台頭が第1次世界大戦の勃発につながった)

Day 1　))CD-A1
Quick Review
答えは左ページ下

- □ epidemic
- □ facility
- □ obstacle
- □ diagnosis
- □ heritage
- □ perspective
- □ alternative
- □ resource
- □ dispute
- □ tribute
- □ emission
- □ circulation
- □ statistics
- □ consistency
- □ literacy
- □ strategy

CHAPTER 1
CHAPTER 2
CHAPTER 3
CHAPTER 4
CHAPTER 5
CHAPTER 6
CHAPTER 7
CHAPTER 8
CHAPTER 9
CHAPTER 10

Day 3 名詞3

Check 1 Listen)) CD-A3

☐ 0033
consensus
/kənsénsəs/

名❶**合意**、総意(≒agreement)(⇔disagreement) ❷(意見などの)一致
名consent：(〜に対する)同意、許可(to 〜)
動consent：(consent toで)〜に同意する、〜を承諾[許可]する

☐ 0034
procedure
/prəsíːdʒər/

名❶(〜の)**手順**、順序(for 〜)(≒process) ❷(法律などの)手続き(≒proceeding)
動proceed：❶(proceed toで)〜へ進む、向かう ❷(proceed withで)〜を続ける
名proceed：(〜s)収益、売上高

☐ 0035
budget
/bʌ́dʒit/

名❶**予算**(案) ❷経費(≒expense, cost) ❸(形容詞的に)予算に合った；安い
動(〜の)予算を立てる(for 〜)
形budgetary：予算上の

☐ 0036
executive
/igzékjətiv/
❶発音注意

名**経営幹部**、重役(≒director)
形❶実施[事務]の ❷重役の
動execute：❶(計画など)を実行する ❷〜を死刑にする
名execution：❶死刑執行 ❷実行、実施

☐ 0037
publicity
/pʌblísəti/

名❶**評判**、知名度(≒popularity)(⇔privacy) ❷宣伝、広報(≒advertising, promotion)
動publicize：〜を公表[広告、宣伝]する、公にする

☐ 0038
initiative
/iníʃiətiv/
❶アクセント注意

名❶(the 〜)**主導権**、イニシアチブ ❷自発性、独創力
動initiate：(計画など)を始める
形initial：最初の
副initially：最初(のうち)は、初めに

☐ 0039
competence
/kʌ́mpətəns/

名(〜の)**能力**；適性(in [for] 〜)(≒capability, ability)(⇔incompetence)
形competent：❶(仕事などに)有能な(at [in] 〜)；(〜する)能力のある(to do)；(〜するのに)適格な(to do) ❷(仕事などが)満足のいく

☐ 0040
habitat
/hǽbitæt/

名(動植物の)**生息地**(≒home)
動inhabit：〜に住む、生息する
名inhabitant：住民、居住者

continued
▼

「3日坊主」にならないためにも、今日と明日の学習がとっても大切！ CDを聞き流すだけでもOKなので、「継続」を心がけよう。

- □ 聞くだけモード　Check 1
- □ しっかりモード　Check 1 ▶ 2
- □ かんぺきモード　Check 1 ▶ 2 ▶ 3

Check 2　Phrase

- □ reach a consensus on ~（~に関して合意に達する）
- □ a consensus of opinion（意見の一致）

- □ follow correct procedure（正しい手順に従う）
- □ legal procedure（訴訟手続き）

- □ the defense budget（防衛予算、防衛費）
- □ the household budget（家計費）

- □ a top executive（最高経営幹部）
- □ a sales executive（販売担当重役）

- □ good [bad] publicity（好評[悪評]）
- □ a publicity campaign（宣伝キャンペーン）

- □ seize the initiative（主導権を握る）
- □ on one's own initiative（自発的に）

- □ competence in programming（プログラミングの能力）
- □ competence as an engineer（エンジニアとしての適性）

- □ the natural habitat of ~（~の自然生息地）

Check 3　Sentence

- □ The two countries have reached a consensus on the matter.（両国はその問題に関して合意に達した）

- □ Employees must follow proper procedures for reporting on-the-job injuries.（従業員は勤務中のけがを報告する際は適切な手順に従わなければならない）

- □ The government was forced to cut its budget because of revenue shortfalls.（政府は歳入不足のため予算を削減せざるを得なかった）

- □ He is an executive in the insurance firm.（彼はその保険会社の経営幹部だ）

- □ The film attracted a lot of publicity before its release.（その映画は公開前に大きな評判を集めた）

- □ Japan should take the initiative in addressing environmental problems.（日本は環境問題への取り組みにおいて主導権を取るべきだ）

- □ She has a high level of competence in English.（彼女には高いレベルの英語の能力がある）

- □ The animal is endangered because its habitat is being destroyed.（その動物は生息地が破壊されつつあるので、絶滅の危機に瀕している）

continued
▼

Day 3

Check 1　Listen 》CD-A3

□ 0041
addiction
/ədíkʃən/

名（麻薬などの）**依存症**、常用癖、中毒(to ～)(≒dependence)
名addict：（麻薬などの）常用者、中毒患者
形addicted：（麻薬などに）中毒の(to ～)
形addictive：（麻薬などが）中毒[習慣]性の

□ 0042
surplus
/sə́ːrplʌs/

名❶**余り**、残り(≒rest, remainder, excess)(⇔deficiency：不足)　❷黒字(⇔deficit)
形残り[余分]の

□ 0043
critic
/krítik/

名**評論[批評]家**(≒reviewer)
動criticize：❶～を（…のことで）非難する(for ...)　❷～を批評[評論]する
名criticism：❶批評、評論　❷非難
形critical：❶重大な　❷批判[批評]的な

□ 0044
outburst
/áutbə̀ːrst/

名（感情などの）**爆発**、噴出(of ～)(≒eruption, explosion)

□ 0045
expertise
/èkspərtíːz/
❶アクセント注意

名（～に関する）**専門的知識**[技術](in ～)(≒know-how)
名expert：（～の）専門家、熟達者(on [in, at] ～)
形expert：❶熟達した　❷専門的な

□ 0046
capital
/kǽpətl/

名❶**資本**(金)(≒finance, fund)　❷首都；（産業などの）中心地　❸大文字
形❶資本の　❷大文字の　❸死刑の、死刑に値する
名capitalism：資本主義
名capitalist：❶資本家　❷資本主義者

□ 0047
triumph
/tráiəmf/

名（～に対する）**勝利**、征服(over ～)(≒victory, win, conquest)(⇔defeat)
動勝利を収める、（～に）打ち勝つ(over ～)
形triumphant：❶勝利を収めた　❷勝ち誇った

□ 0048
fracture
/frǽktʃər/

名❶**骨折**　❷割れ[割け]目(≒crack)
動❶（骨）を折る　❷折れる

| Day 2 》CD-A2
Quick Review
答えは右ページ下 | □ 障害
□ 補償金
□ 禁止
□ 請願書 | □ 見積もり
□ 種
□ インフラ
□ 渋滞 | □ 論争
□ 通勤
□ 住民
□ 資金 | □ 用地
□ 対立
□ 管理
□ 勃発 |

Check 2 Phrase

- □ drug addiction(薬物依存症)

- □ be in surplus(余っている；黒字である)
- □ a budget surplus(財政黒字)

- □ a film [theater] critic(映画[演劇]評論家)

- □ an outburst of anger(怒りの爆発)

- □ expertise in information technology(情報技術の専門的知識)

- □ invested capital(投下資本)
- □ the capital of France(フランスの首都)

- □ a triumph over one's rival(ライバルに対する勝利)
- □ man's triumph over nature(自然に対する人類の勝利)

- □ a compound [simple] fracture(複雑[単純]骨折)
- □ a hairline fracture(細い割れ目、亀裂)

Check 3 Sentence

- □ His addiction to alcohol ruined his career.(アルコール依存症は彼のキャリアを台無しにした)

- □ There is a surplus of workers in the company.(その会社では従業員が余っている)

- □ The novel was well-received by many critics.(その小説は多くの評論家からの好評を博した)

- □ My boss has occasional outbursts of frustration.(私の上司は時々フラストレーションを爆発させることがある)

- □ He has experience and expertise in marketing.(彼はマーケティングの経験と専門的知識を持っている)

- □ The company has sufficient capital to expand its business.(その会社には事業を拡大するのに十分な資本がある)

- □ The party achieved a major triumph in the general election.(その政党は総選挙で大勝利を収めた)

- □ She suffered a leg fracture in the car accident.(彼女はその自動車事故で脚を骨折した)

Day 2 》CD-A2
Quick Review
答えは左ページ下

- □ disorder
- □ compensation
- □ ban
- □ petition
- □ estimate
- □ species
- □ infrastructure
- □ congestion
- □ argument
- □ commute
- □ resident
- □ fund
- □ site
- □ conflict
- □ administration
- □ outbreak

CHAPTER 1
CHAPTER 2
CHAPTER 3
CHAPTER 4
CHAPTER 5
CHAPTER 6
CHAPTER 7
CHAPTER 8
CHAPTER 9
CHAPTER 10

Day 4 名詞4

Check 1 Listen)) CD-A4

0049 property /prάpərti/
- 名 ❶(集合的に)**財産**；不動産(≒real estate) ❷(しばしば~ies)特性(≒quality, characteristic, feature)

0050 hunch /hʌ́ntʃ/
- 名 **予感**、直感(≒feeling, premonition)

0051 compliment /kάmpləmənt/
- 名 (~についての)**褒め言葉**、賛辞；お世辞(on ~)(≒praise, flattery)
- 動 (/kάmpləmènt/)~に賛辞を述べる ⊕complement(~を補完する)と混同しないように注意
- 形 complimentary：❶無料の ❷称賛の

0052 incentive /inséntiv/
- 名 (~する)**動機**(to do)(≒motive, motivation, inducement)；(~への)刺激(to ~)(≒stimulus)

0053 excerpt /éksə:rpt/
- 名 (本などからの)**抜粋**、引用(句)(from ~)(≒extract, quotation, citation)
- 動 (/iksə́:rpt/)~を(…から)抜粋[引用]する(from …)(≒extract, quote, cite)

0054 solution /səlú:ʃən/
- 名 (~の)**解決策**；解答(to ~)(≒answer, resolution)
- 動 solve：❶(困難など)を解決する ❷(問題など)を解く

0055 expense /ikspéns/
- 名 ❶**出費**、費用(≒cost) ❷(~s)経費(≒expenditure) ❸犠牲(≒sacrifice)
- 形 expensive：高価な、値段が高い

0056 majority /mədʒɔ́:rəti/
- 名 (~の)**大多数**、過半数(of ~)(⇔minority)
- 形 major：主要[重要]な
- 動 major：(major inで)~を専攻する
- 名 major：❶専攻科目 ❷専攻学生

continued
▼

同意語・類義語(≒)や反意語・反対語(⇔)もチェックしてる？ 余裕があれば確認して、語彙の数を積極的に増やしていこう。

☐ 聞くだけモード　Check 1
☐ しっかりモード　Check 1 ▶ 2
☐ かんぺきモード　Check 1 ▶ 2 ▶ 3

CHAPTER 1

Check 2　Phrase

☐ private property(私有財産)
☐ chemical properties(化学的特性)

☐ have a hunch (that) ~(~という予感がする)
☐ follow one's hunch(直感に従う)

☐ pay him a compliment(彼を褒める)
☐ take ~ as a compliment(~を褒め言葉として受け取る)

☐ have no [little] incentive to do ~(~する動機が全く[ほとんど]ない)
☐ economic incentives(経済的刺激)

☐ an excerpt from the report(その報告書からの抜粋)

☐ a solution to the issue(その問題の解決策)
☐ the solution to the quiz(そのクイズの解答)

☐ at great expense(多額の費用をかけて)
☐ living [medical] expenses(生活[医療]費)

☐ the majority of people(人々の大多数)
☐ be in a [the] majority(過半数を占めている)

Check 3　Sentence

☐ Intellectual property must be protected by law.(知的財産は法律によって保護されなければならない)

☐ I had a hunch that something bad might happen.(私は何か悪いことが起こるかもしれないという予感がした)

☐ I took what she said as a compliment.(私は彼女が言ったことを褒め言葉として受け取った)

☐ The law will provide incentives for homeowners to install solar panels.(その法律は住宅所有者にソーラーパネルを設置する動機を与えるだろう)

☐ An excerpt from the president's speech appeared in today's newspaper.(大統領の演説の抜粋が今日の新聞に掲載された)

☐ There is no easy solution to global warming.(地球温暖化の簡単な解決策などない)

☐ He spared no expense in educating his children.(彼は彼の子どもたちの教育に出費を惜しまなかった)

☐ Polls show that the majority of American citizens are in favor of the bill.(世論調査では、米国市民の大多数はその法案を支持している)

continued
▼

Day 4

Check 1　Listen 》CD-A4

□ 0057
clause
/klɔ́:z/
　名 (契約・法律などの)**条項** (≒ section)

□ 0058
gender
/dʒéndər/
　名 (文化的・社会的側面から見た)**性**、ジェンダー　❶生物的な「性」はsex

□ 0059
collision
/kəlíʒən/
　名 (〜との／…の間の)**衝突** (with 〜/between …) (≒ crash, clash)　❶比喩的な意味にも用いる
　動 collide：(collide withで)〜と衝突する、ぶつかる

□ 0060
solitude
/sɑ́lətjù:d/
　名 **孤独**；1人でいること(≒ loneliness, isolation, seclusion, privacy)
　形 solitary：❶たった1つの、唯一の　❷1人だけの

□ 0061
edge
/édʒ/
　名 ❶(〜に対する)**優位**、優勢、強み(over [on] 〜) (≒ advantage)　❷縁、へり　❸刃、刃先
　動 ❶少しずつ進む　❷〜を少しずつ移動させる　❸〜を(…で)縁取る(with …)

□ 0062
promotion
/prəmóuʃən/
　名 ❶(〜への)**昇進**(to 〜) (⇔ demotion：降格)　❷促進、助成(≒ encouragement)　❸販売促進
　動 promote：❶〜を促進する　❷(promote A to Bで)AをBに昇進させる　❸〜の販売を促進する
　形 promotional：宣伝[プロモーション]用の

□ 0063
virtue
/vá:rtʃu:/
　名 ❶**美徳**、徳、善(≒ goodness) (⇔ vice：悪)　❷美点、長所(≒ good point, strong point)
　形 virtuous：徳の高い、高潔な

□ 0064
alert
/ələ́:rt/
　名 (警戒)**警報**(≒ warning)；警戒態勢
　動 〜に警戒態勢を取らせる；〜に(…に対して)注意を喚起する(to …)
　形 ❶(〜に)油断のない、用心深い(to 〜)　❷機敏な

Day 3 》CD-A3
Quick Review
答えは右ページ下

□ 合意　□ 評判　□ 依存症　□ 専門的知識
□ 手順　□ 主導権　□ 余り　□ 資本
□ 予算　□ 能力　□ 評論家　□ 勝利
□ 経営幹部　□ 生息地　□ 爆発　□ 骨折

Check 2   Phrase

- ☐ delete [amend] a clause in the treaty（条約の条項を削除[修正]する）

- ☐ gender roles（性別役割分担）
- ☐ gender differences（性差）

- ☐ a head-on collision（正面衝突）
- ☐ a collision of interests（利害の衝突）

- ☐ enjoy one's solitude（孤独を楽しむ）
- ☐ in solitude（1人で）

- ☐ have an [the] edge over [on] ～（～より優位に立っている）
- ☐ a competitive edge（競争上の優位性、競争力）

- ☐ one's promotion to sales manager（販売部長への昇進）
- ☐ the promotion of peace（平和の促進）

- ☐ a person of virtue（徳の高い人）
- ☐ have the virtue of ～（～という長所がある）

- ☐ a flood alert（洪水警報）
- ☐ be on the alert for ～（～を警戒している）

Check 3   Sentence

- ☐ The contract contains a penalty clause.（その契約には違約条項が含まれている）

- ☐ Discrimination on the basis of gender is prohibited.（性に基づく差別は禁止されている）

- ☐ Thirty people were injured in the collision.（その衝突で30人がけがをした）

- ☐ He is the kind of man who likes solitude.（彼は孤独を好むタイプの男性だ）

- ☐ Large companies have an edge over smaller companies in many ways.（大企業はいろいろな点で中小企業よりも優位な立場にある）

- ☐ Promotion should be based on merit rather than seniority.（昇進は、年功ではなく功績に基づくべきだ）

- ☐ Humility is thought to be a virtue in Japan.（謙遜は日本では美徳と考えられている）

- ☐ A smog alert was issued in Beijing today.（今日、北京ではスモッグ警報が発令された）

CHAPTER 1
CHAPTER 2
CHAPTER 3
CHAPTER 4
CHAPTER 5
CHAPTER 6
CHAPTER 7
CHAPTER 8
CHAPTER 9
CHAPTER 10

Day 3))CD-A3
Quick Review
答えは左ページ下

- ☐ consensus
- ☐ procedure
- ☐ budget
- ☐ executive
- ☐ publicity
- ☐ initiative
- ☐ competence
- ☐ habitat
- ☐ addiction
- ☐ surplus
- ☐ critic
- ☐ outburst
- ☐ expertise
- ☐ capital
- ☐ triumph
- ☐ fracture

Day 5 名詞5

Check 1 Listen 》CD-A5

0065
likelihood
/láiklihùd/

名 (〜の／…という)**可能性**、見込み(of 〜/that節 . . .)(≒ probability, chance, possibility, prospect)
形 likely：❶ありそうな、起こりそうな ❷(be likely to doで)〜しそうである ❸本当らしい

0066
condolence
/kəndóuləns/
❶アクセント注意

名 (しばしば〜s)**悔やみ**、哀悼(≒ sympathy)

0067
transportation
/trænspərtéiʃən/

名 **交通**[輸送]**機関**；輸送、運送(≒ conveyance)
動 transport：〜を(…に)輸送[運送]する(to . . .)
名 transport：輸送、運送；輸送機関[手段]

0068
conservation
/kànsərvéiʃən/

名 (自然環境などの)**保護**、保存(≒ protection, preservation)
動 conserve：❶(エネルギーなど)を節約して使う ❷〜を保護[保存]する
形 conservative：❶保守的な ❷(評価などが)控えめな

0069
reserve
/rizə́:rv/

名 ❶(〜の)**蓄え**(of 〜)(≒ store, stock) ❷遠慮
動 ❶〜を予約する(≒ book) ❷(reserve A for Bで)AをBのために取っておく(≒ spare A for B)
名 reservation：❶(ホテルなどの)予約 ❷(野生動物の)保護区

0070
anatomy
/ənǽtəmi/
❶アクセント注意

名 **解剖学**

0071
plot
/plɑ́t/

名 ❶(小説などの)**筋**、構想(≒ story line) ❷(〜しようとする／…に対する)陰謀、策略(to do/against . . .)(≒ scheme, intrigue, conspiracy)
動 ❶〜をたくらむ ❷(plot to doで)〜しようとたくらむ ❸(〜に対して)陰謀を企てる(against 〜)

0072
extinction
/ikstíŋkʃən/

名 **絶滅**(≒ extermination)
形 extinct：絶滅した
動 extinguish：(火など)を消す
名 extinguisher：消火器

continued
▼

Quick Reviewは使ってる？ 昨日覚えた単語でも、記憶に残っているとは限らない。学習の合間に軽くチェックするだけでも効果は抜群！

- ☐ 聞くだけモード　Check 1
- ☐ しっかりモード　Check 1 ▶ 2
- ☐ かんぺきモード　Check 1 ▶ 2 ▶ 3

Check 2　Phrase

- ☐ the likelihood of rain（雨が降る可能性）
- ☐ in all likelihood（間違いなく）

- ☐ a letter of condolence（お悔やみ状）
- ☐ send [offer, extend] one's condolences（哀悼の言葉を述べる）

- ☐ public transportation（公共交通機関）
- ☐ the transportation industry（運送業）

- ☐ the conservation of nature（自然保護）
- ☐ a conservation area（自然保護区域）

- ☐ oil reserves（石油備蓄）
- ☐ break through one's reserve（〜を打ち解けさせる）

- ☐ human anatomy（人体解剖学）

- ☐ the plot of the movie（その映画の筋）
- ☐ a plot to overthrow the government（政府を転覆させようとする陰謀）

- ☐ be in danger of [threatened with] extinction（絶滅の危機に瀕している）

Check 3　Sentence

- ☐ There is an increasing likelihood that the economy will continue to slow.（経済が停滞を続ける可能性が高まっている）

- ☐ Please accept my sincerest condolences on the passing of your beloved.（最愛の人のご逝去に当たり、心からお悔やみ申し上げます）

- ☐ Tokyo's public transportation is very efficient and convenient.（東京の公共交通機関はとても効率的で便利だ）

- ☐ She is interested in wildlife conservation.（彼女は野生生物の保護に関心を持っている）

- ☐ It is important to keep some money in reserve for emergencies.（緊急の場合に備えてお金を蓄えておくことが大切だ）

- ☐ Dr. Moore is a professor of anatomy at the University of Toronto.（ムーア博士はトロント大学の解剖学の教授だ）

- ☐ The plot of the novel was too complicated to understand.（その小説の筋は複雑過ぎて理解できなかった）

- ☐ The extinction of the dinosaurs occurred approximately 65 million years ago.（恐竜の絶滅は約6500万年前に起きた）

continued
▼

Day 5

Check 1　Listen 》CD-A5

0073 inquiry /inkwáiəri/
- 名 ❶(~についての)**問い合わせ**、質問(about ~)(≒question, query)　❷(事件などの)調査(into ~)(≒investigation, examination, probe)
- 動 inquire：❶(inquire aboutで)~について尋ねる、問い合わせる　❷(inquire intoで)~を調査する、調べる

0074 coverage /kʌ́vəridʒ/
- 名 ❶**報道**　❷保険保護[担保]；補償範囲(≒insurance)
- 動 cover：❶(費用など)を賄う　❷~に保険をかける　❸~を取材する　❹~に(…を)かぶせる(with ...)
- 名 cover：❶カバー　❷保険

0075 punctuality /pʌ̀ŋktʃuǽləti/
- 名 **時間厳守**；きちょうめんさ
- 形 punctual：(~の点で)時間を守る(in ~)
- 副 punctually：時間通りに

0076 pollution /pəlúːʃən/
- 名 **汚染**(≒contamination)；公害
- 動 pollute：~を(…で)汚染する(with ...)
- 名 pollutant：汚染物質

0077 fatigue /fətíːg/　❶発音注意
- 名 (心身の)**疲労**(≒tiredness, weariness, exhaustion)
- 形 fatigued：疲れた、疲労した

0078 subsidy /sʌ́bsədi/
- 名 **補助[助成]金**(≒grant)
- 動 subsidize：~に補助[助成]金を与える

0079 breed /bríːd/
- 名 (動植物の)**品種**(≒variety)；血統
- 動 ❶~を飼育[栽培]する(≒rear, raise)　❷繁殖する(≒reproduce)　❸~を引き起こす(≒cause)
- 名 breeding：❶繁殖　❷品種改良
- 名 breeder：繁殖させる人；品種改良家

0080 rivalry /ráivəlri/
- 名 (~との/…の間の)**競争**(with ~/between ...)(≒competition)
- 名 rival：❶競争相手　❷匹敵する人
- 動 rival：~に匹敵する

Day 4 》CD-A4　Quick Review　答えは右ページ下

- □ 財産
- □ 予感
- □ 褒め言葉
- □ 動機
- □ 抜粋
- □ 解決策
- □ 出費
- □ 大多数
- □ 条項
- □ 性
- □ 衝突
- □ 孤独
- □ 優位
- □ 昇進
- □ 美徳
- □ 警報

Check 2　Phrase

- a telephone inquiry（電話での問い合わせ）
- an inquiry into the murder（その殺人事件の調査）

- newspaper coverage（新聞報道）
- healthcare coverage（医療保険）

- be obsessive about punctuality（過度に時間に厳しい）

- water pollution（水質汚染）
- noise pollution（騒音公害）

- physical and mental fatigue（心身の疲労）

- agricultural subsidies（農業補助金）

- a breed of dog（イヌの品種）

- the rivalry between the two companies（両社間の競争）
- be in rivalry（張り合っている）

Check 3　Sentence

- So far, we have received over 100 inquiries about the job.（これまでのところ、その仕事に関して当社は100を超える問い合わせを受けている）

- The event received widespread media coverage.（そのイベントは幅広いメディアで報道された）

- The school places great emphasis on punctuality.（その学校は時間厳守を非常に重要視している）

- Air pollution is one of the most serious environmental problems.（大気汚染は最も深刻な環境問題の1つだ）

- He is suffering from fatigue due to his heavy workload.（彼は重労働による疲労に苦しんでいる）

- The government must reduce wasteful subsidies.（政府は無駄の多い補助金を削減しなければならない）

- What's your favorite breed of cat?（あなたが好きなネコの品種は何ですか？）

- In politics, there is fierce rivalry for political power.（政界では、政治力をめぐる激しい競争がある）

Day 4　))CD-A4
Quick Review
答えは左ページ下

- property
- hunch
- compliment
- incentive
- excerpt
- solution
- expense
- majority
- clause
- gender
- collision
- solitude
- edge
- promotion
- virtue
- alert

Day 6　名詞6

Check 1　Listen 》CD-A6

☐ 0081
fossil
/fásəl/
❶発音注意

名 化石

☐ 0082
priority
/praiɔ́:rəti/

名 ❶ **優先事項**　❷優先(権)(≒preference, precedence)
形 prior：❶(prior to で)〜より前に、〜に先立って　❷前の、先の　❸(〜に)優先する、(〜より)重要な(to 〜)

☐ 0083
dismissal
/dismísəl/

名 (〜からの)**解雇**、免職(from 〜)(≒discharge, displacement)
動 dismiss：❶〜を解雇する　❷(dismiss A as B で)A(提案など)をBだとして退ける、忘れてしまう

☐ 0084
scheme
/skí:m/
❶発音注意

名 ❶ **計画**、案(≒plan, project)　❷たくらみ、陰謀(≒plot, conspiracy, intrigue)
動 (〜しようと／…に対して)たくらむ(to do/against . . .)

☐ 0085
atmosphere
/ǽtməsfìər/
❶アクセント注意

名 ❶ **雰囲気**(≒mood, ambience)　❷(the 〜)大気(≒air)
形 atmospheric：❶大気の　❷雰囲気を感じさせる

☐ 0086
plantation
/plæntéiʃən/

名 (大規模な)**農園**、農場、プランテーション
動 plant：〜を植える
名 plant：❶植物　❷(通例複合語で)工場　❸施設

☐ 0087
remedy
/rémədi/

名 ❶(病気の)**治療**(法)、医薬品(for 〜)(≒treatment, cure, therapy, medicine, medication)　❷(〜の)改善法、救済策(for 〜)(≒solution)
動 (事態など)を改善[修復、矯正]する

☐ 0088
equality
/ikwɔ́ləti/

名 **平等**(⇔inequality)
形 equal：❶同量[同等]の　❷(be equal to で)〜と等しい；〜に匹敵する　❸平等な
動 equal：〜に等しい
動 equalize：〜を(…と)等しくする(with [to] . . .)

continued
▼

「細切れ時間」を有効活用してる？『キクタン』は2分でも学習可能。いつでもどこでもテキストとCDを持ち歩いて、単語・熟語に触れよう！

☐ 聞くだけモード　Check 1
☐ しっかりモード　Check 1 ▶ 2
☐ かんぺきモード　Check 1 ▶ 2 ▶ 3

Check 2　Phrase

☐ dinosaur fossils（恐竜の化石）

☐ a top [first] priority（最優先事項）
☐ have [take, get] priority over ～（～に優先する）

☐ unfair [wrongful] dismissal（不当解雇）
☐ be threatened with dismissal（解雇の危機にさらされている）

☐ a pension scheme（年金計画）
☐ uncover a scheme（陰謀を暴露する）

☐ create a romantic atmosphere（ロマンチックな雰囲気を生み出す）
☐ carbon dioxide in the atmosphere（大気中の二酸化炭素）

☐ a coffee [rubber] plantation（コーヒー［ゴム］農園）

☐ a folk remedy（民間療法）
☐ a remedy for unemployment（失業の改善策）

☐ racial [sexual] equality（人種的［男女の］平等）

Check 3　Sentence

☐ Coal, petroleum, and natural gas are fossil fuels.（石炭、石油、そして天然ガスは化石燃料だ）

☐ Balancing the budget is one of the government's priorities.（予算の均衡化は政府の優先事項の1つだ）

☐ They decided to sue their former employer for unfair dismissal.（彼らは以前の雇用主を不当解雇で訴えることを決めた）

☐ The management gave the go-ahead for the business scheme.（経営陣はその事業計画にゴーサインを出した）

☐ There was a relaxed atmosphere in the restaurant.（そのレストランにはくつろいだ雰囲気が漂っていた）

☐ Many plantations were devastated by the typhoon.（多くの農園がその台風によって壊滅した）

☐ Massage is an excellent home remedy for headaches.（マッサージは頭痛の優れた家庭治療法だ）

☐ Equality is the cornerstone of democracy.（平等は民主主義の基礎だ）

CHAPTER 1
CHAPTER 2
CHAPTER 3
CHAPTER 4
CHAPTER 5
CHAPTER 6
CHAPTER 7
CHAPTER 8
CHAPTER 9
CHAPTER 10

continued

Day 6

Check 1　Listen 》CD-A6

0089 privilege /prívəlidʒ/
- 名 **特権**、特典、名誉(≒prerogative, benefit, honor)
- 動 (be privileged to doで)〜する特権[特典]を与えられている
- 形 privileged：(〜する)特権[特典]を持つ(to do)；特権階級に属する

0090 capacity /kəpǽsəti/
- 名 ❶ **収容能力**；生産能力　❷ 能力(≒ability, capability)　❸ 容量(≒volume)

0091 investment /invéstmənt/
- 名 (〜への)**投資**、出資(in 〜)
- 動 invest：❶ (〜に)投資する(in 〜)　❷ (invest A in Bで) AをBに投資する
- 名 investor：投資家[者]、出資者

0092 popularity /pὰpjulǽrəti/
- 名 **人気**、評判；流行(≒publicity, fashion, trend)
- 形 popular：❶ (〜に) 人気のある、評判のよい(with [among] 〜)　❷ 一般人の、一般民衆の

0093 hospitality /hὰspətǽləti/
- 名 **温かい**[手厚い、親切な]**もてなし**、歓待
- 形 hospitable：❶ (客などを)温かく[手厚く、親切に]もてなす　❷ (環境などが)快適な

0094 ecosystem /ékousìstəm/
❶ アクセント注意
- 名 **生態系**、エコシステム
- 名 ecology：❶ 生態(系)　❷ 生態学、エコロジー

0095 controversy /kántrəvə̀:rsi/
- 名 (社会・政治・道徳上の)**論争**、議論(≒argument, dispute, debate)
- 形 controversial：議論の余地のある、異論の多い[ある]

0096 regulation /règjuléiʃən/
- 名 ❶ (〜に関しての)**規則**、規定(on [about] 〜)(≒rule)　❷ 規制、統制(≒control)
- 動 regulate：❶ 〜を規制[統制、管理]する　❷ 〜を調節[調整]する

Day 5 》CD-A5
Quick Review
答えは右ページ下

- □ 可能性
- □ 悔やみ
- □ 交通機関
- □ 保護
- □ 蓄え
- □ 解剖学
- □ 筋
- □ 絶滅
- □ 問い合わせ
- □ 報道
- □ 時間厳守
- □ 汚染
- □ 疲労
- □ 補助金
- □ 品種
- □ 競争

Check 2 — Phrase

- enjoy privilege（特権を享受する）
- have the privilege of doing ~（~する特権[名誉]を与えられている）

- a capacity crowd（満員の観客）
- be beyond one's capacity（~の能力を超えている、~には理解できない）

- investment in stocks（株式投資）
- capital investment（資本投資）

- win [lose] popularity（人気を得る[失う]）
- gain in popularity（人気が増す）

- generous hospitality（寛大なもてなし）
- extend hospitality to ~（~を歓待する）

- conserve the ecosystem（生態系を保護する）

- controversy over the Iraq war（イラク戦争をめぐる論争）
- cause [arouse] controversy（議論を巻き起こす）

- obey traffic regulations（交通規則に従う）
- regulation of price（価格規制）

Check 3 — Sentence

- Healthcare is a right, not a privilege.（医療は権利であり、特権ではない）

- The theater has a capacity of 1,000.（その劇場は1000人の収容能力がある）

- Japan needs more investment in education.（日本は教育へのより多くの投資が必要だ）

- The popularity of cycling is increasing in Europe.（自転車の人気がヨーロッパで高まっている）

- Thank you very much for your hospitality last night.（昨晩は、温かくおもてなしいただき、誠にありがとうございました）

- Human activities have affected the ecosystem noticeably in the past few centuries.（この数世紀の間で、人間の活動は生態系に著しい影響を及ぼしている）

- There has been a long controversy over the issue.（その問題をめぐっては長い論争が続いている）

- Employees are required to comply with safety regulations.（従業員は安全規則に従うことを求められている）

Day 5　))CD-A5
Quick Review
答えは左ページ下

- likelihood
- condolence
- transportation
- conservation
- reserve
- anatomy
- plot
- extinction
- inquiry
- coverage
- punctuality
- pollution
- fatigue
- subsidy
- breed
- rivalry

Day 7　名詞7

Check 1　Listen 》CD-A7

0097 tip /típ/
名❶(〜についての)**助言**、秘けつ(on [about, for] 〜)　❷先、先端(≒point, end)　❸チップ(≒gratuity)

0098 ingredient /ingríːdiənt/
名(料理などの)**材料**；成分、要素(≒element, component)

0099 backbone /bǽkbòun/
名❶(the 〜)(〜の)**中枢**、重要要素、大黒柱(of 〜)(≒foundation, cornerstone, mainstay)　❷背骨、脊柱(≒spine)

0100 exile /égzail/
名❶**亡命者**；追放者　❷亡命；国外追放(≒banishment)
動〜を(…へ)国外追放する(to …)(≒banish)

0101 debt /dét/
❶発音注意
名**借金**、負債；借金状態
名debtor：債務者、借り主

0102 prescription /priskríp∫ən/
名**処方箋**
動prescribe：(prescribe A for Bで)A(薬)をB(病気・人)に処方する

0103 status /stéitəs/
名❶**地位**、身分(≒position, standing)　❷状態、状況(≒state, condition, situation)

0104 mourning /mɔ́ːrniŋ/
名❶**喪に服すこと**、服喪(≒grief)　❷喪服
動mourn：❶(死などを)悲しむ、嘆く(for [over] 〜)　❷(死など)を悲しむ、嘆く

continued
▼

今日で『キクタン英検準1級』は1週間が終了！残りは9週！ 先はまだまだ長いけど、急がず焦らず学習を進めていこう。

- □ 聞くだけモード　Check 1
- □ しっかりモード　Check 1 ▶ 2
- □ かんぺきモード　Check 1 ▶ 2 ▶ 3

Check 2　Phrase

- □ tips on how to save money（お金の節約の仕方に関する助言）
- □ the tips of one's fingers（指先）

- □ mix the ingredients in a bowl（ボウルの中で材料を混ぜる）
- □ essential ingredients for success（成功に不可欠な要素）

- □ the backbone of the economy（経済の中枢）
- □ an injured backbone（傷ついた背骨）

- □ a political exile（政治亡命者）
- □ live in exile（亡命生活を送る）

- □ pay off one's debts（借金を完済する）
- □ be in debt to ~（~に借金している）

- □ a prescription for antibiotics（抗生物質の処方箋）
- □ on prescription（処方箋に基づいて）

- □ the status of women（女性の地位）
- □ the current status of negotiations（交渉の現在の状況）

- □ be in mourning（喪に服している；喪服を着ている）
- □ go into mourning（喪に服す；喪服を着る）

Check 3　Sentence

- □ He gave me useful tips about skiing.（彼はスキーについて役に立つ助言を私にしてくれた）

- □ All our food is made with fresh, top quality ingredients.（当店の料理はすべて、新鮮で最高品質の材料で作られています）

- □ Manufacturing used to be the backbone of British industry.（製造業はかつては英国の産業の中枢だった）

- □ There are many Cuban exiles in Miami.（マイアミには多くのキューバ人亡命者がいる）

- □ She had run up huge credit card debts.（彼女はクレジットカードで巨額の借金を重ねてしまった）

- □ You need a prescription for this medicine.（この薬には処方箋が必要だ）

- □ Wealth and social status are not important to me.（富や社会的地位は私には重要でない）

- □ The woman is still in mourning for her husband.（その女性はまだ夫の喪に服している）

continued
▼

CHAPTER 1
CHAPTER 2
CHAPTER 3
CHAPTER 4
CHAPTER 5
CHAPTER 6
CHAPTER 7
CHAPTER 8
CHAPTER 9
CHAPTER 10

Day 7

Check 1　Listen 》CD-A7

0105
virus
/váirəs/
❶発音注意

名 ❶ **ウイルス**　❷(コンピューター)ウイルス

0106
captivity
/kæptívəti/

名 **監禁状態**、捕らわれの身(≒imprisonment, confinement)(⇔freedom)
名 captive：❶捕虜　❷とりこ
形 captive：捕虜になった

0107
flaw
/flɔ́ː/

名 (〜の)**欠陥**、欠点(in 〜)(≒defect, fault, shortcoming)
形 flawed：欠点[欠陥]のある
形 flawless：欠点のない、非の打ちどころがない

0108
setback
/sétbæk/

名 (進歩などの)**後退**、妨げ、挫折
動 set back：(計画など)を妨げる、遅らせる

0109
dialect
/dáiəlèkt/

名 **方言**(≒vernacular)

0110
application
/æpləkéiʃən/

名 (〜への)**申し込み**[申請](書)(for 〜)
動 apply：❶(apply forで)〜を申し込む　❷(apply toで)(規則などが)〜に適用される、当てはまる；〜に申し込む　❸(apply A to Bで)AをBに適用[応用、利用]する
名 applicant：(〜への)応募者、志願者(for 〜)

0111
suspect
/sʌ́spekt/

名 **容疑者**、被疑者　➕「被告」はdefendant
動 (/səspékt/)❶〜だと疑う、思う　❷(suspect A of Bで)AにB(犯罪など)の容疑[嫌疑]をかける
名 suspicion：疑い
形 suspicious：❶疑わしい　❷疑い深い

0112
recognition
/rèkəgníʃən/

名 ❶(〜という)**認識**、評価(that節 〜)(≒acknowledgment, realization)　❷承認、認可(≒approval)
動 recognize：❶〜を見分ける、識別する　❷(recognize A as Bで)AをBだと認める

| Day 6 》CD-A6
Quick Review
答えは右ページ下 | □ 化石
□ 優先事項
□ 解雇
□ 計画 | □ 雰囲気
□ 農園
□ 治療
□ 平等 | □ 特権
□ 収容能力
□ 投資
□ 人気 | □ 温かいもてなし
□ 生態系
□ 論争
□ 規則 |

Check 2 Phrase

- a flu virus(インフルエンザ・ウイルス)
- be infected with a virus(ウイルスに感染している)

- release ~ from captivity(~を監禁状態から解放する)
- be in captivity(監禁状態にある)

- a fundamental flaw(根本的な欠陥)
- a character flaw(性格上の欠点)

- suffer [experience] a setback(後退を余儀なくされる、妨げに遭う、挫折する)

- speak in dialect(方言で話す)
- the Kansai dialect(関西弁)

- an application for a housing loan(住宅ローンの申し込み)
- an application form(申込用紙、申請書)

- a murder suspect(殺人容疑者)
- the prime suspect(有力な容疑者)

- in recognition of ~(~を認めて、評価して)
- give [pay] recognition to ~(~を認める)

Check 3 Sentence

- The patient is infected with the Ebola virus.(その患者はエボラ・ウイルスに感染している)

- The hostage has been in captivity for three months.(その人質は3カ月間、監禁状態にある)

- There is a fatal flaw in the hypothesis.(その仮説には致命的な欠陥がある)

- The country's economy suffered a temporary setback due to the financial crisis.(金融危機のため、その国の経済は一時的な後退を余儀なくされた)

- I couldn't understand the old man's dialect.(私はその老人の方言を理解できなかった)

- There were over 30 applications for the job.(その仕事には30を超える申し込みがあった)

- Police released a photograph of the suspect.(警察は容疑者の写真を公表した)

- There is a growing recognition that climate change is taking place.(気候変動が起きているという認識が広まっている)

Day 6 CD-A6
Quick Review
答えは左ページ下

- fossil
- priority
- dismissal
- scheme
- atmosphere
- plantation
- remedy
- equality
- privilege
- capacity
- investment
- popularity
- hospitality
- ecosystem
- controversy
- regulation

CHAPTER 1
CHAPTER 2
CHAPTER 3
CHAPTER 4
CHAPTER 5
CHAPTER 6
CHAPTER 7
CHAPTER 8
CHAPTER 9
CHAPTER 10

Day 8　名詞8

Check 1　Listen ») CD-A8

☐ 0113
correspondence
/kɔ̀:rəspάndəns/

图(〜との)**文通**、通信(with 〜)(≒ communication)
動correspond：❶(correspond toで)〜に一致する；〜に相当する　❷(correspond withで)〜と文通する
图correspondent：(新聞社などの)特派員；通信員

☐ 0114
sanction
/sǽŋkʃən/

图❶(通例〜s)(〜に対する)**制裁**(措置)(against [on] 〜)　❷認可(≒ permission, approval, authorization)
動❶〜を認可[公認]する(≒ permit, approve, authorize)　❷〜に対して制裁措置を取る

☐ 0115
cell phone
/sél fòun/

图**携帯電話**　❶cellphoneと1語でつづることもある(≒ cellular phone, mobile phone, mobile)

☐ 0116
premonition
/prì:mənίʃən/

图(〜の／…という)**予感**(of 〜/that節 . . .)　❶通例、よくないことに関して用いられる(≒ feeling, hunch)

☐ 0117
turbulence
/tə́:rbjələns/

图❶**乱気流**　❷(社会的)動乱、騒乱(≒ upheaval, commotion)
形turbulent：❶騒然とした、不穏な　❷(天候などが)荒れ狂う

☐ 0118
discretion
/diskréʃən/

图❶**慎重さ**、思慮深さ、思慮分別(≒ carefulness, circumspection)　❷自由裁量、判断[行動、選択]の自由
形discreet：慎重な；(〜について)口が堅い(about 〜)

☐ 0119
stance
/stǽns/

图(物事に対する)**立場**、姿勢、態度(on 〜)(≒ position, attitude)

☐ 0120
counterpart
/káuntərpὰ:rt/

图(〜に)**相当**[対応]**するもの**[人](of [to] 〜)(≒ equivalent)

continued
▼

「声を出しながら」CDを聞いてる？ えっ、恥ずかしい?! 恥ずかしがっていては「話せる」ようにならないよ！ もっと口を動かそう！

☐ 聞くだけモード　Check 1
☐ しっかりモード　Check 1 ▶ 2
☐ かんぺきモード　Check 1 ▶ 2 ▶ 3

Check 2　Phrase

☐ be in correspondence with ~（~と文通している）
☐ study by correspondence（通信教育で勉強する）

☐ impose sanctions on ~（~に対して制裁を課す）
☐ give sanction to ~（~を認可する）

☐ talk to ~ on one's cell phone（携帯電話で~と話す）

☐ a premonition of danger（危険の予感）
☐ have a premonition that ~（~という予感がする）

☐ encounter severe turbulence（激しい乱気流に遭遇する）
☐ political turbulence（政治的混乱）

☐ with discretion（慎重に）
☐ leave the decision to his discretion（決定を彼の裁量に委ねる）

☐ take a neutral stance on ~（~に対して中立的な立場を取る）

☐ the Japanese counterpart of the English pub（日本で英国のパブに相当するもの）

Check 3　Sentence

☐ I have been in correspondence with her for several years.（私は数年間、彼女との文通を続けている）

☐ Trade sanctions against the country were lifted.（その国に対する貿易制裁は解除された）

☐ Please make sure your cell phones are turned off prior to the performance.（演奏の前に、携帯電話の電源が切ってあることをお確かめください）

☐ I had a premonition that something bad would happen.（何か悪いことが起こりそうな予感がした）

☐ The plane shuddered violently as it hit turbulence.（乱気流に突入して、その飛行機は激しく揺れた）

☐ Personal information must be handled with extreme discretion.（個人情報は極めて慎重に扱われなければならない）

☐ What is your stance on smoking?（喫煙に対するあなたの立場はどうですか？）

☐ The Japanese *otsukaresama* has no exact counterpart in English.（日本語の「お疲れさま」に正確に相当するものは英語にはない）

CHAPTER 1
CHAPTER 2
CHAPTER 3
CHAPTER 4
CHAPTER 5
CHAPTER 6
CHAPTER 7
CHAPTER 8
CHAPTER 9
CHAPTER 10

continued
▼

Day 8

Check 1　Listen))) CD-A8

0121
advertising
/ǽdvərtàiziŋ/
- 名 ❶(集合的に)**広告** ❷広告業
- 形 広告の
- 名 advertisement：広告、宣伝
- 動 advertise：❶〜を宣伝[広告]する　❷(〜を求める)広告を出す(for 〜)

0122
target
/tá:rgit/
- 名 ❶(計画などの)**目標**(of 〜)(≒objective, goal, aim) ❷標的、的(≒mark)
- 動 〜を標的[目標]にする；〜を(…に)向ける(at [on] …)

0123
inheritance
/inhérətəns/
- 名 **遺産**、相続財産(≒legacy, heritage)
- 動 inherit：(財産など)を(…から)相続する、受け継ぐ(from …)

0124
transfer
/trænsfə:r/
- 名 ❶**転送** ❷転任、異動 ❸乗り換え
- 動 ❶〜を(…に)移す(to …)(≒remove)　❷(〜から/…へ)乗り換える(from 〜/to …)　❸〜を(…へ)転任させる(to …)

0125
erosion
/iróuʒən/
- 名 **浸食**(作用)
- 動 erode：❶〜を浸食する　❷浸食される

0126
archive
/á:rkaiv/
- 名 (通例〜s)❶**記録**[公文書]**保管所** ❷(集合的に)公文書、古文書 ❸(コンピューターの)アーカイブ
- 動 〜を(記録保管所などに)保管する

0127
hub
/hʌ́b/
- 名 (活動などの)**中心**(地)、中核、中枢(of 〜)(≒center, core, heart, focus)

0128
strain
/stréin/
- 名 ❶**重圧**、負担、緊張(≒pressure, tension, stress)　❷(動植物などの)品種、変種(≒variety)
- 動 ❶(体)を使い過ぎて痛める(≒injure, hurt)　❷〜を引っ張る
- 形 strained：緊迫[緊張]した

Day 7))) CD-A7
Quick Review
答えは右ページ下

- ☐ 助言
- ☐ 材料
- ☐ 中枢
- ☐ 亡命者
- ☐ 借金
- ☐ 処方箋
- ☐ 地位
- ☐ 喪に服すこと
- ☐ ウイルス
- ☐ 監禁状態
- ☐ 欠陥
- ☐ 後退
- ☐ 方言
- ☐ 申し込み
- ☐ 容疑者
- ☐ 認識

Check 2 Phrase

- ☐ TV advertising(テレビ広告)
- ☐ a career in advertising(広告業での仕事)

- ☐ meet [achieve] a target(目標を達成する)
- ☐ miss the target(的を外れる)

- ☐ live off one's inheritance(遺産で生計を立てる)
- ☐ an inheritance tax(相続税)

- ☐ the transfer of information(情報の転送)
- ☐ a transfer to an overseas branch(海外支店への転任)

- ☐ soil [coastal] erosion(土壌[海岸]浸食)

- ☐ library's archives(図書館の記録保管所)
- ☐ archive tapes(保管テープ)

- ☐ the hub of the city(その都市の中心地)

- ☐ put a strain on ~(~に重圧[負担]をかける)
- ☐ a new strain of the virus(新種のウイルス)

Check 3 Sentence

- ☐ Advertising on the Internet has become an important marketing tool.(インターネットでの広告は重要なマーケティング手段になっている)

- ☐ The store reached its sales target of $10 million last year.(その店は昨年、1000万ドルの売上目標に達した)

- ☐ He left his daughter an inheritance of $500,000.(彼は娘に50万ドルの遺産を残した)

- ☐ The speed of data transfer is measured in bits per second (bps).(データ転送の速さはビット毎秒[bps]で測定される)

- ☐ Soil erosion can be prevented by planting trees.(土壌浸食は植林によって防ぐことができる)

- ☐ The original copy of the contract is preserved in the company's archives.(その契約書の原本は会社の記録保管所にしまってある)

- ☐ Paris is the hub of the fashion world.(パリはファッション界の中心だ)

- ☐ He has lost weight under the strain of his job.(彼は仕事の重圧で体重が減ってしまった)

Day 7))CD-A7
Quick Review
答えは左ページ下

- ☐ tip
- ☐ ingredient
- ☐ backbone
- ☐ exile
- ☐ debt
- ☐ prescription
- ☐ status
- ☐ mourning
- ☐ virus
- ☐ captivity
- ☐ flaw
- ☐ setback
- ☐ dialect
- ☐ application
- ☐ suspect
- ☐ recognition

CHAPTER 1
CHAPTER 2
CHAPTER 3
CHAPTER 4
CHAPTER 5
CHAPTER 6
CHAPTER 7
CHAPTER 8
CHAPTER 9
CHAPTER 10

Day 9　名詞9

Check 1　Listen 》CD-A9

□ 0129
efficiency
/ifíʃənsi/
❶アクセント注意

名 **効率**、能率
形 efficient：❶効率[能率]的な　❷有能な
副 efficiently：能率[効果]的に

□ 0130
composure
/kəmpóuʒər/

名 **落ち着き**、平静（≒calm）

□ 0131
shortcoming
/ʃɔ́ːrtkÀmiŋ/

名 （通例～s）**欠点**、短所（≒fault, defect, flaw）

□ 0132
existence
/igzístəns/

名 ❶**存在**（≒being）　❷生活（状況）（≒life）
動 exist：❶存在[実在]する　❷（～で）生きていく（on ～）
形 existing：現在の；現存する、既存の

□ 0133
sector
/séktər/

名 （産業などの）**部門**、分野

□ 0134
dismay
/disméi/
❶アクセント注意

名 **失望**、落胆（≒disappointment）
動 ～を失望[落胆]させる（≒disappoint）

□ 0135
reduction
/ridʌ́kʃən/

名 （～の）**削減**；減少（in ～）（≒decrease, cutback）
動 reduce：～を減らす

□ 0136
deficit
/défəsit/
トビラの問題の正解はコレ！

名 **赤字**、不足額（⇔surplus）

continued
▼

単語上のチェックボックスを使ってる？ 確実に押さえた単語にはチェックマーク、自信のないものには?マークをつけて復習に役立てよう。

- □ 聞くだけモード　Check 1
- □ しっかりモード　Check 1 ▶ 2
- □ かんぺきモード　Check 1 ▶ 2 ▶ 3

Check 2　Phrase

- □ fuel efficiency（燃費効率）
- □ improve efficiency（効率を高める）

- □ keep [lose] one's composure（落ち着いている［落ち着きを失う］）

- □ acknowledge one's shortcomings（欠点を認める）
- □ shortcomings of economic policy（経済政策の欠点）

- □ be in existence（存在［現存］している）
- □ lead a miserable existence（哀れな生活を送る）

- □ the private [public] sector（民間［公共］部門）

- □ in [with] dismay（失望［落胆］して）
- □ to one's dismay（がっかりしたことには）

- □ a reduction in costs（経費の削減）
- □ a reduction in the number of ~（~の数の減少）

- □ a budget [trade] deficit（財政［貿易］赤字）
- □ in deficit（赤字の［で］）

Check 3　Sentence

- □ Productivity and efficiency are closely related.（生産力と効率は密接に関連している）

- □ It took a while for her to regain her composure.（落ち着きを取り戻すのに、彼女はしばらく時間がかかった）

- □ He is aware of his own shortcomings.（彼は自分の欠点を自覚している）

- □ Do you believe in the existence of ghosts?（あなたは幽霊の存在を信じますか?）

- □ The financial sector has lost tens of thousands of jobs since the recession began.（景気後退が始まって以降、金融部門では何万もの職が失われている）

- □ He could not hide his dismay at the exam result.（彼はその試験の結果に失望を隠せなかった）

- □ The manufacturer announced a reduction in its workforce.（そのメーカーは従業員の削減を発表した）

- □ The state currently has a budget deficit of $15 billion.（その州は現在、150億ドルの財政赤字を抱えている）

continued
▼

Day 9

Check 1 Listen))) CD-A9

☐ 0137
therapy
/θérəpi/
- 名 (薬や手術を用いない)**治療**、療法(≒ treatment, remedy, cure)
- 名 therapist：治療専門家、セラピスト
- 形 therapeutic：治療(法)の

☐ 0138
ventilation
/vèntəléiʃən/
- 名 **換気**、風通し
- 動 ventilate：(部屋など)を換気する

☐ 0139
global warming
/glòubəl wɔ́ːrmiŋ/
- 名 **地球温暖化**
- 形 global：地球上の、世界的な

☐ 0140
recess
/ríːses/
- 名 (授業間の)**休憩時間**；(議会・法廷などの)休会[休廷]期間(≒ break, rest, adjournment)
- 動 ❶~を休会[休憩]にする ❷休会[休憩]する(≒ adjourn)
- 名 recession：景気後退、一時的不景気

☐ 0141
candidate
/kǽndidət, kǽndidèit/
- 名 (~の)**候補者**；志願者(for ~)(≒ applicant)
- 名 candidacy：(~への)立候補(for ~)

☐ 0142
manuscript
/mǽnjuskrìpt/
- 名 (手書き・タイプの)**原稿**

☐ 0143
conviction
/kənvíkʃən/
- 名 ❶**有罪判決**(≒ sentence)(⇔ acquittal) ❷(~という)確信、信念(of [that節] ~)(≒ confidence, belief)
- 動 convict：(convict A of Bで)AにB(犯罪)の有罪を宣告する
- 名 convict：罪人、囚人

☐ 0144
friction
/fríkʃən/
- 名 ❶(~に対する)**摩擦**(on [against] ~) ❷(~の間の)あつれき、いさかい、不和(between ~)(≒ conflict, disagreement, discord, tension)

Day 8))) CD-A8
Quick Review
答えは右ページ下

- ☐ 交通
- ☐ 制裁
- ☐ 携帯電話
- ☐ 予感
- ☐ 乱気流
- ☐ 慎重さ
- ☐ 立場
- ☐ 相当するもの
- ☐ 広告
- ☐ 目標
- ☐ 遺産
- ☐ 転送
- ☐ 浸食
- ☐ 記録保管所
- ☐ 中心
- ☐ 重圧

Check 2　Phrase	Check 3　Sentence
☐ be in therapy（治療を受けている） ☐ natural therapy（自然療法）	☐ After a few years of therapy, she conquered her sleep disorder.（数年間の治療の後、彼女は睡眠障害を克服した）
☐ have good [poor] ventilation（[部屋などが]換気がいい[悪い]） ☐ a ventilation system（換気システム）	☐ This attic has poor ventilation.（この屋根裏部屋は換気が悪い）
☐ the effects of global warming（地球温暖化の影響）	☐ Greenhouse gases are causing global warming.（温室効果ガスが地球温暖化を引き起こしている）
☐ at recess（休み時間に） ☐ be in recess（[議会などが]休会中である）	☐ There is a 20-minute recess between the second and third period in the elementary school.（その小学校では2時間目と3時間目の間に20分の休憩時間がある）
☐ a presidential candidate（大統領候補者） ☐ the prime candidate（最有力候補者）	☐ There are 48 candidates standing in the city council election.（48人の候補者が市議会議員選挙に立候補している）
☐ the original manuscript（元の原稿）	☐ He sent the manuscript to a London-based publisher.（彼はその原稿をロンドンにある出版社に送った）
☐ a conviction for theft（窃盗の有罪判決） ☐ political [moral] convictions（政治的[道徳的]信念）	☐ The suspect has three previous convictions for similar offenses.（その容疑者は同様の犯罪で以前に3度の有罪判決を受けている）
☐ cause [generate] friction（摩擦を起こす） ☐ friction between the two countries（両国間のあつれき）	☐ Lubricant is used to reduce friction.（潤滑油は摩擦を減らすために使われる）

Day 8　))CD-A8
Quick Review
答えは左ページ下

☐ correspondence　☐ turbulence　☐ advertising　☐ erosion
☐ sanction　☐ discretion　☐ target　☐ archive
☐ cell phone　☐ stance　☐ inheritance　☐ hub
☐ premonition　☐ counterpart　☐ transfer　☐ strain

CHAPTER 1
CHAPTER 2
CHAPTER 3
CHAPTER 4
CHAPTER 5
CHAPTER 6
CHAPTER 7
CHAPTER 8
CHAPTER 9
CHAPTER 10

Day 10　名詞10

Check 1　Listen 》CD-A10

□ 0145
blunder
/blʌ́ndər/

名 **大失敗**、へま(≒ mistake, error)
動 ❶大失敗する　❷まごまごしながら進む；(～に)うっかり入り込む(into ～)

□ 0146
depression
/dipréʃən/

名 ❶**うつ病**　❷(長期の)不景気、不況
動 depress：❶～を憂うつにさせる　❷(be depressed about [over]で)～で憂うつになっている　❸(市場など)を不景気にする
形 depressed：❶元気のない、憂うつな　❷不景気の

□ 0147
preservative
/prizə́ːrvətiv/

名 **保存料**、防腐剤
動 preserve：～を(…から)保護[保存]する(from ...)
名 preservation：保護、保存、維持

□ 0148
consequence
/kánsəkwèns/
❶アクセント注意

名 (通例～s)(～の)**結果**、影響(of ～)(≒ result, outcome, effect, upshot)(⇔ cause)
形 consequent：(～の)結果として起こる(on [upon, to] ～)
副 consequently：その結果、従って

□ 0149
molecule
/máləkjùːl/

名 **分子**　❶「原子」はatom
形 molecular：分子の

□ 0150
satellite
/sǽtəlàit/

名 ❶**衛星**(≒ moon)　❷人工衛星

□ 0151
dosage
/dóusidʒ/

名 (1回分の)**服用量**(≒ dose)

□ 0152
archaeologist
/àːrkiálədʒist/

名 **考古学者**
名 archaeology：考古学
形 archaeological：考古学(上)の

continued
▼

名詞と前置詞の結びつきを確認してる？ 0155のconcession to ～(～への譲歩)のように、名詞の後ろにつく前置詞にも注意していこう。

- □ 聞くだけモード Check 1
- □ しっかりモード Check 1 ▶ 2
- □ かんぺきモード Check 1 ▶ 2 ▶ 3

Check 2　Phrase

- □ make a blunder (大失敗する)
- □ a political blunder (政治的大失態)

- □ suffer from depression (うつ病を患う)
- □ an economic depression (経済不況)

- □ artificial preservatives (人工保存料)
- □ a wood preservative (木材防腐剤)

- □ tragic consequences (悲惨な結果)
- □ as a consequence of ～ (～の結果として)

- □ a molecule of water (水の分子)

- □ satellites of Saturn (土星の衛星)
- □ a spy [weather] satellite (スパイ[気象]衛星)

- □ increase [decrease] the dosage (服用量を増やす[減らす])
- □ the prescribed dosage (規定の服用量)

- □ a renowned archaeologist (著名な考古学者)

Check 3　Sentence

- □ The management blunders led to the company's bankruptcy. (経営上の大失敗がその会社の倒産につながった)

- □ The symptoms of depression are often subtle at first. (うつ病の症状は最初のうちは見つけにくいことが多い)

- □ The product contains no artificial preservatives. (その製品には人工保存料は含まれていない)

- □ You must accept the consequences of your actions. (あなたは自分の行動の結果を受け入れなければならない)

- □ A molecule of carbon dioxide consists of one atom of carbon and two atoms of oxygen. (二酸化炭素の分子は炭素原子1つと酸素原子2つから成り立っている)

- □ Mars has two satellites, Phobos and Deimos. (火星には、フォボスとダイモスという2つの衛星がある)

- □ Do not exceed the recommended dosage. (推奨服用量を超えてはいけません)

- □ The tomb was excavated by archaeologists in 1924. (その墓は考古学者たちによって1924年に発掘された)

continued ▼

Day 10

Check 1 Listen)) CD-A10

0153
makeup
/méikÀp/

名 ❶**構造**、構成(≒composition, constitution, structure) ❷化粧(≒cosmetic)
動make up：❶〜を構成する ❷化粧する

0154
recession
/riséʃən/

名 **景気後退**、一時的不景気
名recess：休憩時間；(議会・法廷などの)休会[休廷]期間
動recess：❶〜を休会[休憩]にする ❷休会[休憩]する

0155
concession
/kənséʃən/

名 (〜への)**譲歩**(to 〜)(≒compromise)
動concede：〜を(正しいと)(渋々)認める

0156
complex
/kámpleks/

名 **複合施設**、総合ビル
形(/kəmpléks/)複雑な(≒complicated, intricate)(⇔simple)
名complexity：複雑さ、複雑性

0157
association
/əsòusiéiʃən/

名 ❶(共通の目的のための)**協会**、団体(≒organization) ❷(〜との)提携、つき合い(with 〜)
動associate：❶(associate A with Bで)AをBと結びつけて考える ❷(be associated withで)〜と関連している
名associate：同僚、仲間

0158
opponent
/əpóunənt/

名 ❶(試合・討論などの)**敵**、相手(≒rival, adversary, competitor) ❷反対者(⇔proponent)
動oppose：(計画など)に反対する
形opposite：❶反対側の ❷(性質などが)正反対の
名opposition：❶反対 ❷(集合的に)対戦チーム

0159
decade
/dékeid/

名 **10年間** ❶「100年間」はcentury、「1000年間」はmillennium

0160
intervention
/intərvénʃən/

名 ❶(〜への)**介入**、干渉(in 〜)(≒interference) ❷(〜への)仲裁、調停(in 〜)(≒mediation)
動intervene：(intervene inで)❶〜に介入[干渉]する、割り込む ❷〜を調停する、とりなす

| Day 9)) CD-A9
Quick Review
答えは右ページ下 | □ 効率
□ 落ち着き
□ 欠点
□ 存在 | □ 部門
□ 失望
□ 削減
□ 赤字 | □ 治療
□ 換気
□ 地球温暖化
□ 休憩時間 | □ 候補者
□ 原稿
□ 有罪判決
□ 摩擦 |

Check 2 Phrase

- the genetic makeup（遺伝子構造）
- put on one's makeup（化粧をする）

- the lingering recession（長引く景気後退）
- remain in recession（いまだに不景気である）

- make a concession to ~（~に譲歩する）
- a major concession（大幅な譲歩）

- a sports complex（複合スポーツ施設）
- an apartment complex（団地）

- the Japan Football Association（日本サッカー協会）
- in association with ~（~と提携して、~と共同で）

- a political opponent（政敵）
- opponents of the reforms（改革の反対者たち）

- the last decade of the 20th century（20世紀の最後の10年間）
- for the past [last] few decades（この数十年の間に）

- military intervention（軍事介入）
- intervention in the dispute（その紛争の仲裁）

Check 3 Sentence

- The DNA makeup differs from one species to another.（DNAの構造は種ごとに異なる）

- The US economy is recovering from the recession.（米国経済は景気後退から回復しつつある）

- The management was forced to make concessions to the union.（経営陣は労働組合に対して譲歩せざるを得なかった）

- A large shopping complex is being built near the station.（駅の近くに大型の複合ショッピング施設が建設されている）

- The Italian Slow Food Association was founded in 1986.（イタリア・スローフード協会は1986年に設立された）

- The champion knocked his opponent down in the third round.（チャンピオンは敵を第3ラウンドでノックダウンした）

- Use of the Internet has expanded dramatically in the last decade.（インターネットの使用はこの10年間で劇的に拡大した）

- Government intervention in economic affairs should be minimal.（経済問題への政府の介入は最小限であるべきだ）

Day 9 CD-A9
Quick Review
答えは左ページ下

- efficiency
- composure
- shortcoming
- existence
- sector
- dismay
- reduction
- deficit
- therapy
- ventilation
- global warming
- recess
- candidate
- manuscript
- conviction
- friction

CHAPTER 1
CHAPTER 2
CHAPTER 3
CHAPTER 4
CHAPTER 5
CHAPTER 6
CHAPTER 7
CHAPTER 8
CHAPTER 9
CHAPTER 10

Day 11　名詞11

Check 1　Listen 》CD-A11

☐ 0161
outcome
/áutkʌm/

名(〜の)**結果**(of 〜)(≒result, consequence, effect, upshot)

☐ 0162
eruption
/irʌ́pʃən/

名(火山の)**噴火**、爆発
動erupt：(火山が)噴火する

☐ 0163
participant
/pɑːrtísəpənt/

名(〜の)**参加者**(in 〜)
動participate：(participate inで)〜に参加する
名participation：(〜への)参加(in 〜)

☐ 0164
assignment
/əsáinmənt/

名❶**宿題**、研究課題(≒homework, project)　❷任務(≒task)；(仕事などの)割り当て(≒allocation)
動assign：❶(assign A to Bで)A(仕事など)をBに割り当てる；AをB(部署など)に配属[任命]する　❷(assign A to doで)Aを〜する仕事に就かせる

☐ 0165
dimension
/diménʃən/

名❶**局面**、側面(≒aspect)　❷(〜s)重要性(≒importance, significance)；規模(≒scale)；大きさ(≒size)　❸寸法(≒measurement)　❹次元

☐ 0166
nuisance
/njúːsns/
❶発音注意

名**迷惑**；迷惑[不愉快]な人[物、事](≒annoyance, trouble)

☐ 0167
credibility
/krèdəbíləti/

名**信用**、信頼性(≒reliability)
形credible：信用[信頼]できる

☐ 0168
ransom
/rǽnsəm/

名**身代金**　❶「誘拐」はkidnapping、「人質」はhostage

continued
▼

今日でChapter 1は最後！ 時間に余裕があったら、章末のReviewにも挑戦しておこう。忘れてしまった単語も結構あるのでは?!

☐ 聞くだけモード Check 1
☐ しっかりモード Check 1 ▶ 2
☐ かんぺきモード Check 1 ▶ 2 ▶ 3

Check 2　Phrase

☐ the final outcome of the negotiations(その交渉の最終結果)

☐ a volcanic eruption(火山噴火)

☐ participants in the contest(そのコンテストの参加者)

☐ finish one's assignment(宿題を終える)
☐ on assignment(任務[仕事]で)

☐ the social dimension of globalization(グローバル化の社会的側面)
☐ a problem of great dimensions(非常に重要な問題)

☐ make a nuisance of oneself (人に迷惑をかける)
☐ What a nuisance!(嫌だな！)

☐ gain [lose] credibility(信用を得る[失う])
☐ undermine the credibility of ~(~の信頼を傷つける)

☐ a ransom demand(身代金の要求)

Check 3　Sentence

☐ He is very worried about the outcome of the trial.(彼はその裁判の結果を非常に心配している)

☐ The last eruption of Mt. Fuji was in 1707.(富士山の最後の噴火は1707年だった)

☐ More than 100 participants attended the seminar.(100人を超える参加者がそのセミナーに出席した)

☐ He forgot to turn in his assignment to his teacher.(彼は宿題を先生に提出するのを忘れた)

☐ Marriage brought a new dimension to his life.(結婚は彼の生活に新しい局面をもたらした)

☐ Noisy dogs can be a nuisance to neighbors.(やかましいイヌは近所の人たちにとって迷惑になることがある)

☐ The scandal has ruined his credibility as a politician.(そのスキャンダルは政治家としての彼の信用を台無しにしてしまった)

☐ The kidnapper demanded a ransom of $2 million for the release of the hostage.(誘拐犯はその人質を解放する代わりに200万ドルの身代金を要求した)

continued
▼

Day 11

Check 1　Listen))) CD-A11

□ 0169 ballot
/bǽlət/

名 ❶**投票**(≒vote, poll, election)　❷投票用紙　❸投票数
動 ❶(〜に賛成／…に反対)投票する(for 〜/against . . .)(≒vote, poll)　❷〜を投票で決める

□ 0170 leftover
/léftòuvər/

名 (通例〜s)(料理などの)**残り物**
形 残りの、食べ残しの

□ 0171 reminder
/rimáindər/

名 (〜を)**思い出させる物**[人]、(〜の)思い出(の品)(of 〜)　⊕remainder(残り)と混同しないように注意
動 remind：(remind A of [about] Bで)AにBを思い出させる、気づかせる

□ 0172 consent
/kənsént/

名 (〜に対する)**同意**、承諾(to 〜)(≒agreement, assent, acceptance, approval, permission)(⇔dissent)
動 (consent toで)〜に同意する、〜を承諾[許可]する(≒agree to, assent to, accept, approve)
名 consensus：❶合意、総意　❷(意見などの)一致

□ 0173 amenity
/əménəti/

名 (通例〜ies)(便利な)**設備**、施設(≒facility)

□ 0174 evaluation
/ivæljuéiʃən/

名 **評価**、査定(≒assessment, appraisal)
動 evaluate：〜を評価する

□ 0175 minor
/máinər/

名 ❶**未成年者**(⇔adult)　❷副専攻科目(⇔major)
形 ❶(比較的)重大[重要]でない、ちょっとした(≒unimportant)　❷小さい[少ない]ほうの(⇔major)
名 minority：❶(通例〜ies)(1国内の)少数民族[集団]　❷少数(の者)　❸少数派

□ 0176 detour
/díːtuər/
❶発音注意

名 **迂回**(路)、回り道(≒diversion)
動 迂回する、回り道する

Day 10))) CD-A10　Quick Review　答えは右ページ下

□ 大失敗　□ うつ病　□ 保存料　□ 結果　□ 分子　□ 衛星　□ 服用量　□ 考古学者　□ 構造　□ 景気後退　□ 譲歩　□ 複合施設　□ 協会　□ 敵　□ 10年間　□ 介入

Check 2　Phrase

- [ ] secret ballot(無記名投票)
- [ ] cast a ballot(投票する)

- [ ] put leftovers into the fridge(残り物を冷蔵庫にしまう)

- [ ] serve as a reminder of ~(~を思い出させる)
- [ ] a constant reminder(いつも思い出させる物)

- [ ] give (one's) consent to ~(~に同意する)
- [ ] without one's consent(~の承諾なしに)

- [ ] the basic amenities(最低限の設備)
- [ ] public amenities(公共施設)

- [ ] job [performance] evaluation(職務[業績]評価)

- [ ] sell cigarettes to minors(未成年者にたばこを売る)
- [ ] take sociology as a minor(社会学を副専攻科目として受講する)

- [ ] make [take] a detour(迂回する)

Check 3　Sentence

- [ ] A new chairperson will be elected by ballot.(新しい議長は投票で選ばれるだろう)

- [ ] I ate yesterday's leftovers for lunch.(私は昨日の残り物を昼食に食べた)

- [ ] The Auschwitz concentration camp serves as a reminder of the Holocaust during World War II.(アウシュビッツ強制収容所は第2次世界大戦中のホロコーストを思い出させる)

- [ ] His silence implied tacit consent to the plan.(彼の沈黙はその計画に対する暗黙の同意を意味していた)

- [ ] The hotel has wonderful amenities.(そのホテルは素晴らしい設備を備えている)

- [ ] Employees receive an annual performance evaluation.(従業員たちは年に1度、業績評価を受ける)

- [ ] It is legally forbidden to sell alcohol to minors.(未成年者にアルコール類を販売するのは法律で禁じられている)

- [ ] I took a detour to avoid the city center.(私は街の中心部を避けるために迂回した)

Day 10))) CD-A10
Quick Review
答えは左ページ下

- [ ] blunder
- [ ] depression
- [ ] preservative
- [ ] consequence
- [ ] molecule
- [ ] satellite
- [ ] dosage
- [ ] archaeologist
- [ ] makeup
- [ ] recession
- [ ] concession
- [ ] complex
- [ ] association
- [ ] opponent
- [ ] decade
- [ ] intervention

Chapter 1 Review

左ページの(1)〜(20)の名詞の同意・類義語（≒）、反意・反対語（⇔）を右ページのA〜Tから選び、カッコの中に答えを書き込もう。意味が分からないときは、見出し番号を参照して復習しておこう（答えは右ページ下）。

- ☐ (1) perspective (0006) ≒は? (　　)
- ☐ (2) ban (0019) ≒は? (　　)
- ☐ (3) consensus (0033) ⇔は? (　　)
- ☐ (4) surplus (0042) ⇔は? (　　)
- ☐ (5) compliment (0051) ≒は? (　　)
- ☐ (6) solitude (0060) ≒は? (　　)
- ☐ (7) conservation (0068) ≒は? (　　)
- ☐ (8) subsidy (0078) ≒は? (　　)
- ☐ (9) scheme (0084) ≒は? (　　)
- ☐ (10) remedy (0087) ≒は? (　　)
- ☐ (11) flaw (0107) ≒は? (　　)
- ☐ (12) recognition (0112) ≒は? (　　)
- ☐ (13) discretion (0118) ≒は? (　　)
- ☐ (14) strain (0128) ≒は? (　　)
- ☐ (15) dismay (0134) ≒は? (　　)
- ☐ (16) conviction (0143) ⇔は? (　　)
- ☐ (17) blunder (0145) ≒は? (　　)
- ☐ (18) consequence (0148) ⇔は? (　　)
- ☐ (19) credibility (0167) ≒は? (　　)
- ☐ (20) evaluation (0174) ≒は? (　　)

A. carefulness
B. deficiency
C. acquittal
D. preservation
E. cause
F. defect
G. viewpoint
H. assessment
I. treatment
J. loneliness
K. acknowledgment
L. disagreement
M. pressure
N. reliability
O. grant
P. praise
Q. disappointment
R. prohibition
S. mistake
T. plan

【解答】(1) G (2) R (3) L (4) B (5) P (6) J (7) D (8) O (9) T (10) I
(11) F (12) K (13) A (14) M (15) Q (16) C (17) S (18) E (19) N (20) H

CHAPTER 2

動詞：超頻出112

Chapter 2では、英検準1級「超頻出」の動詞112を身につけていきます。Chapter 1を終え、学習のペースもだいぶつかめてきたのでは？「英検準1級合格」を目指して、このペースをキープしていきましょう。

Day 12【動詞1】
▶ 62
Day 13【動詞2】
▶ 66
Day 14【動詞3】
▶ 70
Day 15【動詞4】
▶ 74
Day 16【動詞5】
▶ 78
Day 17【動詞6】
▶ 82
Day 18【動詞7】
▶ 86
Chapter 2 Review
▶ 90

こんなの出たよ！

To improve the quality of its courses, the language school asks students to (　　　) their teachers by completing a questionnaire at the end of each semester. (2009年度第1回)

1　evaluate　　2　retrieve
3　postpone　　4　intensify

▼
答えはDay 18でチェック！

Day 12 動詞1

Check 1　Listen))) CD-A12

☐ 0177
boost
/búːst/
▶ 動(生産など)**を増加[増大]させる**、高める、伸ばす(≒ increase, raise, improve, uplift)
名❶(物価などの)増加、上昇(≒ increase, rise)　❷景気づけ

☐ 0178
stimulate
/stímjulèit/
▶ 動**～を刺激する**、活気づける(≒ encourage)
名stimulation:刺激、興奮
名stimulus:刺激(するもの)
名stimulant:興奮剤、刺激剤
形stimulating:刺激的な

☐ 0179
suspend
/səspénd/
▶ 動❶**～を一時停止[中止]する**(≒ stop, postpone, delay, discontinue)　❷～を(…から)停職[停学、出場停止]にする(from ...)　❸～をつるす(≒ hang)
名suspension:❶(活動などの)一時停止[中止]　❷停学、停職、出場停止

☐ 0180
exploit
/ikspl´ɔit/
▶ 動❶**～を搾取する**、食い物にする、不当に使う　❷(資源など)を利用[活用、開発]する(≒ use, utilize)
名exploitation:❶搾取、私的利用　❷(資源などの)利用、開発

☐ 0181
detect
/ditékt/
▶ 動**～を発見する**、感知[探知]する、～に気づく(≒ find, discover, notice, sense)
名detector:探知[検出]器
名detection:発見；探知
名detective:刑事；探偵

☐ 0182
encounter
/inkáuntər/
▶ 動❶(困難など)**に直面[遭遇]する**(≒ face, confront)　❷～に偶然出会う(≒ come across, run across)
名(～との)(偶然の)出会い、遭遇(with ～)

☐ 0183
browse
/bráuz/
▶ 動❶(雑誌などに)**ざっと目を通す**(through ～)(≒ scan, skim)　❷(インターネットで)～を閲覧[検索]する
名browser:ブラウザ

☐ 0184
generate
/dʒénərèit/
▶ 動**～を生み出す**、発生させる、引き起こす(≒ produce, create, cause, give rise to)
名generation:❶(集合的に)同世代の人々　❷一世代　❸発生
名generator:発電機

continued
▼

Chapter 2では、7日をかけて「超頻出」の動詞112をチェック。まずはCDでチャンツを聞いて、単語を「耳」からインプット!

□ 聞くだけモード　Check 1
□ しっかりモード　Check 1 ▶ 2
□ かんぺきモード　Check 1 ▶ 2 ▶ 3

Check 2　Phrase

□ **boost** sales [profits]（売り上げ[利益]を増やす）
□ **boost** one's morale（士気を高める）

□ **stimulate** one's interest（興味を刺激する）
□ **stimulate** the domestic economy（国内経済を活気づける）

□ **suspend** the construction of ~（~の建設を一時停止する）
□ **suspend** the employee for two days（その従業員を2日間の停職にする）

□ **exploit** the poor（貧困層を搾取する）
□ **exploit** natural resources（天然資源を利用する）

□ **detect** enemy aircraft（敵機を発見する）
□ **detect** hazardous gases（有毒ガスを感知する）

□ **encounter** hardship（苦難に直面する）
□ **encounter** an old friend（旧友に偶然出会う）

□ **browse** through the book（本にざっと目を通す）
□ **browse** the website（ウェブサイトを閲覧する）

□ **generate** income（収入を生み出す）
□ **generate** electricity（電気を発生させる）

Check 3　Sentence

□ Tax cuts will **boost** spending and help the country recover from the recession.（減税は支出を増加させ、その国が景気後退から回復するのに役立つだろう）

□ The policy is expected to **stimulate** economic activity.（その政策は経済活動を刺激すると期待されている）

□ The automaker is planning to **suspend** production at one of its assembly plants.（その自動車メーカーは組立工場の1つでの生産を一時停止することを計画している）

□ Many workers were **exploited** during the Industrial Revolution.（産業革命の間、多くの労働者は搾取されていた）

□ Many cancers can be cured if **detected** early.（初期に発見されれば、多くのがんは治癒可能だ）

□ The family is **encountering** money problems.（その家庭は金銭問題に直面している）

□ I spent hours **browsing** through magazines.（私は雑誌にざっと目を通しながら、数時間を過ごした）

□ The steelmaker **generated** record profits last year.（その鉄鋼メーカーは昨年、最高の収益を生み出した）

continued
▼

Day 12

Check 1　Listen 》CD-A12

0185
devise /diváiz/
- 動 ～を考案[案出]する (≒ conceive, formulate, think up)
- 名 device：(～の)装置、機器(for ～)

0186
exterminate /ikstə́ːrmənèit/
- 動 (害虫など)を駆除する、根絶させる、皆殺しにする (≒ wipe out, eradicate)
- 名 extermination：駆除、根絶
- 名 exterminator：害虫駆除業者

0187
compile /kəmpáil/
- 動 ～を編集[編さん]する (≒ edit)
- 名 compilation：編集物；編集

0188
launch /lɔ́ːntʃ/
- 動 ❶(事業など)に着手する (≒ embark on)　❷(ロケットなど)を打ち上げる　❸(新製品)を売り出す　❹(launch intoで)～を(熱心に)始める、やり出す
- 名 ❶(事業などの)開始　❷(ロケットなどの)発射　❸(新製品などの)発売

0189
advocate /ǽdvəkèit/
- 動 ～を支持[擁護、弁護]する (≒ support, back)
- 名 (/ǽdvəkət/)(～の)支持[擁護]者(of [for] ～) (≒ supporter, backer)；弁護士
- 名 advocacy：支持、擁護、弁護

0190
expire /ikspáiər/
- 動 期限が切れる、満期になる (≒ end, run out)
- 名 expiration：(期限の)終了、満期

0191
embrace /imbréis/
- 動 ❶～を抱き締める、抱擁する (≒ hug, cuddle)　❷(意見など)を受け入れる、採用する (≒ accept, adopt, employ)
- 名 抱擁 (≒ hug, cuddle)

0192
cultivate /kʌ́ltəvèit/
- 動 ❶(友情など)をはぐくむ、深める (≒ develop)　❷(土地など)を耕す (≒ farm)　❸～を栽培する (≒ grow)
- 名 cultivation：❶耕作　❷栽培　❸教養、修養
- 形 cultivated：❶教養のある、洗練された　❷耕作された　❸栽培された

Day 11 》CD-A11　Quick Review
答えは右ページ下

- □ 結果
- □ 噴火
- □ 参加者
- □ 宿題
- □ 局面
- □ 迷惑
- □ 信用
- □ 身代金
- □ 投票
- □ 残り物
- □ 思い出させる物
- □ 同意
- □ 設備
- □ 評価
- □ 未成年者
- □ 迂回

Check 2　Phrase

- ☐ devise a new method（新しい方法を考案する）

- ☐ exterminate cockroaches（ゴキブリを駆除する）

- ☐ compile a dictionary（辞書を編さんする）

- ☐ launch a new business（新しい事業に着手する）
- ☐ launch a space shuttle（スペースシャトルを打ち上げる）

- ☐ advocate capital punishment（死刑を支持する）
- ☐ advocate human rights（人権を擁護する）

- ☐ expire on December 31（12月31日に期限が切れる）

- ☐ embrace each other（抱き合う）
- ☐ embrace his opinion（彼の意見を受け入れる）

- ☐ cultivate a relationship with ～（～との関係をはぐくむ）
- ☐ cultivate barren land（不毛の土地を耕す）

Check 3　Sentence

- ☐ Esperanto was devised by Dr. Zamenhof in the 1880s.（エスペラントはザメンホフ博士によって1880年代に考案された）● エスペラント＝人工の国際語

- ☐ This poison is used to exterminate rats.（この毒薬はネズミを駆除するのに使われる）

- ☐ She is working on compiling an encyclopedia.（彼女は百科事典の編集に取り組んでいる）

- ☐ Police have launched an investigation into the incident.（警察はその事件の調査に着手した）

- ☐ The group openly advocates violence.（その団体は公然と暴力を支持している）

- ☐ My passport expires next month.（私のパスポートは来月で期限が切れる）

- ☐ She embraced her daughter tightly.（彼女は娘をしっかりと抱き締めた）

- ☐ Teachers should cultivate the talents of children.（教師は子どもたちの才能をはぐくむべきだ）

Day 11　CD-A11　Quick Review
答えは左ページ下

- ☐ outcome
- ☐ eruption
- ☐ participant
- ☐ assignment
- ☐ dimension
- ☐ nuisance
- ☐ credibility
- ☐ ransom
- ☐ ballot
- ☐ leftover
- ☐ reminder
- ☐ consent
- ☐ amenity
- ☐ evaluation
- ☐ minor
- ☐ detour

Day 13　動詞2

Check 1　Listen » CD-A13

0193
pacify
/pǽsəfài/
- 動 ❶ ～をなだめる(≒ placate, appease, calm down) ❷(国・地域)に平和をもたらす
- 形 pacific：❶平和を好む；平和な ❷穏やかな

0194
disrupt
/disrʌ́pt/
- 動 ～を中断[混乱]させる(≒ interrupt)
- 名 disruption：中断、混乱
- 形 disruptive：❶(生徒などが)問題を起こす ❷混乱をもたらす

0195
shrink
/ʃríŋk/
- 動 ❶縮む(≒ contract) ❷～を縮ませる ❸減少[縮小]する(≒ decrease) ❹～を減少[縮小]させる(≒ reduce)
- 名 shrinkage：減少、縮小

0196
enhance
/inhǽns/
- 動 (価値など)を高める、強める(≒ increase, heighten, intensify)
- 名 enhancement：増大、強化

0197
condemn
/kəndém/
❶発音注意
- 動 ～を(…の理由で)非難する、責める(for ...)(≒ blame, criticize, censure, reprimand, rebuke)

0198
overtake
/òuvərtéik/
- 動 ～を追い越す、上回る(≒ pass)

0199
decay
/dikéi/
- 動 腐る、腐敗する、朽ちる(≒ rot, spoil, go bad, decompose)
- 名 腐敗、腐食(≒ rot, decomposition)

0200
reveal
/rivíːl/
- 動 (秘密など)を明らかにする、暴露する(≒ disclose, expose, uncover, unearth)(⇔ hide, conceal：～を秘密にする)
- 名 revelation：❶暴露 ❷意外な新事実、新発見

continued ▼

音と意味がつながるまでは「使える」ようになったとは言えない。チャンツの最初の「英語」の部分で意味がすぐに浮かぶか試してみよう。

☐ 聞くだけモード　Check 1
☐ しっかりモード　Check 1 ▶ 2
☐ かんぺきモード　Check 1 ▶ 2 ▶ 3

Check 2　　Phrase

☐ pacify angry customers（怒っている客をなだめる）
☐ pacify Afghanistan（アフガニスタンに平和をもたらす）

☐ disrupt train service（列車の運行を中断させる）
☐ disrupt society（社会を混乱させる）

☐ a shrunken sweater（縮んだセーター）
☐ shrinking economy（縮小する経済）

☐ enhance one's reputation（評判を高める）

☐ condemn his actions ＝ condemn him for his actions（彼の行動を非難する）

☐ overtake the car ahead（前方の車を追い越す）

☐ decayed food（腐った食べ物）
☐ a decayed tree（朽ちた木）

☐ reveal secrets to ~（~に秘密を明かす）

Check 3　　Sentence

☐ She tried to pacify her crying baby.（彼女は泣いている赤ん坊をなだめようとした）

☐ The game was disrupted by rain.（その試合は雨のため中断された）

☐ My favorite shirt shrank in the wash.（私のお気に入りのシャツは洗濯したら縮んでしまった）

☐ The company is trying to enhance its productivity.（その会社は生産性を高めようと努力している）

☐ The UN has condemned the country for its human rights violations.（国連はその国を人権侵害で非難した）

☐ China overtook the US in CO_2 emissions in 2007.（中国は2007年に二酸化炭素排出量で米国を追い越した）

☐ I found tomatoes decaying in my fridge.（私はトマトが冷蔵庫で腐りかけているのを見つけた）

☐ The details of the incident were revealed in court.（その事件の詳細が法廷で明らかにされた）

continued
▼

Check 1 Listen))) CD-A13

☐ 0201
eliminate
/ilímənèit/

▶ 動 **〜を(…から)取り除く**、除去[排除]する(from . . .) (≒ remove, get rid of, exclude)
　名 elimination：(〜からの)除去、排除(from 〜)

☐ 0202
escalate
/éskəlèit/

▶ 動 ❶(問題などが)(〜に)**エスカレートする**、だんだん悪化する(into 〜) ❷〜をエスカレート[悪化]させる
　名 escalation：(問題などが)エスカレートすること
　名 escalator：エスカレーター

☐ 0203
alter
/ɔ́ːltər/

▶ 動 ❶**〜を変える**、改める(≒ change, modify) ❷変わる
　名 alteration：変更、修正

☐ 0204
exaggerate
/igzǽdʒərèit/

▶ 動 **〜を誇張する**、大げさに言う(≒ overstate)
　名 exaggeration：誇張
　形 exaggerated：誇張した、大げさな

☐ 0205
capture
/kǽptʃər/

▶ 動 ❶**〜を捕まえる**(≒ catch, arrest, seize) ❷〜を獲得する(≒ get, acquire) ❸〜を攻略する(≒ occupy)
　名 ❶逮捕(≒ arrest, seizure) ❷獲得 ❸攻略
　名 captive：❶捕虜 ❷とりこ
　形 captive：捕虜になった

☐ 0206
sustain
/səstéin/

▶ 動 ❶**〜を維持する**、持続させる(≒ maintain, continue) ❷(損害など)を被る、負う(≒ suffer)
　形 sustainable：持続可能な
　名 sustainability：持続可能性
　名 sustenance：(生命維持のための)食物、栄養(物)

☐ 0207
ensure
/inʃúər/

▶ 動 **〜を保証する**、確実にする(≒ guarantee, make sure, secure) ⊕insure(〜に保険をかける)と混同しないように注意

☐ 0208
shatter
/ʃǽtər/

▶ 動 ❶(ガラスなど)**を粉々にする**(≒ smash) ❷粉々になる

Day 12))) CD-A12
Quick Review
答えは右ページ下

☐ 〜を増加させる ☐ 〜を発見する ☐ 〜を考案する ☐ 〜を支持する
☐ 〜を刺激する ☐ 〜に直面する ☐ 〜を駆除する ☐ 期限が切れる
☐ 〜を一時停止する ☐ ざっと目を通す ☐ 〜を編集する ☐ 〜を抱き締める
☐ 〜を搾取する ☐ 〜を生み出す ☐ 〜に着手する ☐ 〜をはぐくむ

Check 2　Phrase

- ☐ eliminate fat from one's diet（脂肪を食事から取り除く）
- ☐ eliminate the possibility that ~（~という可能性を排除する）

- ☐ escalate into violence（暴力ざたへとエスカレートする）
- ☐ escalate the situation（状況を悪化させる）

- ☐ alter the plan（計画を変える）
- ☐ considerably [dramatically, drastically] alter（大幅に変わる）

- ☐ greatly [grossly] exaggerate ~（~を著しく誇張する）
- ☐ exaggerate the importance of ~（~の重要性を誇張する）

- ☐ capture the criminal（その犯人を捕まえる）
- ☐ capture 45 percent of the vote（投票数の45パーセントを獲得する）

- ☐ sustain a relationship with ~（~との関係を維持する）
- ☐ sustain damage（損害を被る）

- ☐ ensure safety（安全性を保証する）
- ☐ ensure (that) ~（~ということを保証する、確実にする）

- ☐ shatter a vase（花瓶を粉々に割る）
- ☐ shatter into pieces（粉々になる）

Check 3　Sentence

- ☐ Terrorism risks cannot be completely eliminated.（テロの危険性は完全に取り除くことはできない）

- ☐ The tension between the two countries escalated into war.（両国の緊張状態は戦争へとエスカレートした）

- ☐ Prices may be altered without notice.（価格は予告なく変わることがある）

- ☐ Some people say that the media exaggerates the threat of global warming.（マスメディアは地球温暖化の脅威を誇張していると言う人たちもいる）

- ☐ The suspect has not yet been captured.（その容疑者はまだ捕まっていない）

- ☐ China has sustained economic growth of 8-10 percent.（中国は8から10パーセントの経済成長を維持している）

- ☐ Gender equality must be ensured in all areas.（男女の平等はすべての分野で保証されなければならない）

- ☐ Windows of neighboring houses were shattered by the explosion.（近隣の住宅の窓はその爆発で粉々になった）

Day 12 》CD-A12
Quick Review
答えは左ページ下

- ☐ boost
- ☐ stimulate
- ☐ suspend
- ☐ exploit
- ☐ detect
- ☐ encounter
- ☐ browse
- ☐ generate
- ☐ devise
- ☐ exterminate
- ☐ compile
- ☐ launch
- ☐ advocate
- ☐ expire
- ☐ embrace
- ☐ cultivate

Day 14　動詞3

Check 1　Listen)) CD-A14

0209
thrive
/θráiv/
動 ❶ **繁栄する**、栄える、成功する (≒ flourish, prosper, succeed)　❷ (植物などが)よく成長[生育]する
形 thriving：繁栄している

0210
accommodate
/əkámədèit/
動 ❶ (建物などが)**～を収容する** (≒ hold)　❷ (要求など)を受け入れる (≒ accept)
名 accommodation：(通例～s)宿泊設備
形 accommodating：親切な、世話好きな

0211
extinguish
/ikstíŋgwiʃ/
動 (火など)**を消す** (≒ put out) (⇔ light：～に火をつける)
名 extinguisher：消火器
名 extinction：絶滅
形 extinct：絶滅した

0212
accumulate
/əkjú:mjəlèit/
動 ❶ (金など)**をためる**、蓄積する (≒ save, collect, gather, amass)　❷ たまる、積もる
名 accumulation：蓄積

0213
surpass
/sərpǽs/
動 **～を超える**、～に勝る、～より優れている (≒ excel, exceed)

0214
devastate
/dévəstèit/
動 ❶ (場所)**を壊滅[荒廃]させる** (≒ destroy, ruin)　❷ (人)に立ち直れないほどのショックを与える (≒ shock, stun)
形 devastating：❶ 壊滅的な　❷ 衝撃的な
名 devastation：荒廃(状態)

0215
impersonate
/impə́:rsənèit/
動 ❶ **～に成り済ます**、～を装う　❷ ～の物まねをする (≒ imitate, mimic, copy)

0216
compromise
/kámprəmàiz/
❶ アクセント注意
動 ❶ (～と／…のことで)**妥協する** (with ～/on …)　❷ ～を損なう、汚す (≒ damage, undermine)　❸ (主義など)を曲げる
名 妥協、歩み寄り

continued
▼

余裕があるときは、派生語・関連語も覚えておこう。そうすれば、1つの単語から、2倍、3倍と語彙が増えていくよ！

□ 聞くだけモード　Check 1
□ しっかりモード　Check 1 ▶ 2
□ かんぺきモード　Check 1 ▶ 2 ▶ 3

Check 2　Phrase

□ thrive on tourism（[都市などが]観光で繁栄する）
□ thrive in dry conditions（[植物などが]乾燥状態でよく成長する）

□ accommodate up to 500 guests（最大500人の客を収容する）
□ accommodate employees' requests（従業員の要望を受け入れる）

□ extinguish a cigarette（たばこの火を消す）

□ accumulate money（お金をためる）
□ accumulate on roads（[雪が]路上に積もる）

□ surpass expectations（予想を上回る）
□ surpass him in ability（能力で彼に勝る）

□ areas devastated by the earthquake（その地震で壊滅した地域）
□ be devastated by the news（そのニュースにショックを受ける）

□ impersonate a security guard（警備員に成り済ます）
□ impersonate a famous person（有名人の物まねをする）

□ compromise with ~ on the issue（~とその問題のことで妥協する）
□ compromise one's reputation（評判を落とす）

Check 3　Sentence

□ The country is thriving economically.（その国は経済的に繁栄している）

□ The stadium can accommodate about 80,000 spectators.（そのスタジアムは約8万人の観客を収容できる）

□ Firefighters tried in vain to extinguish the fire.（消防士たちはその火事を消そうとしたが無駄だった）

□ He has accumulated $10,000 in debt.（彼は1万ドルまで借金をためてしまった）

□ India's population will surpass China's in the future.（インドの人口は将来、中国の人口を超えるだろう）

□ The village was devastated by the tsunami.（その村は津波で壊滅した）

□ The man was arrested for impersonating a police officer.（その男は警官に成り済ましたかどで逮捕された）

□ We don't compromise on the quality of our products.（当社は製品の品質の点では妥協しない）

continued
▼

Day 14

Check 1　Listen))) CD-A14

0217 resume /rizjúːm/
- 動 ❶ ~を再開する (≒ restart, reopen, renew) ❷ 再開する
- 名 resumption：再開

0218 designate /dézignèit/
- 動 ~を(…として)指定[指名、任命]する (as ...) ⊕ この as は省略可能 (≒ appoint, nominate)
- 名 designation：指定、指名、任命

0219 unearth /ʌnə́ːrθ/
- 動 ❶ ~を発掘する、掘り出す (≒ dig up, excavate) ❷ (秘密などを)明らかにする、暴く (≒ disclose, reveal, expose, uncover)；~を発見する (≒ discover)

0220 modify /mάdəfài/
- 動 ~を(部分的に)修正[変更]する (≒ change, alter)
- 名 modification：修正、変更

0221 anticipate /æntísəpèit/
- 動 ❶ ~を予想[予期、期待]する (≒ expect, predict, foresee) ❷ ~に前もって対処する
- 名 anticipation：期待、予想

0222 reciprocate /risíprəkèit/
- 動 ❶ ~に報いる、返礼する (≒ reward, repay, pay) ❷ 報いる、返礼する
- 名 reciprocation：返礼、お返し
- 名 reciprocity：相互(依存)関係、互恵主義

0223 evacuate /ivǽkjuèit/
- 動 ❶ ~を(…から)避難させる (from ...) (≒ remove) ❷ ~から避難する (≒ leave) ❸ 避難する
- 名 evacuation：避難

0224 stray /stréi/
- 動 ❶ (~から)迷い出る、はぐれる (from ~) (≒ wander, get lost) ❷ (話題などが)(~から)それる、脱線する (from ~) (≒ digress, deviate)
- 形 (動物などが)道に迷った
- 名 迷子の動物

Day 13))) CD-A13
Quick Review
答えは右ページ下

- □ ~をなだめる
- □ ~を中断させる
- □ 縮む
- □ ~を高める
- □ ~を非難する
- □ ~を追い越す
- □ 腐る
- □ ~を明らかにする
- □ ~を取り除く
- □ エスカレートする
- □ ~を変える
- □ ~を誇張する
- □ ~を捕まえる
- □ ~を維持する
- □ ~を保証する
- □ ~を粉々にする

Check 2 Phrase

- [ ] resume negotiations(交渉を再開する)

- [ ] designate the area as a national park(その地域を国立公園に指定する)
- [ ] designate him as chairperson(彼を議長に任命する)

- [ ] unearth treasures(財宝を発掘する)
- [ ] unearth evidence(証拠を明らかにする)

- [ ] modify the original plan(当初の計画を変更する)
- [ ] genetically modified foods(遺伝子組み換え食品)

- [ ] anticipate the worst(最悪の事態を予想する)
- [ ] anticipate customers' needs(顧客の要望に前もって応える)

- [ ] reciprocate her hospitality(彼女の温かいもてなしに報いる)

- [ ] evacuate residents from flooded areas(洪水地域から住民を避難させる)
- [ ] evacuate one's home(自宅から避難する)

- [ ] stray from the path(道に迷う)
- [ ] stray from the main topic(本題からそれる)

Check 3 Sentence

- [ ] Both countries agreed to resume peace talks.(両国は和平協議を再開することで同意した)

- [ ] Horyuji was designated as a cultural World Heritage site in 1993.(法隆寺は1993年に世界文化遺産に指定された)

- [ ] The archaeologist unearthed pottery dating back 4,000 years.(その考古学者は4000年前の陶器を発掘した)

- [ ] Do you think that the constitution should be modified?(憲法は修正されるべきだと思いますか?)

- [ ] It is anticipated that corporate tax will be reduced.(法人税は引き下げられると予想されている)

- [ ] His love for her was not reciprocated.(彼女への彼の愛は報われなかった)

- [ ] Over 10,000 refugees were evacuated from combat areas.(1万人を超える難民が戦闘地域から避難した)

- [ ] The soldiers strayed into enemy territory.(兵士たちは敵の領土へ迷い出た)

Day 13))CD-A13
Quick Review
答えは左ページ下

- [ ] pacify
- [ ] disrupt
- [ ] shrink
- [ ] enhance
- [ ] condemn
- [ ] overtake
- [ ] decay
- [ ] reveal
- [ ] eliminate
- [ ] escalate
- [ ] alter
- [ ] exaggerate
- [ ] capture
- [ ] sustain
- [ ] ensure
- [ ] shatter

Day 15　動詞4

Check 1　Listen)) CD-A15

☐ 0225
forfeit
/fɔ́:rfit/
❶発音注意

動 (所有物)**を没収される**、(権利など)をはく奪される(≒ lose, surrender, relinquish)　❶「~を没収する」は confiscate
名 ❶没収、はく奪　❷没収物、罰金

☐ 0226
contaminate
/kəntǽmənèit/

動 **~を汚染する**(≒ pollute)
名 contamination：汚染
名 contaminant：汚染物質

☐ 0227
prosper
/prɑ́spər/

動 **繁栄[繁盛]する**、栄える、成功する(≒ flourish, thrive, succeed)
名 prosperity：繁栄、繁盛
形 prosperous：繁栄している

☐ 0228
clarify
/klǽrəfài/

動 (意味など)**をはっきりさせる**、明らか[明確]にする
名 clarity：(表現などの)明快さ

☐ 0229
loiter
/lɔ́itər/

動 (目的もなく)**うろつく**、ぶらつく(≒ wander, roam, stroll)

☐ 0230
verify
/vérəfài/

動 ❶**~を**(正しいかどうか)**確かめる**、確認する(≒ check)　❷~を立証[実証]する(≒ confirm, prove)
名 verification：確認、証明

☐ 0231
hinder
/híndər/

動 **~を妨げる**、遅らせる(≒ hamper, obstruct, prevent, delay)
名 hindrance：(~の)障害、障壁、妨害、邪魔(to ~)

☐ 0232
absorb
/əbzɔ́:rb, æbsɔ́:rb/

動 ❶**~を吸収する**　❷(be absorbed inで)~に夢中になっている、没頭している
名 absorption：❶吸収　❷(~への)没頭(in [with] ~)
形 absorbing：非常に面白い

continued
▼

チャンツを聞く際には、「英語→日本語→英語」の2回目の「英語」の部分で声に出して読んでみよう。定着度が倍増するはず！

- □ 聞くだけモード　Check 1
- □ しっかりモード　Check 1 ▶ 2
- □ かんぺきモード　Check 1 ▶ 2 ▶ 3

Check 2　Phrase

- □ **forfeit** one's property（財産を没収される）
- □ **forfeit** the right to do ～（～する権利をはく奪される）

- □ **contaminate** soil [groundwater]（土壌[地下水]を汚染する）

- □ a **prospering** economy（繁栄している経済）
- □ **prosper** in business（事業に成功する）

- □ **clarify** an issue（問題点をはっきりさせる）
- □ **clarify** one's position（自分の立場を明確にする）

- □ **loiter** in the mall（ショッピングセンターの中をぶらつく）

- □ **verify** the accuracy of ～（～の正確さを確かめる）
- □ **verify** his testimony（彼の証言を立証する）

- □ **hinder** economic growth（経済成長を妨げる）

- □ **absorb** nutrients（栄養を吸収する）
- □ be **absorbed** in music（音楽に夢中になっている）

Check 3　Sentence

- □ If you cancel your order, you will **forfeit** your deposit.（注文を取り消す場合は、手付金は没収される）

- □ The land is **contaminated** by hazardous waste.（その土地は有害廃棄物で汚染されている）

- □ The movie industry **prospered** during the Great Depression.（映画産業は世界大恐慌の間に繁栄した）

- □ He was asked to **clarify** what he meant.（彼は言おうとしていることをはっきりさせるよう求められた）

- □ Please report suspicious persons **loitering** near schools.（学校の近くでうろついている不審者がいたら通報してください）

- □ NASA's Mars lander **verified** the existence of water on Mars.（NASAの火星探査機は火星に水があることを確かめた）

- □ The high cost of fuel cells has **hindered** their commercialization.（燃料電池のコスト高がその商品化を妨げている）

- □ Black **absorbs** more heat than any other color.（黒は他のどんな色よりも多くの熱を吸収する）

continued
▼

Day 15

Check 1　Listen 》CD-A15

□ 0233
scrutinize
/skrúːtənàiz/
▶ 動 **〜を綿密に調べる**、吟味[精査]する(≒examine, inspect, survey, investigate)
名 scrutiny：綿密な調査、吟味、精査

□ 0234
demolish
/dimáliʃ/
▶ 動 (建物など)**を取り壊す**、破壊する(≒destroy, knock down, pull down, take down)
名 demolition：(建物などの)取り壊し、破壊、解体

□ 0235
mimic
/mímik/
▶ 動 **〜の物まねをする**、〜をまねる(≒imitate, copy, impersonate)
名 物まね芸人
名 mimicry：物まね

□ 0236
endorse
/indɔ́ːrs/
▶ 動 ❶**〜を承認[是認、支持]する**(≒approve, support, back)　❷(小切手など)に裏書きする
名 endorsement：❶承認、是認、支持　❷(小切手などの)裏書き

□ 0237
discharge
/distʃáːrdʒ/
▶ 動 ❶**〜を(…へ)排出[放出]する**(into . . .)(≒emit)　❷〜を(…から)退院[除隊]させる、釈放する(from . . .)(≒release, free, dismiss)
名 (/dístʃɑːrdʒ/)❶排出、放出　❷退院、除隊、釈放

□ 0238
implement
/ímpləmènt/
❶アクセント注意
▶ 動 (計画など)**を実行[実施、履行]する**(≒execute, carry out, fulfill)
名 (/ímpləmənt/)道具、用具(≒tool, instrument, utensil)
名 implementation：実行、実施、履行

□ 0239
provoke
/prəvóuk/
▶ 動 (感情など)**を引き起こす**、誘発する(≒cause, evoke, arouse)
名 provocation：挑発
形 provocative：挑発的な

□ 0240
withhold
/wiðhóuld/
▶ 動 **〜を(…に)与えずにおく**(from . . .)、〜を保留する(≒hold back, keep back)

| Day 14 》CD-A14
Quick Review
答えは右ページ下 | □ 繁栄する
□ 〜を収容する
□ 〜を消す
□ 〜をためる | □ 〜を超える
□ 〜を壊滅させる
□ 〜に成り済ます
□ 妥協する | □ 〜を再開する
□ 〜を指定する
□ 〜を発掘する
□ 〜を修正する | □ 〜を予想する
□ 〜に報いる
□ 〜を避難させる
□ 迷い出る |

Check 2 Phrase

- □ scrutinize the contents of ~（~の中身を綿密に調べる）

- □ demolish the old building（その古いビルを取り壊す）

- □ mimic famous singers（有名歌手の物まねをする）
- □ mimic the sound of a bass drum（バスドラムの音をまねる）

- □ endorse her proposal（彼女の提案を承認する）
- □ endorse a check（小切手に裏書きする）

- □ discharge sewage into rivers（下水を川へ排出する）
- □ be discharged from the hospital（退院する）

- □ implement reforms（改革を実行する）

- □ provoke discussion [debate]（議論を巻き起こす）
- □ provoke protests（抗議を引き起こす）

- □ withhold information from ~（情報を~に与えずにおく）
- □ withhold judgment（判断を保留する）

Check 3 Sentence

- □ The detective scrutinized the crime scene.（その刑事は犯行現場を綿密に調べた）

- □ The school will be demolished so that a new school can be built.（新しい校舎を建てるために、その学校は取り壊される予定だ）

- □ He likes mimicking people.（彼は人の物まねをするのが好きだ）

- □ The project plan was endorsed by the board of directors.（その事業計画は取締役会で承認された）

- □ The factory was fined for discharging toxic substances into the river.（その工場は有毒物質を川に排出したかどで罰金を科された）

- □ The government should implement policies to reduce inequality in income.（政府は所得格差を減らすための政策を実行するべきだ）

- □ The decision to close the hospital provoked anger among local residents.（その病院を閉鎖する決定は地元住民の怒りを引き起こした）

- □ The company was accused of withholding overtime pay from some employees.（その会社は従業員数名に残業代を与えずにいたことで告訴された）

Day 14))) CD-A14
Quick Review
答えは左ページ下

- □ thrive
- □ accommodate
- □ extinguish
- □ accumulate
- □ surpass
- □ devastate
- □ impersonate
- □ compromise
- □ resume
- □ designate
- □ unearth
- □ modify
- □ anticipate
- □ reciprocate
- □ evacuate
- □ stray

Day 16　動詞5

Check 1　Listen 》CD-A16

☐ 0241
roam
/róum/

動 (目的もなく)(〜を)**歩き回る**、放浪する、ぶらつく
(around [through, over] 〜)(≒ wander, loiter, stroll)

☐ 0242
overlook
/òuvərlúk/

動 ❶**〜を見落とす**、見逃す(≒ miss)　❷(場所が)〜を見渡せる、見下ろせる
名 (/óuvərlùk/)(景色が見渡せる)高台

☐ 0243
underestimate
/ʌ̀ndəréstəmèit/

動 ❶**〜を過小評価する**(≒ underrate, undervalue)
(⇔ overestimate:〜を過大評価する)　❷〜を安く[少なく]見積もり過ぎる
名 (/ʌ̀ndəréstəmət/)安過ぎる見積もり；過小評価
動 estimate: ❶〜を見積もる　❷〜を評価する

☐ 0244
justify
/dʒʌ́stəfài/

動 **〜を正当化する**
名 justification: 正当化；(〜を)正当とする理由(for 〜)

☐ 0245
plunge
/plʌ́ndʒ/

動 ❶(〜に)**飛び込む**、突っ込む(into 〜)(≒ dive, jump)　❷急落する(≒ plummet, slump)
名 ❶落下、転落(≒ fall)　❷急落(≒ drop, slump)

☐ 0246
exceed
/iksí:d/

動 **〜を超える**、上回る(≒ surpass)
名 excess:(〜の)超過(量)(of 〜)
形 excess: 超過した、余分の
形 excessive: 過度の、極端[法外]な

☐ 0247
conserve
/kənsə́:rv/

動 ❶(エネルギーなど)**を節約して使う**(≒ save)　❷〜を保護[保存]する(≒ preserve, protect)
名 conservation:(自然環境などの)保護、保存
形 conservative: ❶保守的な　❷(評価などが)控えめな
名 conservative: 保守的な人

☐ 0248
register
/rédʒistər/
❶アクセント注意

動 ❶**〜を登録[登記]する**(≒ record)　❷(register for で)〜の入学[受講]手続きをする(≒ enroll in [for])
名 登録[記録](簿)
名 registration: 登録、登記
形 registered: ❶登録[登記]された　❷(郵便が)書留の

continued
▼

1つの単語に1つの品詞の用法しかないとは限らない。複数の品詞の用法がある場合には、その意味もなるべく確認しておこう。

☐ 聞くだけモード　Check 1
☐ しっかりモード　Check 1 ▶ 2
☐ かんぺきモード　Check 1 ▶ 2 ▶ 3

Check 2　Phrase

☐ roam around the city（市内を歩き回る）

☐ overlook an important fact（重要な事実を見落とす）
☐ a room overlooking the ocean（海を見渡せる部屋）

☐ underestimate one's opponent（相手を見くびる）
☐ underestimate the cost of ~（~の費用を安く見積もり過ぎる）

☐ justify one's actions（自分の行為を正当化する）

☐ plunge into the pool（プールに飛び込む）
☐ plunging stock prices（急落する株価）

☐ exceed the speed limit（制限速度を超える）
☐ exceed expectations（期待を上回る）

☐ conserve water [energy]（水[エネルギー]を節約して使う）
☐ conserve wildlife（野生生物を保護する）

☐ register a trademark（商標を登録する）
☐ register for the university（その大学の入学手続きをする）

Check 3　Sentence

☐ Cows are allowed to roam through the streets in India.（インドではウシは通りを歩き回ることを許されている）

☐ The importance of sleep is often overlooked.（睡眠の大切さは見落とされることが多い）

☐ The research shows that women tend to underestimate their abilities compared to men.（男性と比べて女性は自分の能力を過小評価する傾向があることをその研究は示している）

☐ Whatever the reason, war cannot be justified.（どんな理由であれ、戦争は正当化できない）

☐ The boy ran down to the beach and plunged into the sea.（その少年は浜辺へと走って、海に飛び込んだ）

☐ The vote exceeded the two-thirds majority needed to approve a constitutional amendment.（投票は憲法改正の承認に必要とされる3分の2の多数を超えた）

☐ It is everyone's responsibility to conserve natural resources.（天然資源を節約して使うことはすべての人の責任だ）

☐ The car was registered in my father's name.（その車は私の父親の名義で登録された）

continued
▼

Day 16

Check 1　Listen))) CD-A16

0249 emerge /imə́ːrdʒ/
- 動 ❶(事実などが)**明らかになる**(≒transpire) ❷現れる、出てくる(≒appear)
- 名 emergence：出現、発生
- 形 emergent：新興[新生]の
- 名 emergency：緊急時、緊急[非常]事態

0250 monopolize /mənápəlàiz/
❶アクセント注意
- 動 **〜を独占する**
- 名 monopoly：❶(〜の)独占(on [of, in] 〜) ❷独占企業
- 名 monopolization：独占

0251 waver /wéivər/
- 動 (判断などに/…の間で)**迷う**、ためらう、揺らぐ(in 〜/between …)(≒hesitate) ◆waiver(権利放棄証書)と混同しないように注意

0252 grasp /grǽsp/
- 動 ❶**〜を理解[把握]する**(≒understand, comprehend) ❷〜を(しっかり)握る、つかむ(≒hold, grip, clutch, clasp)
- 名 ❶理解(力)(≒understanding, comprehension) ❷握ること

0253 resent /rizént/
- 動 **〜に憤慨する**、〜を恨む(≒grudge)
- 形 resentful：(〜に)憤慨した(at [of, about] 〜)
- 名 resentment：(〜に対する)憤慨(at [against, toward] 〜)

0254 mingle /míŋgl/
- 動 ❶(〜と)**歓談する**、歓談して回る(with 〜)(≒socialize, circulate) ❷(〜と)混ざる(with 〜) ❸〜を(…と)混ぜ合わせる(with …)(≒mix, blend)

0255 supervise /súːpərvàiz/
- 動 (人・仕事など)**を監督[指揮、管理]する**(≒direct, manage, oversee)
- 名 supervisor：監督[管理]者、上司
- 名 supervision：監督、指揮、管理

0256 invest /invést/
- 動 ❶(〜に)**投資する**(in 〜) ❷(invest A in Bで)AをBに投資する
- 名 investment：(〜への)投資、出資(in 〜)
- 名 investor：投資家[者]、出資者

Day 15))) CD-A15 Quick Review
答えは右ページ下

- □ 〜を没収される
- □ 〜を汚染する
- □ 繁栄する
- □ 〜をはっきりさせる
- □ うろつく
- □ 〜を確かめる
- □ 〜を妨げる
- □ 〜を吸収する
- □ 〜を綿密に調べる
- □ 〜を取り壊す
- □ 〜の物まねをする
- □ 〜を承認する
- □ 〜を排出する
- □ 〜を実行する
- □ 〜を引き起こす
- □ 〜を与えずにおく

Check 2　Phrase

- It emerges that ~.（~ということが明らかになる）
- emerge from the water（水面から現れる）

- monopolize the market [conversation]（市場[会話]を独占する）

- waver in one's judgment（判断に迷う）
- waver between going and not going（行くか行かないか心が揺らぐ）

- grasp the importance of ~（~の重要性を理解する）
- grasp her hand（彼女の手を握る）

- resent the fact that ~（~という事実に憤慨する）
- resent being treated like a child（子どものように扱われることに憤慨する）

- mingle with old friends（旧友たちと歓談する）
- mingle with water（水と混ざる）

- supervise construction work（建設工事を監督する）

- invest in the stock market（株式市場に投資する）
- invest $2 million in the company（その会社に200万ドルを投資する）

Check 3　Sentence

- New evidence emerged during the trial.（新しい証拠が裁判中に明らかになった）

- Antitrust laws forbid one company from monopolizing an entire industry.（独占禁止法は1つの企業が産業全体を独占するのを禁じている）

- He has never wavered in his decision.（彼は決断に迷ったことが一度もない）

- Abstract concepts are difficult for children to grasp.（抽象的な概念は子どもには理解するのが難しい）

- Good employees resent lazy employees.（優秀な従業員たちは怠惰な従業員たちに憤慨している）

- The guests were mingling in the garden after the ceremony.（式典の後、招待客たちは庭で歓談していた）

- He is in charge of supervising the project.（彼はそのプロジェクトの監督を任されている）

- Now is not a good time to invest in the real estate market.（今は不動産市場に投資するのに適した時ではない）

Day 15))CD-A15
Quick Review
答えは左ページ下

- forfeit
- contaminate
- prosper
- clarify
- loiter
- verify
- hinder
- absorb
- scrutinize
- demolish
- mimic
- endorse
- discharge
- implement
- provoke
- withhold

CHAPTER 1
CHAPTER 2
CHAPTER 3
CHAPTER 4
CHAPTER 5
CHAPTER 6
CHAPTER 7
CHAPTER 8
CHAPTER 9
CHAPTER 10

Day 17　動詞6

Check 1　Listen 》CD-A17

0257 pamper /pæmpər/
- 動 〜を(過度に)**甘やかす**、〜の好きなようにさせる(≒ spoil, indulge, cosset)

0258 duplicate /djúːpləkèit/
- 動 〜を複製[コピー]する(≒ copy)
- 名 (/djúːpləkət/) 複製、コピー(≒ copy)
- 形 (/djúːpləkət/) 複製[コピー]の

0259 merge /mə́ːrdʒ/
- 動 (〜と)**合併する**(with 〜)(≒ amalgamate)
- 名 merger：(〜との／…の間の)合併(with 〜/between …)

0260 flare /fléər/
- 動 ❶ **ぱっと燃え上がる**(≒ blaze, flash)　❷ (人が)かっとなる、語気が荒くなる　❸ (感情などが)突発[激発]する(≒ erupt)
- 名 ❶ ぱっと燃え上がる炎(≒ blaze, flash)　❷ (感情などの)激発(≒ burst)

0261 demonstrate /démənstrèit/
❶アクセント注意
- 動 ❶ 〜を証明[実証]する(≒ prove, show)　❷ (商品)を実演する　❸ (〜に反対の)デモをする(against 〜)(≒ protest, rally)
- 名 demonstration：❶ デモ　❷ (商品の)実演
- 名 demonstrator：❶ デモ参加者　❷ 実演する人

0262 manufacture /mæ̀njufǽktʃər/
❶アクセント注意
- 動 (機械で大規模に)〜を**製造[生産]する**(≒ produce, make)
- 名 ❶ 製造、生産(≒ production)　❷ (通例〜s) 製品(≒ product)
- 名 manufacturer：製造会社、メーカー

0263 dread /dréd/
- 動 ❶ 〜を怖がる、恐れる(≒ fear)　❷ (dread doing で)〜するのが怖い、全然〜したくない
- 名 恐怖、恐れ(≒ fear)
- 形 dreadful：ひどい、ひどく悪い
- 副 dreadfully：ひどく、非常に

0264 relieve /rilíːv/
- 動 (苦痛など)**を和らげる**、軽減する(≒ ease, alleviate, mitigate)
- 名 relief：❶ 安心　❷ (苦痛などの)緩和　❸ 救済
- 形 relieved：(be relieved to do で)〜して安心している

continued
▼

同意語・類義語(≒)や反対語・反意語(⇔)もチェックしてる? 余裕があれば確認して、語彙の数を積極的に増やしていこう。

- ☐ 聞くだけモード　Check 1
- ☐ しっかりモード　Check 1 ▶ 2
- ☐ かんぺきモード　Check 1 ▶ 2 ▶ 3

Check 2　Phrase

- ☐ a pampered child（甘やかされて育った子ども）
- ☐ pamper oneself（気ままに振る舞う）

- ☐ duplicate CDs（CDを複製する）
- ☐ duplicate the document（その書類をコピーする）

- ☐ merge with a foreign company（外資系企業と合併する）

- ☐ flare in the darkness（暗闇の中でぱっと燃え上がる）
- ☐ flare (up) at him（彼に八つ当たりする）

- ☐ demonstrate the link between ~（~の間の関連を証明する）
- ☐ demonstrate a new product（新製品を実演する）

- ☐ manufacture computers（コンピューターを製造する）
- ☐ manufactured goods（製品）

- ☐ dread failure（失敗を恐れる）
- ☐ dread meeting him（彼に会うのが怖い）

- ☐ relieve anxiety [stress]（不安[ストレス]を和らげる）

Check 3　Sentence

- ☐ Parents nowadays pamper their children too much.（最近の親は子どもを甘やかし過ぎる）

- ☐ It is illegal to duplicate a copyrighted image without permission from its owner.（著作権のある画像を所有者の許可なく複製することは違法だ）

- ☐ In 1999, Exxon and Mobile merged to form Exxon Mobile.（1999年に、エクソンとモービルは合併してエクソンモービルになった）

- ☐ The candle flared, flickered, and then went out.（ろうそくはぱっと燃え上がり、揺らめき、それから消えた）

- ☐ These data demonstrate that climate change is real.（これらのデータは気候変動が現実のものであることを証明している）

- ☐ The plant manufactures 500 cars per month.（その工場は1カ月に500台の車を製造する）

- ☐ I dread the thought of having to go to the dentist.（私は歯医者に行かなくてはならないと思うと怖くなる）

- ☐ The drug relieves the symptoms of influenza.（その薬はインフルエンザの症状を和らげる）

continued

Day 17

Check 1　Listen)) CD-A17

☐ 0265
guarantee
/gæ̀rəntíː/
❶アクセント注意

動 **〜を保証[保障]する**(≒ensure)
名 保証(書)(≒warranty)

☐ 0266
plead
/plíːd/

動 ❶(有罪・無罪の)**申し立て[主張]をする**　❷(plead forで)〜を嘆願する、請う(≒beg for)

☐ 0267
cherish
/tʃériʃ/

動 **〜を大切[大事]にする**(≒treasure)

☐ 0268
envision
/invíʒən/

動 (将来のこと)**を想像する**、心に描く(≒imagine, envisage, visualize)

☐ 0269
boast
/bóust/

動 ❶(地域などが)**〜を誇りにしている**　❷(〜を)自慢する(about [of] 〜)(≒brag)
名 自慢(の種)、誇りとする物[事](≒brag, pride)

☐ 0270
humiliate
/hjuːmílièit/

動 **〜に恥をかかせる**、屈辱を与える(≒embarrass, shame, mortify)
名 humiliation：恥、屈辱
形 humiliating：屈辱的な、不面目な

☐ 0271
dispatch
/dispǽtʃ/

動 ❶(軍隊など)**を**(…に)**派遣する**(to . . .)　❷(手紙など)を(…に)発送する、送る(to . . .)(≒send, post, mail)
名 ❶公文書、伝達文書　❷(特派員からの)記事、特電　❸ 派遣、発送

☐ 0272
scatter
/skǽtər/

動 ❶**〜を**(…に)**まき散らす**、ばらまく(over [on] . . .)(≒sprinkle, spread, strew)　❷(群衆などが)四散する(≒disperse)

| Day 16)) CD-A16
Quick Review
答えは右ページ下 | ☐ 歩き回る
☐ 〜を見落とす
☐ 〜を過小評価する
☐ 〜を正当化する | ☐ 飛び込む
☐ 〜を超える
☐ 〜を節約して使う
☐ 〜を登録する | ☐ 明らかになる
☐ 〜を独占する
☐ 迷う
☐ 〜を理解する | ☐ 〜に憤慨する
☐ 歓談する
☐ 〜を監督する
☐ 投資する |

Check 2 — Phrase

- ☐ **guarantee** products against defects（欠陥に対して製品を保証する）

- ☐ **plead** guilty（罪状を認める）
- ☐ **plead** for help（助けを求める）

- ☐ **cherish** one's child（子どもを大切に育てる）
- ☐ one's most **cherished** possession（最も大事な持ち物）

- ☐ **envision** the future（将来を想像する）
- ☐ **envision** a day when ～（～する日を想像する）

- ☐ **boast** historic buildings（[街などが]歴史的建築物を誇りにしている）
- ☐ **boast** about one's achievement（自分の業績を自慢する）

- ☐ **humiliate** him in public（人前で彼に恥をかかせる）
- ☐ feel **humiliated**（屈辱を感じる）

- ☐ **dispatch** troops to ～（軍隊を～に派遣する）
- ☐ **dispatch** goods to ～（商品を～に送る）

- ☐ **scatter** seeds over the soil（土壌に種をまく）
- ☐ **scatter** in all directions（四方八方に散る）

Check 3 — Sentence

- ☐ The constitution **guarantees** free speech.（憲法は言論の自由を保障している）

- ☐ The defendant **pleaded** not guilty to the charge.（被告は罪状に対して無罪の申し立てをした）

- ☐ Most people **cherish** good memories of childhood.（ほとんどの人は子どものころのいい思い出を大切にしている）

- ☐ Sometimes I **envision** a world free from poverty.（時々、私は貧困のない世界を想像する）

- ☐ The hotel **boasts** excellent recreational facilities.（そのホテルは素晴らしい娯楽施設を誇りにしている）

- ☐ I was **humiliated** in front of my colleagues.（私は同僚たちの前で恥をかいた）

- ☐ A fact-finding delegation was **dispatched** to the country.（現地調査団がその国に派遣された）

- ☐ Several papers were **scattered** on the floor.（いくつかの書類が床にまき散らされていた）

Day 16 CD-A16
Quick Review
答えは左ページ下

- ☐ roam
- ☐ overlook
- ☐ underestimate
- ☐ justify
- ☐ plunge
- ☐ exceed
- ☐ conserve
- ☐ register
- ☐ emerge
- ☐ monopolize
- ☐ waver
- ☐ grasp
- ☐ resent
- ☐ mingle
- ☐ supervise
- ☐ invest

CHAPTER 1
CHAPTER 2
CHAPTER 3
CHAPTER 4
CHAPTER 5
CHAPTER 6
CHAPTER 7
CHAPTER 8
CHAPTER 9
CHAPTER 10

Day 18　動詞7

Check 1　Listen ») CD-A18

□ 0273
gleam
/glíːm/
- 動 **光る**、輝く（≒ shine, glimmer, glint, glitter, sparkle, twinkle）
- 名 輝き、きらめき（≒ shine, glimmer, glint, glitter, sparkle, twinkle）

□ 0274
capsize
/kǽpsaiz/
- 動 ❶（船などが）**転覆する**　❷（船など）を転覆させる（≒ overturn, turn over）

□ 0275
endure
/indjúər/
- 動 ❶（困難など）**に耐える**、〜を我慢する（≒ put up with, tolerate, bear）　❷続く、持続する（≒ last, continue）
- 名 endurance：❶耐久[持久]力　❷忍耐
- 形 endurable：（痛みなどが）耐えられる、我慢できる

□ 0276
install
/instɔ́ːl/
- 動 ❶**〜を取りつける**、設置する（≒ put in）　❷〜をインストールする
- 名 installation：（機械などの）取りつけ、設置

□ 0277
disclose
/disklóuz/
- 動 （秘密など）**を明らかにする**、暴露する（≒ reveal, expose, uncover, unearth）（⇔ hide, conceal：〜を秘密にする）
- 名 disclosure：❶暴露　❷発覚した事柄

□ 0278
renew
/rinjúː/
- 動 ❶（契約など）**を更新する**　❷〜を再開する（≒ resume, restart, reopen）
- 名 renewal：❶更新　❷再開
- 形 renewable：❶（エネルギーなどが）再生可能な　❷（契約などが）更新[延長]可能な

□ 0279
disguise
/disɡáiz/
- 動 ❶**〜を変装させる**　❷（事実など）を隠す（≒ hide, conceal）
- 名 変装、偽装

□ 0280
grumble
/ɡrʌ́mbl/
- 動 （〜のことで）（ぶつぶつ）**不平**[文句]**を言う**（about [at, over] 〜）（≒ complain, whine）
- 名 不平（≒ complaint）

continued
▼

今日でChapter 2は最後！ 時間に余裕があったら、章末のReviewにも挑戦しておこう。忘れてしまった単語も結構あるのでは?!

- ☐ 聞くだけモード　Check 1
- ☐ しっかりモード　Check 1 ▸ 2
- ☐ かんぺきモード　Check 1 ▸ 2 ▸ 3

Check 2　Phrase

☐ gleam with sweat（[肌などが]汗で光る）
☐ gleam with joy（[目などが]喜びで輝く）

☐ capsize in the storm（嵐の中で転覆する）
☐ a capsized ship（転覆した船）

☐ endure a great deal of pain（激しい痛みに耐える）
☐ endure forever（永久に続く）

☐ install a security camera（防犯カメラを取りつける）
☐ install software（ソフトウエアをインストールする）

☐ disclose the scandal（そのスキャンダルを暴露する）
☐ It was disclosed that ～.（～ということが明らかにされた）

☐ renew one's passport（パスポートを更新する）
☐ renew an attack（攻撃を再開する）

☐ disguise oneself as ～（～に変装する）
☐ disguise the fact that ～（～という事実を隠す）

☐ grumble about the noise（騒音のことで文句を言う）

Check 3　Sentence

☐ The grass was gleaming with the morning dew.（芝生は朝露で光っていた）

☐ The ship capsized after hitting a reef.（その船は岩礁に乗り上げて転覆した）

☐ Many immigrants had to endure great hardship.（多くの移民たちは厳しい苦難に耐えなければならなかった）

☐ I had an air conditioner installed in my room last week.（私は先週、自分の部屋にエアコンを取りつけてもらった）

☐ The firm didn't disclose details of the deal.（その会社は取引の詳細を明らかにしなかった）

☐ The license must be renewed annually.（その許可証は毎年更新されなければならない）

☐ The bomber was disguised as a woman.（その爆破犯は女性に変装していた）

☐ He is always grumbling about his work.（彼はいつも仕事のことで不平を言っている）

continued
▼

Day 18

Check 1　Listen 》CD-A18

☐ 0281
reinforce
/riːinfɔ́ːrs/

動 **〜を補強[強化]する**(≒strengthen, fortify)
名reinforcement：補強、強化

☐ 0282
distort
/distɔ́ːrt/

動 (事実など)**をゆがめる**、歪曲する
名distortion：❶(事実などの)歪曲 ❷ゆがみ、ひずみ
形distorted：❶(事実などが)歪曲された ❷ゆがんだ、ひずんだ

☐ 0283
halt
/hɔ́ːlt/

動 ❶**〜を中止[停止]する** ❷止まる(≒stop)
名中止、停止(≒stop)

☐ 0284
accelerate
/əksélərèit/

動 ❶**〜を加速させる**、促進する(≒hasten, facilitate, expedite) ❷加速する(≒speed up)(⇔slow down, decelerate)
名acceleration：加速、促進
名accelerator：アクセル、加速装置

☐ 0285
forbid
/fərbíd/

動 ❶**〜を禁じる**(≒ban, prohibit)(⇔allow, permit)
❷(forbid A to do [from doing]で)Aが〜するのを禁じる
(≒ban A from doing, prohibit A from doing)
形forbidden：禁じられた、禁制の

☐ 0286
migrate
/máigreit/

動 ❶(動物が)(〜から/…へ)**移動する**、渡る(from 〜/to …)(≒travel) ❷(人が)(〜から/…へ)移住する(from 〜/to …)(≒emigrate, immigrate)
名migration：移動、移住
名migrant：❶移住者 ❷移動動物、渡り鳥

☐ 0287
commence
/kəméns/

動 ❶**始まる** ❷〜を始める(≒start, begin)
名commencement：❶開始、始まり ❷(大学・高校の)卒業式

☐ 0288
evaluate
/ivǽljuèit/

動 **〜を評価する**(≒assess, appraise)
名evaluation：評価、査定

トビラの問題の正解はコレ！

Day 17 》CD-A17
Quick Review
答えは右ページ下

☐ 〜を甘やかす　☐ 〜を証明する　☐ 〜を保証する　☐ 〜を誇りにしている
☐ 〜を複製する　☐ 〜を製造する　☐ 申し立てをする　☐ 〜に恥をかかせる
☐ 合併する　☐ 〜を怖がる　☐ 〜を大切にする　☐ 〜を派遣する
☐ ぱっと燃え上がる　☐ 〜を和らげる　☐ 〜を想像する　☐ 〜をまき散らす

Check 2 Phrase

- ☐ reinforce a wall(壁を補強する)
- ☐ reinforce troops(軍隊を増強する)

- ☐ distort the truth(真実をゆがめる)

- ☐ halt operations(操業を中止する)
- ☐ Halt!(止まれ！)

- ☐ accelerate the structural reform(構造改革を加速させる)
- ☐ accelerate quickly(急加速する)

- ☐ forbid photography(写真撮影を禁じる)
- ☐ forbid her to go out(彼女に外出を禁じる)

- ☐ migrating birds(渡り鳥)
- ☐ migrate in search of work(仕事を求めて移住する)

- ☐ commence with a welcome([会合などが]歓迎の言葉で始まる)
- ☐ commence production(生産を開始する)

- ☐ evaluate employees' performance(従業員の業績を評価する)

Check 3 Sentence

- ☐ The bridge was reinforced with steel beams and pillars.(その橋は鋼鉄の梁と柱で補強された)

- ☐ The article distorts the facts.(その記事は事実をゆがめている)

- ☐ The two countries agreed to halt nuclear testing.(両国は核実験を中止することに同意した)

- ☐ Biofuels may accelerate global warming.(バイオ燃料は地球温暖化を加速させる可能性がある)

- ☐ Smoking in public places is forbidden.(公共の場所での喫煙は禁じられている)

- ☐ Reindeer migrate south in the fall and north in the spring.(トナカイは秋に南へ、春に北へ移動する)

- ☐ The conference will commence at 1 p.m.(その会議は午後1時に始まる予定だ)

- ☐ We need to evaluate how well the program is working.(私たちはその計画がどの程度うまくいっているか評価する必要がある)

Day 17))CD-A17
Quick Review
答えは左ページ下

- ☐ pamper
- ☐ duplicate
- ☐ merge
- ☐ flare
- ☐ demonstrate
- ☐ manufacture
- ☐ dread
- ☐ relieve
- ☐ guarantee
- ☐ plead
- ☐ cherish
- ☐ envision
- ☐ boast
- ☐ humiliate
- ☐ dispatch
- ☐ scatter

CHAPTER 1
CHAPTER 2
CHAPTER 3
CHAPTER 4
CHAPTER 5
CHAPTER 6
CHAPTER 7
CHAPTER 8
CHAPTER 9
CHAPTER 10

Chapter 2 Review

左ページの(1)〜(20)の動詞の同意・類義語（≒）、反意・反対語（⇔）を右ページのA〜Tから選び、カッコの中に答えを書き込もう。意味が分からないときは、見出し番号を参照して復習しておこう（答えは右ページ下）。

- ☐ (1) boost (0177) ≒は？ (　　)
- ☐ (2) compile (0187) ≒は？ (　　)
- ☐ (3) advocate (0189) ≒は？ (　　)
- ☐ (4) condemn (0197) ≒は？ (　　)
- ☐ (5) decay (0199) ≒は？ (　　)
- ☐ (6) sustain (0206) ≒は？ (　　)
- ☐ (7) extinguish (0211) ⇔は？ (　　)
- ☐ (8) resume (0217) ≒は？ (　　)
- ☐ (9) anticipate (0221) ≒は？ (　　)
- ☐ (10) contaminate (0226) ≒は？ (　　)
- ☐ (11) prosper (0227) ≒は？ (　　)
- ☐ (12) scrutinize (0233) ≒は？ (　　)
- ☐ (13) underestimate (0243) ⇔は？ (　　)
- ☐ (14) exceed (0246) ≒は？ (　　)
- ☐ (15) grasp (0252) ≒は？ (　　)
- ☐ (16) duplicate (0258) ≒は？ (　　)
- ☐ (17) dread (0263) ≒は？ (　　)
- ☐ (18) envision (0268) ≒は？ (　　)
- ☐ (19) disclose (0277) ⇔は？ (　　)
- ☐ (20) grumble (0280) ≒は？ (　　)

A. maintain
B. copy
C. flourish
D. support
E. complain
F. rot
G. overestimate
H. examine
I. edit
J. surpass
K. imagine
L. expect
M. blame
N. hide
O. light
P. pollute
Q. understand
R. fear
S. increase
T. restart

【解答】 (1) S (2) I (3) D (4) M (5) F (6) A (7) O (8) T (9) L (10) P
(11) C (12) H (13) G (14) J (15) Q (16) B (17) R (18) K (19) N (20) E

CHAPTER 3
形容詞：超頻出112

Chapter 3では、英検準1級「超頻出」の形容詞112をマスターしていきます。このChapterが終われば、「超頻出」の名詞・動詞・形容詞400が身についたことになります。

Day 19【形容詞1】
▶ 94
Day 20【形容詞2】
▶ 98
Day 21【形容詞3】
▶ 102
Day 22【形容詞4】
▶ 106
Day 23【形容詞5】
▶ 110
Day 24【形容詞6】
▶ 114
Day 25【形容詞7】
▶ 118
Chapter 3 Review
▶ 122

こんなの出たよ！

The real estate agent told the couple that the outlook for the housing market was (　　　). He said it would be difficult to sell their house for a good price now.（2009年度第1回）

1　serene　　2　vintage
3　bleak　　 4　hardy

▼
答えはDay 19でチェック！

Day 19 形容詞1

Check 1　Listen))) CD-A19

0289
potential
/pəténʃəl/

形 **潜在的な**、可能性のある (≒possible)
名 (〜の)可能性、潜在性[力] (for 〜) (≒possibility)
名 potentiality：(〜の)可能性、潜在性[力] (for 〜)
副 potentially：潜在的に

0290
relevant
/réləvənt/

形 (当面の問題などに)**関係[関連]のある** (to 〜) (≒related, pertinent) (⇔irrelevant)

0291
significant
/signífikənt/
❶アクセント注意

形 ❶**重要[重大]な** (≒important, vital, crucial)　❷かなりの；著しい (≒notable, remarkable)　❸意味ありげな (≒suggestive, meaningful)
副 significantly：❶著しく　❷重要なこと(に)は
名 significance：❶重要[重大]性　❷意味、意義

0292
chronological
/krànəládʒikəl/

形 **年代順の**
副 chronologically：年代順に

0293
intact
/intǽkt/

形 **無傷の** (≒undamaged)

0294
bleak
/blíːk/
トビラの問題の正解はコレ！

形 ❶(見通しなどが)**暗い** (≒gloomy, grim, somber)　❷(場所などが)荒涼とした (≒bare, desolate)　❸(天気が)寒々しい (≒cold)

0295
widespread
/wáidspréd/

形 **広範囲に及ぶ**；広く行き渡った (≒extensive, comprehensive, prevailing)
動 spread：❶広がる；広まる　❷〜を広げる；〜を広める
名 spread：広がり、広まり、普及

0296
chronic
/kránik/

形 ❶(病気が)**慢性の** (⇔acute：急性の)　❷(社会問題などが)慢性的な、長期にわたる (⇔temporary：一時的な)
副 chronically：慢性的に

continued
▼

Chapter 3では、7日をかけて「超頻出」の形容詞112をチェック。まずはCDでチャンツを聞いて、単語を「耳」からインプット！

☐ 聞くだけモード　Check 1
☐ しっかりモード　Check 1 ▶ 2
☐ かんぺきモード　Check 1 ▶ 2 ▶ 3

Check 2　Phrase

☐ a potential risk（潜在的な危険性）
☐ a potential customer（潜在客、見込み客）

☐ the relevant authorities（関係当局）
☐ relevant information（関連情報）

☐ a significant discovery（重要な発見）
☐ a significant increase（著しい増加）

☐ in chronological order（年代順に）
☐ a chronological table（年表）

☐ remain intact（無傷のままである）
☐ arrive intact（[荷物などが]無傷のまま届けられる）

☐ a bleak outlook [prospect]（暗い見通し）
☐ a bleak landscape（荒涼とした風景）

☐ the widespread use of ～（～の広範囲に及ぶ使用；～の普及）
☐ widespread support（幅広い支持）

☐ chronic asthma（慢性ぜんそく）
☐ a chronic unemployment problem（慢性的な失業問題）

Check 3　Sentence

☐ Doctors have to warn patients about the potential side effects of drugs.（医者は患者に薬の潜在的な副作用について知らせなければならない）

☐ Interview questions must be relevant to the company and the job.（面接での質問はその会社と仕事に関係のあるものでなければならない）

☐ Impressionism played a significant role in the history of painting.（印象主義は絵画史において重要な役割を果たした）

☐ I remember all the presidents in chronological order.（私はすべての大統領を年代順に覚えている）

☐ The building survived World War II almost intact.（その建物は第2次世界大戦をほぼ無傷で切り抜けた）

☐ The current state of the world economy is bleak.（世界経済の現在の状況は暗い）

☐ The hurricane caused widespread damage throughout Virginia.（そのハリケーンはバージニア州一帯に広範囲に及ぶ被害をもたらした）

☐ She has been suffering from chronic fatigue.（彼女は慢性疲労に悩んでいる）

continued
▼

Day 19

Check 1　Listen))) CD-A19

0297 articulate /ɑːrtíkjulət/
- 形 ❶**理路整然とした**、優れた表現力のある(≒eloquent)　❷明確な、分かりやすい(≒clear, comprehensible, understandable)(⇔inarticulate)
- 動 (/ɑːrtíkjulèit/)はっきり話す[発音する]
- 名articulation：❶(はっきりした)発音　❷表現

0298 spacious /spéiʃəs/
- 形 **広々とした**、広い(≒broad, capacious, roomy)
- 名space：❶空間　❷場所　❸間隔　❹宇宙
- 動space：❶〜を間隔を置いて配置する　❷(文字・行など)の間を空ける

0299 brisk /brísk/
- 形 ❶(動きが)**きびきびした**、活発な(≒quick, energetic, lively, vigorous)　❷(商売が)活況の、繁盛した(≒busy)

0300 deliberate /dilíbərət/ ❶アクセント注意
- 形 ❶**意図[計画]的な**、故意の(≒intentional)　❷(話し方などが)慎重な、ゆっくりした(≒careful)
- 動 (/dilíbərèit/)❶〜を熟考する(≒consider)　❷(deliberate about [on, over]で)〜について熟考する
- 副deliberately：❶意図的に、故意に　❷慎重に

0301 innovative /ínəvèitiv/ ❶アクセント注意
- 形 **革新[刷新]的な**；創意に富む
- 動innovate：刷新[革新]する
- 名innovation：革新、刷新；斬新な考え

0302 frail /fréil/
- 形 ❶(老齢などで)**体の弱った**、やせ衰えた(≒weak)　❷壊れやすい、もろい(≒fragile)
- 名frailty：❶衰弱　❷(性格の)弱さ、弱点

0303 persistent /pərsístənt/
- 形 ❶**粘り[根気]強い**、不屈の(≒tenacious)　❷しつこい、慢性的な(≒chronic)
- 動persist：❶(persist inで)〜に固執する、〜を貫く　❷(persist withで)〜をし続ける　❸持続[存続]する
- 名persistence：❶粘り強さ　❷持続、存続

0304 comprehensive /kàmprihénsiv/
- 形 **包括[総合]的な**(≒inclusive)　✚comprehensible(分かりやすい)と混同しないように注意
- 動comprehend：〜を理解する
- 名comprehension：理解(力)

Day 18))) CD-A18　Quick Review　答えは右ページ下

- □ 光る
- □ 転覆する
- □ 〜に耐える
- □ 〜を取り付ける
- □ 〜を明らかにする
- □ 〜を更新する
- □ 〜を変装させる
- □ 不平を言う
- □ 〜を補強する
- □ 〜をゆがめる
- □ 〜を中止する
- □ 〜を加速させる
- □ 〜を禁じる
- □ 移動する
- □ 始まる
- □ 〜を評価する

Check 2 Phrase

- an articulate speech（理路整然とした演説）
- an articulate explanation of ~（~の分かりやすい説明）

- a spacious garden [room]（広々とした庭[部屋]）

- walk at a brisk pace（きびきびと歩く）
- brisk sales（好調な売れ行き）

- a deliberate lie（意図的なうそ）
- a deliberate manner of speaking（慎重な話し方）

- an innovative design（革新的なデザイン）

- a frail old man（体の弱った老人）
- the country's frail economy（その国のもろい経済）

- persistent efforts（粘り強い努力）
- a persistent cough（しつこいせき）

- comprehensive talks（包括的協議）
- comprehensive insurance（総合保険）

Check 3 Sentence

- She is an intelligent and highly articulate woman.（彼女は聡明で、非常に理路整然とした女性だ）

- The car is compact, but surprisingly spacious inside.（その車は小型だが、内部は驚くほど広々としている）

- He starts his day with a brisk walk through a park.（彼は公園をきびきびと歩くことで1日を始める）

- She made a deliberate effort to be more social.（彼女はもっと社交的になろうと意図的に努力した）

- Innovative technology is the key to long-term profitability.（革新的な技術は長期的な収益性への鍵だ）

- The patient looked extremely frail.（その患者は非常に体が弱っているように見えた）

- Be persistent and you will eventually succeed.（粘り強くあれば、あなたはいつかは成功するだろう）

- This book is a comprehensive study of the rise and development of Buddhism.（この本は仏教の誕生と発展を包括的に研究したものだ）

Day 18 》CD-A18
Quick Review
答えは左ページ下

- gleam
- capsize
- endure
- install
- disclose
- renew
- disguise
- grumble
- reinforce
- distort
- halt
- accelerate
- forbid
- migrate
- commence
- evaluate

Day 20　形容詞2

Check 1　Listen ») CD-A20

☐ 0305
soothing
/súːðɪŋ/

形 ❶**心休まる**、気持ちを落ち着かせる(≒relaxing, restful)　❷痛みを和らげる
動soothe：❶～を落ち着かせる、なだめる　❷(薬などが)(痛みなど)を和らげる
副soothingly：なだめるように；和らげるように

☐ 0306
obsolete
/ὰbsəlíːt/

形 **時代遅れの**、廃れた(≒outdated, out-of-date)

☐ 0307
environmental
/ɪnvàɪərənméntl/

形 **環境(上)の**
名environment：❶(the ～)自然環境　❷環境
名environmentalist：環境保護論者
副environmentally：環境的に、環境上
形environmentally-friendly：環境に優しい

☐ 0308
overall
/òuvərɔ́ːl, óuvərɔ̀ːl/

形 **全体[総合]的な**、全体[全部]の(≒entire, total, general, comprehensive)
副 ❶全体的に見て(≒generally)　❷全体で(≒altogether)

☐ 0309
genetic
/dʒənétɪk/

形 **遺伝子の**、遺伝学の
名gene：遺伝子
名genetics：❶遺伝学　❷遺伝的特徴
副genetically：遺伝子上、遺伝学的に

☐ 0310
federal
/fédərəl/

形 **連邦(制)の**、連邦政府の
名federalism：連邦主義
名federalist：連邦主義者
名federation：❶連盟、同盟　❷連邦(政府)

☐ 0311
drastic
/drǽstɪk/

形 (措置などが)**思い切った**、徹底[抜本]的な、ドラスティックな(≒thorough)
副drastically：徹底[抜本]的に、思い切って、ドラスティックに

☐ 0312
superficial
/sùːpərfíʃəl/

形 **表面的な**、うわべだけの(≒shallow, surface)

continued
▼

Quick Reviewは使ってる？ 昨日覚えた単語でも、記憶に残っているとは限らない。学習の合間に軽くチェックするだけでも効果は抜群！

☐ 聞くだけモード　Check 1
☐ しっかりモード　Check 1 ▶ 2
☐ かんぺきモード　Check 1 ▶ 2 ▶ 3

Check 2　Phrase

- ☐ a soothing voice (心休まる声)
- ☐ a soothing effect (鎮痛効果)

- ☐ obsolete technology (時代遅れの技術)
- ☐ become obsolete (時代遅れになる)

- ☐ environmental issues [problems] (環境問題)
- ☐ an environmental group (環境保護団体)

- ☐ an overall improvement (全体的な改善)
- ☐ have overall responsibility for ~ (~の全責任を負う)

- ☐ genetic engineering (遺伝子工学)
- ☐ a genetic disease (遺伝病)

- ☐ federal law (連邦法)
- ☐ a federal republic (連邦共和国)

- ☐ drastic measures (思い切った処置、抜本的対策)

- ☐ on a superficial level (表面的には)
- ☐ a superficial knowledge (うわべだけの知識)

Check 3　Sentence

- ☐ I like soothing piano music. (私は心休まるピアノ音楽が好きだ)

- ☐ Pagers have become obsolete and have been replaced by cell phones. (ポケベルは時代遅れになり、携帯電話に取って代わられた)

- ☐ People have become increasingly aware of the importance of environmental preservation. (人々は環境保護の重要性をますます意識するようになっている)

- ☐ The overall mood of the conference was optimistic. (その会議の全体的なムードは楽観的だった)

- ☐ We inherit our genetic characteristics from our parents. (私たちは遺伝的特徴を両親から受け継ぐ)

- ☐ Social Security, at present, accounts for about 25 percent of the federal budget. (社会保障は現在、連邦予算の約25パーセントを占めている)

- ☐ The government should take drastic action to reduce carbon emissions. (政府は炭素排出量を減らすために思い切った措置を講じるべきだ)

- ☐ The general public often has only a superficial understanding of political issues. (一般市民は政治問題について表面的にしか理解していないことが多い)

continued
▼

Day 20

Check 1　Listen 》CD-A20

0313 genuine /dʒénjuin/
❶アクセント注意
- 形 ❶**本物の**(≒real, authentic)(⇔fake)　❷誠実な(≒sincere, honest)
- 副 genuinely：心から、本当に

0314 radical /rǽdikəl/
- 形 ❶**急進的な**、過激な(≒extreme)(⇔conservative：保守的な)　❷根本的な(≒fundamental)　❸徹底的な(≒thorough)
- 名 急進主義者、過激派
- 名 radicalism：急進主義

0315 cosmopolitan /kàzməpálətn/
❶発音注意
- 形 **国際色豊かな**、国際的な(≒international)
- 名 国際人、コスモポリタン

0316 massive /mǽsiv/
- 形 ❶**巨大な**(≒huge, enormous, vast, immense)(⇔tiny)　❷大規模な、(規模・程度などが)大きい、甚だしい
- 名 mass：❶(a mass of で)多数[多量]の〜　❷塊、集まり

0317 feasible /fíːzəbl/
- 形 **実現[実行]可能な**(≒practicable, viable)
- 名 feasibility：実現性

0318 rigid /rídʒid/
- 形 ❶(規則などが)**厳しい**、厳格な、柔軟性のない(≒strict, rigorous, stern, stringent, inflexible)　❷(人が)(〜に関して)頑固な、柔軟でない(in 〜)(≒inflexible)　❸硬い、硬くて曲がらない(≒stiff, hard, firm)
- 副 rigidly：❶厳格に　❷頑固に　❸硬く

0319 amicable /ǽmikəbl/
- 形 **友好[平和]的な**、円満な(≒friendly)

0320 hostile /hástl/
- 形 ❶(環境などが)**適さない**、好ましくない(≒unfavorable, adverse)　❷(〜に)敵意のある(to [toward] 〜)(⇔friendly)　❸敵[敵国]の
- 名 hostility：❶(〜に対する)敵意(to [toward] 〜)　❷(〜に対する)反対(to [toward] 〜)　❸(〜ies)戦闘

Day 19 》CD-A19
Quick Review
答えは右ページ下

- □ 潜在的な
- □ 関係のある
- □ 重要な
- □ 年代順の
- □ 無傷の
- □ 暗い
- □ 広範囲に及ぶ
- □ 慢性の
- □ 理路整然とした
- □ 広々とした
- □ きびきびした
- □ 意図的な
- □ 革新的な
- □ 体の弱った
- □ 粘り強い
- □ 包括的な

Check 2 Phrase

- a genuine Picasso（本物のピカソの作品）
- a genuine person（誠実な人）

- a radical politician（急進的な政治家）
- radical changes（根本的な変更）

- a cosmopolitan atmosphere（国際色豊かな雰囲気）
- a cosmopolitan resort（国際的なリゾート）

- a massive rock（巨大な岩）
- on a massive scale（大規模に）

- a feasible idea [plan]（実現可能なアイデア［計画］）
- It is feasible to do ~.（~することは可能だ）

- rigid discipline（厳しいしつけ）
- be rigid in one's opinions（意見を頑として変えない）

- be on amicable terms（友好的な間柄である）
- reach an amicable settlement（円満な解決に至る）

- hostile weather conditions（悪天候）
- a hostile look（敵意のある表情）

Check 3 Sentence

- The ring is set with three genuine diamonds.（その指輪には3つの本物のダイヤモンドがはめ込まれている）

- Young people tend to be radical in their political views.（若者は政治的な考えにおいて急進的になる傾向がある）

- Sydney is a cosmopolitan city.（シドニーは国際色豊かな都市だ）

- A massive earthquake hit southwestern China.（巨大地震が中国南西部を襲った）

- Solar energy has only become economically feasible in the past few decades.（太陽エネルギーはこの数十年でようやく経済的に実現可能になった）

- Some etiquette rules are too rigid and outdated.（礼儀作法の中には厳し過ぎて時代遅れのものもある）

- Japan must maintain amicable relations with its neighboring countries.（日本は近隣諸国と友好的な関係を維持しなければならない）

- The desert is a hostile environment for most plants to grow in.（砂漠はほとんどの植物にとって生育に適さない環境だ）

Day 19)) CD-A19
Quick Review
答えは左ページ下

- [ ] potential
- [ ] relevant
- [ ] significant
- [ ] chronological
- [ ] intact
- [ ] bleak
- [ ] widespread
- [ ] chronic
- [ ] articulate
- [ ] spacious
- [ ] brisk
- [ ] deliberate
- [ ] innovative
- [ ] frail
- [ ] persistent
- [ ] comprehensive

Day 21　形容詞3

Check 1　Listen)) CD-A21

0321
fragile
/frǽdʒəl/
形 ❶ **壊れやすい**、もろい(≒delicate, frail)　❷不安定な(≒insecure)
名 fragility：壊れやすさ、もろさ

0322
hilarious
/hiléəriəs/
形 **とても面白い**、実に愉快な

0323
ceaseless
/síːslis/
形 **絶え間ない**、やむことのない、不断の(≒constant, continuous, continual)
副 ceaselessly：絶え間なく、連続して
動 cease：❶〜を中止する、やめる　❷終わる、やむ

0324
subsequent
/sʌ́bsikwənt/
❶アクセント注意
形 **その後の**、以降の(≒following)(⇔previous)
副 subsequently：その後、後になって

0325
obnoxious
/əbnɑ́kʃəs/
形 (とても)**不快な**、嫌な(≒unpleasant, disgusting, disagreeable)

0326
dormant
/dɔ́ːrmənt/
形 **活動休止中の**、休止状態の、休眠中の(≒inactive)(⇔active)

0327
random
/rǽndəm/
形 **無作為の**、手当たり次第の(≒arbitrary)

0328
agricultural
/ǽgrikʌ́ltʃərəl/
形 **農業の**
名 agriculture：農業

continued
▼

形容詞の用法は、名詞を修飾する「限定用法」と、補語となる「叙述用法」の2つ。Check 2, 3 でそれぞれの用法を確認しておこう。

- ☐ 聞くだけモード　Check 1
- ☐ しっかりモード　Check 1 ▶ 2
- ☐ かんぺきモード　Check 1 ▶ 2 ▶ 3

Check 2　Phrase

☐ Fragile — Handle with care（壊れ物——取り扱い注意）
☐ a fragile relationship（不安定な関係）

☐ a hilarious story（とても面白い話）

☐ ceaseless rain（絶え間ない雨）

☐ subsequent investigations（その後の調査）
☐ subsequent to ~（~の後で、~に続いて）

☐ obnoxious smells（不快なにおい）

☐ a dormant volcano（休火山）
☐ lie dormant（活動を休止している）

☐ random drug tests（無作為の薬物検査）
☐ at random（無作為に、手当たり次第に）

☐ agricultural policy（農業政策）
☐ agricultural land（農地）

Check 3　Sentence

☐ The wine glass is very fragile.（そのワイングラスはとても壊れやすい）

☐ The movie was hilarious from beginning to end.（その映画は最初から最後までとても面白かった）

☐ I'm fed up with her ceaseless chattering.（私は彼女の絶え間ないおしゃべりにうんざりしている）

☐ The phenomenon was demonstrated by subsequent experiments.（その現象はその後の実験で実証された）

☐ People who know him say he is an obnoxious man.（彼を知っている人たちは、彼は不快な人物だと言っている）

☐ The volcano has been dormant since the last eruption in 1952.（その火山は1952年の最後の噴火以降、活動を休止している）

☐ The poll was conducted by random sampling.（その世論調査は無作為抽出で行われた）

☐ Agricultural workers account for almost one-third of the total workers in that country.（農業従事者はその国の全労働者のほぼ3分の1を占めている）

continued
▼

Day 21

Check 1　Listen))) CD-A21

0329 irrelevant /írélǝvǝnt/
形 (〜と)**無関係の**(to 〜)、不適切な(≒unrelated) (⇔relevant)

0330 traumatic /trǝmǽtik/ ❶発音注意
形 **心的外傷[トラウマ]となる**、心に傷を残すような
名 trauma：心的外傷、トラウマ

0331 courteous /kə́ːrtiǝs/
形 **礼儀正しい**、丁重[丁寧]な(≒polite, well-mannered, civil)(⇔rude, discourteous)
名 courtesy：❶礼儀(正しさ)、丁重さ　❷儀礼的なこと
副 courteously：礼儀正しく、丁重[丁寧]に

0332 lenient /líːniǝnt/
形 (〜に)**寛大な**、甘い(with 〜)(≒merciful, generous, tolerant)
名 leniency：寛大[寛容]さ

0333 acute /ǝkjúːt/
形 ❶(感覚などが)**鋭い**(≒keen, sharp)　❷(痛みなどが)激しい、強烈な(≒severe)　❸(病気が)急性の(⇔chronic)

0334 mandatory /mǽndǝtɔ̀ːri/
形 **義務[強制]的な**、必須の(≒compulsory, obligatory, essential)(⇔voluntary：自発的な)
動 mandate：❶〜を命令する；〜に(…するように)命令する(to do)　❷〜に(…する)権限を与える(to do)
名 mandate：❶(公式の)命令、指示　❷信任、負託

0335 distinguished /distíŋgwiʃt/
形 ❶(経歴などが)**優れた**、卓越した(≒prominent)　❷著名[有名]な(≒famous, eminent, renowned)
動 distinguish：❶〜を(…から)区別する(from …)　❷(〜を)見分ける(between 〜)
名 distinction：(〜の間の)区別；相違(between 〜)

0336 precarious /prikɛ́ǝriǝs/
形 (状況などが)**危険な**、不安定な(≒dangerous, risky, hazardous, insecure, unstable, uncertain)

Day 20))) CD-A20
Quick Review
答えは右ページ下

- □ 心休まる
- □ 時代遅れの
- □ 環境の
- □ 全体的な
- □ 遺伝子の
- □ 連邦の
- □ 思い切った
- □ 表面的な
- □ 本物の
- □ 急進的な
- □ 国際色豊かな
- □ 巨大な
- □ 実現可能な
- □ 厳しい
- □ 友好的な
- □ 適さない

Check 2 Phrase

- ☐ be totally [completely] irrelevant to ~(~と全く関係がない)
- ☐ irrelevant remarks(不適切な発言)

- ☐ a traumatic experience(心的外傷となる経験)

- ☐ a courteous young man(礼儀正しい若者)
- ☐ courteous language(丁寧な言葉遣い)

- ☐ a lenient sentence(寛大な判決)

- ☐ acute intelligence(鋭い知性)
- ☐ acute pain(激痛)

- ☐ mandatory education(義務教育)

- ☐ a distinguished career(優れた経歴)
- ☐ a distinguished scholar(著名な学者)

- ☐ a precarious situation(危険な状況)
- ☐ a precarious living(不安定な生活)

Check 3 Sentence

- ☐ Age is irrelevant when it comes to learning.(学ぶことに関する限り、年齢は無関係だ)

- ☐ Divorce is often traumatic for children.(離婚は子どもたちにとって心的外傷となることが多い)

- ☐ The hotel staff were friendly and courteous.(そのホテルの従業員たちは親切で礼儀正しかった)

- ☐ Some parents are too lenient with their children.(子どもに対して寛大過ぎる親もいる)

- ☐ Dogs and cats have acute senses of hearing and smell.(イヌやネコは鋭い聴覚と嗅覚を持っている)

- ☐ It is mandatory for riders to wear helmets when riding.(運転中にヘルメットを着用するのはライダーたちの義務だ)

- ☐ He has a distinguished career in the IT field.(彼はIT分野での優れた経歴を持っている)

- ☐ The company is in a financially precarious position.(その会社は財政的に危険な状態にある)

Day 20))) CD-A20
Quick Review
答えは左ページ下

- ☐ soothing
- ☐ obsolete
- ☐ environmental
- ☐ overall
- ☐ genetic
- ☐ federal
- ☐ drastic
- ☐ superficial
- ☐ genuine
- ☐ radical
- ☐ cosmopolitan
- ☐ massive
- ☐ feasible
- ☐ rigid
- ☐ amicable
- ☐ hostile

CHAPTER 1
CHAPTER 2
CHAPTER 3
CHAPTER 4
CHAPTER 5
CHAPTER 6
CHAPTER 7
CHAPTER 8
CHAPTER 9
CHAPTER 10

Day 22 形容詞4

Check 1　Listen ») CD-A22

0337 exhausted /ɪɡzɔ́ːstɪd/ ❶発音注意
- 形 ❶(～で)**疲れ切った**(from [by] ～)(≒tired, worn-out) ❷使い尽くされた
- 動exhaust：❶～を疲れさせる ❷～を使い尽くす
- 名exhaustion：❶極度の疲労 ❷枯渇

0338 compulsory /kəmpʌ́lsəri/
- 形 **義務[強制]的な**、必須[必修]の(≒mandatory, obligatory)(⇔voluntary)
- 動compel：(compel A to doで)Aに～することを強いる

0339 stable /stéɪbl/
- 形 **安定した**(≒steady, secure, firm)(⇔unstable)
- 名stability：安定(性)
- 動stabilize：～を安定させる

0340 appropriate /əpróʊpriət/
- 形 (～に)**適切な**、ふさわしい(for [to] ～)(≒suitable, proper)(⇔inappropriate)
- 副appropriately：適切に、ふさわしく

0341 incompatible /ìnkəmpǽtəbl/
- 形 ❶(～と)**相いれない**、両立しない(with ～)(≒conflicting, irreconcilable) ❷(人が)(～と)気が合わない、折り合いが悪い(with ～)(≒unsuited) ❸(コンピューターが)互換性がない(⇔compatible)

0342 intensive /ɪnténsɪv/
- 形 ❶**集中[徹底]的な**(≒thorough, extended) ❷(農業などが)集約的な
- 形intense：激しい、強烈[猛烈]な
- 名intensity：激しさ、強烈さ
- 動intensify：❶強まる ❷～を強める

0343 conditional /kəndíʃənl/
- 形 **条件つきの**(⇔unconditional：無条件の)；(～を)条件として、(～)次第で(on [upon] ～)(≒contingent, dependent)
- 名condition：❶状態 ❷(～s)状況、事情 ❸(～の)(必要)条件(of [for] ～)

0344 remarkable /rɪmɑ́ːrkəbl/
- 形 (～で)**注目すべき**、驚くべき、目覚ましい(for ～)(≒outstanding, extraordinary, amazing, astonishing)
- 名remark：(～についての)発言(about [on] ～)
- 動remark：～と述べる、言う
- 副remarkably：驚くほど、著しく

continued
▼

「細切れ時間」を有効活用してる？『キクタン』は2分でも学習可能。いつでもどこでもテキストとCDを持ち歩いて、単語・熟語に触れよう！

- ☐ 聞くだけモード　Check 1
- ☐ しっかりモード　Check 1 ▶ 2
- ☐ かんぺきモード　Check 1 ▶ 2 ▶ 3

Check 2　Phrase

- ☐ be exhausted from running（走って疲れ切っている）
- ☐ exhausted land（やせた土地）

- ☐ It is compulsory for ~ to do ...（~が…するのは義務だ）
- ☐ a compulsory subject（必修科目）

- ☐ a stable relationship（安定した関係）
- ☐ be in a stable condition（[患者などが]安定した状態にある）

- ☐ appropriate attire for the occasion（その場に適した服装）
- ☐ It is appropriate to do ~.（~するのが適切である）

- ☐ two incompatible views（相いれない2つの見解）
- ☐ be incompatible with one's boss（上司と気が合わない）

- ☐ an intensive care unit（集中治療室）⊕ICUはこの略
- ☐ intensive farming [agriculture]（集約農業）

- ☐ conditional approval（条件つきの承諾）
- ☐ be conditional on passing ~（[入学などが]~の合格を条件としている）

- ☐ a remarkable discovery（注目すべき発見）
- ☐ It is remarkable that ~.（~ということは驚くべきことだ）

Check 3　Sentence

- ☐ I am exhausted from working all night.（私は一晩中仕事をして疲れ切っている）

- ☐ It is compulsory to attend the workshop.（その研修会への出席は義務となっている）

- ☐ Every child would benefit from living in a stable family environment.（すべての子どもは安定した家族環境で暮らすことで恩恵を受けるだろう）

- ☐ Now is an appropriate time to discuss the issue.（今こそその問題について話し合うのに適切な時だ）

- ☐ War is incompatible with Christ's teachings.（戦争はキリストの教えとは相いれないものだ）

- ☐ I am taking a one-week intensive Spanish course this summer.（私は今年の夏、1週間の集中スペイン語講座を受講するつもりだ）

- ☐ Delivery is conditional on payment in full in advance.（配達は前金での全額支払いの条件つきだ）

- ☐ The boy has a remarkable talent for mathematics.（その少年は注目すべき数学の才能を持っている）

continued ▼

Day 22

Check 1　Listen)) CD-A22

□ 0345
gullible
/gʌ́ləbl/

形 **だまされやすい**(≒naive, credulous)

□ 0346
vicious
/víʃəs/

形 ❶ **凶悪な**、(動物が)どう猛な(≒brutal, violent, fierce, ferocious)　❷悪意のある、意地の悪い(≒malicious, malevolent)
名vice：❶堕落行為、非行　❷悪癖　❸欠点

□ 0347
extensive
/iksténsiv/

形 ❶ **広範囲にわたる**(≒widespread, comprehensive)　❷(損害などが)大規模な、甚だしい(≒large-scale)
名extension：❶延長、延期　❷(電話の)内線　❸拡張
動extend：❶～を拡大する　❷～を延長する
副extensively：広範囲に、幅広く

□ 0348
proficient
/prəfíʃənt/

形 (～に)**熟達[熟練]した**、堪能な(in [at] ～)(≒skilled, accomplished)
名proficiency：(～の)熟達、熟練、堪能(in [at] ～)

□ 0349
bizarre
/bizá:r/

形 **奇妙な**、風変わりな、とっぴな(≒strange, odd, queer, eccentric, peculiar, weird)

□ 0350
legible
/lédʒəbl/

形 (筆跡などが)**読みやすい**、判読できる(≒readable)(⇔illegible)

□ 0351
tranquil
/trǽŋkwil/

形 **穏やかな**、静かな(≒calm, peaceful, serene, placid)
名tranquillity：穏やかさ、静けさ
名tranquilizer：精神安定剤、トランキライザー

□ 0352
chaotic
/keiátik/
❶発音注意

形 **混沌とした**、無秩序な(≒disorderly)
名chaos：混沌、無秩序

Day 21)) CD-A21
Quick Review
答えは右ページ下

□ 壊れやすい　□ 不快な　□ 無関係の　□ 鋭い
□ とても面白い　□ 活動休止中の　□ 心的外傷となる　□ 義務的な
□ 絶え間ない　□ 無作為の　□ 礼儀正しい　□ 優れた
□ その後の　□ 農業の　□ 寛大な　□ 危険な

Check 2 Phrase

- □ gullible tourists(だまされやすい観光客)

- □ a vicious killer(凶悪な殺人犯)
- □ a vicious rumor(悪意のあるうわさ)

- □ extensive research(広範囲にわたる調査)
- □ extensive damage(大規模な被害)

- □ a proficient worker(熟練工)
- □ be proficient in Chinese(中国語が堪能である)

- □ a bizarre incident(奇妙な出来事)

- □ legible characters(読みやすい文字)

- □ the tranquil sea(穏やかな海)
- □ a tranquil life(平穏な生活)

- □ chaotic social conditions(混沌とした社会状況)

Check 3 Sentence

- □ The swindlers preyed on gullible elderly people.(詐欺師たちはだまされやすい高齢者たちを食い物にした)

- □ The number of vicious crimes has been increasing in the past few years.(凶悪犯罪の数がここ数年、増え続けている)

- □ She has extensive knowledge of classical music.(彼女はクラシック音楽について広範囲にわたる知識がある)

- □ He is very proficient at his job.(彼は自分の仕事にとても熟達している)

- □ The pianist was famous for his bizarre behavior.(そのピアニストは奇妙な振る舞いで有名だった)

- □ Her handwriting is very legible.(彼女の筆跡はとても読みやすい)

- □ There was little wind and the lake was tranquil.(風はほとんどなく、湖は穏やかだった)

- □ Things are getting increasingly chaotic.(事態はますます混沌としてきている)

Day 21))CD-A21
Quick Review
答えは左ページ下

- □ fragile
- □ hilarious
- □ ceaseless
- □ subsequent
- □ obnoxious
- □ dormant
- □ random
- □ agricultural
- □ irrelevant
- □ traumatic
- □ courteous
- □ lenient
- □ acute
- □ mandatory
- □ distinguished
- □ precarious

Day 23　形容詞5

Check 1　Listen 》CD-A23

0353 redundant /ridʌ́ndənt/
形 **余分な**、不要[余分]となった(≒extra, superfluous, unnecessary)
名 redundancy：❶余剰人員(の解雇)　❷余分[不要]であること

0354 excessive /iksésiv/
形 **過度の**、極端[法外]な(≒extravagant, exorbitant, extreme, unreasonable)(⇔moderate：適度の)
動 exceed：〜を超える、上回る
名 excess：(〜の)超過(量)(of 〜)
形 excess：超過した、余分の

0355 illicit /ilísit/
形 **不法[違法]な**(≒illegal, unlawful, illegitimate)(⇔legal, lawful)

0356 indecisive /ìndisáisiv/
形 **決断力のない**、優柔不断な(≒hesitant, irresolute)(⇔decisive)

0357 equivalent /ikwívələnt/
❶アクセント注意
形 (〜に)**相当する**、(〜と)同等[同価値]の(to 〜)(≒equal)
名 相当するもの、同等のもの(≒counterpart)

0358 spotless /spɑ́tlis/
形 ❶(評価などが)**非の打ちどころのない**(≒flawless, blameless)　❷染み[汚れ]のない(≒immaculate)
名 spot：❶場所　❷斑点　❸染み
動 spot：❶〜を見つけ出す　❷〜の才能[可能性]を見抜く

0359 illogical /ilɑ́dʒikəl/
形 **非論理的な**、不合理な(≒irrational, unreasonable)(⇔logical)
名 logic：❶論理　❷論理学

0360 undeniable /ʌ̀ndináiəbl/
形 **否定できない**、明白な、確かな(≒indisputable, unquestionable, certain, true)
動 deny：〜を否定する
名 denial：否定

continued
▼

見出し語の下にある「❶アクセント注意」や「❶発音注意」を見てる？ 少しの違いで相手に伝わらないこともあるので要チェック！

- ☐ 聞くだけモード　Check 1
- ☐ しっかりモード　Check 1 ▶ 2
- ☐ かんぺきモード　Check 1 ▶ 2 ▶ 3

Check 2　Phrase

- ☐ a redundant church（不要となった教会）
- ☐ redundant employees（余剰従業員）

- ☐ excessive drinking（過度の飲酒）
- ☐ excessive speed（スピードの出し過ぎ）

- ☐ illicit drugs（違法麻薬）

- ☐ an indecisive leader（決断力のないリーダー）

- ☐ be almost equivalent to ~（ほぼ~に相当する）
- ☐ an equivalent sum of money（同額の金）

- ☐ a spotless reputation（非の打ちどころのない評判）
- ☐ a spotless shirt（染みのないシャツ）

- ☐ an illogical explanation（非論理的な説明）
- ☐ an illogical demand（不合理な要求）

- ☐ an undeniable fact（否定できない事実）
- ☐ It is undeniable that ~.（~ということは否定できない）

Check 3　Sentence

- ☐ The word "unmarried" in "an unmarried single man" is redundant.（「未婚の独身男性」のうち「未婚の」という単語は余分だ）

- ☐ Excessive exercise can lead to injuries.（過度の運動はけがにつながることがある）

- ☐ The actor was prosecuted for illicit possession of drugs.（その俳優は麻薬の不法所持で起訴された）

- ☐ My boss is weak and indecisive.（私の上司は気弱で決断力がない）

- ☐ One mile is equivalent to approximately 1.6 kilometers.（1マイルは約1.6キロメートルに相当する）

- ☐ No one has a spotless character.（非の打ちどころのない性格の人などいない）

- ☐ The English spelling system is irregular and seems illogical.（英語のつづり方は不規則で、非論理的に見える）

- ☐ It is undeniable that global temperatures are rising.（地球の気温が上昇していることは否定できない）

continued
▼

Day 23

Check 1　Listen))) CD-A23

0361 moderate /mάdərət/
形❶(程度などが)**適度の**、中くらいの、並の(≒modest, average, ordinary, common)(⇔excessive)　❷穏健な、極端に走らない(⇔extreme)
動(/mάdərèit/)❶~を和らげる　❷和らぐ
副moderately：適度に、節度を守って

0362 decent /díːsnt/ ❶発音注意
形❶**まともな**、まずまずの(≒satisfactory, reasonable, fair)　❷礼儀正しい、慎み深い(≒polite, modest)(⇔indecent)
名decency：礼儀正しさ
副decently：❶まともに　❷礼儀正しく

0363 psychological /sàikəlάdʒikəl/
形❶**精神[心理]的な**、心の(≒mental)(⇔physical)　❷心理学(上)の
名psychology：心理学
名psychologist：心理学者
副psychologically：心理[精神]的に

0364 fierce /fíərs/
形❶(競争などが)**激しい**(≒intense)　❷(動物などが)凶暴[どう猛]な(≒brutal, violent, vicious, ferocious)
副fiercely：激しく、強烈に

0365 adverse /ædvə́ːrs/
形**都合の悪い**、不利な、逆の(≒unfavorable, disadvantageous)
名adversary：敵；対戦相手

0366 tense /téns/
形❶(雰囲気などが)**緊迫した**、張り詰めた　❷(人などが)緊張した(≒anxious, nervous)　❸(筋肉などが)凝り固まった(≒tight, taut)
名tension：❶緊迫[緊張]状態　❷緊張、不安

0367 utmost /ʌ́tmòust/
形(程度などの点で)**最大[最高]の**(≒greatest, maximum)
名(the [one's] ~)(程度などの)最大限(≒maximum, limit)

0368 diverse /divə́ːrs/
形**さまざまな**、多様な(≒various)
名diversity：❶多様性　❷(a diversity of で)多種多様な~
動diversify：❶~を多様化する　❷(投資)を多角的にする　❸経営を多角化する

Day 22))) CD-A22　Quick Review
答えは右ページ下

□ 疲れ切った　□ 相いれない　□ だまされやすい　□ 奇妙な
□ 義務的な　□ 集中的な　□ 凶悪な　□ 読みやすい
□ 安定した　□ 条件つきの　□ 広範囲にわたる　□ 穏やかな
□ 適切な　□ 注目すべき　□ 熟達した　□ 混沌とした

Check 2 Phrase	Check 3 Sentence
☐ moderate speed（適度なスピード） ☐ moderate views（穏健な考え）	☐ The room was kept at a moderate temperature.（その部屋は適度な温度に保たれていた）
☐ a decent meal（まともな食事） ☐ a decent young man（礼儀正しい若者）	☐ Everyone wants to make a decent living.（誰もがまともな暮らしをしたいと思っている）
☐ a psychological state（精神状態） ☐ psychological terms（心理学用語）	☐ Depression is caused by physical, psychological, or social factors.（うつ病は、身体的、精神的、もしくは社会的要因によって引き起こされる）
☐ a fierce attack（激しい攻撃） ☐ a fierce dog（どう猛なイヌ）	☐ The competition for natural resources has become fierce.（天然資源をめぐる競争は激しくなっている）
☐ have an adverse effect on ~（~に悪影響をもたらす） ☐ adverse weather conditions（悪天候）	☐ During a product liability lawsuit, the company will face adverse publicity.（製造物責任訴訟の間、その会社は都合の悪い評判を受けることになるだろう）
☐ a tense situation（緊迫した状況） ☐ feel tense（緊張する）	☐ There was a tense atmosphere in the meeting room.（会議室には緊迫した空気が流れていた）
☐ with the utmost care（最大の注意を払って） ☐ a matter of the utmost importance（最重要の問題）	☐ The president was treated with the utmost respect.（大統領は最大の敬意をもってもてなされた）
☐ diverse topics（さまざまな話題） ☐ a culturally diverse city（文化的に多様な都市）	☐ There are diverse opinions about the issue.（その問題に関してはさまざまな意見がある）

Day 22))) CD-A22
Quick Review
答えは左ページ下

☐ exhausted
☐ compulsory
☐ stable
☐ appropriate
☐ incompatible
☐ intensive
☐ conditional
☐ remarkable
☐ gullible
☐ vicious
☐ extensive
☐ proficient
☐ bizarre
☐ legible
☐ tranquil
☐ chaotic

CHAPTER 1
CHAPTER 2
CHAPTER 3
CHAPTER 4
CHAPTER 5
CHAPTER 6
CHAPTER 7
CHAPTER 8
CHAPTER 9
CHAPTER 10

Day 24　形容詞6

Check 1　Listen 》CD-A24

0369
intense
/inténs/
- 形 **激しい**、強烈[猛烈]な(≒fierce)
- 名 intensity：激しさ、強烈さ
- 動 intensify：❶強まる　❷～を強める
- 形 intensive：❶集中[徹底]的な　❷(農業などが)集約的な

0370
fake
/féik/
- 形 **偽の**、偽造[模造]の(≒forged, counterfeit)(⇔real, genuine, authentic)
- 名 偽物(≒forgery, counterfeit)
- 動 ❶～を偽造する(≒forge, counterfeit)　❷～を偽る、装う(≒pretend, feign)

0371
substantial
/səbstǽnʃəl/
- 形 (数量などが)**かなりの**、相当な(≒considerable, significant)
- 名 substance：❶物質　❷本質、内容
- 副 substantially：❶かなり、大幅に　❷本質[実質]的に

0372
preliminary
/prilímənèri/
- 形 **予備的な**、準備の(≒preparatory)
- 名 (通例～ies)❶予備段階；準備　❷予選

0373
imminent
/ímənənt/
- 形 **差し迫った**、切迫した(≒impending)　⊕eminent (著名な)と混同しないように注意
- 名 imminence：切迫

0374
consecutive
/kənsékjətiv/
- 形 **連続した**(≒straight, successive)
- 副 consecutively：連続して

0375
sly
/slái/
- 形 **ずる賢い**、ずるい(≒cunning, crafty)

0376
experimental
/ikspèrəméntl/
- 形 **実験の**、実験に基づく；実験的な
- 名 experiment：実験
- 動 experiment：(～の)実験をする、(～を)試みる(with [on] ～)

continued
▼

「声を出しながら」CDを聞いてる？ えっ、恥ずかしい?! 恥ずかしがっていては「話せる」ようにならないよ！ もっと口を動かそう！

☐ 聞くだけモード　Check 1
☐ しっかりモード　Check 1 ▶ 2
☐ かんぺきモード　Check 1 ▶ 2 ▶ 3

Check 2　Phrase

☐ an intense discussion（激しい議論）
☐ intense heat（猛烈な暑さ）

☐ a fake bill [note]（偽札）
☐ a fake passport（偽造パスポート）

☐ a substantial number of ~（かなりの数の~）
☐ substantial improvement（かなりの改善）

☐ preliminary talks（予備会談）
☐ be at a preliminary stage（[計画などが]準備段階にある）

☐ an imminent crisis（差し迫った危機）
☐ be in imminent danger of ~（~の危険が差し迫っている）

☐ for five consecutive days（5日間連続して）
☐ one's fifth consecutive win [defeat]（5連勝[連敗]目）

☐ a sly con man（ずる賢い詐欺師）
☐ a sly look（ずるそうな顔つき）

☐ experimental data（実験データ）

Check 3　Sentence

☐ With more people out of work, competition for jobs has become intense.（より多くの人が失業しており、職を求める競争は激しくなっている）

☐ Two men were arrested for selling fake designer goods.（偽のブランド品を売ったかどで男性2人が逮捕された）

☐ In that country, a substantial proportion of people live in poverty.（その国では、かなりの割合の人々が貧困生活を送っている）

☐ Preliminary experimental results show that the drug is effective and safe.（予備実験の結果は、その薬が効き目があり安全であることを示している）

☐ Endangered species are those in imminent danger of extinction.（絶滅危惧種とは絶滅の危険が差し迫っている種のことだ）

☐ She was absent from work for seven consecutive days.（彼女は7日間連続して仕事を休んだ）

☐ He has a sly personality.（彼はずる賢い性格だ）

☐ The device is still in the experimental stage.（その装置はまだ実験段階にある）

continued

Day 24

Check 1 Listen)) CD-A24

0377 legitimate /lidʒítəmət/
形❶**正当な**、もっともな(≒valid, sound, justifiable, reasonable) ❷合法[適法]の(≒legal, lawful)
動(/lidʒítəmèit/)❶~を正当化する ❷~を合法と認める ❸~を嫡出子と認める
名legitimacy：合法[正当]性

0378 trivial /tríviəl/
形**ささいな**、取るに足りない(≒unimportant, insignificant, trifling)
名trivia：❶雑学(的知識) ❷ささいなこと

0379 enviable /énviəbl/
形**うらやましい**、ねたましい
動envy：~をうらやむ、ねたむ
名envy：うらやましさ、羨望
形envious：(be envious ofで)~をうらやんでいる

0380 indigenous /indídʒənəs/
形(ある土地などに)**原産[固有]の**(to ~)(≒native)(⇔exotic)；現地の

0381 renowned /rináund/
形(~で/…として)**著名[有名]な**(for ~/as …)(≒famous, eminent, distinguished)
名renown：名声、有名

0382 fluid /flú:id/
形❶(状況などが)**流動的な**、不安定な、変わりやすい(≒fluctuating, changeable) ❷(動きが)滑らかな、流れるような(≒smooth)
名液体、水分(≒liquid)

0383 unsanitary /ʌnsǽnətèri/
形**不衛生な**、不潔な(≒insanitary, unhygienic, unclean, dirty)(⇔sanitary)
名sanitation：❶公衆衛生 ❷衛生設備

0384 deceptive /diséptiv/
形**当てにならない**、人を惑わせるような(≒misleading)
名deception：詐欺(行為)、だますこと
動deceive：~をだます、欺く

Day 23)) CD-A23
Quick Review
答えは右ページ下

- □ 余分な
- □ 過度の
- □ 不法な
- □ 決断力のない
- □ 相当する
- □ 非の打ちどころのない
- □ 非論理的な
- □ 否定できない
- □ 適度の
- □ まともな
- □ 精神的な
- □ 激しい
- □ 都合の悪い
- □ 緊迫した
- □ 最大の
- □ さまざまな

Check 2　Phrase

- a legitimate demand（正当な要求）
- the legitimate government（合法政府）

- a trivial problem（ささいな問題）

- an enviable reputation（うらやましいほどの名声）
- be in the enviable position（うらやましい立場にある）

- a plant indigenous to Australia（オーストラリア原産の植物）
- the indigenous language（現地語）

- a renowned author（著名な作家）
- a hotel renowned for its hospitality（温かいもてなしで有名なホテル）

- the fluid political situation（流動的な政治情勢）
- fluid movements（滑らかな動き）

- an unsanitary kitchen（不衛生な台所）

- deceptive information（当てにならない情報）
- deceptive advertising（人を惑わせるような広告、虚偽広告）

Check 3　Sentence

- The student had a legitimate reason for missing the class.（その生徒には授業を休んだ正当な理由があった）

- My wife and I quarreled over a trivial matter last night.（妻と私は昨夜、ささいなことでけんかをした）

- He is in the enviable position of being able to make a living doing what he loves.（彼は大好きなことをしながら生計を立てられるといううらやましい立場にある）

- Tomatoes are indigenous to South America.（トマトは南米原産だ）

- Her father is a renowned architect.（彼女の父親は著名な建築家だ）

- The situation in Afghanistan is still fluid.（アフガニスタンの情勢はいまだに流動的だ）

- More than 50 dogs were found caged in unsanitary conditions.（50頭以上のイヌが不衛生な状態でおりに入れられているのが見つかった）

- Appearances are often deceptive.（見かけは当てにならないことが多い）

Day 23))) CD-A23
Quick Review
答えは左ページ下

- redundant
- excessive
- illicit
- indecisive
- equivalent
- spotless
- illogical
- undeniable
- moderate
- decent
- psychological
- fierce
- adverse
- tense
- utmost
- diverse

CHAPTER 1
CHAPTER 2
CHAPTER 3
CHAPTER 4
CHAPTER 5
CHAPTER 6
CHAPTER 7
CHAPTER 8
CHAPTER 9
CHAPTER 10

Day 25　形容詞7

Check 1　Listen ») CD-A25

☐ 0385
prestigious
/prestíːdʒəs/

形 **一流**[名門]**の**、名声のある（≒ respected, admired）
名 prestige：威信、名声

☐ 0386
inconsiderate
/ìnkənsídərət/

形 **配慮**[思いやり]**のない**（≒ thoughtless, unkind）
（⇔ considerate）

☐ 0387
enormous
/inɔ́ːrməs/

形 **巨大**[莫大、膨大]**な**（≒ huge, vast, immense, gigantic, massive）
副 enormously：非常に

☐ 0388
confidential
/kɑ̀nfədénʃəl/

形 **秘密**[機密、内密]**の**（≒ secret, private, classified）
副 confidentially：内密に
名 confidentiality：内密であること、機密保持

☐ 0389
debatable
/dibéitəbl/

形 **議論の余地のある**、異論のある（≒ controversial, arguable, disputable, questionable）
名 debate：（～に関しての）議論、論争、討論（on [about] ～）
動 debate：～を議論[討論]する

☐ 0390
scarce
/skéərs/

形 **不足している**、乏しい、不十分な（≒ short, insufficient, inadequate）（⇔ plentiful）
副 scarcely：ほとんど～ない

☐ 0391
barren
/bǽrən/

形 **不毛の**（⇔ fertile：肥沃な）

☐ 0392
mainstream
/méinstriːm/

形 **主流**(派)**の**
名 (the ～)主流(派)

continued
▼

今日でChapter 3は最後！ 時間に余裕があったら、章末のReviewにも挑戦しておこう。忘れてしまった単語も結構あるのでは?!

- ☐ 聞くだけモード　Check 1
- ☐ しっかりモード　Check 1 ▶ 2
- ☐ かんぺきモード　Check 1 ▶ 2 ▶ 3

Check 2　Phrase

☐ a prestigious hotel（一流ホテル）

☐ It is inconsiderate of ~ to do...（…するとは~は配慮がない）
☐ inconsiderate remarks（配慮のない発言）

☐ an enormous temple（巨大寺院）
☐ an enormous amount [number] of ~（莫大な量[数]の~）

☐ strictly confidential（極秘の）
☐ confidential documents（機密文書）

☐ It is debatable whether ~.（~かどうかは議論の余地がある）
☐ a debatable issue（議論の余地のある問題）

☐ become scarce（不足する、乏しくなる）
☐ scarce resources（乏しい資源）

☐ barren land（不毛の土地）

☐ mainstream opinion（主流の意見）
☐ become mainstream（主流になる）

Check 3　Sentence

☐ Oxford University is one of the most prestigious universities in the world.（オックスフォード大学は世界の超一流大学の1つだ）

☐ It was inconsiderate of him to say such a thing to her.（そんなことを彼女に言うとは彼は配慮がなかった）

☐ He lives in an enormous house with lots of rooms.（彼はたくさんの部屋がある巨大な家に住んでいる）

☐ You must keep this information confidential.（あなたはこの情報を秘密にしておかなければならない）

☐ It is debatable whether the witness's testimony is credible.（その目撃者の証言が信頼できるかどうかは議論の余地がある）

☐ Land is scarce in urban areas.（都市部では土地が不足している）

☐ The Sahara Desert is the most barren environment in the world.（サハラ砂漠は世界で最も不毛な環境だ）

☐ An eco-friendly lifestyle is becoming mainstream in Japan.（環境に優しい生活様式が日本では主流になりつつある）

continued
▼

Day 25

Check 1　Listen))) CD-A25

0393 harsh
/hάːrʃ/

形 (気候などが)**厳しい**、過酷な (≒ severe, bitter, hard)
副 harshly: ❶厳しく　❷耳[目]障りになるほど

0394 conventional
/kənvénʃənl/

形 **従来の**、慣習[慣例]的な (≒ orthodox, traditional)
(⇔ unconventional: 慣例にとらわれない)
名 convention: ❶(各種団体などの)大会、総会　❷慣習、しきたり

0395 outrageous
/autréidʒəs/

形 **とんでもない**、法外な、常軌を逸した (≒ shocking, scandalous, unreasonable)
名 outrage: (〜に対する)激しい怒り (at [over] 〜)
動 outrage: 〜を激怒させる
形 outraged: 激怒した

0396 durable
/djúərəbl/

形 ❶**耐久性[力]のある**　❷永続的な、恒久的な (≒ long-lasting)
名 durability: 耐久性

0397 obedient
/oubíːdiənt/

形 (〜に)**従順[素直]な** (to 〜) (≒ compliant, docile)
(⇔ disobedient)
名 obedience: (〜に対する)従順さ (to 〜)
副 obediently: 従順に
動 obey: 〜に従う

0398 competitive
/kəmpétətiv/

形 ❶(市場などが)**競争の激しい**　❷(価格などが)競争力のある、他に負けない、格安の
名 competition: (〜を求める)競争 (for 〜)
名 competitor: 競争相手、競合他社
動 compete: (〜と)競争する (with 〜)

0399 spectacular
/spektǽkjələr/

形 **壮大な**、目を見張るような (≒ magnificent, impressive, breathtaking)
名 豪華ショー、超大作
名 spectacle: ❶(大規模な)見せ物、ショー　❷壮観

0400 credible
/krédəbl/

形 **信用[信頼]できる** (≒ reliable, believable)
名 credibility: 信用、信頼性

Day 24))) CD-A24　Quick Review
答えは右ページ下

- ☐ 激しい
- ☐ 偽の
- ☐ かなりの
- ☐ 予備的な
- ☐ 差し迫った
- ☐ 連続した
- ☐ ずる賢い
- ☐ 実験の
- ☐ 正当な
- ☐ ささいな
- ☐ うらやましい
- ☐ 原産の
- ☐ 著名な
- ☐ 流動的な
- ☐ 不衛生な
- ☐ 当てにならない

Check 2 Phrase

- ☐ harsh winter（厳しい冬）
- ☐ harsh criticism（厳しい批評、酷評）

- ☐ conventional methods [medicine]（従来の方法[医学]）

- ☐ It is outrageous that ~.（~とはとんでもないことだ）
- ☐ an outrageous price（法外な値段）

- ☐ durable plastics（耐久性のあるプラスチック）
- ☐ a durable peace（恒久的平和）

- ☐ an obedient dog（従順なイヌ）

- ☐ a competitive market（競争の激しい市場）
- ☐ competitive prices（他社に負けない価格）

- ☐ spectacular scenery（壮大な景色）

- ☐ a credible explanation [report]（信用できる説明[報道]）

Check 3 Sentence

- ☐ Desert plants and animals survive by adapting to the harsh environment.（砂漠の植物や動物は厳しい自然環境に適応することで生き延びている）

- ☐ More and more people are choosing to buy hybrid cars instead of conventional ones.（従来の車ではなくハイブリッド車の購入を選ぶ人がさらに増えている）

- ☐ It is outrageous that the government has ignored the concerns of local people.（地元住民の懸念を政府が無視しているとはとんでもないことだ）

- ☐ Aluminum is more durable than iron.（アルミニウムは鉄よりも耐久性がある）

- ☐ She is obedient to her parents.（彼女は両親に従順だ）

- ☐ Tourism is a highly competitive industry.（観光業は非常に競争の激しい産業だ）

- ☐ The fireworks display was truly spectacular.（その花火大会は本当に壮大だった）

- ☐ Do you think his story is credible?（彼の話は信用できると思いますか？）

Day 24))) CD-A24
Quick Review
答えは左ページ下

- ☐ intense
- ☐ fake
- ☐ substantial
- ☐ preliminary
- ☐ imminent
- ☐ consecutive
- ☐ sly
- ☐ experimental
- ☐ legitimate
- ☐ trivial
- ☐ enviable
- ☐ indigenous
- ☐ renowned
- ☐ fluid
- ☐ unsanitary
- ☐ deceptive

Chapter 3 Review

左ページの(1)〜(20)の形容詞の同意・類義語（≒）、反意・反対語（⇔）を右ページのA〜Tから選び、カッコの中に答えを書き込もう。意味が分からないときは、見出し番号を参照して復習しておこう（答えは右ページ下）。

- □ (1) relevant (0290) ≒は? (　　)
- □ (2) chronic (0296) ⇔は? (　　)
- □ (3) deliberate (0300) ≒は? (　　)
- □ (4) genuine (0313) ⇔は? (　　)
- □ (5) massive (0316) ≒は? (　　)
- □ (6) feasible (0317) ≒は? (　　)
- □ (7) subsequent (0324) ⇔は? (　　)
- □ (8) courteous (0331) ≒は? (　　)
- □ (9) precarious (0336) ≒は? (　　)
- □ (10) compulsory (0338) ≒は? (　　)
- □ (11) remarkable (0344) ≒は? (　　)
- □ (12) bizarre (0349) ≒は? (　　)
- □ (13) illicit (0355) ⇔は? (　　)
- □ (14) spotless (0358) ≒は? (　　)
- □ (15) psychological (0363) ≒は? (　　)
- □ (16) substantial (0371) ≒は? (　　)
- □ (17) imminent (0373) ≒は? (　　)
- □ (18) indigenous (0380) ⇔は? (　　)
- □ (19) confidential (0388) ≒は? (　　)
- □ (20) spectacular (0399) ≒は? (　　)

A. previous
B. exotic
C. fake
D. outstanding
E. flawless
F. mandatory
G. related
H. impressive
I. legal
J. viable
K. considerable
L. intentional
M. secret
N. dangerous
O. polite
P. mental
Q. strange
R. acute
S. impending
T. huge

【解答】 (1) G (2) R (3) L (4) C (5) T (6) J (7) A (8) O (9) N (10) F
(11) D (12) Q (13) I (14) E (15) P (16) K (17) S (18) B (19) M (20) H

CHAPTER 4
名詞：頻出176

Chapter 4では、英検準1級「頻出」の名詞176をマスターします。「超」が抜けても、どれも重要な単語ばかり。本試験で慌てることがないよう、1語1語を着実に身につけていきましょう。

Day 26【名詞12】
▶ 126
Day 27【名詞13】
▶ 130
Day 28【名詞14】
▶ 134
Day 29【名詞15】
▶ 138
Day 30【名詞16】
▶ 142
Day 31【名詞17】
▶ 146
Day 32【名詞18】
▶ 150
Day 33【名詞19】
▶ 154
Day 34【名詞20】
▶ 158
Day 35【名詞21】
▶ 162
Day 36【名詞22】
▶ 166
Chapter 4 Review
▶ 170

こんなの出たよ！

The (　　　) of the opinion poll about the war was questioned when it was discovered that only people who had served in the military had been contacted.（2008年度第2回）

1　persistence　2　validity
3　likelihood　　4　temperament

答えはDay 26でチェック！

Day 26　名詞12

Check 1　Listen)) CD-A26

0401 contribution
/kàntrəbjúːʃən/

名❶(〜への)**貢献**、寄与、助力(to [toward] 〜)　❷(〜への)寄付金、献金(to [toward] 〜)(≒donation)
動contribute：❶(contribute toで)〜の一因[一助]となる；〜に貢献[寄与]する　❷(contribute A to Bで)AをBに寄付[寄贈]する

0402 artifact
/áːrtifækt/

名(特に考古学的な)**工芸品**、(人工)遺物(≒relic)　➕artefactとつづることもある

0403 predecessor
/prédəsèsər/

名❶**前任者**(⇔successor：後継者)　❷前の物、前身、前作、旧型(≒precursor)

0404 subject
/sʌ́bdʒikt/

名❶**被験者**　❷話題；主題；テーマ(≒theme, topic)　❸科目、学科
形(be subject toで)❶〜に左右される；〜を受けやすい　❷〜に服従している
形subjective：主観的な

0405 guideline
/gáidlàin/

名(通例〜s)(政策などの)**指針**、ガイドライン(for [on] 〜)

0406 validity
/vəlídəti/
トビラの問題の正解はコレ！

名(〜の)**妥当**[正当、有効]**性**(of 〜)
形valid：❶(契約などが)有効な　❷(議論などが)妥当[正当]な
動validate：〜を証明[立証]する
名validation：証明、立証

0407 colleague
/káliːg/

名**同僚**(≒co-worker, associate, fellow worker)

0408 legislation
/lèdʒisléiʃən/

名❶(集合的に)(制定された)**法律**(≒law)　❷法律制定、立法(≒lawmaking)
名legislator：法律制定者、立法府議員
名legislature：議会、立法府
形legislative：❶立法上の　❷立法権のある

continued
▼

Chapter 4では、11日をかけて「頻出」名詞176をチェック。まずはCDでチャンツを聞いて、単語を「耳」からインプット!

☐ 聞くだけモード Check 1
☐ しっかりモード Check 1 ▶ 2
☐ かんぺきモード Check 1 ▶ 2 ▶ 3

Check 2 Phrase

☐ make a contribution to ~(~に貢献する)
☐ collect contributions(寄付金を集める)

☐ gold artifacts(金の工芸品)

☐ take over the work of one's predecessor(前任者の仕事を引き継ぐ)
☐ be better than its predecessor(前の物よりも優れている)

☐ a hypnotic subject(催眠術の被験者)
☐ a subject of debate(議題)

☐ follow guidelines(指針に従う)
☐ issue guidelines(指針を発表する)

☐ the validity of the experiment(その実験の妥当性)
☐ give [lend] validity to ~(~を妥当とする)

☐ colleagues from the office(職場の同僚)

☐ gun control legislation(銃規制法)
☐ the power of legislation(立法権)

Check 3 Sentence

☐ The organization has made a significant contribution to world peace.(その団体は世界平和に大きく貢献してきた)

☐ The museum has numerous artifacts from ancient Egypt, Rome, and Greece.(その美術館には古代エジプト、ローマ、そしてギリシャの工芸品がたくさんある)

☐ The new CEO is much younger than his predecessor.(新しいCEOは前任者よりもかなり若い)

☐ A total of 80 subjects participated in the experiment.(計80人の被験者がその実験に参加した)

☐ All employees must follow the safety guidelines.(全従業員は安全指針に従わなければならない)

☐ The scientific validity of the study is in question.(その研究の科学的妥当性が問題になっている)

☐ He invited some of his colleagues to his wedding.(彼は同僚の何人かを結婚式に招待した)

☐ New legislation on immigration will be introduced next year.(移民に関する新しい法律は来年、施行される予定だ)

continued
▼

Day 26

Check 1　Listen)) CD-A26

0409 venture /véntʃər/
名(リスクを伴う)**投機[冒険]的事業**、ベンチャー(≒ enterprise, undertaking)

0410 distress /distrés/ ❶アクセント注意
名❶**苦悩**、心痛(≒suffering, anguish, torment)　❷遭難
動〜を苦しめる、悲しませる(≒torment)
形distressed：(〜に／…して)悩んで、苦しんで(about [at, over] 〜/to do)

0411 retailer /rí:tèilər/ ❶発音注意
名**小売業者**、小売店(⇔wholesaler：卸売業者)
名retail：小売り、小売業
動retail：(〜の値で)小売りされる(for [at] 〜)

0412 inhabitant /inhǽbətənt/
名**住民**、居住者(≒resident, dweller)
動inhabit：〜に住む、生息する

0413 real estate /rí:əl istèit/
名**不動産**
名estate：財産

0414 isolation /àisəléiʃən/
名❶**孤立**、隔絶、隔離　❷孤独(感)
動isolate：〜を(…から)孤立させる、引き離す(from …)
形isolated：孤立した

0415 confrontation /kànfrəntéiʃən/
名(〜との／…の間の)**対立**、対決(with 〜/between …)(≒conflict, clash)
動confront：❶(困難など)に立ち向かう　❷(困難などが)(人)に立ちはだかる

0416 storage /stɔ́:ridʒ/
名**保管**、貯蔵
動store：❶〜を保管[貯蔵]する　❷(エネルギーなど)を蓄える
名store：❶店　❷(〜の)貯蔵、蓄積(of 〜)

Day 25)) CD-A25　Quick Review　答えは右ページ下

- □ 一流の
- □ 配慮のない
- □ 巨大な
- □ 秘密の
- □ 議論の余地のある
- □ 不足している
- □ 不毛の
- □ 主流の
- □ 厳しい
- □ 従来の
- □ とんでもない
- □ 耐久性のある
- □ 従順な
- □ 競争の激しい
- □ 壮大な
- □ 信用できる

Check 2　Phrase

- a joint venture（合併事業）

- be in distress（悲しみに暮れている）
- a distress signal [call]（遭難信号）

- the nation's second-largest retailer（国内第2位の小売業者）

- a town of approximately 20,000 inhabitants（住民数約2万の町）

- a real estate agency（不動産業者）

- be in isolation（孤立している、隔離されている）
- a feeling of isolation（孤独感）

- confrontation between labor and management（労使間の対立）

- a storage facility（保管[貯蔵]施設）
- be in storage（保管[貯蔵]されている）

Check 3　Sentence

- Investments in ventures involve risks.（投機的事業への投資は危険を伴う）

- Children's problems can be a source of distress for parents.（子どもの問題は親にとって苦悩の原因になることがある）

- Toys"R"Us is one of the world's biggest toy retailers.（トイザらスは世界最大のおもちゃの小売業者の1つだ）

- Most of the inhabitants of the village are engaged in agriculture.（その村の住民のほとんどは農業に従事している）

- Real estate prices have been dropping for the past two years.（この2年間、不動産価格は下がり続けている）

- The tribe lives in almost complete isolation from civilization.（その部族は文明からほぼ完全に孤立して生活している）

- The country wants to avoid direct confrontation with the US.（その国は米国との直接的な対立を避けたがっている）

- The warehouse is used for the storage of imported goods.（その倉庫は輸入品の保管に使われている）

CHAPTER 1
CHAPTER 2
CHAPTER 3
CHAPTER 4
CHAPTER 5
CHAPTER 6
CHAPTER 7
CHAPTER 8
CHAPTER 9
CHAPTER 10

Day 25 》CD-A25
Quick Review
答えは左ページ下

- prestigious
- inconsiderate
- enormous
- confidential
- debatable
- scarce
- barren
- mainstream
- harsh
- conventional
- outrageous
- durable
- obedient
- competitive
- spectacular
- credible

Day 27 名詞13

Check 1　Listen 》 CD-A27

☐ 0417
celebrity
/səlébrəti/
❶アクセント注意

名 ❶ **有名**[著名]**人**　❷名声(≒fame)

☐ 0418
sensation
/senséiʃən/

名 ❶ **感覚**、感じ(≒feeling, sense)　❷センセーション、物議、大騒ぎ
形 sensational：❶センセーショナルな、人騒がせな　❷素晴らしい

☐ 0419
abuse
/əbjúːs/

名 ❶ **乱用**、悪用(≒misuse)　❷虐待(≒mistreatment)
動 (/əbjúːz/)❶〜を乱用[悪用]する(≒misuse)　❷〜を虐待する(≒mistreat)

☐ 0420
correlation
/kɔ̀ːrəléiʃən/

名 (〜との／…の間の)**相関**[相互]**関係**(with 〜/between . . .)(≒connection, association, relation)
動 correlate：(〜と)相互関係にある(with 〜)

☐ 0421
emergency
/imə́ːrdʒənsi/

名 **緊急時**、緊急[非常]事態
動 emerge：❶(事実などが)明らかになる　❷現れる、出てくる
名 emergence：出現、発生
形 emergent：新興[新生]の

☐ 0422
ovation
/ouvéiʃən/

名 (聴衆の)**拍手喝采**(≒applause)

☐ 0423
spending
/spéndiŋ/

名 (〜への)**支出**、出費(on 〜)
動 spend：❶(金)を(…に)使う(on . . .)　❷(時間)を過ごす、費やす

☐ 0424
integration
/ìntəgréiʃən/

名 (〜との／…への)**統合**、統一(with 〜/into . . .)(≒unification)
動 integrate：❶〜を(…と)統合する(with . . .)　❷(社会などに)融合する、溶け込む(into 〜)
形 integrated：統合[統一]された

continued
▼

勉強する気分になれないときは、CDを「聞き流す」だけでもOK。家で、車内で、いつでもどこでも語彙に「触れる」時間を作ってみよう。

- ☐ 聞くだけモード　Check 1
- ☐ しっかりモード　Check 1 ▶ 2
- ☐ かんぺきモード　Check 1 ▶ 2 ▶ 3

Check 2　Phrase

- ☐ a sport celebrity（有名スポーツ選手）
- ☐ gain celebrity（名声を得る）

- ☐ lose all sensation（すべての感覚を失う）
- ☐ cause [create] a sensation（センセーションを巻き起こす）

- ☐ drug abuse（麻薬の乱用）
- ☐ child abuse（幼児虐待）

- ☐ the correlation between smoking and lung cancer（喫煙と肺がんの間の相関関係）

- ☐ in an emergency（緊急時に）
- ☐ emergency landing（緊急着陸）

- ☐ give ~ an ovation（~に拍手喝采を送る）
- ☐ a standing ovation（スタンディングオベーション）

- ☐ public spending（公共支出）
- ☐ cut [reduce] spending（支出を削減する）

- ☐ the integration of East and West Germany（東西ドイツの統合）

Check 3　Sentence

- ☐ Many people are interested in celebrities' lives.（多くの人は有名人たちの生活に興味を持っている）

- ☐ Local anesthesia is used to block sensation in certain areas of the body.（局部麻酔は体の特定の部分の感覚を遮断するために用いられる）

- ☐ Alcohol abuse often leads to serious health disorders.（アルコールの乱用は深刻な健康障害につながることが多い）

- ☐ There is a strong correlation between poverty and malnutrition.（貧困と栄養失調の間には強い相関関係がある）

- ☐ It is important to set some money aside in case of an emergency.（緊急時に備えていくらかお金を蓄えておくことが大切だ）

- ☐ She was given a warm ovation at the end of her speech.（彼女はスピーチの最後に温かい拍手喝采を浴びた）

- ☐ Government spending on education should be increased.（教育への政府支出は引き上げられるべきだ）

- ☐ Integration into the EU will benefit the country's economy.（EUへの統合はその国の経済に利益をもたらすだろう）

continued
▼

Day 27

Check 1　Listen))) CD-A27

□ 0425
admiration
/ǽdməréiʃən/

名❶(〜に対する)**称賛**、感嘆(for 〜)(≒respect, praise, applause)　❷(the 〜)称賛の的
動admire：〜を(…の点で)称賛する(for . . .)
名admirer：(〜の)ファン、称賛者(of 〜)

□ 0426
workplace
/wɔ́ːrkplèis/

名**職場**、仕事場

□ 0427
mayor
/méiər/

名**市長**、町長　✚「知事」はgovernor

□ 0428
clue
/klúː/

名(難問などの)**手がかり**、糸口(to [about, as to] 〜)(≒hint)

□ 0429
uproar
/ʌ́prɔ̀ːr/

名**大騒ぎ**、騒動(≒turmoil, tumult)

□ 0430
drawback
/drɔ́ːbæ̀k/

名(〜の)**欠点**、障害、不利な点(of [to] 〜)(≒disadvantage, obstacle)

□ 0431
routine
/ruːtíːn/
❶アクセント注意

名**日常の仕事**、日課
形❶いつもの、日常的な　❷単調な、退屈な

□ 0432
deception
/disépʃən/

名**詐欺**(行為)、だますこと(≒deceit, fraud, fraudulence)
動deceive：〜をだます、欺く
形deceptive：当てにならない、人を惑わせるような

Day 26))) CD-A26
Quick Review
答えは右ページ下

□ 貢献
□ 工芸品
□ 前任者
□ 被験者

□ 指針
□ 妥当性
□ 同僚
□ 法律

□ 投機的事業
□ 苦悩
□ 小売業者
□ 住民

□ 不動産
□ 孤立
□ 対立
□ 保管

Check 2　Phrase

- watch ~ in admiration（~を感嘆して見つめる）
- be the admiration of ~（~の称賛の的である）

- gender discrimination in the workplace（職場での性差別）

- the Mayor of London（ロンドン市長）

- search [look] for clues（手がかりを探す）
- leave a clue（[犯人などが]手がかりを残す）

- be in (an) uproar（[部屋などが]大騒ぎになっている）
- cause [provoke] (an) uproar（騒動を引き起こす）

- a major [serious] drawback（重大な[深刻な]欠点）

- a daily routine（日課）
- as a matter of routine（習慣として）

- an elaborate deception（手の込んだ詐欺）

Check 3　Sentence

- His scientific achievements have won worldwide admiration.（彼の科学的業績は世界中で称賛されている）

- Smoking in the workplace is prohibited except in designated smoking areas.（職場での喫煙は指定された喫煙場所以外では禁止されている）

- Four candidates are running for mayor.（4人の候補者が市長に立候補している）

- Police searched the crime scene for clues.（警察は手がかりを求めて犯罪現場を捜索した）

- There was uproar in the court when the sentence was announced.（判決が言い渡されると、法廷は大騒ぎになった）

- One of the biggest drawbacks of an electric car is the limited driving range.（電気自動車の最大の欠点の1つは短い走行距離だ）

- She is tired of the routine in the office.（彼女は職場での日常の仕事にうんざりしている）

- The man was arrested for obtaining money by deception.（その男は詐欺で金を手に入れた容疑で逮捕された）

Day 26))) CD-A26
Quick Review
答えは左ページ下

- contribution
- artifact
- predecessor
- subject
- guideline
- validity
- colleague
- legislation
- venture
- distress
- retailer
- inhabitant
- real estate
- isolation
- confrontation
- storage

CHAPTER 1
CHAPTER 2
CHAPTER 3
CHAPTER 4
CHAPTER 5
CHAPTER 6
CHAPTER 7
CHAPTER 8
CHAPTER 9
CHAPTER 10

Day 28　名詞14

Check 1　Listen))) CD-A28

0433 symptom /símptəm/
图❶(〜の)**症状**(of 〜)(≒manifestation)　❷(〜の)兆候、兆し(of 〜)(≒sign)

0434 innovation /ìnəvéiʃən/
图**革新**、刷新；斬新な考え
形innovative：革新[刷新]的な；創意に富む
動innovate：刷新[革新]する

0435 reputation /rèpjutéiʃən/
图(〜との／…としての)**評判**、名声(for [of] 〜/as ...)
形reputable：評判のよい

0436 component /kəmpóunənt/
图❶(薬などの)**成分**(≒ingredient)　❷(機械類の)部品、構成要素(≒part, element, constituent)

0437 proximity /prɑksíməti/
图(〜に)**近いこと**(to 〜)、近接(≒closeness, nearness, vicinity)

0438 workforce /wə́ːrkfɔ̀ːrs/
图(全)**従業員**(数)、(全)労働人口、労働力(≒staff, personnel, labor force, manpower)

0439 incident /ínsədənt/
图**出来事**、事件、事故(≒event, accident)
形(〜に)付随する(to 〜)
图incidence：(病気・犯罪などの)発生率
形incidental：❶付随[二次]的な　❷(〜に)付随して起こる(to 〜)

0440 rainforest /réinfɔ̀ːrist/
图**熱帯雨林**　●rain forestと2語に分けることもある

continued
▼

「分散学習」も効果的。朝起きたら Check 1、昼食後に Check 2、寝る前に Check 3といった具合に、学習時間を作る工夫をしてみよう。

☐ 聞くだけモード　Check 1
☐ しっかりモード　Check 1 ▶ 2
☐ かんぺきモード　Check 1 ▶ 2 ▶ 3

Check 2　Phrase

☐ symptoms of diabetes（糖尿病の症状）
☐ symptoms of recession（景気後退の兆候）

☐ technological innovation（技術革新）

☐ a good [bad] reputation（好評[悪評]）
☐ earn [establish, gain] a reputation as ~（~としての名声を得る）

☐ chemical components（化学成分）
☐ electrical components（電気部品）

☐ in close proximity to ~（~のすぐ近くに[で]）

☐ cut the workforce by 10 percent（従業員数を10パーセント削減する）
☐ enter the workforce（労働人口に加わる）

☐ an unexpected incident（思いがけない出来事）
☐ without incident（何事もなく、無事に）

☐ the Amazon rainforest（アマゾンの熱帯雨林）

Check 3　Sentence

☐ Chronic coughing is the most common symptom of tuberculosis.（慢性的なせきは結核の最も一般的な症状だ）

☐ Innovations in information technology have revolutionized business practices.（情報技術の革新はビジネス手法に革命的変化をもたらした）

☐ Japan has a reputation for being one of the safest societies in the world.（日本は世界で最も安全な社会の1つであるとの評判を得ている）

☐ Amino acids are the basic components of proteins.（アミノ酸はタンパク質の主成分だ）

☐ We chose the house for its proximity to the station.（私たちは駅に近いことでその家を選んだ）

☐ The firm has a workforce of around 400 people.（その会社には約400人の従業員がいる）

☐ Most of the movie is based on true incidents.（その映画の大部分は実際の出来事に基づいている）

☐ Rainforests are disappearing at a terrifying rate.（熱帯雨林は恐ろしいほどのペースで消失している）

continued
▼

Day 28

Check 1　Listen 》CD-A28

0441 shift /ʃíft/
- 名 ❶(考えなどの)(〜への)**転換**、変化、移行(to [toward] 〜)(≒change, alteration)　❷(交代制の)勤務時間
- 動 ❶移動する　❷〜を移動する(≒move)　❸〜を変える　❹変わる(≒change, alter)

0442 craving /kréiviŋ/
- 名 (〜への)**切望**、渇望、飢え(for 〜)(≒desire, longing, yearning)
- 動 crave: 〜を切望[渇望]する

0443 breakthrough /bréikθrù:/
- 名 (研究などの)**飛躍的な進展**、大発見、躍進(in 〜)(≒advance, development)

0444 theft /θéft/
- 名 **窃盗**(罪)、盗み(≒stealing, burglary)　❶「強盗」はrobbery
- 動 thieve: 〜を盗む
- 名 thief: 泥棒、窃盗犯

0445 applicant /ǽplikənt/
- 名 (〜への)**応募者**、志願者(for 〜)(≒candidate)
- 名 application: (〜への)申し込み[申請](書)(for 〜)
- 動 apply: ❶(apply forで)〜を申し込む　❷(apply toで)(規則などが)〜に適用される、当てはまる；〜に申し込む　❸(apply A to Bで)AをBに適用[応用、利用]する

0446 hostage /hάstidʒ/
- 名 **人質**　❶「誘拐」はkidnapping、「身代金」はransom

0447 portion /pɔ́:rʃən/
- 名 ❶(〜の)**部分**、一部(of 〜)(≒part, segment)　❷(食べ物の)1人前(of 〜)(≒serving, helping)

0448 awareness /əwéərnis/
- 名 (〜の)**意識**、認識、自覚(of 〜)(≒consciousness, recognition, realization)
- 形 aware: (be aware ofで)〜に気づいている、〜を承知している

Day 27 》CD-A27　Quick Review　答えは右ページ下

- □ 有名人
- □ 感覚
- □ 乱用
- □ 相関関係
- □ 緊急時
- □ 拍手喝采
- □ 支出
- □ 統合
- □ 称賛
- □ 職場
- □ 市長
- □ 手がかり
- □ 大騒ぎ
- □ 欠点
- □ 日常の仕事
- □ 詐欺

Check 2   Phrase

- ☐ a **shift** in public opinion（世論の変化）
- ☐ finish one's **shift**（自分の勤務時間を終える）

- ☐ have a **craving** for ～（～を切望する、～が欲しくてたまらない）
- ☐ a **craving** to be loved（愛されたいという渇望）

- ☐ a **breakthrough** in cancer research（がん研究の飛躍的な進展）
- ☐ make a **breakthrough**（飛躍的な進展を遂げる、大発見をする）

- ☐ car [auto] **theft**（自動車窃盗）

- ☐ **applicants** for admission（入学志願者）
- ☐ job **applicants**（求職者）

- ☐ take ～ **hostage**（～を人質に取る）
- ☐ be held **hostage**（人質になっている）

- ☐ a substantial [significant] **portion** of ～（～の大部分）
- ☐ four **portions** of pasta（4人前のパスタ）

- ☐ raise **awareness** of [about] ～（～についての意識を高める）
- ☐ political **awareness**（政治意識）

Check 3   Sentence

- ☐ The **shift** to environmentally sustainable economies will require public support.（環境面で持続可能な経済への転換には国民の支持が必要となるだろう）

- ☐ I have no **craving** for fame or power.（私は名声や権力を切望していない）

- ☐ The discovery of insulin was a remarkable medical **breakthrough**.（インシュリンの発見は注目すべき医学の飛躍的な進展だった）

- ☐ The man has four previous convictions for **theft**.（その男は窃盗で以前に4回有罪判決を受けている）

- ☐ He was selected from dozens of **applicants** for the job.（彼はその仕事への何十人もの応募者の中から選ばれた）

- ☐ The **hostages** were released unharmed last night.（人質たちは昨夜、無事に解放された）

- ☐ The country spends a considerable **portion** of its budget on education.（その国は予算のかなりの部分を教育に費やしている）

- ☐ There is a growing **awareness** of climate change.（気候変動への意識が高まってきている）

Day 27))) CD-A27
Quick Review
答えは左ページ下

- ☐ celebrity
- ☐ sensation
- ☐ abuse
- ☐ correlation
- ☐ emergency
- ☐ ovation
- ☐ spending
- ☐ integration
- ☐ admiration
- ☐ workplace
- ☐ mayor
- ☐ clue
- ☐ uproar
- ☐ drawback
- ☐ routine
- ☐ deception

Day 29　名詞15

Check 1　Listen 》CD-A29

□ 0449
achievement
/ətʃíːvmənt/

名❶**業績**、成果　❷達成、成就(≒attainment, accomplishment)
動achieve：❶(名声など)を獲得する、勝ち取る　❷〜を成し遂げる、達成する

□ 0450
refund
/ríːfʌnd/
❶アクセント注意

名**返金**、払い戻し金(≒repayment, reimbursement)
動(/rifʌ́nd/)(料金など)を払い戻す(≒repay, pay back, reimburse)

□ 0451
sentence
/séntəns/

名❶**刑**、刑罰、判決(≒punishment, penalty)　❷文
動〜に判決を下す

□ 0452
compassion
/kəmpǽʃən/

名(〜への)**同情**、哀れみ、思いやり(for 〜)(≒pity, sympathy)

□ 0453
aptitude
/ǽptətjùːd/

名(〜の)**才能**、素質、適性(for 〜)

□ 0454
source
/sɔ́ːrs/

名❶(〜の)**源**(of 〜)(≒origin)　❷(〜の)原因(of 〜)(≒cause)

□ 0455
limitation
/lìmətéiʃən/

名❶(通例〜s)(能力などの)**限界**　❷(〜に対する)制約、規制、制限(on [to] 〜)(≒restriction)
名limit：❶限度、制限　❷(通例〜s)範囲、区域
動limit：〜を(…に)制限する(to ...)
形limited：限られた、有限の

□ 0456
tuition
/tjuːíʃən/

名❶**授業料**(≒tuition fee)　❷指導、授業(≒teaching, instruction)

continued
▼

同意語・類義語(≒)や反意語・反対語(⇔)もチェックしてる? 余裕があれば確認して、語彙の数を積極的に増やしていこう。

□ 聞くだけモード　Check 1
□ しっかりモード　Check 1 ▶ 2
□ かんぺきモード　Check 1 ▶ 2 ▶ 3

Check 2　Phrase

□ academic achievements(学業成績、学問的業績)
□ a sense of achievement(達成感)

□ receive [demand] a refund(返金を受け取る[要求する])

□ a light [heavy] sentence(軽い[重い]刑)
□ a jail [prison] sentence(実刑)

□ feel [show, have] compassion for ~(~に同情する)
□ with compassion(哀れみを持って)

□ an aptitude for music(音楽の才能)
□ an aptitude test(適性検査)

□ an energy source(エネルギー源)
□ the source of the trouble(トラブルの原因)

□ have one's limitations(限界がある)
□ impose limitations on ~(~に制限を課す)

□ can afford tuition(授業料を払う余裕がある)
□ private tuition(個人指導)

Check 3　Sentence

□ The professor was awarded the prize in recognition of his scientific achievements.(その教授は科学上の業績を認められて賞を授与された)

□ A full refund will be given if the product is faulty.(製品に欠陥がある場合、全額が返金される)

□ The defendant was given a 10-year sentence.(その被告は10年の刑を言い渡された)

□ I feel a deep compassion for her.(私は彼女に深く同情している)

□ She has a special aptitude for languages.(彼女は言語に対する特別な才能がある)

□ Milk is an excellent source of calcium.(牛乳は優れたカルシウム源だ)

□ He is fully aware of his own limitations.(彼は自分の限界を十分に自覚している)

□ The university raised tuition by 5 percent last year.(その大学は昨年、授業料を5パーセント引き上げた)

continued ▼

Day 29

Check 1　Listen))) CD-A29

☐ 0457
insight
/ínsàit/
> 名(〜に対する／…についての)**洞察力**、見識(into 〜/ about . . .)(≒intuition, penetration, acumen)

☐ 0458
scholarship
/skάlərʃip/
> 名❶(大学などの)**奨学金**(to 〜)(≒grant)　❷学識、学問(≒learning, knowledge)
> 名scholar：❶学者　❷奨学生
> 形scholarly：❶学術的な　❷博学な

☐ 0459
circumstance
/sə́:rkəmstæns/
> 名(通例〜s)**状況**、事情(≒condition, situation)

☐ 0460
extension
/iksténʃən/
> 名❶**延長**、延期(≒postponement, prolongation)　❷(電話の)内線　❸拡張(≒expansion)
> 動extend：❶〜を拡大する　❷〜を延長する
> 形extensive：❶広範囲にわたる　❷大規模な、甚だしい
> 副extensively：広範囲に、幅広く

☐ 0461
requirement
/rikwáiərmənt/
> 名(〜の)**必要条件**、資格(for 〜)(≒prerequisite)
> 動require：❶〜を必要とする　❷〜を要求する、義務づける

☐ 0462
carbon dioxide
/kὰ:rbən daiάksaid/
> 名**二酸化炭素**　❶「酸素」はoxygen
> 名carbon：炭素

☐ 0463
violation
/vàiəléiʃən/
> 名❶(法律などの)**違反**(of 〜)(≒breach, offense)　❷(権利などの)侵害(of 〜)(≒invasion, infringement)
> 動violate：❶(法律など)に違反する　❷(権利など)を侵害する

☐ 0464
irrigation
/ìrəɡéiʃən/
> 名**灌漑**(かんがい)
> 動irrigate：(土地)を灌漑する

Day 28))) CD-A28
Quick Review
答えは右ページ下

☐ 症状　☐ 近いこと　☐ 転換　☐ 応募者
☐ 革新　☐ 従業員　☐ 切望　☐ 人質
☐ 評判　☐ 出来事　☐ 飛躍的な進展　☐ 部分
☐ 成分　☐ 熱帯雨林　☐ 窃盗　☐ 意識

Check 2 Phrase

- a person of great insight(洞察力の鋭い人)

- win [get] a scholarship(奨学金を得る)
- a man of great scholarship(学識の深い人)

- political [economic] circumstances(政治[経済]状況)
- suspicious circumstances(不審な状況)

- an extension of the contract(契約の延長)
- an extension number(内線番号)

- meet requirements(必要条件を満たす)
- requirements for admission(入学資格)

- reduce the amount of carbon dioxide in the atmosphere(大気中の二酸化炭素量を減らす)

- in violation of ~(~に違反して)
- a violation of privacy(プライバシーの侵害)

- an irrigation channel [canal](灌漑用水路)

Check 3 Sentence

- The book gives us a deep insight into the cause of the current economic crisis.(その本は現在の経済危機の原因に対する深い洞察力を私たちに与えてくれる)

- She won a scholarship to Columbia University.(彼女はコロンビア大学の奨学金を得た)

- Police will investigate the circumstances of the incident.(警察はその事件をめぐる状況を調査する予定だ)

- He applied for an extension of his student visa.(彼は学生ビザの延長を申請した)

- Fluency in English and Spanish is a requirement of the position.(英語とスペイン語に堪能であることがその職の必要条件だ)

- Plants absorb carbon dioxide and release oxygen.(植物は二酸化炭素を吸収して、酸素を放出する)

- The company was charged with violation of intellectual property law.(その会社は知的財産法違反のかどで告発された)

- Ancient Egyptians developed complex irrigation systems.(古代エジプト人は複雑な灌漑システムを開発した)

Day 28))) CD-A28
Quick Review
答えは左ページ下

- symptom
- innovation
- reputation
- component
- proximity
- workforce
- incident
- rainforest
- shift
- craving
- breakthrough
- theft
- applicant
- hostage
- portion
- awareness

CHAPTER 1
CHAPTER 2
CHAPTER 3
CHAPTER 4
CHAPTER 5
CHAPTER 6
CHAPTER 7
CHAPTER 8
CHAPTER 9
CHAPTER 10

Day 30 名詞16

Check 1　Listen))) CD-A30

☐ 0465
profile
/próufail/
❶発音注意

名❶**横顔**　❷プロフィール、人物紹介　❸(会社などの)評判、イメージ
動〜のプロフィールを紹介する

☐ 0466
coincidence
/kouínsidəns/

名❶**偶然の一致**(≒accident, chance)　❷(〜の)一致(of 〜)(≒agreement, accord)
動coincide: (coincide withで)❶〜と同時に起こる　❷(意見などが)〜と一致する
形coincidental：偶然の

☐ 0467
orbit
/ɔ́:rbit/

名**軌道**
動❶(軌道に沿って)〜の周りを回る　❷軌道を描いて回る

☐ 0468
supplement
/sʌ́pləmənt/

名❶(〜への)**補足**、補充(to 〜)　❷(ビタミンなどの)補給剤　❸(書物などの)補遺、付録(≒appendix)
動(/sʌ́pləmènt/)〜を補う
形supplementary：補足[追加]の

☐ 0469
voucher
/váutʃər/

名(商品)**引換券**、割引券、クーポン(≒coupon, token)

☐ 0470
divorce
/divɔ́:rs/

名**離婚**(≒separation)(⇔marriage)
動❶〜と離婚する　❷離婚する(≒separate)

☐ 0471
context
/kántekst/

名❶**文脈**、(文章の)前後関係　❷(出来事などの)背景、状況(≒circumstance, condition, situation, background)

☐ 0472
identification
/aidèntifəkéiʃən/

名❶**身分証明書**　❶略語はID　❷(犠牲者などの)身元確認　❸(〜との)同一感、共感(with 〜)(≒empathy)
動identify：〜を(…であると)確認する(as …)
名identity：❶身元、正体　❷個性、アイデンティティー

continued
▼

チャンツを聞く際には、「英語→日本語→英語」の2回目の「英語」の部分で声に出して読んでみよう。定着度が倍増するはず！

- □ 聞くだけモード　Check 1
- □ しっかりモード　Check 1 ▶ 2
- □ かんぺきモード　Check 1 ▶ 2 ▶ 3

Check 2　Phrase

- □ in profile（横顔で、横から）
- □ a profile of the actor（その俳優のプロフィール）

- □ What a coincidence!（何という偶然なんでしょう！）
- □ a coincidence of interests（利害の一致）

- □ put a satellite into orbit（人工衛星を軌道に乗せる）
- □ in orbit（軌道上に）

- □ a supplement to one's income（収入を補うもの）
- □ vitamin supplements（ビタミン補給剤）

- □ a voucher for a free lunch（無料の昼食の引換券）
- □ a travel voucher（旅行引換券）

- □ get a divorce（離婚する）
- □ divorce proceedings（離婚手続き）

- □ in this context（この文脈[状況]では）
- □ political [social] context（政治[社会]的背景）

- □ show one's identification（身分証明書を見せる）
- □ the identification of the suspect（その容疑者の身元確認）

Check 3　Sentence

- □ She has a beautiful profile.（彼女は美しい横顔をしている）

- □ Life is full of strange coincidences.（人生は不可思議な偶然の一致に満ちている）

- □ The lunar probe is now in orbit around the moon.（その月面探査機は現在、月を周回する軌道上にある）

- □ This document is a supplement to that report.（この書類はその報告書を補足するものだ）

- □ This voucher expires 12 months from date of issue.（この引換券は発行日の12カ月後に期限が切れる）

- □ The divorce rate in the US is around 50 percent.（米国の離婚率は約50パーセントだ）

- □ Words have a variety of meanings depending on the context.（単語は文脈によってさまざまな意味を持つ）

- □ Can I see your identification, please?（身分証明書を見せてもらえますか？）

continued ▼

Day 30

Check 1　Listen)) CD-A30

0473
discipline
/dísəplin/
❶アクセント注意

- 名 ❶**規律**、しつけ(≒order)　❷訓練、鍛錬、修練(≒training)
- 動 ❶(違反者)を懲戒する(≒punish)　❷〜をしつける(≒train)

0474
productivity
/pròudʌktívəti/

- 名 **生産性**[力]
- 形 productive：❶生産力のある、生産的な　❷実りの多い
- 名 product：製品
- 名 production：❶製造、生産　❷生産量[高]
- 動 produce：〜を製造[生産]する

0475
menace
/ménis/
❶発音注意

- 名 (〜に対する)**脅威**、危険な人[物] (to 〜)(≒threat)
- 動 〜を危険にさらす、脅かす(≒threaten)

0476
retirement
/ritáiərmənt/

- 名 (〜からの)**退職**、引退(from 〜)(≒resignation)
- 動 retire：(〜から)退職[引退]する(from 〜)
- 形 retired：退職[引退]した
- 名 retiree：退職[引退]者

0477
invasion
/invéiʒən/

- 名 ❶(〜への)**侵略**、侵攻(of 〜)　❷(権利などの)侵害(of 〜)(≒violation, infringement)
- 動 invade：❶〜を侵略する、〜に侵攻する　❷(権利など)を侵害する
- 名 invader：侵略[侵入]者

0478
commodity
/kəmádəti/

- 名 **商品**、生産物(≒item, product)

0479
famine
/fǽmin/
❶発音注意

- 名 **飢饉**(ききん)

0480
contentment
/kənténtmənt/

- 名 **満足**(≒satisfaction, content)(⇔discontent)
- 形 content：(〜に)満足している(with 〜)
- 動 content：❶(content oneselfで)(〜で)満足する、(〜に)甘んじる(with 〜)　❷〜を満足させる

Day 29)) CD-A29
Quick Review
答えは右ページ下

- □ 業績
- □ 返金
- □ 刑
- □ 同情
- □ 才能
- □ 源
- □ 限界
- □ 授業料
- □ 洞察力
- □ 奨学金
- □ 状況
- □ 延長
- □ 必要条件
- □ 二酸化炭素
- □ 違反
- □ 灌漑

Check 2 — Phrase

- ☐ maintain discipline(規律を保つ)
- ☐ self-discipline(自己鍛錬[修養]；自制)

- ☐ boost productivity(生産性を高める)
- ☐ agricultural productivity(農業生産性)

- ☐ a menace to society [peace](社会[平和]に対する脅威)

- ☐ take early retirement(早期退職する)
- ☐ retirement age(定年)

- ☐ the Soviet invasion of Afghanistan(ソ連のアフガニスタン侵攻)
- ☐ an invasion of privacy(プライバシーの侵害)

- ☐ commodity management(商品管理)
- ☐ agricultural commodities(農産物)

- ☐ a severe famine(深刻な飢饉)
- ☐ famine relief(飢饉の救済)

- ☐ a look of contentment(満足した表情)
- ☐ in perfect contentment(満足し切って)

Check 3 — Sentence

- ☐ The school is famous for its strict discipline.(その学校は厳しい規律で有名だ)

- ☐ An untidy working environment will decrease productivity.(乱雑な職場環境は生産性を下げるだろう)

- ☐ The president believed that Saddam Hussein was a menace to world peace.(サダム・フセインは世界平和に対する脅威だとその大統領は信じていた)

- ☐ He took early retirement and moved to Florida.(彼は早期退職して、フロリダに引っ越した)

- ☐ Poland has suffered many invasions during its history.(ポーランドはその歴史の中で多くの侵略を受けた)

- ☐ Commodity prices have been declining steadily over the last few years.(商品価格はこの数年にわたって徐々に下がっている)

- ☐ The region is threatened by famine due to poor harvests.(その地域は凶作による飢饉に脅かされている)

- ☐ I find contentment in my circumstances.(私は自分の境遇に満足している)

CHAPTER 1
CHAPTER 2
CHAPTER 3
CHAPTER 4
CHAPTER 5
CHAPTER 6
CHAPTER 7
CHAPTER 8
CHAPTER 9
CHAPTER 10

Day 29))) CD-A29
Quick Review
答えは左ページ下

- ☐ achievement
- ☐ refund
- ☐ sentence
- ☐ compassion
- ☐ aptitude
- ☐ source
- ☐ limitation
- ☐ tuition
- ☐ insight
- ☐ scholarship
- ☐ circumstance
- ☐ extension
- ☐ requirement
- ☐ carbon dioxide
- ☐ violation
- ☐ irrigation

Day 31　名詞17

Check 1　Listen)) CD-A31

☐ 0481
removal
/rimúːvəl/

名 (〜の／…からの) **撤去**、除去 (of 〜/from . . .) (≒ elimination)
動 remove：〜を(…から)取り除く、取り外す (from . . .)

☐ 0482
powerhouse
/páuərhàus/

名 **強大な国** [組織] (≒ superpower)

☐ 0483
catastrophe
/kətǽstrəfi/
❶アクセント注意

名 ❶ **大災害**、大惨事 (≒ disaster, calamity)　❷ 破滅、破局 (≒ ruin)
形 catastrophic：❶悲惨な、最悪の　❷壊滅的な

☐ 0484
ethics
/éθiks/

名 ❶ (職業などの) **倫理** [道徳] (規範) (≒ moral)　❷ 倫理学
形 ethical：倫理 [道徳] 上の；倫理 [道徳] 的な

☐ 0485
quota
/kwóutə/

名 (生産などの) **ノルマ**、割当量 (≒ allocation, allotment)

☐ 0486
interaction
/ìntərǽkʃən/

名 (〜との／…の間の) **交流**、触れ合い、相互作用 (with 〜/between . . .)
動 interact：❶ (〜と)交流する (with 〜)　❷ (〜と)相互に作用する (with 〜)
形 interactive：双方向の、インタラクティブな

☐ 0487
valuable
/vǽljuəbl/

名 (通例〜s) **貴重品**
形 ❶貴重な (≒ precious, priceless)　❷高価な (≒ costly, expensive)　❸有益な (≒ useful, helpful)
名 value：❶価値　❷価格　❸ (〜s) 価値観
動 value：〜を高く評価する、尊重する

☐ 0488
memento
/məméntou/

名 (〜の) **思い出の品**、記念品 (of 〜) (≒ souvenir)

continued
▼

「声に出す」練習は続けてる？ えっ、周りに人がいてできない?! そんなときは「口パク」でもOK。「耳＋口」の練習を忘れずに！

☐ 聞くだけモード　Check 1
☐ しっかりモード　Check 1 ▶ 2
☐ かんぺきモード　Check 1 ▶ 2 ▶ 3

Check 2　Phrase

☐ the removal of a tumor（腫瘍の切除）
☐ stain removal（染み抜き）

☐ an economic powerhouse（経済大国）

☐ a terrible catastrophe（恐ろしい大惨事）
☐ move toward a catastrophe（破滅へと向かう）

☐ professional ethics（職業倫理）
☐ major in ethics（倫理学を専攻する）

☐ fill [meet] a quota（ノルマを果たす）
☐ an import quota（輸入割当量）

☐ interaction between the management and employees（経営陣と従業員たちの交流）

☐ put valuables in a safe（貴重品を金庫にしまう）

☐ a memento of one's trip to France（フランス旅行の思い出の品）

Check 3　Sentence

☐ Local people are demanding the removal of the dam.（地元住民はそのダムの撤去を要求している）

☐ China has become a powerhouse of manufacturing in the world.（中国は世界の製造業の大国になった）

☐ The earthquake was one of the worst catastrophes in Japanese history.（その地震は日本の歴史の中で最悪の大災害の1つだった）

☐ The ethics of journalism have been widely debated.（ジャーナリズムの倫理が幅広く議論されている）

☐ He met his sales quota for two consecutive quarters.（彼は2四半期連続で販売ノルマを果たした）

☐ Interaction between parents and teachers is very important in achieving educational goals.（親と教師たちの交流は教育目標を達成する上で非常に重要だ）

☐ Please keep an eye on your valuables at all times.（常に貴重品から目を離さないでください）

☐ Her room is full of mementos of her childhood.（彼女の部屋は子どものころの思い出の品であふれている）

continued ▼

Day 31

Check 1　Listen))) CD-A31

0489 conversion /kənvə́ːrʒən/
- 名 (〜から／…への)**変換**、転換、改造、改装(from 〜/to [into] ...)(≒ change, transformation, adaptation, alteration)
- 動 convert：(convert A into [to] Bで)AをBに変える、AをBに変換[転換、改造、改装]する

0490 balance /bǽləns/
❶アクセント注意
- 名 ❶(預金口座の)**残高** ❷均衡、釣り合い、バランス(≒ equilibrium)
- 動 ❶バランスを取る ❷〜のバランスを取る
- 形 balanced：❶バランス[均衡]の取れた ❷公平[公正]な、偏りのない

0491 preference /préfərəns/
- 名 (〜に対する)**好み**(for 〜)(≒ liking)
- 動 prefer：(…よりも)〜のほうを好む(to ...)
- 形 preferable：(〜より)好ましい(to 〜)
- 副 preferably：できれば

0492 testimony /téstəmòuni/
- 名 (法廷などでの)**証言**、陳述(≒ evidence)
- 動 testify：(〜に有利な／…に不利な)証言をする(for 〜/against ...)

0493 overhaul /óuvərhɔ̀ːl/
- 名 (機械などの)**分解修理**、整備、オーバーホール(of 〜)(≒ service, maintenance, repair)
- 動 (/òuvərhɔ́ːl/)(機械など)を分解修理する、整備する、オーバーホールする(≒ service, maintain, repair)

0494 enterprise /éntərpràiz/
❶アクセント注意
- 名 ❶**企業**、会社(≒ company, business, firm, corporation) ❷事業(≒ undertaking, venture)

0495 consumption /kənsʌ́mpʃən/
- 名 **消費量**[高]；消費
- 動 consume：〜を消費する
- 名 consumer：消費者

0496 prediction /pridíkʃən/
- 名 (〜の／…についての)**予測**、予想(of 〜/about ...)(≒ forecast)
- 動 predict：〜を予測[予想]する
- 形 predictable：❶予測可能な ❷予想通りの

Day 30))) CD-A30
Quick Review
答えは右ページ下

- □ 横顔
- □ 偶然の一致
- □ 軌道
- □ 補足
- □ 引換券
- □ 離婚
- □ 文脈
- □ 身分証明書
- □ 規律
- □ 生産性
- □ 脅威
- □ 退職
- □ 侵略
- □ 商品
- □ 飢饉
- □ 満足

Check 2 — Phrase

- the conversion of sunlight into energy(日光のエネルギーへの変換)
- the conversion of the building(そのビルの改装)

- bank balance(銀行預金残高)
- keep [lose] one's balance(バランスを保つ[失う])

- have no particular preference for ~(特に~に対する好みはない)
- have a preference for ~(~を好む)

- give testimony(証言する)
- the defendant's testimony(被告の証言)

- a major overhaul(大がかりな分解修理)

- a state-owned enterprise(国営企業)
- public enterprise(公営事業)

- oil consumption(石油消費量)
- the consumption of fossil fuels(化石燃料の消費)

- make a prediction about ~(~を予想[予測]する)
- future predictions(未来予測)

Check 3 — Sentence

- Conversion from analog to digital television is under way.(アナログテレビからデジタルテレビへの変換が進行している)

- You can call our toll-free number to check your balance.(当社のフリーダイヤルにお電話いただくと残高をご確認になれます)

- Personal preference varies from person to person.(個人的な好みは人によって異なる)

- The witness's testimony was adverse to the defendant.(その目撃者の証言は被告にとって不利なものだった)

- The engine needs a complete overhaul.(そのエンジンは徹底した分解修理が必要だ)

- A large number of small and medium-sized enterprises are on the verge of bankruptcy.(多くの中小企業が倒産寸前になっている)

- We need to reduce energy consumption for environmental reasons.(私たちは環境上の理由からエネルギー消費量を減らす必要がある)

- Government predictions of 3-percent economic growth this year seem overly optimistic.(今年の3パーセントの経済成長という政府の予測は楽観的過ぎるように思われる)

Day 30 》CD-A30
Quick Review
答えは左ページ下

- profile
- coincidence
- orbit
- supplement
- voucher
- divorce
- context
- identification
- discipline
- productivity
- menace
- retirement
- invasion
- commodity
- famine
- contentment

Day 32　名詞18

Check 1　Listen 》CD-A32

0497 sequence /síːkwəns/
- 名❶(物事の)**一連**、連続(≒series, succession)　❷順序(≒order)
- 形 sequential：連続的な

0498 forecast /fɔ́ːrkæst/
- 名 **予測**、予想、予報(≒prediction)
- 動 ～を予測[予想、予報]する(≒predict)

0499 coauthor /kòuɔ́ːθər/
- 名 **共著者**(≒joint author)　◐co-authorとつづることもある
- 名 author：著者

0500 pursuit /pərsúːt/
- 名❶**追跡**(≒chase)　❷追求(≒quest, search)
- 動 pursue：❶～を追跡する　❷～を追い求める

0501 itinerary /aitínərèri/
- 名 **旅行計画**、旅程(≒travel plan)
- ◐アクセント注意

0502 restriction /ristríkʃən/
- 名(～に対する)**制限**、規制(on ～)(≒limitation)
- 動 restrict：～を(…に)制限する(to …)、～を規制する
- 形 restricted：(～に)限られた、制限された(to ～)

0503 expansion /ikspǽnʃən/
- 名(～の)**拡大**、拡張(of ～)(≒enlargement)(⇔contraction：収縮)
- 動 expand：❶～を拡大する　❷拡大する
- 名 expanse：(海などの)広がり(of ～)

0504 negligence /néɡlidʒəns/
- 名 **過失**、怠慢(≒error, mistake)
- 動 neglect：❶～を無視[軽視]する　❷～を怠る、おろそかにする
- 名 neglect：❶無視、軽視　❷怠慢、放置
- 形 negligent：怠慢な

continued

単語はフレーズやセンテンスの中で覚えると、定着度が飛躍的にアップする。そのためにも、Check 2、3での確認を忘れずに！

- □ 聞くだけモード　Check 1
- □ しっかりモード　Check 1 ▶ 2
- □ かんぺきモード　Check 1 ▶ 2 ▶ 3

Check 2　Phrase

- □ the sequence of events（一連の出来事［事件］）
- □ in sequence（順に）

- □ sales forecast（売上予測）
- □ the weather forecast（天気予報）

- □ the coauthor of the book（その本の共著者）

- □ in pursuit of ～（～を追跡して；～を求めて）
- □ the pursuit of happiness [profit]（幸福［利益］の追求）

- □ make up an itinerary（旅行計画を立てる）
- □ alter the itinerary（旅行計画を変更する）

- □ speed [import] restriction（速度［輸入］制限）
- □ impose restrictions on ～（～に規制を加える）

- □ the expansion of the Internet（インターネットの拡大）
- □ the expansion of the stadium（そのスタジアムの拡張）

- □ medical negligence（医療過失）
- □ negligence of duty（職務怠慢）

Check 3　Sentence

- □ Police are investigating the sequence of events that led to the accident.（警察はその事故につながった一連の出来事を調査している）

- □ The government lowered economic growth forecasts for this year.（政府は今年の経済成長予測を引き下げた）

- □ Friedrich Engels is the coauthor of "The Communist Manifesto."（フリードリッヒ・エンゲルスは『共産党宣言』の共著者だ）

- □ The officer was shot while in pursuit of the suspect.（その警官は容疑者を追跡中に銃で撃たれた）

- □ The itinerary includes a visit to the Louvre.（その旅行計画にはルーブル美術館の見学が含まれている）

- □ There are restrictions on the size and weight of luggage that passengers can carry onto the aircraft.（乗客が機内に持ち込める手荷物の大きさと重量には制限がある）

- □ The pace of economic expansion has slowed in recent months.（景気拡大のペースはこの数カ月で落ちてきている）

- □ Most car accidents are caused by negligence.（ほとんどの自動車事故は過失によって起こる）

continued ▼

Day 32

Check 1 Listen))) CD-A32

□ 0505
infant
/ínfənt/

名 **乳児**、幼児、赤ん坊 (≒baby, newborn)
形 初期 (段階) の

□ 0506
corruption
/kərʌ́pʃən/

名 ❶ **汚職**、買収 (≒bribery, scandal) ❷ 堕落、腐敗 (≒decadence, degradation)
形 corrupt：堕落 [腐敗] した、不正な
動 corrupt：～を堕落させる、買収する

□ 0507
alliance
/əláiəns/

名 (～との／…の間の) **同盟**、提携、連携 (with ～/between . . .) (≒union, league, association, confederation)
名 ally：❶ 同盟国 ❷ 協力者、味方
動 ally：(ally oneself to [with] で) ～と同盟を結ぶ

□ 0508
precaution
/prikɔ́ːʃən/

名 (～に対する) **予防措置** [対策]、用心、警戒 (against ～) (≒caution, safeguard)

□ 0509
representative
/rèprizéntətiv/
❶ アクセント注意

名 ❶ **代表者**、代理人 (≒delegate) ❷ (R～)(米国の) 下院議員 ➕「上院議員」は senator
形 ❶ 典型的な (≒typical) ❷ (～を) 代表する (of ～)
動 represent：❶ ～を代表する ❷ ～を表す
名 representation：❶ 代表、代理 ❷ 表現、描写

□ 0510
livelihood
/láivlihùd/

名 **生計**、暮らし (≒living)

□ 0511
registration
/rèdʒistréiʃən/

名 **登録**、登記
動 register：❶ ～を登録 [登記] する ❷ (register for で) ～の入学 [受講] 手続きをする
名 register：登録 [記録] (簿)
形 registered：❶ 登録 [登記] された ❷ (郵便が) 書留の

□ 0512
vault
/vɔ́ːlt/

名 ❶ (地下) **金庫室** ❷ (教会などの) アーチ形天井 [屋根]

Day 31))) CD-A31
Quick Review
答えは右ページ下

□ 撤去
□ 強大な国
□ 大災害
□ 倫理

□ ノルマ
□ 交流
□ 貴重品
□ 思い出の品

□ 変換
□ 残高
□ 好み
□ 証言

□ 分解修理
□ 企業
□ 消費量
□ 予測

Check 2　Phrase

- ☐ **infants** under one year of age(1歳未満の乳児)
- ☐ an **infant** prodigy(天才児)

- ☐ bribery and **corruption**(贈収賄)
- ☐ political **corruption**(政治の腐敗)

- ☐ military **alliance**(軍事同盟)
- ☐ in **alliance** with ~(~と提携して)

- ☐ take **precautions** against ~(~に対する予防措置を講じる)
- ☐ as a **precaution**(用心[念]のために)

- ☐ send a **representative** to ~(~に代表者を送る)
- ☐ the House of **Representatives**([米国の]下院;[日本の]衆議院)

- ☐ depend on ~ for one's **livelihood**(~に生計を頼る;~で生計を立てる)
- ☐ lose one's **livelihood**(生計を失う)

- ☐ a **registration** fee(登録[登記]料)
- ☐ voter **registration**(選挙人登録)

- ☐ a bank **vault**(銀行の金庫室)

Check 3　Sentence

- ☐ **Infants** have an innate capacity for acquiring language.(乳児は生まれつき言語を習得する能力を持っている)

- ☐ The mayor was arrested on charges of **corruption**.(その市長は汚職の容疑で逮捕された)

- ☐ Both leaders have agreed to strengthen the **alliance** between Japan and the US.(両首脳は日米間の同盟を強化することで意見が一致した)

- ☐ You should take **precautions** against theft.(あなたは泥棒に対する予防措置を講じたほうがいい)

- ☐ **Representatives** from nearly 200 countries gathered to discuss climate change.(200カ国近くの代表者たちが気候変動について話し合うために集まった)

- ☐ The majority of the villagers depend on agriculture for their **livelihood**.(村民たちの大半は農業で生計を立てている)

- ☐ The **registration** deadline for the seminar is October 20.(そのセミナーの登録締め切り日は10月20日だ)

- ☐ The **vault** is protected by armed guards.(その金庫室は武装警備員たちによって守られている)

Day 31 ♪)) CD-A31
Quick Review
答えは左ページ下

- ☐ removal
- ☐ powerhouse
- ☐ catastrophe
- ☐ ethics
- ☐ quota
- ☐ interaction
- ☐ valuable
- ☐ memento
- ☐ conversion
- ☐ balance
- ☐ preference
- ☐ testimony
- ☐ overhaul
- ☐ enterprise
- ☐ consumption
- ☐ prediction

Day 33　名詞19

Check 1　Listen ») CD-A33

0513 contamination /kəntæmənéiʃən/
- 名 汚染（≒pollution）
- 動 contaminate：〜を汚染する
- 名 contaminant：汚染物質

0514 immigrant /ímigrənt/
- 名（外国からの）移民、移住者（≒settler）　⊕外国への「移民、移住者」はemigrant
- 動 immigrate：（〜から／…へ）移住する（from 〜/to ...）
- 名 immigration：❶移住、移民　❷入国管理［審査］

0515 proportion /prəpɔ́ːrʃən/
- 名 ❶割合、部分（≒part, portion）　❷比率（≒ratio）　❸釣り合い、バランス（≒balance）

0516 enforcement /infɔ́ːrsmənt/
- 名（法律などの）施行、実施（≒operation, administration）
- 動 enforce：❶（法律など）を守らせる、施行する　❷（服従など）を（…に）強要する、押しつける（on ...）

0517 confession /kənféʃən/
- 名（犯罪などの）自白、自供、白状（of 〜）（≒admission, acknowledgment）
- 動 confess：❶〜を自白［自供、白状］する　❷（confess toで）〜を自白［自供、白状］する

0518 intuition /ìntjuːíʃən/
- 名 直感、勘（≒instinct）
- 形 intuitive：❶直感的な　❷直感力のある

0519 poll /póul/
- 名 ❶世論調査　❷（the 〜s）投票所
- 動 〜に世論調査をする

0520 esteem /istíːm/
- 名 尊敬、尊重、評価（≒respect, admiration）
- 動 〜を尊敬［尊重、評価］する（≒respect, admire）
- 名 self-esteem：自尊心

continued ▼

単語が難しくなればなるほど、「繰り返し」の学習が大切。1度で覚えられたと安心せず、2度、3度と語彙に触れる回数を増やそう！

- ☐ 聞くだけモード　Check 1
- ☐ しっかりモード　Check 1 ▶ 2
- ☐ かんぺきモード　Check 1 ▶ 2 ▶ 3

Check 2　Phrase

☐ radioactive [food] contamination（放射能[食品]汚染）

☐ illegal immigrants（不法移民）
☐ German immigrants（ドイツ人移民）

☐ a large proportion of ~（~の大部分）
☐ in proportion to ~（~に比べて、比例して）

☐ law enforcement（法の執行）

☐ make a confession（自白[自供、白状]する）
☐ a confession of murder（殺害の自白）

☐ women's intuition（女性の直感）
☐ by intuition（勘で）

☐ conduct [carry out] a poll（世論調査を行う）
☐ go to the polls（投票[選挙]に行く）

☐ be held in esteem（尊敬[尊重、評価]されている）
☐ as a token of one's esteem（尊敬の印として）

Check 3　Sentence

☐ The groundwater in the area was tested for contamination.（その地域の地下水は汚染されていないかどうか検査された）

☐ The US is a country of immigrants.（米国は移民の国だ）

☐ Elderly people make up a high proportion of the village population.（高齢者はその村の人口のかなりの割合を占めている）

☐ Strict enforcement of laws is necessary in order to maintain social stability.（法の厳格な施行は社会の安定を維持するために必要だ）

☐ The suspect made a full confession of the crime.（その容疑者は犯行を全面的に自白した）

☐ My intuition told me something was wrong.（何かがおかしいと私は直感で分かった）

☐ The poll shows a steep decline in support for the government.（政府への支持が急激に下がっていることをその世論調査は示している）

☐ He is held in high esteem by his colleagues.（彼は同僚たちにとても尊敬されている）

continued
▼

Day 33

Check 1　Listen 》CD-A33

0521
gene /dʒíːn/
- 名 **遺伝子**
- 形 genetic：遺伝子の、遺伝学の
- 名 genetics：❶遺伝学　❷遺伝的特徴
- 副 genetically：遺伝子上、遺伝学的に

0522
currency /kə́ːrənsi/
- 名 **通貨**、貨幣（≒money）
- 形 current：現在の、今の
- 名 current：（川などの）流れ
- 副 currently：現在は、現在のところ

0523
evolution /èvəlúːʃən/
- 名 ❶**進化**　❷発展、発達（≒development, progress, growth）
- 動 evolve：❶（〜に）進化[発展]する（into 〜）　❷〜を進化[発展]させる
- 形 evolutionary：進化[発展]の

0524
objective /əbdʒéktiv/
- 名 **目標**、目的（≒aim, goal, target）
- 形 客観的な（⇔subjective）
- 名 object：❶物体　❷対象　❸目的
- 動 object：（object toで）〜に反対する
- 名 objection：（〜に対する）反対、異議（to [against] 〜）

0525
hindrance /híndrəns/
- 名 （〜の）**障害**、障壁、妨害、邪魔（to 〜）（≒obstacle, barrier, impediment）
- 動 hinder：〜を妨げる、遅らせる

0526
dependency /dipéndənsi/
- 名 （〜への）**依存**（on [upon] 〜）（≒dependence, reliance）
- 動 depend：（depend on [upon]で）❶〜に頼る、依存する　❷〜によって決まる、〜次第である
- 形 dependable：信頼できる、当てになる

0527
surrounding /səráundiŋ/
- 名 （〜s）（周囲の）**環境**（≒environment, setting）
- 形 周囲[周辺]の
- 動 surround：〜を囲む、取り巻く

0528
adolescent /ædəlésnt/
- 名 **十代**[青春期、思春期]**の若者**（≒teenager）
- 形 青春[思春]期の
- 名 adolescence：青春[思春]期

Day 32 》CD-A32　Quick Review
答えは右ページ下

- ☐ 一連
- ☐ 予測
- ☐ 共著者
- ☐ 追跡
- ☐ 旅行計画
- ☐ 制限
- ☐ 拡大
- ☐ 過失
- ☐ 乳児
- ☐ 汚職
- ☐ 同盟
- ☐ 予防措置
- ☐ 代表者
- ☐ 生計
- ☐ 登録
- ☐ 金庫室

Check 2　Phrase

- ☐ a dominant [recessive] gene（優性[劣性]遺伝子）

- ☐ local currency（国内[現地]通貨）
- ☐ foreign currency（外貨）

- ☐ the theory of evolution（進化論）
- ☐ the evolution of democracy（民主主義の発展）

- ☐ the main [primary, principal] objective（主要な目標）
- ☐ achieve [meet] an objective（目標を達成する）

- ☐ a hindrance to economic growth（経済成長の障害）
- ☐ without hindrance（支障なく）

- ☐ dependency on one's parents（親への依存）

- ☐ adjust to one's new surroundings（新しい環境に慣れる）

- ☐ a normal adolescent（普通の十代の若者）

Check 3　Sentence

- ☐ Scientists think that a human has about 20,000 to 25,000 genes.（ヒトは約2万から2万5000の遺伝子を持っていると科学者たちは考えている）

- ☐ The currency in Germany is the euro.（ドイツの通貨はユーロだ）

- ☐ Natural selection is central to Darwin's theory of evolution.（自然淘汰はダーウィンの進化論の中核を成している）

- ☐ Objectives should be realistic and attainable.（目標は現実的で達成可能であるべきだ）

- ☐ The lack of irrigation facilities is a major hindrance to agricultural development in the region.（灌漑施設の不足がその地域の農業開発の大きな障害となっている）

- ☐ We must reduce our dependency on oil.（私たちは石油への依存を減らさなければならない）

- ☐ Everyone wants to live in pleasant surroundings.（誰もが気持ちのよい環境で暮らしたいと思っている）

- ☐ Steroid abuse is increasingly common among adolescents.（ステロイドの乱用は十代の若者の間でますます一般化している）

Day 32))CD-A32
Quick Review
答えは左ページ下

- ☐ sequence
- ☐ forecast
- ☐ coauthor
- ☐ pursuit
- ☐ itinerary
- ☐ restriction
- ☐ expansion
- ☐ negligence
- ☐ infant
- ☐ corruption
- ☐ alliance
- ☐ precaution
- ☐ representative
- ☐ livelihood
- ☐ registration
- ☐ vault

Day 34　名詞20

Check 1　Listen ») CD-A34

0529 interference /ìntərfíərəns/
名 (〜への)**干渉**、口出し(in 〜)(≒intrusion, intervention)
動 interfere：❶(interfere inで)〜に干渉する　❷(interfere withで)〜を妨害する

0530 consolation /kànsəléiʃən/
名 **慰め**(≒comfort, solace)
動 console：〜を(…で)慰める(with …)

0531 self-esteem /sèlfistí:m/
名 **自尊心**(≒self-respect, self-worth, pride)
名 esteem：尊敬、尊重、評価
動 esteem：〜を尊敬[尊重、評価]する

0532 downturn /dáuntə̀:rn/
名 (景気の)**後退**、(生産などの)減少(in 〜)(≒downswing)(⇔upturn)

0533 welfare /wélfèər/
名 ❶**福祉**、福利(≒well-being)　❷生活保護(≒social security)

0534 boundary /báundəri/
名 **境界**(線)(≒border)

0535 fragment /frǽgmənt/
名 (〜の)**破片**、かけら(of 〜)
動 (/frægmènt/)❶ばらばらになる　❷〜をばらばらにする(≒break up)

0536 usher /ʎʃər/
名 (劇場などの)**案内係**(≒guide, attendant)
動 〜を(…へ)案内する(to [into] …)(≒guide, escort, accompany)

continued
▼

Quick Reviewは使ってる? 昨日覚えた単語でも、記憶に残っているとは限らない。学習の合間に軽くチェックするだけでも効果は抜群!

- ☐ 聞くだけモード Check 1
- ☐ しっかりモード Check 1 ▶ 2
- ☐ かんぺきモード Check 1 ▶ 2 ▶ 3

Check 2　　Phrase

☐ **interference** in personal affairs(私事への干渉)

☐ words of **consolation**(慰めの言葉)
☐ take **consolation** from [in] ~(〜に慰められる)

☐ have high [low] **self-esteem**(自尊心が高い[低い])

☐ the economic **downturn**(景気後退)
☐ a **downturn** in sales(売り上げの減少)

☐ **welfare** benefits(福祉手当)
☐ live on **welfare**(生活保護を受けて暮らす)

☐ the **boundary** between California and Nevada(カリフォルニア州とネバダ州の境界)

☐ **fragments** of glass(ガラスの破片)

☐ a theater **usher**(劇場の案内係)

Check 3　　Sentence

☐ The country protested the foreign **interference** in its domestic affairs.(その国は国内問題への外国からの干渉に抗議した)

☐ Many people find **consolation** in music.(音楽に慰めを見いだす人は多い)

☐ Children with low **self-esteem** tend to be overly critical of themselves.(自尊心の低い子どもは自分を過度に批判する傾向がある)

☐ There has been a severe **downturn** in the domestic economy.(国内経済の深刻な後退が続いている)

☐ The government needs to reform the **welfare** system.(政府は福祉制度を改革する必要がある)

☐ The Mississippi River forms the **boundary** between Illinois and Missouri.(ミシシッピ川はイリノイ州とミズーリ州の境界を成している)

☐ The floor was littered with **fragments** of broken dishes.(床は割れた皿の破片で散らかっていた)

☐ The **usher** took me to my seat.(案内係は私を席へと連れて行ってくれた)

continued
▼

Day 34

Check 1　Listen))) CD-A34

0537 complexity /kəmpléksəti/
- 名 **複雑さ**、複雑性(⇔simplicity)
- 形 complex：複雑な
- 名 complex：複合施設、総合ビル

0538 prosperity /prɑspérəti/
- 名 **繁栄**、繁盛
- 動 prosper：繁栄[繁盛]する、栄える、成功する
- 形 prosperous：繁栄している

0539 additive /ǽdətiv/
- 名 **添加物**[剤]

0540 lawsuit /lɔ́ːsùːt/
- 名 **訴訟**(≒suit)

0541 deficiency /difíʃənsi/ ❶アクセント注意
- 名 **不足**、欠乏(≒lack, shortage, want, dearth)
- 形 deficient：(〜が)不足している、不十分な(in 〜)

0542 subordinate /səbɔ́ːrdənət/
- 名 **部下**(≒inferior)(⇔boss, supervisor, superior)
- 形 ❶(〜より)下位[下級]の(to 〜)(≒junior, lower)　❷副次的な(≒secondary)

0543 curator /kjúərèitər/
- 名 (博物館などの)**学芸員**

0544 refugee /rèfjudʒíː/ ❶アクセント注意
- 名 (戦争などの)**難民**、亡命者
- 名 refuge：❶避難所　❷避難

Day 33))) CD-A33　Quick Review　答えは右ページ下

- □ 汚染
- □ 移民
- □ 割合
- □ 施行
- □ 自白
- □ 直感
- □ 世論調査
- □ 尊敬
- □ 遺伝子
- □ 通貨
- □ 進化
- □ 目標
- □ 障害
- □ 依存
- □ 環境
- □ 十代の若者

Check 2 — Phrase

- ☐ an issue of great **complexity** (非常に複雑な問題)
- ☐ economic **prosperity** (経済的繁栄)
- ☐ food **additives** (食品添加物)
- ☐ file a **lawsuit** against ~ (~に対して訴訟を起こす)
- ☐ iron **deficiency** (鉄分不足)
- ☐ a **deficiency** of nutrition (栄養不足)
- ☐ the relationship between **subordinates** and superiors (部下と上司の関係)
- ☐ one's work as a **curator** (学芸員としての仕事)
- ☐ a **refugee** camp (難民キャンプ)
- ☐ a political **refugee** (政治亡命者)

Check 3 — Sentence

- ☐ We were overwhelmed by the **complexity** of the problem. (私たちはその問題の複雑さに圧倒された)
- ☐ The Roman Empire enjoyed 200 years of peace and **prosperity** known as the Pax Romana. (ローマ帝国はパックス・ロマーナとして知られる200年にわたる平和と繁栄を享受した)
- ☐ This product is free of **additives** and preservatives. (この製品には添加物と保存料は入っていない)
- ☐ He dropped his **lawsuit** against the firm. (彼はその会社に対する訴訟を取り下げた)
- ☐ Vitamin **deficiency** can cause insomnia. (ビタミン不足は不眠症を引き起こすことがある)
- ☐ **Subordinates** must obey their supervisor's orders. (部下は上司の指示に従わなければならない)
- ☐ My sister is a **curator** at the Museum of Contemporary Art. (私の姉は現代美術館の学芸員だ)
- ☐ Since 1945, Australia has accepted over 600,000 **refugees**. (1945年以降、オーストラリアは60万人以上の難民を受け入れてきた)

Day 33 》CD-A33
Quick Review
答えは左ページ下

- ☐ contamination
- ☐ immigrant
- ☐ proportion
- ☐ enforcement
- ☐ confession
- ☐ intuition
- ☐ poll
- ☐ esteem
- ☐ gene
- ☐ currency
- ☐ evolution
- ☐ objective
- ☐ hindrance
- ☐ dependency
- ☐ surrounding
- ☐ adolescent

CHAPTER 1
CHAPTER 2
CHAPTER 3
CHAPTER 4
CHAPTER 5
CHAPTER 6
CHAPTER 7
CHAPTER 8
CHAPTER 9
CHAPTER 10

Day 35　名詞21

Check 1　Listen 》CD-A35

☐ 0545
finding
/fáindiŋ/

名 (通例~s)(調査などの)**結果**、発見(≒discovery)
動 find：~を見つける、発見する

☐ 0546
utility
/juːtíləti/

名 ❶(通例~ies)(水道などの)**公共料金**；公共施設；公共事業　❷有用[実用]性(≒usefulness)
動 utilize：~を(…として)利用[活用]する(as ...)
名 utilization：利用、活用

☐ 0547
hardship
/háːrdʃip/

名 **苦難**、困窮(≒difficulty, privation, austerity)

☐ 0548
assembly
/əsémbli/

名 ❶(機械の)**組み立て**(≒construction)　❷集会、会合(≒meeting, gathering)　❸議会(≒congress, parliament)
動 assemble：❶(機械など)を組み立てる　❷集まる、集合する　❸~を集める

☐ 0549
ignorance
/ígnərəns/

名 ❶(~を)**知らないこと**(of [about] ~)　❷無知、無学
形 ignorant：(be ignorant of [about]で)~を知らない
動 ignore：~を無視する

☐ 0550
summary
/sʌ́məri/

名 (~の)**要約**、概要(of ~)(≒digest, outline, synopsis, abstract)
形 ❶略式[即決]の(≒immediate, instant)　❷要約した、手短な(≒abridged, abbreviated)
動 summarize：~を要約する

☐ 0551
completion
/kəmplíːʃən/

名 **完成**、完了(≒perfection, accomplishment)
形 complete：❶完全な　❷全部の　❸完成した
動 complete：~を完成させる
副 completely：完全に、すっかり

☐ 0552
hypnosis
/hipnóusis/
❶発音注意

名 ❶ **催眠術**(≒hypnotism)　❷催眠(状態)
動 hypnotize：~に催眠術をかける
名 hypnotist：催眠術師

continued
▼

今日で『キクタン英検準1級』は前半戦が終了！ここまで一緒に学習を続けてくれてありがとう！ あと5週間、頑張ろう！

- ☐ 聞くだけモード　Check 1
- ☐ しっかりモード　Check 1 ▶ 2
- ☐ かんぺきモード　Check 1 ▶ 2 ▶ 3

Check 2　Phrase

- ☐ the findings of the survey（調査結果）

- ☐ a utility company（公益事業会社）
- ☐ be of no utility（役に立たない）

- ☐ economic [financial] hardship（経済[財政]的苦難）
- ☐ It is no hardship to do ~.（~するのは大したことではない）

- ☐ an assembly line（組み立てライン）
- ☐ freedom of assembly（集会の自由）

- ☐ in ignorance of ~（~を知らずに）
- ☐ out of [through] ignorance（無知のために）

- ☐ a summary of the book（その本の要約）
- ☐ in summary（要約すると、要するに）

- ☐ be nearing completion（完成間近である）
- ☐ on completion of ~（~が完成[終了]次第）

- ☐ under hypnosis（催眠術にかかって；催眠状態で）

Check 3　Sentence

- ☐ The findings of this study will be published in a scientific journal.（この研究の結果は科学雑誌に掲載される予定だ）

- ☐ The rent includes utilities, cable, and Internet.（家賃には、公共料金、ケーブルテレビ、そしてインターネットが含まれている）

- ☐ Many immigrants faced hardship and discrimination in their new country.（多くの移民たちは新しい国で苦難と差別に直面した）

- ☐ The automaker has 20 assembly plants in five countries.（その自動車メーカーは5カ国に20の組み立て工場を持っている）

- ☐ Ignorance of the law is no excuse for violating it.（法律を知らないことが法律違反の言い訳にはならない）

- ☐ The professor wrapped up his lecture with a summary of the important points.（その教授は重要な点を要約して講義を終えた）

- ☐ The bridge is due for completion next year.（その橋は来年、完成予定だ）

- ☐ Hypnosis is often used to boost confidence and self-esteem.（催眠術は自信や自尊心を高めるためにしばしば用いられる）

continued

Day 35

Check 1　Listen 》CD-A35

0553
session
/séʃən/

名❶ **会議**、会合(≒ meeting, assembly)　❷会、集まり(≒ gathering)　❸(大学の)学期(≒ term, semester)

0554
dignity
/dígnəti/

名 **威厳**、尊厳(≒ nobility, majesty)
動dignify：～に(…で)威厳をつける(with ...)
形dignified：威厳のある

0555
abolition
/æbəlíʃən/

名(制度などの) **廃止**、撤廃(of ～)
動abolish：(制度など)を廃止[撤廃]する

0556
investigation
/invèstəgéiʃən/

名(犯罪などの) **捜査**、調査(into [of] ～)(≒ examination, inquiry, inspection)
動investigate：～を調査[捜査]する
名investigator：調査員、捜査官

0557
segment
/ségmənt/

名 **部分**、区分(≒ part, portion)
動(/ségment/)～を分割[区分]する
名segmentation：分割、区分

0558
deposit
/dipázit/

名❶(～の) **頭金**、手付金、保証金(on ～)(≒ down payment)　❷預金(⇔withdrawal：預金の引き出し)
動～を預金する(⇔withdraw：[預金]を引き出す)

0559
possession
/pəzéʃən/

名❶(通例～s) **所有物**、財産(≒ belonging, property, asset)　❷所有、所持(≒ ownership)
動possess：～を所有する、持っている
形possessive：所有[独占]欲の強い

0560
firm
/fə́ːrm/

名 **会社**、企業(≒ company, business, enterprise, corporation)；(組織としての)事務所
形堅い(≒ hard)

Day 34 》CD-A34
Quick Review
答えは右ページ下

- ☐ 干渉
- ☐ 慰め
- ☐ 自尊心
- ☐ 後退
- ☐ 福祉
- ☐ 境界
- ☐ 破片
- ☐ 案内係
- ☐ 複雑さ
- ☐ 繁栄
- ☐ 添加物
- ☐ 訴訟
- ☐ 不足
- ☐ 部下
- ☐ 学芸員
- ☐ 難民

Check 2　Phrase

- □ in session（開会[開廷]中で）
- □ a training session（研修会）

- □ with dignity（威厳を込めて、堂々と）
- □ human dignity（人間の尊厳）

- □ the abolition of slavery（奴隷制度の廃止）
- □ the abolition of nuclear weapons（核兵器の廃絶）

- □ a criminal investigation（犯罪捜査）
- □ an investigation into the cause of the accident（その事故の原因の調査）

- □ a large segment of ~（~の大部分）

- □ put a deposit on ~（~の頭金[手付金]を払う）
- □ make a deposit（預金をする）

- □ personal possessions（私物）
- □ be in possession of ~（~を所有している）

- □ a large firm（大企業）
- □ an accounting firm（会計事務所）

Check 3　Sentence

- □ The new committee held its first plenary session last week.（新しい委員会は先週、最初の本会議を開催した）

- □ He is a man of dignity and warmth.（彼は威厳と優しさを持った人だ）

- □ The human-rights group is calling for the abolition of the death penalty.（その人権団体は死刑の廃止を求めている）

- □ The police have completed their investigations into the incident.（警察はその事件の捜査を終えた）

- □ The over-65 group is the fastest growing segment of the country's population.（65歳以上のグループはその国の人口で最も急速に増えている部分だ）

- □ I put a $3,000 deposit on my new car.（私は新車の3000ドルの頭金を払った）

- □ The family lost all their possessions in the fire.（その家族は火事ですべての所有物を失った）

- □ My father works for an insurance firm.（私の父は保険会社に勤務している）

Day 34))) CD-A34
Quick Review
答えは左ページ下

- □ interference
- □ consolation
- □ self-esteem
- □ downturn
- □ welfare
- □ boundary
- □ fragment
- □ usher
- □ complexity
- □ prosperity
- □ additive
- □ lawsuit
- □ deficiency
- □ subordinate
- □ curator
- □ refugee

CHAPTER 1
CHAPTER 2
CHAPTER 3
CHAPTER 4
CHAPTER 5
CHAPTER 6
CHAPTER 7
CHAPTER 8
CHAPTER 9
CHAPTER 10

Day 36　名詞22

Check 1　Listen 》CD-B1

0561 brochure /bróuʃúər/ ❶発音注意
名 **パンフレット**、小冊子(≒ pamphlet, booklet)

0562 treaty /tríːti/
名 (国家間の)**条約**、協定(≒ agreement, pact)

0563 hazard /hǽzərd/
名 **危険**(≒ danger, risk, peril)；(〜への)危険要素(to 〜)
形 hazardous：(〜にとって)有害な、危険な(to 〜)

0564 architect /ɑ́ːrkətèkt/
名 **建築家**
名 architecture：❶建築様式　❷建築(学)
形 architectural：建築上の；建築学の

0565 fine /fáin/
名 (〜に対する)**罰金**(for 〜)(≒ penalty)
動 (fine A for Bで)AにBのかどで罰金を科す

0566 offspring /ɔ́ːfsprìŋ/
名 **子**、子孫　❶単複同形(≒ child, descendant)

0567 wreck /rék/
名 ❶**残骸**、(乗り物などの)壊れた物(≒ debris)　❷(衝突)事故(≒ accident)
動 ❶(計画など)を台無しにする(≒ ruin, spoil)　❷〜を大破させる
名 wreckage：(集合的に)残骸

0568 deforestation /diːfɔ̀ːristéiʃən/
名 **森林破壊**[伐採]

continued ▼

今日でChapter 4は最後！ 時間に余裕があったら、章末のReviewにも挑戦しておこう。忘れてしまった単語も結構あるのでは?!

☐ 聞くだけモード　Check 1
☐ しっかりモード　Check 1 ▶ 2
☐ かんぺきモード　Check 1 ▶ 2 ▶ 3

Check 2　　Phrase

☐ a travel brochure（旅行パンフレット）

☐ sign [ratify] a treaty（条約に署名する[条約を批准する]）
☐ a peace treaty（平和条約）

☐ an occupational hazard（職業上の危険）
☐ a safety hazard（安全上の問題、安全を脅かすもの）

☐ the architect of London's St. Paul's Cathedral（ロンドンのセントポール大聖堂の建築家）⊕Christopher Wren

☐ a parking fine（駐車違反の罰金）
☐ a heavy fine（重い罰金）

☐ produce and raise offspring（子を産み育てる）

☐ the burnt-out wreck of a car（燃え尽きた車の残骸）
☐ a train wreck（列車衝突事故）

☐ massive deforestation（大規模な森林破壊）

Check 3　　Sentence

☐ Our product brochures are available on our website.（当社の製品パンフレットは当社のウェブサイトで入手できます）

☐ The US and Japan concluded a security treaty in 1951.（米国と日本は1951年に安全保障条約を締結した）

☐ Most smokers are aware of the hazards of smoking and want to quit.（ほとんどの喫煙者は喫煙の危険性を自覚しており、禁煙したいと思っている）

☐ My cousin is studying to be an architect.（私のいとこは建築家になるために勉強している）

☐ He paid a $130 fine for speeding.（彼はスピード違反で130ドルの罰金を払った）

☐ African elephants produce one offspring at a time.（アフリカゾウは1度に1頭の子を産む）

☐ Some passengers are still trapped in the wreck.（何人かの乗客がまだ残骸の中に閉じ込められている）

☐ Deforestation is affecting the environment around the world.（森林破壊は世界中の自然環境に影響を及ぼしている）

continued
▼

Day 36

Check 1　Listen))) CD-B1

0569 crisis /kráisis/
- 名 **危機**、重大局面
- 形 critical：❶(～にとって)重大な(to ～)　❷批判[批評]的な

0570 quarantine /kwɔ́:rəntì:n/
- 名 (伝染病予防のための)**隔離**(期間)(≒isolation)
- 動 ～を隔離[検疫]する(≒isolate)

0571 fame /féim/
- 名 **名声**(≒renown, celebrity)
- 形 famous：(～で／…として)有名な(for ～/as …)

0572 motive /móutiv/
- 名 **動機**(≒incentive, inducement)
- 動 motivate：(motivate A to doで)Aを～する気にさせる；Aに～する動機を与える
- 名 motivation：❶やる気、意欲　❷動機、動機づけ

0573 warehouse /wéərhàus/
- 名 **倉庫**(≒depot)

0574 fraud /frɔ́:d/
- 名 **詐欺**(≒fraudulence, deceit, deception)
- 形 fraudulent：詐欺の

0575 intake /íntèik/
- 名 ❶**摂取量**　❷採用[入学]者(数)

0576 activist /ǽktəvist/
- 名 **活動[運動]家**
- 名 activity：活動

Day 35))) CD-A35
Quick Review
答えは右ページ下

- ☐ 結果
- ☐ 公共料金
- ☐ 苦難
- ☐ 組み立て
- ☐ 知らないこと
- ☐ 要約
- ☐ 完成
- ☐ 催眠術
- ☐ 会議
- ☐ 威厳
- ☐ 廃止
- ☐ 捜査
- ☐ 部分
- ☐ 頭金
- ☐ 所有物
- ☐ 会社

Check 2 Phrase

- ☐ a political [financial] crisis (政治[金融]危機)
- ☐ crisis management (危機管理)

- ☐ in quarantine (隔離されて)
- ☐ quarantine regulations (検疫規則)

- ☐ achieve [win, gain] fame (名声を得る)
- ☐ fame and fortune (名声と富)

- ☐ the motive behind ~ (~の裏にある動機)
- ☐ an ulterior motive (隠された動機)

- ☐ convert an old warehouse into a restaurant (古い倉庫をレストランに変える)

- ☐ insurance fraud (保険金詐欺)
- ☐ fraud charges (詐欺罪)

- ☐ a daily intake of vitamin C (ビタミンCの1日の摂取量)
- ☐ the annual student intake (年間入学者数)

- ☐ an environmental activist (環境保護の活動家)

Check 3 Sentence

- ☐ The country's economy is in crisis. (その国の経済は危機に陥っている)

- ☐ He was diagnosed as having cholera and kept in quarantine for two weeks. (彼はコレラに感染していると診断され、2週間隔離された)

- ☐ She gained international fame as a ballet dancer. (彼女はバレエダンサーとして国際的な名声を得た)

- ☐ The exact motive for the crime remains a mystery. (その犯罪の正確な動機は謎のままだ)

- ☐ The building is currently used as a warehouse. (その建物は現在は倉庫として使われている)

- ☐ The defendant was convicted of credit card fraud. (その被告はクレジットカード詐欺で有罪判決を受けた)

- ☐ The recommended daily intake of calories is 2,000 for women and 2,500 for men. (1日の推奨カロリー摂取量は、女性が2000、男性が2500だ)

- ☐ The author is also known as a human-rights activist. (その作家は人権活動家としても知られている)

Day 35 》CD-A35
Quick Review
答えは左ページ下

- ☐ finding
- ☐ utility
- ☐ hardship
- ☐ assembly
- ☐ ignorance
- ☐ summary
- ☐ completion
- ☐ hypnosis
- ☐ session
- ☐ dignity
- ☐ abolition
- ☐ investigation
- ☐ segment
- ☐ deposit
- ☐ possession
- ☐ firm

CHAPTER 1
CHAPTER 2
CHAPTER 3
CHAPTER 4
CHAPTER 5
CHAPTER 6
CHAPTER 7
CHAPTER 8
CHAPTER 9
CHAPTER 10

Chapter 4 Review

左ページの(1)〜(20)の名詞の同意・類義語（≒）、反意・反対語（⇔）を右ページのA〜Tから選び、カッコの中に答えを書き込もう。意味が分からないときは、見出し番号を参照して復習しておこう（答えは右ページ下）。

- □ (1) predecessor (0403) ⇔は？（　）
- □ (2) inhabitant (0412) ≒は？（　）
- □ (3) abuse (0419) ≒は？（　）
- □ (4) deception (0432) ≒は？（　）
- □ (5) proximity (0437) ≒は？（　）
- □ (6) compassion (0452) ≒は？（　）
- □ (7) violation (0463) ≒は？（　）
- □ (8) divorce (0470) ⇔は？（　）
- □ (9) contentment (0480) ≒は？（　）
- □ (10) ethics (0484) ≒は？（　）
- □ (11) enterprise (0494) ≒は？（　）
- □ (12) expansion (0503) ⇔は？（　）
- □ (13) infant (0505) ≒は？（　）
- □ (14) esteem (0520) ≒は？（　）
- □ (15) adolescent (0528) ≒は？（　）
- □ (16) complexity (0537) ⇔は？（　）
- □ (17) subordinate (0542) ⇔は？（　）
- □ (18) session (0553) ≒は？（　）
- □ (19) segment (0557) ≒は？（　）
- □ (20) brochure (0561) ≒は？（　）

A. breach
B. part
C. resident
D. respect
E. satisfaction
F. marriage
G. simplicity
H. closeness
I. baby
J. boss
K. misuse
L. pamphlet
M. pity
N. contraction
O. moral
P. fraud
Q. teenager
R. company
S. meeting
T. successor

【解答】 (1) T (2) C (3) K (4) P (5) H (6) M (7) A (8) F (9) E (10) O
(11) R (12) N (13) I (14) D (15) Q (16) G (17) J (18) S (19) B (20) L

CHAPTER 5
動詞：頻出112

Chapter 5では、英検準1級で頻出の動詞112を見ていきます。本書もいよいよ後半戦に突入！ ゴール（＝英検準1級合格）を目指して、これからも着実に学習を進めていきましょう。

Day 37【動詞8】
▶ 174
Day 38【動詞9】
▶ 178
Day 39【動詞10】
▶ 182
Day 40【動詞11】
▶ 186
Day 41【動詞12】
▶ 190
Day 42【動詞13】
▶ 194
Day 43【動詞14】
▶ 198
Chapter 5 Review
▶ 202

こんなのが出たよ！

A : Wow, what a party that was! It'll take hours to clean up the mess.
B : Well, let's (　　) the kitchen now and leave the rest until tomorrow morning.
（2008年度第3回）

1　tackle　　2　prompt
3　offend　　4　strain

▼
答えはDay 37でチェック！

Day 37　動詞8

Check 1　Listen 》CD-B2

□ 0577
intrude
/intrúːd/

動 (〜の)**邪魔をする**、(〜に)立ち入る(on [upon, in] 〜)(≒ disturb, interrupt, interfere)
名 intruder：❶侵入者　❷邪魔者
名 intrusion：邪魔、侵害

□ 0578
certify
/sə́ːrtəfài/

動 ❶**〜を証明[保証]する**(≒ prove, confirm, verify, guarantee)　❷〜に証明書[免許状]を与える(≒ license)
名 certificate：❶証明書　❷修了証；免許状
形 certified：❶公認の、免許を持っている　❷保証された

□ 0579
seize
/síːz/
❶発音注意

動 ❶**〜を押収する**、差し押さえる(≒ confiscate)　❷〜を(ぐいと)つかむ(≒ grab, grasp)
名 seizure：❶(権力などの)奪取　❷押収、差し押さえ

□ 0580
whine
/hwáin/

動 (〜のことで)**泣き言を言う**、愚痴をこぼす(about 〜)(≒ complain, grumble)
名 泣き言、愚痴

□ 0581
retain
/ritéin/

動 **〜を保つ**、保持[維持]する(≒ keep, maintain, preserve)
名 retention：保持、維持

□ 0582
demote
/dimóut/

動 **〜を(…に)降格する**(to . . .)(≒ downgrade, relegate)(⇔ promote)
名 demotion：降格

□ 0583
analyze
/ǽnəlàiz/

動 **〜を分析する**
名 analysis：(〜の)分析(of 〜)
名 analyst：分析者、アナリスト
形 analytical：分析の、分析的な

□ 0584
tackle
/tǽkl/
トビラの問題の正解はコレ！

動 ❶**〜に取り組む**、対処する(≒ address, handle, deal with)　❷〜にタックルする
名 ❶タックル　❷器具、用具(≒ gear, equipment, apparatus, kit)；釣り道具

continued
▼

Chapter 5では、7日をかけて「頻出」動詞112をチェック。まずはCDでチャンツを聞いて、単語を「耳」からインプット！

- □ 聞くだけモード Check 1
- □ しっかりモード Check 1 ▶ 2
- □ かんぺきモード Check 1 ▶ 2 ▶ 3

Check 2 Phrase

- □ I'm sorry to intrude, but ~.（お邪魔して申し訳ありませんが~）
- □ intrude on her privacy（彼女のプライバシーに立ち入る）

- □ I hereby certify that ~.（ここに~であることを証明[保証]する）
- □ be certified as ~（~の資格を持っている）

- □ seize illegal drugs（違法薬物を押収する）
- □ seize her hand（彼女の手をつかむ）

- □ whine about one's job（仕事のことで泣き言を言う）
- □ Stop whining!（泣き言を言うな！）

- □ retain one's independence（自立を保つ）
- □ retain control of ~（~の支配を維持する）

- □ be demoted to a subordinate position（下級職に降格される）

- □ analyze the situation（状況を分析する）

- □ tackle environmental problems（環境問題に取り組む）

Check 3 Sentence

- □ I hope I am not intruding.（お邪魔でなければいいのですが）

- □ All new vehicles sold in the US must be certified as meeting emission standards.（米国で販売されるすべての新車は排気ガス基準を満たしていることを証明されていなければならない）

- □ The authorities seized a personal computer from the suspect's home.（当局はその容疑者の家からパソコンを押収した）

- □ She is always whining about her husband.（彼女はいつも夫のことで泣き言を言っている）

- □ The cathedral still retains its original beauty.（その大聖堂はいまだに建築当時の美しさを保っている）

- □ The officer was demoted from lieutenant to sergeant.（その警官は警部補から巡査部長に降格された）

- □ We analyzed data obtained from questionnaires.（私たちはアンケートから得られたデータを分析した）

- □ The government should tackle poverty and inequality.（政府は貧困と格差に取り組むべきだ）

continued ▼

Day 37

Check 1   Listen))) CD-B2

0585 convene /kənvíːn/
- 動 ❶ **～を招集する**(≒summon) ❷会議[会合]を開く、集まる(≒assemble, gather)
- 名 convention：❶(各種団体などの)大会、総会 ❷慣習、しきたり

0586 reconcile /rékənsàil/ ❶アクセント注意
- 動 ❶ **～を**(…と)**両立[一致、調和]させる**(with …)(≒harmonize) ❷(be reconciled withで)～と和解[仲直り]する ❸和解する、仲直りする
- 名 reconciliation：❶(～との／…の間の)和解、調停(with ～/between …) ❷両立、調和

0587 undertake /ʌ̀ndərtéik/
- 動 ❶(仕事など)**を引き受ける**(≒take on) ❷(計画などに)着手する(≒embark on) ❸(undertake to doで)～することを約束する(≒promise to do)
- 名 undertaking：❶事業、仕事 ❷約束、保証

0588 retrieve /ritríːv/
- 動 ❶ **～を**(…から)**回収する**、取り戻す(from …)(≒recover) ❷(情報)を検索する
- 名 retrieval：❶(情報などの)検索 ❷回収

0589 trigger /trígər/
- 動 **～を引き起こす**、誘発する、～の引き金となる(≒cause, prompt)
- 名 ❶引き金 ❷(～の)きっかけ、誘因(for ～)

0590 grant /grǽnt/
- 動 ❶ **～を**(…に)**与える**、授ける(to …)(≒give, award) ❷～を認める(≒admit)
- 名 補助[助成]金、奨学金(≒subsidy, scholarship)

0591 undermine /ʌ̀ndərmáin/
- 動 ❶(制度など)**を揺るがす**、脅かす(≒threaten) ❷(名声・信用など)を傷つける(≒damage, hurt, injure)

0592 define /difáin/
- 動 **～を**(…と)**定義する**(as …)
- 名 definition：定義

Day 36))) CD-B1
Quick Review
答えは右ページ下

- □ パンフレット
- □ 条約
- □ 危険
- □ 建築家
- □ 罰金
- □ 子
- □ 残骸
- □ 森林破壊
- □ 危機
- □ 隔離
- □ 名声
- □ 動機
- □ 倉庫
- □ 詐欺
- □ 摂取量
- □ 活動家

Check 2　Phrase

- ☐ convene a commission（委員会を招集する）
- ☐ convene once a year（1年に1度会議を開く）

- ☐ reconcile theory with practice（理論を実践と一致させる）
- ☐ be reconciled with one's boyfriend（彼氏と仲直りする）

- ☐ undertake a dangerous assignment（危険な任務を引き受ける）
- ☐ undertake a new business（新しい事業に着手する）

- ☐ retrieve the situation（事態を収拾する）
- ☐ retrieve information（情報を検索する）

- ☐ trigger a war [riot]（戦争[暴動]を引き起こす）
- ☐ trigger a memory（記憶をよみがえらせる）

- ☐ be granted US citizenship（米国市民権を与えられる）
- ☐ I grant you (that) ～.（～ということは認めよう）

- ☐ undermine public confidence（国民の信頼を揺るがす）
- ☐ undermine his reputation（彼の評判を傷つける）

- ☐ a term difficult to define（定義するのが難しい語）

Check 3　Sentence

- ☐ Congress will be convened within one week.（議会が1週間以内に招集される予定だ）

- ☐ He finds it difficult to reconcile his work with his family.（彼は自分の仕事を家庭と両立させるのが難しいと感じている）

- ☐ She willingly undertook the task.（彼女は快くその仕事を引き受けた）

- ☐ The satellite was retrieved by the space shuttle.（その人工衛星はスペースシャトルによって回収された）

- ☐ The massive explosion was triggered by a gas leak.（その大爆発はガス漏れによって引き起こされた）

- ☐ He was granted a Fulbright scholarship in 1962.（彼は1962年にフルブライト奨学金を与えられた）

- ☐ The scandal has undermined the prime minister's position.（そのスキャンダルは首相の立場を揺るがしている）

- ☐ The dictionary defines "define" as "to explain the exact meaning of a particular word."（その辞書は「～を定義する」を「特定の語の正確な意味を説明すること」と定義している）

Day 36))) CD-B1
Quick Review
答えは左ページ下

- ☐ brochure
- ☐ treaty
- ☐ hazard
- ☐ architect
- ☐ fine
- ☐ offspring
- ☐ wreck
- ☐ deforestation
- ☐ crisis
- ☐ quarantine
- ☐ fame
- ☐ motive
- ☐ warehouse
- ☐ fraud
- ☐ intake
- ☐ activist

Day 38　動詞9

Check 1　Listen 》CD-B3

☐ 0593
scan
/skǽn/
- 動❶(文書など)**にざっと目を通す**(≒skim)　❷〜をスキャンする
- 名scanner：スキャナー

☐ 0594
acknowledge
/æknɑ́lidʒ/
- 動❶(過失など)**を認める**(≒admit, accept)(⇔deny)　❷(手紙など)を受け取ったことを知らせる
- 名acknowledgment：❶承認　❷感謝；(〜s)謝辞

☐ 0595
populate
/pɑ́pjulèit/
- 動(場所)**に居住する**、住む(≒inhabit)
- 名population：❶人口　❷(特定地域の)(全)住民
- 形populous：人口の多い、人口密度の高い

☐ 0596
betray
/bitréi/
- 動**〜を裏切る**
- 名betrayal：裏切り(行為)
- 名betrayer：裏切り者

☐ 0597
restore
/ristɔ́:r/
- 動❶**〜を修復**[復元]**する**(≒repair, fix, mend)　❷(秩序など)を回復する(≒recover, return)
- 名restoration：❶修復　❷回復　❸返還

☐ 0598
accompany
/əkʌ́mpəni/
- 動❶**〜に同行する**、ついて行く　❷〜に伴う、付随する

☐ 0599
slash
/slǽʃ/
- 動❶(予算など)**を大幅に削減する**(≒cut, reduce, lower)　❷〜に深く切りつける(≒gash, slit)
- 名❶切りつけること　❷切り傷　❸スラッシュ、斜線

☐ 0600
contradict
/kɑ̀ntrədíkt/
- 動**〜と矛盾する**、相反する
- 名contradiction：(〜の間の)矛盾(between 〜)
- 形contradictory：(〜と)矛盾した(to 〜)

continued
▼

「細切れ時間」を有効活用してる?『キクタン』は2分でも学習可能。いつでもどこでもテキストとCDを持ち歩いて、単語・熟語に触れよう!

- ☐ 聞くだけモード　Check 1
- ☐ しっかりモード　Check 1 ▶ 2
- ☐ かんぺきモード　Check 1 ▶ 2 ▶ 3

Check 2　Phrase

- ☐ scan the document(書類にざっと目を通す)
- ☐ scan a bar code(バーコードをスキャンする)

- ☐ acknowledge one's mistake(間違いを認める)
- ☐ acknowledge his letter(彼の手紙を受け取ったことを知らせる)

- ☐ be populated by ~([地域などに]~が居住している)
- ☐ a densely populated country(人口密度の高い国)

- ☐ betray his trust(彼の信頼を裏切る)

- ☐ restore an old church(古い教会を修復する)
- ☐ restore order [peace](治安[平和]を回復する)

- ☐ accompany him on his trip(彼の旅行に同行する)
- ☐ nausea accompanied by fever(熱を伴う吐き気)

- ☐ slash costs(コストを大幅に削減する)
- ☐ a slashed tire(深く切りつけられたタイヤ)

- ☐ contradict oneself(矛盾したことを言う)

Check 3　Sentence

- ☐ She scanned the want ads.(彼女は求人広告にざっと目を通した)

- ☐ The company acknowledged that toxic chemicals had been released into the river.(その会社は有毒化学物質が川に流されていたことを認めた)

- ☐ The city is populated by approximately 100,000 people.(その都市には約10万人が居住している)

- ☐ He lied to her and betrayed her.(彼は彼女にうそをつき、彼女を裏切った)

- ☐ The painting was restored by an expert.(その絵画は専門家によって修復された)

- ☐ Her mother accompanied her to the audition.(彼女の母親はそのオーディションまで彼女に同行した)

- ☐ The government slashed next year's budget.(政府は来年度予算を大幅に削減した)

- ☐ His behavior contradicts his words.(彼の行動は彼の言葉と矛盾している)

continued
▼

Day 38

Check 1　Listen))) CD-B3

□ 0601
dominate
/dάmənèit/
- 動 ~を支配する (≒control)
- 名 domination：支配
- 形 dominant：支配的な；優勢な

□ 0602
extract
/ikstrǽkt/
- 動 ❶ ~を(…から)引き抜く (from . . .) (≒take out, pull out)　❷ ~を(…から)抽出する (from . . .)　❸ ~を(…から)抜粋する (from . . .) (≒quote, excerpt)
- 名 (/ékstrækt/) ❶ 抽出物　❷ (~からの)抜粋 (from ~) (≒quotation, excerpt)

□ 0603
curb
/kə́:rb/
- 動 ~を抑制[制限]する (≒restrain, restrict, limit)
- 名 ❶ (歩道の)縁石　❷ (~に対する)抑制、制限 (on ~) (≒restraint, restriction)

□ 0604
reassure
/rì:əʃúər/
- 動 ~を安心させる
- 名 reassurance：安心(させるもの[言葉])

□ 0605
commemorate
/kəmémərèit/
- 動 ~を記念する
- 名 commemoration：❶ 記念　❷ 記念式；記念物
- 形 commemorative：記念の、記念となる

□ 0606
withdraw
/wiðdrɔ́:/
- 動 ❶ (預金)を(…から)引き出す (from . . .) (⇔deposit：~を預金する)　❷ ~を撤回する (≒take back)　❸ (~から)撤退する (from ~) (≒retreat)
- 名 withdrawal：❶ 預金の引き出し　❷ 撤退　❸ 撤回

□ 0607
hamper
/hǽmpər/
- 動 ~を妨げる、妨害する (≒prevent, hinder)
- 名 洗濯[買い物]かご (≒basket)

□ 0608
negotiate
/nigóuʃièit/
- 動 ❶ (~と/…のことで)交渉する (with ~ /for [about, over] . . .) (≒bargain)　❷ (契約など)を取り決める (≒arrange)
- 名 negotiation：交渉
- 形 negotiable：交渉の余地がある

Day 37))) CD-B2
Quick Review
答えは右ページ下

- □ 邪魔をする
- □ ~を証明する
- □ ~を押収する
- □ 泣き言を言う
- □ ~を保つ
- □ ~を降格する
- □ ~を分析する
- □ ~に取り組む
- □ ~を招集する
- □ ~を両立させる
- □ ~を引き受ける
- □ ~を回収する
- □ ~を引き起こす
- □ ~を与える
- □ ~を揺るがす
- □ ~を定義する

Check 2 Phrase	Check 3 Sentence
☐ dominate the market(市場を支配する) ☐ dominate the conversation(会話を独り占めする)	☐ Information technology is a field that is largely dominated by men.(情報技術は男性にほぼ支配されている分野だ)
☐ extract a decayed tooth(虫歯を引き抜く) ☐ extract DNA from a cell(細胞からDNAを抽出する)	☐ I had my wisdom tooth extracted.(私は親知らずを引き抜いてもらった)
☐ curb inflation(インフレを抑制する)	☐ The government should curb the fiscal deficit.(政府は財政赤字を抑制すべきだ)
☐ reassure her that ~(~と言って彼女を安心させる)	☐ My doctor reassured me that everything was fine.(医者は、何も問題はないと言って私を安心させた)
☐ commemorate the 50th anniversary of ~(~の50周年を記念する)	☐ The Statue of Liberty was built to commemorate the 100th anniversary of American Independence.(自由の女神像は米国独立100周年を記念して建てられた)
☐ withdraw $100 from one's account(口座から100ドルを引き出す) ☐ withdraw one's remarks(発言を撤回する)	☐ He withdrew $5,000 to put a deposit on a new car.(彼は新車の頭金を払うために5000ドルを引き出した)
☐ hamper rescue efforts([悪天候などが]救助活動を妨げる)	☐ The search for the missing people was hampered by bad weather.(行方不明者の捜索は悪天候に妨げられた)
☐ refuse to negotiate(交渉を拒否する) ☐ negotiate a settlement [contract](合意[契約]を取り決める)	☐ "We will not negotiate with terrorists," the president said.(「テロリストとは交渉しない」と大統領は言った)

Day 37 ♪CD-B2
Quick Review
答えは左ページ下

☐ intrude ☐ retain   ☐ convene   ☐ trigger
☐ certify ☐ demote   ☐ reconcile   ☐ grant
☐ seize   ☐ analyze ☐ undertake   ☐ undermine
☐ whine   ☐ tackle   ☐ retrieve   ☐ define

CHAPTER 1
CHAPTER 2
CHAPTER 3
CHAPTER 4
CHAPTER 5
CHAPTER 6
CHAPTER 7
CHAPTER 8
CHAPTER 9
CHAPTER 10

Day 39　動詞10

Check 1　Listen 》CD-B4

□ 0609
confront
/kənfrʌ́nt/
▶ 動❶(困難など)**に立ち向かう**(≒face up to)　❷(困難などが)(人)に立ちはだかる
名confrontation：(～との／…の間の)対立、対決(with ～/between ...)

□ 0610
revive
/riváiv/
▶ 動❶**～を復興**[復活]**させる**(≒re-establish)　❷復興[復活]する　❸～を生き返らせる(≒resuscitate)、～の意識を回復させる　❹生き返る、意識を回復する(≒come to)
名revival：❶復興、復活　❷再上演[上映]

□ 0611
escort
/iskɔ́ːrt/
▶ 動❶**～を護衛**[護送]**する**(≒convoy)　❷(人)を案内する(≒guide, usher)　❸～につき添う(≒accompany)
名(/éskɔːrt/)❶護衛(団)(≒guard)　❷つき添い、同伴者

□ 0612
deflect
/diflékt/
▶ 動❶**～を**(…から)**そらす**(from ...)(≒divert, avert)　❷それる
名deflection：❶それること　❷(計器などの)ふれ

□ 0613
formulate
/fɔ́ːrmjuleit/
▶ 動**～を策定**[考案、案出]**する**、練り上げる(≒devise, conceive, think up)
名formula：❶(～の)解決策(for ～)　❷(～の)公式(for ～)　❸(薬などの)製法

□ 0614
transplant
/trænsplǽnt/
▶ 動**～を**(…に)**移植する**(into [to] ...)(≒implant)
名(/trǽnsplænt/)移植
名transplantation：移植
形transplanted：移植された

□ 0615
classify
/klǽsəfài/
▶ 動❶**～を**(…に)**分類する**(as ...)(≒categorize, group)　❷(文書など)を機密扱いにする
名classification：分類、区分
形classified：(文書などが)機密の、極秘扱いの

□ 0616
evolve
/ivɑ́lv/
▶ 動❶(～に)**進化**[発展]**する**(into ～)　❷～を進化[発展]させる(≒develop)
名evolution：❶進化　❷発展、発達
形evolutionary：進化[発展]の

continued
▼

他動詞は後ろに来る目的語、自動詞は後ろに来る前置詞・副詞とセットで覚えるのが効果的。そのためにもCheck 2の学習を忘れずに！

- □ 聞くだけモード　Check 1
- □ しっかりモード　Check 1 ▶ 2
- □ かんぺきモード　Check 1 ▶ 2 ▶ 3

Check 2　Phrase

□ confront one's fears(恐怖に立ち向かう)
□ the problem that confronts us(私たちの前に立ちはだかる問題)

□ revive the economy(経済を復興させる)
□ revive ~ with cardiac massage(~を心臓マッサージで生き返らせる)

□ escort the president(大統領を護衛する)
□ escort her to the table(彼女をテーブルまで案内する)

□ deflect criticism [attention](批判[注意]をそらす)
□ deflect the blow(一撃をそらす)

□ formulate a policy [plan](政策[計画]を策定する)

□ transplant a liver into ~(肝臓を~に移植する)

□ classify dinosaurs as reptiles(恐竜をは虫類に分類する)
□ classify the information(その情報を機密扱いにする)

□ evolve into a major manufacturer(大手メーカーに進化する)
□ evolve a theory(理論を発展させる)

Check 3　Sentence

□ He has the courage to confront reality head-on.(彼は現実に真っ正面から立ち向かう勇気を持っている)

□ The country is trying to revive its car industry.(その国は自国の自動車産業を復興させようとしている)

□ A NATO warship escorted a cargo vessel to a port in Somalia.(NATO軍の戦艦が貨物船をソマリアの港まで護衛した)

□ The prime minister deflected questions about the scandal.(首相はそのスキャンダルに関する質問をそらした)

□ He formulated sales strategies.(彼は販売戦略を策定した)

□ The surgeon successfully transplanted a kidney into a 20-year-old woman.(その外科医は無事に腎臓を20歳の女性に移植した)

□ The platypus is classified as a mammal.(カモノハシは哺乳類に分類される)

□ Birds evolved from dinosaurs.(鳥類は恐竜から進化した)

continued ▼

Day 39

Check 1　Listen)) CD-B4

☐ 0617
recruit
/rikrúːt/

- 動 (新入社員など)**を採用する**(≒hire, employ)
- 名 ❶新兵　❷新人(≒rookie)

☐ 0618
discard
/diskάːrd/

- 動 (不用品など)**を捨てる**、処分[廃棄]する(≒throw away, dispose of, get rid of)
- 名 (/dískɑːrd/)捨てられた物[人]

☐ 0619
outweigh
/àutwéi/

- 動 **～より重要である**[価値がある、大きい]

☐ 0620
evaporate
/ivǽpərèit/

- 動 ❶**蒸発する**　❷～を蒸発させる　❸(希望などが)消える(≒disappear)
- 名 evaporation：蒸発
- 名 vapor：蒸気

☐ 0621
contend
/kənténd/

- 動 ❶**～だと主張する**(≒claim, maintain, assert)　❷(contend forで)～をかけて競う、戦う、争う　❸(contend withで)(困難などに)対処する(≒cope with, deal with)
- 名 contention：❶主張　❷論争、議論
- 名 contender：競争[競技]者

☐ 0622
linger
/líŋɡər/

- 動 ❶**いつまでも残る**、残存する　❷立ち去らずにいる、居残る
- 形 lingering：なかなか消えない

☐ 0623
overlap
/òuvərlǽp/

- 動 ❶(～と)(一部)**重なり合う**(with ～)　❷～と(一部)重なり合う
- 名 (/óuvərlæp/)❶重複　❷重複部分

☐ 0624
depict
/dipíkt/

- 動 **～を**(…として)**描く**、描写[表現]する(as ...)(≒describe, represent, portray)
- 名 depiction：描写、表現

Day 38))) CD-B3
Quick Review
答えは右ページ下

- ☐ ～にざっと目を通す
- ☐ ～を認める
- ☐ ～に居住する
- ☐ ～を裏切る
- ☐ ～を修復する
- ☐ ～に同行する
- ☐ ～を大幅に削減する
- ☐ ～と矛盾する
- ☐ ～を支配する
- ☐ ～を引き抜く
- ☐ ～を抑制する
- ☐ ～を安心させる
- ☐ ～を記念する
- ☐ ～を引き出す
- ☐ ～を妨げる
- ☐ 交渉する

Check 2 Phrase

- ☐ recruit more staff（より多くのスタッフを採用する）

- ☐ discard old clothes（古着を捨てる）

- ☐ outweigh all else（他の何よりも重要である）

- ☐ evaporate completely（完全に蒸発する）
- ☐ evaporate sea water（海水を蒸発させる）

- ☐ contend that he is innocent（彼は無実だと主張する）
- ☐ contend for a gold medal（金メダルをかけて競う）

- ☐ linger for a long time（長い間残存する[居残る]）

- ☐ overlap slightly [considerably]（少し[かなり]重なり合う）
- ☐ overlap each other（互いに重なり合う）

- ☐ depict her as a tragic heroine（彼女を悲劇のヒロインとして描く）

Check 3 Sentence

- ☐ The insurance firm recruited 100 new employees this year.（その保険会社は今年、100名の新入社員を採用した）

- ☐ She discarded her old shoes.（彼女は古い靴を捨てた）

- ☐ Quality outweighs quantity.（質は量より重要だ）

- ☐ Alcohol evaporates much faster than water.（アルコールは水よりもはるかに速く蒸発する）

- ☐ The plaintiff contended that the driver was exceeding the speed limit.（その運転手は制限速度を超えていたと原告は主張した）

- ☐ The sweet smell of her perfume lingered in the room.（彼女の香水の甘い香りが部屋にいつまでも残っていた）

- ☐ My musical tastes don't overlap with my wife's at all.（私の音楽の趣味は妻のものと全く重なり合わない）

- ☐ The painting depicts the Virgin Mary.（その絵画は聖母マリアを描いている）

Day 38))) CD-B3
Quick Review
答えは左ページ下

- ☐ scan
- ☐ acknowledge
- ☐ populate
- ☐ betray
- ☐ restore
- ☐ accompany
- ☐ slash
- ☐ contradict
- ☐ dominate
- ☐ extract
- ☐ curb
- ☐ reassure
- ☐ commemorate
- ☐ withdraw
- ☐ hamper
- ☐ negotiate

CHAPTER 1
CHAPTER 2
CHAPTER 3
CHAPTER 4
CHAPTER 5
CHAPTER 6
CHAPTER 7
CHAPTER 8
CHAPTER 9
CHAPTER 10

Day 40　動詞11

Check 1　Listen 》CD-B5

0625
revoke
/rivóuk/
動 **〜を無効にする**、取り消す(≒cancel, repeal)
名revocation：取り消し、廃止

0626
expel
/ikspél/
動 ❶ **〜を**(…から)**除名[追放]する**(from . . .)　❷〜を(…から)国外退去させる(from . . .)
名expulsion：(〜からの)追放、強制退去(from 〜)

0627
skim
/skím/
動 ❶(〜を)**ざっと読む**(through 〜)　❷〜をざっと読む(≒scan)　❸(浮遊物)を(…から)すくい取る、取り除く(from . . .)(≒remove)

0628
foster
/fɔ́:stər/
動 ❶ **〜を促進[育成]する**(≒promote, encourage)　❷〜を(里親として)養育する(≒bring up, raise, rear)　➕「〜を養子にする」はadopt
形 里親[里子]の

0629
sacrifice
/sǽkrəfàis/
動 **〜を**(…のために)**犠牲にする**(for . . .)
名 ❶犠牲　❷いけにえ

0630
disperse
/dispə́:rs/
動 ❶(群衆など)**を追い散らす**　❷(群衆などが)散り散りになる、解散する(≒scatter, break up)

0631
prevail
/privéil/
動 ❶(〜に)**広がっている**、普及している(in [among] 〜)；支配的[優勢]である　❷(〜に)勝つ(over [against] 〜)(≒win, triumph)
形prevailing：広く行き渡っている、一般的な
形prevalent：一般的な、流行している

0632
emphasize
/émfəsàiz/
動 **〜を強調[力説]する**(≒stress, highlight, underline)
名emphasis：(〜の)強調(on 〜)
形emphatic：❶断固とした、語気の強い　❷(勝利などが)圧倒的な

continued
▼

「声を出しながら」CDを聞いてる？ えっ、恥ずかしい?! 恥ずかしがっていては「話せる」ようにならないよ！ もっと口を動かそう！

- □ 聞くだけモード　Check 1
- □ しっかりモード　Check 1 ▶ 2
- □ かんぺきモード　Check 1 ▶ 2 ▶ 3

Check 2　Phrase

□ revoke the sentence（判決を無効にする）

□ be expelled from school（退学処分を受ける）
□ expel illegal immigrants（不法移民を国外退去させる）

□ skim through the report（報告書をざっと読む）
□ skim the scum（あくをすくい取る）

□ foster world peace（世界平和を促進する）
□ foster an orphan（孤児を養育する）

□ sacrifice everything [one's life] for ~（~のためにすべて[一生]を犠牲にする）

□ disperse the demonstrators（デモ参加者たちを追い散らす）
□ disperse in all directions（四方八方に散る）

□ customs prevailing in the society（その社会に広まっている習慣）
□ prevail over the enemy（敵に勝つ）

□ emphasize the importance of ~（~の重要性を強調する）

Check 3　Sentence

□ His driver's license was revoked for 60 days.（彼の運転免許は60日間、無効になった）

□ The politician was expelled from his party.（その政治家は党から除名された）

□ She skimmed through the article.（彼女はその記事をざっと読んだ）

□ The workshop aims to foster better communication between labor and management.（その研修会は労使間のよりよいコミュニケーションを促進することを目指している）

□ He has sacrificed his family for his career.（彼は仕事のために家族を犠牲にしてきた）

□ The police dispersed the crowd using tear gas.（警察は催涙ガスを使って群衆を追い散らした）

□ After the concert, a very pleasant atmosphere prevailed in the audience.（コンサートの後、とても心地よい雰囲気が聴衆の中に広がっていた）

□ The prime minister emphasized that there are no plans to increase the consumption tax.（消費税を引き上げる計画はないことを首相は強調した）

CHAPTER 1
CHAPTER 2
CHAPTER 3
CHAPTER 4
CHAPTER 5
CHAPTER 6
CHAPTER 7
CHAPTER 8
CHAPTER 9
CHAPTER 10

continued
▼

Day 40

Check 1 Listen)) CD-B5

0633 transmit /trænzmít/
- 動 ❶(データなど)**を送る**、通信する(≒transfer, convey) ❷(番組など)を放送する(≒broadcast, air) ❸(病気など)を伝染[感染]させる
- 名 transmission：❶(データなどの)送信、通信、放送 ❷(自動車の)変速装置 ❸(病気などの)伝染、感染

0634 inspire /inspáiər/
- 動 ❶**〜を鼓舞**[刺激、触発]**する**(≒stimulate, motivate, encourage) ❷(inspire A to doで)Aを触発[刺激]して〜する気にさせる(≒stimulate A to do, motivate A to do, encourage A to do)
- 名 inspiration：着想、ひらめき、インスピレーション

0635 assess /əsés/
- 動 ❶**〜を評価する**(≒evaluate, appraise) ❷〜を(…と)査定する(at . . .)(≒estimate, value)
- 名 assessment：❶評価 ❷査定

0636 worsen /wə́ːrsn/
- 動 ❶**悪化する**(≒deteriorate) ❷〜を悪化させる(≒aggravate)
- 形 worse：より悪い
- 副 worse：より悪く
- 名 worse：一層悪い事[物、状態]

0637 imply /implái/
- 動 **〜をほのめかす**、示唆[暗示]する(≒hint, suggest, insinuate)
- 名 implication：❶示唆、含意 ❷(通例〜s)影響、結果

0638 simulate /símjulèit/
- 動 **〜をシミュレートする**、〜の模擬実験をする
- 名 simulation：シミュレーション、模擬実験

0639 diminish /dimíniʃ/
- 動 ❶**減少する**、少なくなる ❷〜を減らす、少なくする(≒decrease, reduce, lessen)

0640 paralyze /pǽrəlàiz/
- 動 **〜を麻痺させる** ❶比喩的な意味にも用いる
- 名 paralysis：麻痺

Day 39)) CD-B4
Quick Review
答えは右ページ下

- □ 〜に立ち向かう
- □ 〜を復興させる
- □ 〜を護衛する
- □ 〜をそらす
- □ 〜を策定する
- □ 〜を移植する
- □ 〜を分類する
- □ 進化する
- □ 〜を採用する
- □ 〜を捨てる
- □ 〜より重要である
- □ 蒸発する
- □ 〜だと主張する
- □ いつまでも残る
- □ 重なり合う
- □ 〜を描く

Check 2　Phrase

- ☐ **transmit** the data（そのデータを送る）
- ☐ be **transmitted** live（[番組などが]生放送される）

- ☐ **inspire** the team（チームを鼓舞する）
- ☐ **inspire** students to study（生徒を触発して勉強する気にさせる）

- ☐ **assess** students' ability（生徒の能力を評価する）
- ☐ **assess** the land at $1 million（その土地を100万ドルと査定する）

- ☐ **worsen** considerably [significantly]（かなり[著しく]悪化する）
- ☐ **worsen** the situation（状況を悪化させる）

- ☐ **imply** one's intention to do ～（～する意図をほのめかす）
- ☐ an **implied** criticism（言外の非難）

- ☐ **simulate** future climate change（将来の気候変動をシミュレートする）

- ☐ **diminish** with time（時がたつにつれて減少する）
- ☐ **diminish** the risk of ～（～の危険性を減らす）

- ☐ **paralyze** traffic（交通を麻痺させる）
- ☐ be **paralyzed** from the waist down（下半身が麻痺している）

Check 3　Sentence

- ☐ Visual information is **transmitted** to the brain via the optic nerve.（視覚情報は視神経を通じて脳へ送られる）

- ☐ The most important function of the supervisor is to **inspire** his subordinates.（上司の最も重要な役割は部下を鼓舞することだ）

- ☐ Each employee's performance is **assessed** annually.（各従業員の業績は年1回評価される）

- ☐ The country's economy is **worsening** rapidly.（その国の経済は急速に悪化している）

- ☐ His silence **implied** tacit approval.（彼の沈黙は暗黙の承認をほのめかしていた）

- ☐ The training aircraft can **simulate** zero gravity.（その練習機は無重力状態をシミュレートできる）

- ☐ The world's natural resources are **diminishing** rapidly.（地球の天然資源は急速に減少している）

- ☐ The city's subway system was **paralyzed** by the strike.（ストによってその都市の地下鉄網は麻痺した）

CHAPTER 1
CHAPTER 2
CHAPTER 3
CHAPTER 4
CHAPTER 5
CHAPTER 6
CHAPTER 7
CHAPTER 8
CHAPTER 9
CHAPTER 10

Day 39))CD-B4
Quick Review
答えは左ページ下

- ☐ confront
- ☐ revive
- ☐ escort
- ☐ deflect
- ☐ formulate
- ☐ transplant
- ☐ classify
- ☐ evolve
- ☐ recruit
- ☐ discard
- ☐ outweigh
- ☐ evaporate
- ☐ contend
- ☐ linger
- ☐ overlap
- ☐ depict

Day 41　動詞12

Check 1　Listen 》CD-B6

0641
startle
/stá:rtl/
- 動 **〜をびっくりさせる**(≒surprise, frighten, astonish)
- 形 startling：驚くべき

0642
flourish
/flə́:riʃ/
- 動 **栄える**、繁盛する(≒prosper, thrive, succeed)
- 形 flourishing：(商売などが)繁盛している、成功した

0643
cite
/sáit/
- 動 ❶〜を(…として)**引き合いに出す**、挙げる(as . . .)(≒mention, refer to)　❷〜を引用する(≒quote)
- 名 citation：❶(裁判所への)召喚　❷引用　❸表彰

0644
liberate
/líbərèit/
- 動 **〜を解放する**、自由にする(≒free, release, emancipate)
- 名 liberty：❶自由　❷解放
- 形 liberal：❶寛大[寛容]な　❷自由主義の

0645
ridicule
/rídikjù:l/
- 動 **〜をあざ笑う**、あざける、嘲笑する(≒laugh at, mock, deride)
- 名 あざ笑い、あざけり、嘲笑(≒mockery, derision)
- 形 ridiculous：ばかげた、おかしい

0646
elude
/ilú:d/
- 動 (追及など)**を逃れる**、避ける(≒avoid, evade)
- 形 elusive：❶捕まえにくい　❷達成し難い　❸分かりにくい

0647
retreat
/ritrí:t/
- 動 (〜から／…へ)**撤退[退却]する**(from 〜/to . . .)(≒withdraw)
- 名 (〜からの)撤退、退却(≒withdrawal)

0648
utilize
/jú:təlàiz/
- 動 〜を(…として)**利用[活用]する**(as . . .)(≒use, make use of)
- 名 utilization：利用、活用
- 名 utility：❶(通例〜ies)(水道などの)公共料金；公共施設；公共事業　❷有用[実用]性

continued
▼

動詞は受動態の文中で過去分詞形で使われることも多い。今日は6つの動詞が受動態で使われている。Check 3でチェック！

- ☐ 聞くだけモード　Check 1
- ☐ しっかりモード　Check 1 ▶ 2
- ☐ かんぺきモード　Check 1 ▶ 2 ▶ 3

Check 2　Phrase

☐ You startled me!（びっくりするじゃないか！）
☐ be startled to do ～（～してびっくりする）

☐ begin to flourish（栄え始める、繁盛し始める）

☐ cite a reason（理由を挙げる）
☐ cite a passage from the Bible（聖書の1節を引用する）

☐ liberate prisoners [slaves]（捕虜[奴隷]を解放する）

☐ ridicule his idea（彼の考えをあざ笑う）
☐ out of fear of being ridiculed（笑われるのを恐れて）

☐ elude the police（警察の手を逃れる）

☐ retreat from the front（前線から撤退する）

☐ utilize waste oil as fuel（廃油を燃料として利用する）

Check 3　Sentence

☐ The sharp bell of my alarm clock startled me awake.（目覚まし時計の鋭いベルにびっくりして私は目を覚ました）

☐ The Indus civilization flourished from about 2500 B.C. to 1500 B.C.（インダス文明はおよそ紀元前2500年から紀元前1500年まで栄えた）

☐ Paris is often cited as the fashion capital of the world.（パリは世界のファッションの中心地として引き合いに出されることが多い）

☐ Belgium was liberated by the Allied Forces in September 1944.（ベルギーは1944年9月に連合軍によって解放された）

☐ She was ridiculed for her ignorance.（彼女は無知ぶりをあざ笑われた）

☐ A murder suspect who had eluded capture for 10 years was arrested yesterday.（10年間逮捕を逃れてきた殺人容疑者が昨日、逮捕された）

☐ The terrorists retreated to the high mountains.（テロリストたちは高山地帯へ撤退した）

☐ You should utilize your time wisely.（あなたは時間を賢く利用するべきだ）

continued ▼

Day 41

Check 1　Listen 》CD-B6

0649 extend /iksténd/
- 動 ❶ ～を拡大する (≒expand, enlarge) ❷ ～を延長する (≒prolong, lengthen)
- 名 extension：❶延長、延期　❷(電話の)内線　❸拡張
- 形 extensive：❶広範囲にわたる　❷大規模な、甚だしい
- 副 extensively：広範囲に、幅広く

0650 scrap /skrǽp/
- 動 ❶ (制度など)を廃止[中止]する (≒abolish, abandon)　❷ ～を廃棄処分する、スクラップにする (≒throw away, dispose of, get rid of)
- 名 ❶切れ端 (≒fragment)　❷スクラップ、廃物

0651 deploy /diplói/
- 動 (部隊など)を配置[配備]する、展開させる
- 名 deployment：(部隊などの)配置、配備、展開

0652 submit /səbmít/
- 動 ❶ ～を(…に)提出する (to ...) (≒hand in, turn in)　❷ (submit to で)～に服従する (≒yield to, give in to)
- 名 submission：❶(～の)提出 (of ～)　❷(～への)服従 (to ～)
- 形 submissive：従順な

0653 amplify /ǽmpləfài/
- 動 ❶ ～を詳しく説明する、詳述する (≒elaborate on)　❷ (音声など)を増幅する
- 名 amplifier：アンプ、増幅器

0654 reschedule /rì:skédʒu:l/
- 動 ～の予定[日程]を(…に)変更する (for ...)

0655 impair /impéər/
- 動 (能力など)を低下させる、(健康など)を損なう (≒damage, harm)
- 形 impaired：障害のある

0656 dictate /díkteit/
- 動 ❶ (物・事が)～を決定[左右]する (≒determine)　❷ ～を(…に)口述する (to ...)　❸ ～を指図する (≒order, command)
- 名 命令
- 名 dictation：口述、書き取り、ディクテーション

Day 40 》CD-B5　Quick Review　答えは右ページ下

- □ ～を無効にする
- □ ～を除名する
- □ ざっと読む
- □ ～を促進する
- □ ～を犠牲にする
- □ ～を追い散らす
- □ 広がっている
- □ ～を強調する
- □ ～を送る
- □ ～を鼓舞する
- □ ～を評価する
- □ 悪化する
- □ ～をほのめかす
- □ ～をシミュレートする
- □ 減少する
- □ ～を麻痺させる

Check 2 — Phrase

- ☐ extend power（勢力を拡大する）
- ☐ extend one's stay in London（ロンドンでの滞在を延長する）

- ☐ scrap the seniority system（年功序列制度を廃止する）
- ☐ scrap an old car（古い車を廃棄処分する）

- ☐ deploy soldiers（兵士を配置する）
- ☐ deploy missiles（ミサイルを配備する）

- ☐ submit a budget to the board（予算案を役員会に提出する）
- ☐ submit to the police（警察に服従する）

- ☐ amplify one's opinion（自分の意見を詳しく説明する）
- ☐ amplify the sound（音を大きくする）

- ☐ reschedule the meeting for next week（会議の予定を来週に変更する）

- ☐ impair eyesight（視力を低下させる）
- ☐ impair one's health（健康を損なう）

- ☐ dictate the result of ~（~の結果を左右する）
- ☐ dictate a letter to ~（~に手紙を口述する）

Check 3 — Sentence

- ☐ Last year, the company extended its business to China.（昨年、その会社は事業を中国に拡大した）

- ☐ The government has decided to scrap the dam project.（政府はそのダム計画を廃止することを決めた）

- ☐ A team of UN observers were deployed in the country to monitor a truce.（停戦を監視するため、国連の監視団がその国に配置された）

- ☐ All assignments must be submitted by the deadline of July 11.（すべての研究課題は締め切り日の7月11日までに提出されなければならない）

- ☐ Can you amplify that point?（その点を詳しく説明してくれますか?）

- ☐ The press conference was rescheduled for 10 p.m.（記者会見の予定は午後10時に変更された）

- ☐ A lack of sleep impairs job performance.（寝不足は仕事の遂行能力を低下させる）

- ☐ The relationship between supply and demand dictates price.（供給と需要の関係が価格を決定する）

CHAPTER 1
CHAPTER 2
CHAPTER 3
CHAPTER 4
CHAPTER 5
CHAPTER 6
CHAPTER 7
CHAPTER 8
CHAPTER 9
CHAPTER 10

Day 40 》CD-B5
Quick Review
答えは左ページ下

- ☐ revoke
- ☐ expel
- ☐ skim
- ☐ foster
- ☐ sacrifice
- ☐ disperse
- ☐ prevail
- ☐ emphasize
- ☐ transmit
- ☐ inspire
- ☐ assess
- ☐ worsen
- ☐ imply
- ☐ simulate
- ☐ diminish
- ☐ paralyze

Day 42 動詞13

Check 1　Listen)) CD-B7

☐ 0657
restrain
/ristréin/

動 ❶**〜を抑制する**、抑える(≒control, curb, limit) ❷(restrain oneself from doingで)〜するのを我慢する
名restraint：❶自制、慎み　❷抑制
形restrained：❶控えめな　❷抑えられた

☐ 0658
collaborate
/kəlǽbərèit/

動 ❶(〜と／〜を)**共同制作[研究]する**、協力する(with 〜/on . . .)(≒work together, cooperate)
名collaboration：共同制作[研究]、協力
名collaborator：❶(敵国などへの)協力者　❷共同制作[研究]者

☐ 0659
tolerate
/tάlərèit/

動 ❶**〜に耐える**、〜を我慢する(≒put up with, endure, bear)　❷〜を容認する(≒allow, permit, accept)
名tolerance：❶(〜に対する)寛容、寛大(for [of, toward] 〜)　❷(〜に対する)忍耐、我慢(for [of, to] 〜)
形tolerant：(〜に対して)寛大[寛容]な(of [toward] 〜)

☐ 0660
dissolve
/dizάlv/
❶発音注意

動 ❶**〜を(…に)溶かす**(in . . .)　❷(〜に)溶ける(in 〜)(≒melt, thaw)　❸(議会など)を解散する(≒disband)　❹(契約など)を解消する(≒annul)
名dissolution：❶(議会の)解散　❷(契約などの)解消　❸溶解

☐ 0661
wither
/wíðər/

動 ❶**枯れる**、しおれる(≒shrivel, wilt, droop)　❷〜を枯らす、しおれさせる

☐ 0662
precede
/prisíːd/

動 **〜より先に起こる[存在する]**、〜に先行する(⇔follow)
名precedent：(〜に対する)前例、先例(for 〜)
形preceding：(通例the 〜)前の、先の
名precedence：優先、優位

☐ 0663
assemble
/əsémbl/

動 ❶(機械など)**を組み立てる**(≒construct)　❷集まる、集合する　❸〜を集める(≒gather, collect)
名assembly：❶(機械の)組み立て　❷集会、会合　❸議会

☐ 0664
manipulate
/mənípjulèit/
❶アクセント注意

動 (世論など)**を**(不正に)**操る**、操作する
名manipulation：❶(〜の)操作、扱い(of 〜)　❷不正操作、改ざん
形manipulative：人を操る、ずるい

continued
▼

同意語・類義語(≒)や反意語・反対語(⇔)もチェックしてる? 余裕があれば確認して、語彙の数を積極的に増やしていこう。

☐ 聞くだけモード　Check 1
☐ しっかりモード　Check 1 ▶ 2
☐ かんぺきモード　Check 1 ▶ 2 ▶ 3

Check 2　Phrase

☐ restrain one's anger(怒りを抑える)
☐ restrain oneself from laughing(笑うのを我慢する)

☐ collaborate on a movie(映画を共同制作する)
☐ collaborate on the project(そのプロジェクトで協力する)

☐ tolerate the noise(騒音に耐える)
☐ tolerate him doing 〜(彼が〜するのを容認する)

☐ dissolve the sugar in water(砂糖を水に溶かす)
☐ dissolve in water(水に溶ける)

☐ wither in the sun(日を浴びてしおれる)
☐ wither flowers(花をしおれさせる)

☐ precede the movie([コマーシャルなどが]その映画の前に流される)

☐ assemble a bookcase(本棚を組み立てる)
☐ assemble at 10 a.m.(午前10時に集合する)

☐ manipulate public opinion(世論を操る)

Check 3　Sentence

☐ The government has taken steps to restrain inflation.(政府はインフレを抑制する対策を講じている)

☐ He collaborated with her on the song.(彼は彼女とその歌を共同制作した)

☐ I can no longer tolerate his behavior.(私は彼の態度にもう耐えられない)

☐ Dissolve the yeast in warm water.(ぬるめのお湯にイーストを溶かしてください)

☐ Crops have withered from lack of water.(水不足のため作物は枯れてしまった)

☐ A large explosion preceded the fire.(大爆発がその火事より先に起こった)

☐ Many "foreign" cars are assembled in the US.(多くの「外」車が米国で組み立てられている)

☐ The politician is good at manipulating the media.(その政治家はメディアを操るのがうまい)

continued
▼

Day 42

Check 1　Listen)) CD-B7

0665 disengage /dìsingéidʒ/
- 動 ❶(接続した機械の一部)**を外す**、抜く(≒remove, detach)　❷～を解放する、自由にする(≒free, liberate)　❸(～から)撤退する(from ～)(≒withdraw, retreat)
- 名 disengagement：❶(～からの)解放(from ～)　❷(～からの)撤退、撤収(from ～)

0666 slaughter /slɔ́ːtər/
❶発音注意
- 動 ❶(多数の人)**を虐殺する**(≒massacre)　❷(食肉用に)(家畜など)を殺す(≒kill, butcher)
- 名 ❶大量虐殺　❷(家畜の)食肉処理、畜殺

0667 convey /kənvéi/
- 動 ❶(情報など)**を**(…に)**伝える**(to . . .)(≒communicate, pass on)　❷～を運ぶ(≒carry, transport)
- 名 conveyance：❶乗り物、輸送機関　❷運搬、輸送

0668 activate /ǽktəvèit/
- 動 ❶**～を作動させる**(≒set off)　❷～を活性化する
- 名 activity：活動
- 形 active：❶活動的な　❷積極的な　❸活動中の

0669 rot /rɑ́t/
- 動 **腐る**、腐敗する(≒decay, spoil, go bad, decompose)
- 名 ❶腐敗(≒decay, decomposition)　❷腐敗物
- 形 rotten：腐った、腐敗した

0670 enforce /infɔ́ːrs/
- 動 ❶(法律など)**を守らせる**、施行する(≒administer)　❷(服従など)を(…に)強要する、押しつける(on . . .)
- 名 enforcement：(法律などの)施行、実施

0671 conceal /kənsíːl/
- 動 **～を隠す**(≒hide)(⇔reveal)
- 名 concealment：隠すこと、隠匿

0672 relocate /riːlóukèit/
❶アクセント注意
- 動 ❶**～を**(…に)**移転[転勤]させる**(to . . .)　❷(～に)移転[転勤]する(to ～)
- 名 relocation：移転、転勤

Day 41)) CD-B6　Quick Review　答えは右ページ下
- □ ～をびっくりさせる
- □ 栄える
- □ ～を引き合いに出す
- □ ～を解放する
- □ ～をあざ笑う
- □ ～を逃れる
- □ 撤退する
- □ ～を利用する
- □ ～を拡大する
- □ ～を廃止する
- □ ～を配置する
- □ ～を提出する
- □ ～を詳しく説明する
- □ ～の予定を変更する
- □ ～を低下させる
- □ ～を決定する

Check 2 Phrase

- ☐ **disengage** the brake(ブレーキを外す)
- ☐ **disengage** oneself from ~(~から解放される)

- ☐ **slaughter** innocent people(罪のない人々を虐殺する)
- ☐ **slaughter** pigs([食肉用に]ブタを殺す)

- ☐ **convey** the information to him(その情報を彼に伝える)
- ☐ **convey** weapons(武器を運ぶ)

- ☐ **activate** the alarm system(警報システムを作動させる)
- ☐ **activate** local economy(地方経済を活性化する)

- ☐ begin to **rot**(腐り始める)
- ☐ the smell of **rotting** fish(腐りかけた魚のにおい)

- ☐ **enforce** the speed limit(制限速度を守らせる)
- ☐ **enforce** obedience(服従を強要する)

- ☐ **conceal** the fact that ~(~という事実を隠す)
- ☐ **conceal** one's feelings(感情を隠す)

- ☐ **relocate** him to Sapporo(彼を札幌へ転勤させる)
- ☐ **relocate** from Osaka to Tokyo(大阪から東京へ移転する)

Check 3 Sentence

- ☐ **Disengage** the gears when you start the car.(車のエンジンをかける時は、ギアを外してください)

- ☐ Over a million people were **slaughtered** at Auschwitz.(100万を超える人々がアウシュビッツで虐殺された)

- ☐ Please **convey** my regards to your parents.(ご両親によろしくお伝えください)

- ☐ The security system is **activated** by movement.(その防犯システムは動きに反応して作動する)

- ☐ Fruit was left to **rot** on the trees.(果実は木々についたまま腐るに任されていた)

- ☐ The primary role of the police is to **enforce** the law.(警察の最も重要な役割は法律を守らせることだ)

- ☐ Are you **concealing** anything from me?(あなたは私に何かを隠していませんか?)

- ☐ The firm **relocated** its headquarters from New York to Chicago.(その会社は本社をニューヨークからシカゴへ移転させた)

Day 41))CD-B6
Quick Review
答えは左ページ下

- ☐ startle
- ☐ flourish
- ☐ cite
- ☐ liberate
- ☐ ridicule
- ☐ elude
- ☐ retreat
- ☐ utilize
- ☐ extend
- ☐ scrap
- ☐ deploy
- ☐ submit
- ☐ amplify
- ☐ reschedule
- ☐ impair
- ☐ dictate

CHAPTER 1
CHAPTER 2
CHAPTER 3
CHAPTER 4
CHAPTER 5
CHAPTER 6
CHAPTER 7
CHAPTER 8
CHAPTER 9
CHAPTER 10

Day 43　動詞14

Check 1　Listen)) CD-B8

0673 undergo /ʌ̀ndərgóu/
動 (治療など)**を受ける**；(苦難など)を経験する(≒experience, go through)

0674 disregard /dìsrigá:rd/
動 **～を無視[軽視]する**(≒ignore, neglect)
名 (～の)無視、軽視(for [of] ～)(≒neglect)

0675 litter /lítər/
動 ❶(場所)**を**(…で)**散らかす**(with ...)(≒mess up, clutter up)　❷ごみを散らかす[捨てる]
名 ごみ、くず(≒garbage, trash, rubbish)

0676 delete /dilí:t/
動 **～を**(…から)**削除[消去]する**(from ...)(≒erase)
名 deletion：❶削除　❷削除部分[個所]

0677 resign /rizáin/
動 ❶(組織から/役職を)**辞職[辞任]する**(from ～/as ...)(≒leave, retire, quit)　❷(地位など)を辞める
名 resignation：❶辞職、辞任　❷辞表

0678 elevate /éləvèit/
動 ❶**～を**(…に)**昇進させる**(to ...)(≒promote)　❷(水準など)を(…まで)向上させる(to ...)　❸～を持ち上げる(≒raise, lift)
名 elevation：❶海抜、標高　❷(～への)昇進、登用(to ～)　❸(水準などの)上昇、増大(in ～)

0679 shoplift /ʃáplìft/
動 ❶**万引きする**　❷～を万引きする
名 shoplifting：万引き
名 shoplifter：万引き犯

0680 infect /infékt/
動 ❶(人)**を**(病気に)**感染させる**、(人)に(病気を)うつす(with ...)　❷～を(有毒物などで)汚染する(with ...)(≒contaminate, pollute)
名 infection：❶感染[伝染]病　❷感染、伝染
形 infectious：❶感染[伝染]性の　❷すぐに伝わる

continued
▼

今日でChapter 5は最後！ 時間に余裕があったら、章末のReviewにも挑戦しておこう。忘れてしまった単語も結構あるのでは?!

- □ 聞くだけモード Check 1
- □ しっかりモード Check 1 ▶ 2
- □ かんぺきモード Check 1 ▶ 2 ▶ 3

Check 2　　Phrase

□ undergo treatment(治療を受ける)
□ undergo hardship(苦難を経験する)

□ disregard safety rules(安全規則を無視する)

□ litter the floor with books(床を本で散らかす)
□ No littering(ごみを捨てないでください)●掲示

□ delete his name from the list(彼の名前をリストから削除する)

□ resign as CEO(CEOを辞任する)
□ resign one's position as ~(~の職を辞する)

□ elevate him to vice president(彼を副社長に昇進させる)
□ elevate the spirit(精神を高揚させる)

□ witness someone shoplifting(誰かが万引きしているのを目撃する)
□ shoplift goods(商品を万引きする)

□ infect others with flu(他人にインフルエンザをうつす)
□ infect the atmosphere(大気を汚染する)

Check 3　　Sentence

□ She underwent four hours of heart surgery.(彼女は4時間にわたる心臓手術を受けた)

□ He completely disregarded my advice.(彼は私の助言を完全に無視した)

□ Her room was littered with clothes.(彼女の部屋は服で散らかっていた)

□ I accidentally deleted important files from my computer.(私は重要なファイルをコンピューターから誤って削除してしまった)

□ The minister resigned for health reasons.(その大臣は健康上の理由で辞職した)

□ She was elevated to sales manager last month.(彼女は先月、販売部長に昇進した)

□ The boy was caught shoplifting by a store manager.(その少年は万引きしているところを店長に見つかった)

□ The patient is infected with tuberculosis.(その患者は結核に感染している)

continued
▼

Day 43

Check 1　Listen)) CD-B8

☐ 0681
prosecute
/prάsikjùːt/

動 ～を(罪状などで)**起訴する**(for ...)(≒charge, indict)
名prosecution：起訴(手続き)
名prosecutor：検察官、検事

☐ 0682
update
/ʌ̀pdéit/

動❶～を**更新**[改訂]**する**、アップデートする　❷～に(…の)最新情報を伝える(on ...)
名(/ʌ́pdèit/)❶(～に関する)最新情報(on ～)　❷最新版
形up-to-date：❶最新(式)の　❷現代的な

☐ 0683
exert
/igzə́ːrt/
❶発音注意

動❶(権力など)**を**(…に)**行使する**(on ...)(≒exercise)　❷(exert oneselfで)努力する、頑張る(≒make an effort)
名exertion：❶(権力などの)行使　❷努力

☐ 0684
administer
/ədmínistər/

動❶～を**管理**[運営、統治]**する**(≒manage, direct)　❷～を施す、実施する　❸(薬など)を投与する
名administration：❶管理、経営；(the ～)経営陣　❷行政；(しばしばthe A～)政権、内閣
形administrative：❶管理[経営]の　❷行政の

☐ 0685
outsource
/àutsɔ́ːrs/

動(業務)**を外部委託する**；(部品など)を外部調達する、外注する(≒contract out)
名outsourcing：外注、アウトソーシング

☐ 0686
displace
/displéis/

動❶～を(…から)**立ち退かせる**、退去させる(from ...)　❷～に取って代わる(≒replace)　❸～を解雇[解任]する(≒dismiss)
名displacement：強制退去

☐ 0687
sweep
/swíːp/

動❶(嵐などが)**～を襲う**(≒engulf)　❷～を掃除する、掃く(≒brush, clean)

☐ 0688
cease
/síːs/
❶発音注意

動❶**～を中止する**、やめる　❷終わる、やむ(≒stop, end)
形ceaseless：絶え間ない、やむことのない、不断の
副ceaselessly：絶え間なく、連続して

| Day 42)) CD-B7
Quick Review
答えは右ページ下 | ☐ ～を抑制する
☐ 共同制作する
☐ ～に耐える
☐ ～を溶かす | ☐ 枯れる
☐ ～より先に起こる
☐ ～を組み立てる
☐ ～を操る | ☐ ～を外す
☐ ～を虐殺する
☐ ～を伝える
☐ ～を作動させる | ☐ 腐る
☐ ～を守らせる
☐ ～を隠す
☐ ～を移転させる |

Check 2 Phrase

- [ ] **prosecute** the suspect for tax evasion(その容疑者を脱税で起訴する)

- [ ] **update** software(ソフトウエアをアップデートする)
- [ ] **update** him on what's going on(彼に最新の状況を伝える)

- [ ] **exert** authority on ~(~に権力を行使する)
- [ ] **exert** oneself to please her(彼女を喜ばせようと努力する)

- [ ] **administer** a charity(慈善団体を運営する)
- [ ] **administer** first aid(応急手当を施す)

- [ ] **outsource** components from China(部品を中国から外部調達する)

- [ ] **displace** refugees(難民たちを立ち退かせる)
- [ ] **displace** old technology([新しい技術が]古い技術に取って代わる)

- [ ] **sweep** the Kyushu area([台風などが]九州地方を襲う)
- [ ] **sweep** the floor(床を掃除する)

- [ ] **cease** military operations(軍事行動を中止する)
- [ ] **cease** abruptly(突然終わる)

Check 3 Sentence

- [ ] The politician was **prosecuted** for bribery.(その政治家は収賄で起訴された)

- [ ] I **update** my blog every day.(私は自分のブログを毎日更新している)

- [ ] Microsoft **exerts** a huge influence on the computer industry.(マイクロソフト社はコンピューター産業に非常に大きな影響力を行使している)

- [ ] The bankruptcy trustee **administers** the bankrupt party's estate.(破産管財人は破産者の財産を管理する)

- [ ] Many large companies **outsource** their customer service.(多くの大企業は顧客サービスを外部委託している)

- [ ] More than 200,000 people have been **displaced** from their homes by the hurricane.(20万以上の人々がそのハリケーンによって自宅を立ち退いている)

- [ ] The Black Death **swept** Europe in the 1340s.(黒死病は1340年代にヨーロッパを襲った)

- [ ] The electronics manufacturer has decided to **cease** production of cell phones.(その電子機器メーカーは携帯電話の生産を中止することを決定した)

Day 42))) CD-B7
Quick Review
答えは左ページ下

- [ ] restrain
- [ ] collaborate
- [ ] tolerate
- [ ] dissolve
- [ ] wither
- [ ] precede
- [ ] assemble
- [ ] manipulate
- [ ] disengage
- [ ] slaughter
- [ ] convey
- [ ] activate
- [ ] rot
- [ ] enforce
- [ ] conceal
- [ ] relocate

Chapter 5 Review

左ページの(1)〜(20)の動詞の同意・類義語（≒）、反意・反対語（⇔）を右ページのA〜Tから選び、カッコの中に答えを書き込もう。意味が分からないときは、見出し番号を参照して復習しておこう（答えは右ページ下）。

- ☐ (1) retain (0581) ≒は? (　　)
- ☐ (2) demote (0582) ⇔は? (　　)
- ☐ (3) tackle (0584) ≒は? (　　)
- ☐ (4) acknowledge (0594) ≒は? (　　)
- ☐ (5) curb (0603) ≒は? (　　)
- ☐ (6) withdraw (0606) ⇔は? (　　)
- ☐ (7) escort (0611) ≒は? (　　)
- ☐ (8) recruit (0617) ≒は? (　　)
- ☐ (9) depict (0624) ≒は? (　　)
- ☐ (10) emphasize (0632) ≒は? (　　)
- ☐ (11) assess (0635) ≒は? (　　)
- ☐ (12) worsen (0636) ≒は? (　　)
- ☐ (13) startle (0641) ≒は? (　　)
- ☐ (14) liberate (0644) ≒は? (　　)
- ☐ (15) scrap (0650) ≒は? (　　)
- ☐ (16) precede (0662) ⇔は? (　　)
- ☐ (17) conceal (0671) ⇔は? (　　)
- ☐ (18) disregard (0674) ≒は? (　　)
- ☐ (19) delete (0676) ≒は? (　　)
- ☐ (20) administer (0684) ≒は? (　　)

A. ignore
B. address
C. abolish
D. describe
E. admit
F. free
G. convoy
H. erase
I. promote
J. follow
K. deteriorate
L. deposit
M. manage
N. highlight
O. reveal
P. restrain
Q. keep
R. frighten
S. appraise
T. hire

【解答】 (1) Q (2) I (3) B (4) E (5) P (6) L (7) G (8) T (9) D (10) N
(11) S (12) K (13) R (14) F (15) C (16) J (17) O (18) A (19) H (20) M

CHAPTER 6

形容詞：頻出112

Chapter 6では、英検準1級で頻出の形容詞112をマスター。そしてこのChapterが終われば、50日が終了。マラソンに例えるなら、30キロ地点を過ぎたころ。ここを乗り切れば、ゴールが少しずつ見えてくる！

Day 44【形容詞8】
▶ 206
Day 45【形容詞9】
▶ 210
Day 46【形容詞10】
▶ 214
Day 47【形容詞11】
▶ 218
Day 48【形容詞12】
▶ 222
Day 49【形容詞13】
▶ 226
Day 50【形容詞14】
▶ 230
Chapter 6 Review
▶ 234

こんなの出たよ！

After scientists announced that there were only 500 of the rare eagles left in the wild, the government declared them an (　　) species and introduced measures to protect them.（2009年度第1回）

1　indifferent　2　incisive
3　accessible　4　endangered

▼
答えはDay 47でチェック！

Day 44 形容詞8

Check 1　Listen 》CD-B9

0689 costly /kɔ́:stli/
- 形 ❶ **高価な**、費用のかかる (≒expensive)　❷ 損失[犠牲]の大きい、手痛い
- 名 cost：❶ (しばしば~s) (必要) 経費、費用　❷ (時間などの) 犠牲
- 動 cost：❶ (時間・費用が) かかる　❷ ~を犠牲にする

0690 elaborate /ilǽbərət/
- 形 ❶ **手の込んだ**、凝った　❷ 入念な (≒careful)
- 動 (/ilǽbərèit/) (~について) 詳しく述べる (on ~)
- 名 elaboration：念入りに作ること；推敲
- 副 elaborately：精巧に、入念に

0691 advanced /ædvǽnst/
- 形 ❶ (技術などが) **先進の**、進歩した、高度な (≒developed, state-of-the-art)　❷ (課程などが) 上級[高等]の (⇔elementary：初歩の)
- 名 advance：❶ 進歩　❷ 前進
- 動 advance：❶ 前進する　❷ 進歩する

0692 hazardous /hǽzərdəs/
- 形 (~にとって) **有害な**、危険な (to ~) (≒dangerous, risky, perilous)
- 名 hazard：危険；(~への) 危険要素 (to ~)

0693 obscure /əbskjúər/
- 形 ❶ **分かりにくい**、あいまいな (≒unclear, vague) (⇔clear)　❷ 世に知られていない、無名の (≒unknown)
- 動 ❶ ~を分かりにくくする　❷ ~を見えなくする
- 名 obscurity：❶ あいまいさ、不明瞭さ　❷ 世に知られていないこと、無名

0694 complicated /kɑ́mpləkèitid/
- ❶ アクセント注意
- 形 **複雑な**、込み入った (≒complex, intricate) (⇔simple)
- 動 complicate：❶ ~を複雑にする　❷ (病気) を悪化させる
- 名 complication：❶ 面倒な事態[問題]　❷ (通例~s) 合併症

0695 decisive /disáisiv/
- 形 ❶ **決定的な** (≒deciding, conclusive, crucial)　❷ 決断力のある、断固たる (≒resolute) (⇔indecisive)
- 動 decide：~を決める、決定する
- 名 decision：❶ 決定、決断　❷ 判決、裁定

0696 secure /sikjúər/
- 形 ❶ (~に対して) **安全な** (from [against] ~) (≒safe)　❷ (仕事などが) 安定した (≒stable)
- 動 ❶ ~を確保する (≒obtain, acquire, gain)　❷ ~を (…から) 守る (from …) (≒protect)
- 名 security：❶ 警備　❷ 安全

continued
▼

Chapter 6では、7日をかけて「頻出」形容詞112をチェック。まずはCDでチャンツを聞いて、単語を「耳」からインプット！

- □ 聞くだけモード　Check 1
- □ しっかりモード　Check 1 ▶ 2
- □ かんぺきモード　Check 1 ▶ 2 ▶ 3

Check 2　Phrase

- □ costly goods（高価な商品）
- □ a costly mistake [failure]（手痛いミス［失敗］）

- □ elaborate design（手の込んだデザイン）
- □ an elaborate plan（入念な計画）

- □ advanced technology（先進技術）
- □ advanced students of mathematics（数学の学習が進んだ生徒）

- □ hazardous chemicals [waste]（有害化学物質［廃棄物］）
- □ be hazardous to one's health（健康に有害である）

- □ obscure legal terms（分かりにくい法律用語）
- □ an obscure painter（無名の画家）

- □ the complicated tax system（複雑な税制）

- □ a decisive victory（決定的な勝利）
- □ take decisive steps（断固たる措置を取る）

- □ a secure place（安全な場所）
- □ a secure income（安定した収入）

Check 3　Sentence

- □ For most people, a house is the most costly purchase of a lifetime.（ほとんどの人にとって、家は人生で最も高価な買い物だ）

- □ She prepared an elaborate meal for us.（彼女は私たちに手の込んだ食事を用意してくれた）

- □ Advanced countries should take the lead in tackling climate change.（先進諸国は気候変動への取り組みにおいて主導的な役割を担うべきだ）

- □ Nuclear waste will remain hazardous for thousands of years.（核廃棄物は何千年も有害なまま残るだろう）

- □ The professor's lecture was very obscure.（その教授の講義はとても分かりにくかった）

- □ The plot of the play is too complicated to explain.（その劇の筋は複雑過ぎて説明できない）

- □ He played a decisive role in the negotiations.（彼はその交渉で決定的な役割を果たした）

- □ Australia is one of the most secure countries in the world.（オーストラリアは世界で最も安全な国の1つだ）

continued

Day 44

Check 1　Listen)) CD-B9

0697 beneficial /bènəfíʃəl/
- 形 (～にとって)**有益な**、(～の)ためになる(to ～)(≒ advantageous, favorable, useful)
- 名 benefit：❶利益　❷(通例～s)給付金、手当
- 動 benefit：❶～のためになる　❷(benefit from [by]で)～によって利益を得る

0698 versatile /və́ːrsətl/
- 形 ❶**多才な**、多芸の(≒all-around)　❷用途の広い(≒all-purpose)
- 名 versatility：❶多才　❷用途の広さ

0699 flexible /fléksəbl/
- 形 (考えなどが)**柔軟な**；(予定が)融通の利く(≒adaptable)(⇔rigid, inflexible)
- 名 flexibility：柔軟性

0700 unauthorized /ʌnɔ́ːθəràizd/
- 形 **無許可の**、無認可の(⇔authorized)

0701 contagious /kəntéidʒəs/
- 形 ❶(笑いなどが)**伝染しやすい**、うつりやすい　❷(接触)伝染性の(≒infectious)
- 名 contagion：❶接触伝染　❷接触伝染病

0702 crucial /krúːʃəl/
- 形 (～にとって)**非常に重要[重大]な**、決定的な(to [for] ～)(≒vital, critical, decisive)
- 副 crucially：決定的に

0703 mature /mətjúər/
- 形 ❶(人が)**大人びた**、分別のある(≒sensible)(⇔immature)　❷(生物が)十分に成長した、成熟した(≒grown-up)　❸熟した(≒ripe)
- 動 ❶成熟する(≒grow up)　❷(保険などが)満期になる
- 名 maturity：❶成熟(期)　❷満期(日)

0704 questionable /kwéstʃənəbl/
- 形 ❶**疑わしい**、疑問の余地のある(≒doubtful, controversial)　❷いかがわしい、不審な(≒suspicious)
- 名 question：❶質問　❷問題　❸疑問
- 動 question：❶～を疑う　❷～に(…について)質問する(about [as to] ...)

Day 43)) CD-B8　Quick Review　答えは右ページ下

- □ ～を受ける
- □ ～を無視する
- □ ～を散らかす
- □ ～を削除する
- □ 辞職する
- □ ～を昇進させる
- □ 万引きする
- □ ～を感染させる
- □ ～を起訴する
- □ ～を更新する
- □ ～を行使する
- □ ～を管理する
- □ ～を外部委託する
- □ ～を立ち退かせる
- □ ～を襲う
- □ ～を中止する

Check 2　Phrase

☐ beneficial information（有益な情報）

☐ a versatile musician（多才な音楽家）
☐ versatile material（用途の広い材料）

☐ a flexible approach（柔軟な取り組み）
☐ a flexible work schedule（融通の利く仕事の予定）

☐ the unauthorized use of ～（～の無許可の使用）

☐ a contagious laugh（人から人へとうつりやすい笑い）
☐ a contagious disease（接触伝染病）

☐ a crucial issue（非常に重要な問題）
☐ It is crucial that ～．（～ということは非常に重要である）

☐ a mature attitude（分別のある態度）
☐ a mature tree（成長した木）

☐ It is questionable whether ～．（～かどうか疑わしい）
☐ questionable activities（不審な行動）

Check 3　Sentence

☐ A balanced diet is beneficial to health.（バランスの取れた食事は健康にとって有益だ）

☐ She is a versatile actress who can play a wide variety of parts.（彼女はさまざまな役を演じることができる多才な女優だ）

☐ You need to be more flexible in your thinking.（あなたは考え方をもっと柔軟にする必要がある）

☐ The unauthorized copying of computer software is prohibited.（コンピューターソフトウエアの無許可のコピーは禁じられている）

☐ Fear is highly contagious.（恐怖は非常に伝染しやすい）

☐ Parents play a crucial role in their child's social development.（親は子どもの社会性の発達において非常に重要な役割を果たす）

☐ He is mature for his age.（彼は年齢の割には大人びている）

☐ It is questionable whether the project will ever materialize.（そのプロジェクトが実現するかどうか疑わしい）

Day 43))) CD-B8
Quick Review
答えは左ページ下

☐ undergo　☐ resign　☐ prosecute　☐ outsource
☐ disregard　☐ elevate　☐ update　☐ displace
☐ litter　☐ shoplift　☐ exert　☐ sweep
☐ delete　☐ infect　☐ administer　☐ cease

CHAPTER 1
CHAPTER 2
CHAPTER 3
CHAPTER 4
CHAPTER 5
CHAPTER 6
CHAPTER 7
CHAPTER 8
CHAPTER 9
CHAPTER 10

Day 45　形容詞9

Check 1　Listen)) CD-B10

0705 indispensable /ìndispénsəbl/
形 (〜に)**不可欠な**、絶対必要な、必須の(to [for] 〜)(≒ essential, necessary)

0706 corrupt /kərʌ́pt/
形 **堕落[腐敗]した**、不正な(≒ dishonest)
動 〜を堕落させる、買収する(≒ deprave)
名 corruption: ❶汚職、買収　❷堕落、腐敗

0707 prevailing /privéiliŋ/
形 **広く行き渡っている**、一般的な(≒ widespread)
動 prevail: ❶(〜に)広がっている、普及している(in [among] 〜); 支配的[優勢]である　❷(〜に)勝つ(over [against] 〜)
形 prevalent: 一般的な、流行している

0708 coherent /kouhíərənt/
形 **首尾一貫した**、筋の通った(≒ logical, reasoned, reasonable)(⇔ incoherent)
副 coherently: 首尾一貫して
名 coherence: 首尾一貫性
動 cohere: 首尾一貫する、筋が通る

0709 fertile /fə́ːrtl/
形 **肥沃な**(≒ rich)(⇔ barren: 不毛の)
動 fertilize: (土地)を肥沃にする
名 fertilizer: 肥料

0710 vibrant /váibrənt/
形 ❶**活気に満ちた**、活発な(≒ lively, active)　❷(色などが)鮮やかな(≒ vivid, bright)　❸(音が)よく響く、響き渡る(≒ resonant)

0711 majestic /mədʒéstik/
形 **雄大[壮麗]な**、堂々とした(≒ magnificent, grand, splendid, stately, dignified)
名 majesty: ❶雄大さ、壮麗さ　❷(敬称として)陛下

0712 bankrupt /bǽŋkrʌpt/
形 **破産[倒産]した**(≒ broke, insolvent)
名 破産者
名 bankruptcy: 破産、倒産

continued
▼

チャンツを聞く際には、「英語→日本語→英語」の2回目の「英語」の部分で声に出して読んでみよう。定着度が倍増するはず!

- □ 聞くだけモード Check 1
- □ しっかりモード Check 1 ▶ 2
- □ かんぺきモード Check 1 ▶ 2 ▶ 3

Check 2　Phrase

- □ be indispensable to [for] the success of ~（~の成功に不可欠である）
- □ an indispensable item（必須アイテム）

- □ a corrupt society（腐敗した社会）
- □ corrupt practices（不正行為）

- □ prevailing customs（広く行き渡っている習慣）
- □ the prevailing view（一般的な見方）

- □ a coherent explanation [argument]（首尾一貫した説明[主張]）

- □ fertile land（肥沃な土地）

- □ a vibrant young man（活気に満ちた若者）
- □ a vibrant purple（鮮やかな紫色）

- □ the majestic Alps（雄大なアルプス山脈）

- □ go bankrupt（破産する）

Check 3　Sentence

- □ The Internet has become an indispensable part of our lives.（インターネットは私たちの生活に不可欠なものになった）

- □ Corrupt officials accepted bribes from the company.（堕落した役人たちはその会社から賄賂を受け取っていた）

- □ The prevailing mood among investors is uncertainty and skepticism.（投資家たちの間に広く行き渡っている雰囲気は不確かさと疑念だ）

- □ The movie lacks a coherent plot.（その映画には首尾一貫した筋がない）

- □ The soil of the area is very fertile.（その地域の土壌はとても肥沃だ）

- □ Los Angeles is a vibrant and cosmopolitan city.（ロサンゼルスは活気に満ちた国際色豊かな都市だ）

- □ The hotel overlooks the majestic Mississippi River.（そのホテルからは雄大なミシシッピ川が見渡せる）

- □ The bank was declared bankrupt.（その銀行は破産を宣告された）

continued
▼

Day 45

Check 1   Listen)) CD-B10

0713 stern /stə́ːrn/
形 ❶ **厳格な**、厳しい(≒strict, severe, rigid) ❷ (表情などが)いかめしい(≒serious, unsmiling)

0714 dubious /djúːbiəs/
形 ❶ (〜について) **疑っている** (about 〜) (≒suspicious, skeptical) ❷ 疑わしい、不審な(≒doubtful)

0715 vigorous /vígərəs/
形 ❶ (活動などが) **活発な**、盛んな(≒strenuous) ❷ 元気[健康、丈夫]な(≒robust, healthy, strong)
名 vigor : 精力、活力、元気
副 vigorously : 精力的に、力強く

0716 infectious /infékʃəs/
形 ❶ **感染[伝染]性の** ❷ (感情などが)すぐに伝わる[広まる](≒contagious)
動 infect : ❶ 〜を(病気に)感染させる(with ...) ❷ 〜を(有毒物などで)汚染する(with ...)
名 infection : ❶ 感染[伝染]病 ❷ 感染、伝染

0717 commendable /kəméndəbl/
形 **称賛に値する**、褒めるに足る(≒admirable, praiseworthy)
動 commend : ❶ 〜を(…のことで)褒める、称賛する(for ...) ❷ 〜を(…に)推薦[推奨]する(to ...)
名 commendation : ❶ 称賛 ❷ 推薦

0718 gravitational /ɡrævətéiʃənl/
形 **重力[引力]の**
名 gravity : ❶ 重力、引力 ❷ 重大さ ❸ 厳粛さ
名 gravitation : 重力、引力

0719 nutritious /njuːtríʃəs/
形 **栄養のある**
名 nutrition : ❶ 栄養補給[摂取] ❷ 栄養学
名 nutrient : 栄養物[素]

0720 subtle /sʌ́tl/
❶発音注意
形 ❶ **微妙な**(≒fine) ❷ (香りなどが)かすかな、ほのかな(≒faint)
副 subtly : 微妙に、かすかに
名 subtlety : ❶ 微妙さ ❷ 微妙な点

Day 44)) CD-B9
Quick Review
答えは右ページ下

- [ ] 高価な
- [ ] 手の込んだ
- [ ] 先進の
- [ ] 有害な
- [ ] 分かりにくい
- [ ] 複雑な
- [ ] 決定的な
- [ ] 安全な
- [ ] 有益な
- [ ] 多才な
- [ ] 柔軟な
- [ ] 無許可の
- [ ] 伝染しやすい
- [ ] 非常に重要な
- [ ] 大人びた
- [ ] 疑わしい

Check 2 — Phrase

- ☐ stern measures(厳格な措置)
- ☐ a stern look [expression](いかめしい表情)

- ☐ be dubious about his story(彼の話を疑っている)
- ☐ dubious business dealings(不審な商取引)

- ☐ vigorous exercise(活発な運動)
- ☐ a vigorous old man(元気な老人)

- ☐ an infectious disease(感染[伝染]病)
- ☐ infectious yawning(思わずつられてしまうあくび)

- ☐ commendable behavior(称賛に値する行為)
- ☐ be highly commendable(非常に立派である)

- ☐ a gravitational field(重力場)
- ☐ a gravitational pull(重力、引力)

- ☐ nutritious foods(栄養のある食べ物)

- ☐ a subtle difference(微妙な違い)
- ☐ a subtle scent of roses(ほのかなバラの香り)

Check 3 — Sentence

- ☐ She was raised by a stern father.(彼女は厳格な父親に育てられた)

- ☐ Some analysts are dubious about the effectiveness of the economic policy.(その経済政策の有効性を疑っているアナリストもいる)

- ☐ They had a vigorous debate on the issue.(彼らはその問題をめぐって活発な議論をした)

- ☐ Influenza is highly infectious and spreads easily from person to person.(インフルエンザは感染力が強く、人から人へとすぐに広がる)

- ☐ Her efforts are commendable.(彼女の努力は称賛に値する)

- ☐ The gravitational pull of the Moon is about one-sixth that of the Earth.(月の重力は地球の重力の約6分の1だ)

- ☐ It is very important to have a nutritious diet.(栄養のある食事をすることは非常に大切だ)

- ☐ There are subtle differences between American and Canadian English.(アメリカ英語とカナダ英語の間には微妙な違いがある)

Day 44))) CD-B9
Quick Review
答えは左ページ下

- ☐ costly
- ☐ elaborate
- ☐ advanced
- ☐ hazardous
- ☐ obscure
- ☐ complicated
- ☐ decisive
- ☐ secure
- ☐ beneficial
- ☐ versatile
- ☐ flexible
- ☐ unauthorized
- ☐ contagious
- ☐ crucial
- ☐ mature
- ☐ questionable

CHAPTER 1
CHAPTER 2
CHAPTER 3
CHAPTER 4
CHAPTER 5
CHAPTER 6
CHAPTER 7
CHAPTER 8
CHAPTER 9
CHAPTER 10

Day 46　形容詞10

Check 1　Listen 》CD-B11

□ 0721
dejected
/didʒéktid/

形 **落胆した**、がっかりした、意気消沈した(≒disappointed, downcast)
名 dejection：落胆

□ 0722
binding
/báindiŋ/

形 (契約などが)**拘束力のある**
動 bind：(bind A to doで)Aに〜することを義務づける

□ 0723
infamous
/ínfəməs/
❶発音注意

形 (〜で)**悪名高い**(for 〜)(≒notorious)

□ 0724
exotic
/igzátik/

形 ❶(動植物などが)**外来の**(≒foreign)(⇔native, indigenous：原産の)　❷異国情緒の、エキゾチックな

□ 0725
numerous
/njúːmərəs/
❶発音注意

形 **数多くの**、たくさんの(≒many, a lot of)

□ 0726
conservative
/kənsə́ːrvətiv/

形 ❶**保守的な**　❷控えめな；地味な(≒modest)
名 保守的な人
名 conservation：(自然環境などの)保護、保存
動 conserve：❶(エネルギーなど)を節約して使う　❷〜を保護[保存]する

□ 0727
profound
/prəfáund/

形 ❶(影響などが)**重大[重要]な**　❷(悲しみなどが)深い (≒deep)
副 profoundly：❶非常に、大いに　❷ひどく、とても

□ 0728
ambiguous
/æmbígjuəs/

形 **あいまいな**、両義[多義]的な(≒unclear, obscure, equivocal)
副 ambiguously：あいまいに
名 ambiguity：(意味などの)あいまいさ、両義[多義]性

continued
▼

英字新聞・英字雑誌などを使って、語彙との出合いを増やそう。学習した語彙ともきっと遭遇するはず。出合いの数と定着度は正比例する！

☐ 聞くだけモード　Check 1
☐ しっかりモード　Check 1 ▶ 2
☐ かんぺきモード　Check 1 ▶ 2 ▶ 3

Check 2　Phrase

☐ a dejected look（落胆した表情）

☐ a binding agreement（拘束力のある協定）

☐ an infamous murderer（悪名高い殺人犯）

☐ exotic plants（外来植物）
☐ an exotic restaurant（異国情緒あふれるレストラン）

☐ be too numerous to count（あまりに数が多くて数え切れない）
☐ on numerous occasions（何度も）

☐ conservative views（保守的な見解）
☐ a conservative estimate（控えめな見積もり）

☐ have a profound effect [influence, impact] on ～（～に重大な影響を与える）
☐ profound grief（深い悲しみ）

☐ an ambiguous explanation（あいまいな説明）

Check 3　Sentence

☐ He looked so dejected when he failed the exam.（その試験に落ちた時、彼はとても落胆した様子だった）

☐ The contract is legally binding.（その契約には法的拘束力がある）

☐ The city is infamous for its high crime rate.（その都市は高い犯罪率で悪名高い）

☐ The zoo has many exotic animals.（その動物園には数多くの外来動物がいる）

☐ The author has published numerous novels.（その作家は数多くの小説を発表している）

☐ The politician belongs to the conservative wing of the party.（その政治家は党の保守派に属している）

☐ Divorce can have a profound impact on the parent-child relationship.（離婚は親子の関係に重大な影響を与えることがある）

☐ The wording of the sentence is somewhat ambiguous.（その文の言い回しは少しあいまいだ）

continued ▼

CHAPTER 1
CHAPTER 2
CHAPTER 3
CHAPTER 4
CHAPTER 5
CHAPTER 6
CHAPTER 7
CHAPTER 8
CHAPTER 9
CHAPTER 10

Day 46

Check 1　Listen))) CD-B11

0729 impressive /imprésiv/
- 形 **印象的な**、素晴らしい
- 名 impression：❶印象　❷(〜という)感じ(that 節 〜)
- 動 impress：❶〜を感動[感心]させる　❷(be impressed by [with]で)〜に感動[感心]している

0730 invaluable /invǽljuəbl/
- 形 **非常に貴重な**(≒valuable, precious)(⇔valueless)
- 名 value：❶価値　❷価格　❸(〜s)価値観
- 動 value：〜を高く評価する、尊重する
- 名 valuable：(通例〜s)貴重品

0731 comparable /kámpərəbl/ ❶アクセント注意
- 形 (〜と)**同等の**、(〜に)匹敵する(with [to] 〜)(≒similar, equal)
- 動 compare：〜を(…と)比較する(with [to] …)
- 名 comparison：(〜との)比較(with 〜)
- 副 comparatively：比較的

0732 qualified /kwάləfàid/
- 形 (〜の／…する)**資格[免許]を有する**(for 〜/to do)(≒certified, licensed)
- 名 qualification：❶(〜する)資格(to do)　❷(〜の)適性、資質(for 〜)
- 動 qualify：(qualify as で)〜の資格を取る

0733 disoriented /disɔ́:rièntid/
- 形 ❶**方向感覚を失った**(≒lost)　❷混乱した、まごついた(≒confused)

0734 viable /váiəbl/
- 形 **実現[実行]可能な**(≒feasible, practicable)
- 名 viability：実現[実行]可能性

0735 adjoining /ədʒɔ́iniŋ/
- 形 **隣接した**、隣り合った、隣の(≒adjacent)
- 動 adjoin：〜に隣接する

0736 ongoing /άngòuiŋ/
- 形 **進行[継続]中の**(≒in progress, under way)

Day 45))) CD-B10
Quick Review
答えは右ページ下

- □ 不可欠な
- □ 堕落した
- □ 広く行き渡っている
- □ 首尾一貫した
- □ 肥沃な
- □ 活気に満ちた
- □ 雄大な
- □ 破産した
- □ 厳格な
- □ 疑っている
- □ 活発な
- □ 感染性の
- □ 称賛に値する
- □ 重力の
- □ 栄養のある
- □ 微妙な

Check 2　Phrase

- □ an impressive performance（印象的な演奏）

- □ invaluable information（非常に貴重な情報）

- □ comparable incomes（同等の収入）
- □ people of comparable ages（同じ年代の人々）

- □ a qualified teacher [accountant]（資格を持った教師[公認会計士]）

- □ become disoriented in fog（霧の中で方向感覚を失う）
- □ feel disoriented（頭が混乱する）

- □ commercially [economically] viable（商業的[経済的]に実現可能な）
- □ a viable alternative（実行可能な代案）

- □ adjoining hotel rooms（隣り合ったホテルの部屋）

- □ an ongoing problem（進行中の問題）
- □ ongoing negotiations（継続中の交渉）

Check 3　Sentence

- □ The view from the top floor of the building was impressive.（そのビルの最上階からの眺めは印象的だった）

- □ The internship has provided me with invaluable experience.（その実務研修は私に非常に貴重な経験をもたらした）

- □ Companies are required to pay comparable wages to employees in the same job classifications.（企業は同じ職階の従業員に対して同等の賃金を払うよう求められている）

- □ He is fully qualified for the job.（彼はその仕事に十分な資格を持っている）

- □ Whales can become disoriented in shallow water.（クジラは浅瀬で方向感覚を失うことがある）

- □ Electric cars are becoming commercially viable.（電気自動車は商業的に実現可能になりつつある）

- □ The fire rapidly spread to adjoining houses.（その火災は隣接した家々にすぐに広がった）

- □ The police investigation into the incident is ongoing.（その事件の警察の捜査は進行中だ）

Day 45))CD-B10
Quick Review
答えは左ページ下

- □ indispensable
- □ corrupt
- □ prevailing
- □ coherent
- □ fertile
- □ vibrant
- □ majestic
- □ bankrupt
- □ stern
- □ dubious
- □ vigorous
- □ infectious
- □ commendable
- □ gravitational
- □ nutritious
- □ subtle

Day 47　形容詞11

Check 1　Listen 》CD-B12

□ 0737
accessible
/æksésəbl/

形 ❶(場所などが)**行きやすい**、近づきやすい(⇔inaccessible)　❷(〜にとって)入手しやすい、利用できる(to 〜)(≒available)
名access：❶アクセス権　❷面会の許可[機会]
動access：❶〜にアクセスする　❷〜に入る、近づく

□ 0738
spontaneous
/spɑntéiniəs/

形 **自発的な**、自然(発生的)な(≒voluntary)
副spontaneously：自発的に、自然(発生的)に

□ 0739
hasty
/héisti/

形 **性急**[軽率]**な**(≒rash)
名haste：大急ぎ
動hasten：❶(行動など)を早める　❷急いで行く

□ 0740
peculiar
/pikjú:ljər/

形 **奇妙な**、変な、妙な(≒strange, odd, queer, eccentric, bizarre, weird)
副peculiarly：妙に、変に
名peculiarity：❶特性、特質　❷奇妙な癖、風変わりな点

□ 0741
cautious
/kɔ́:ʃəs/

形 (〜について)**慎重な**、注意[用心]深い(about 〜)(≒careful)
名caution：❶用心、警戒　❷警告、注意
動caution：❶(caution A about [against] Bで)AにBを警告する　❷(caution A to doで)Aに〜するよう警告する

□ 0742
modest
/mɑ́dist/

形 ❶(〜に関して)**控えめな**、謙遜した(about 〜)(≒humble)(⇔immodest, boastful)　❷あまり大きく[多く]ない、並の(≒moderate)
名modesty：謙遜、謙虚
副modestly：控えめに、謙遜して

□ 0743
authentic
/ɔ:θéntik/

形 ❶**本物の**(≒real, genuine)(⇔fake)　❷本格的な
名authenticity：本物であること

□ 0744
painstaking
/péinztèikiŋ/

形 (仕事などが)**骨の折れる**、(研究などが)入念な(≒meticulous)

continued
▼

「書いて覚える」のも効果的！「聞く+音読する」に加えて、「書く」学習もしてみよう。そう、語彙学習には「あの手この手」が大切！

- □ 聞くだけモード　Check 1
- □ しっかりモード　Check 1 ▶ 2
- □ かんぺきモード　Check 1 ▶ 2 ▶ 3

Check 2　Phrase

- □ be accessible by car（[場所などが]車で行くことができる）
- □ readily accessible（すぐに入手できる）

- □ a spontaneous offer of help（援助の自発的申し出）
- □ spontaneous applause（自然にわき起こる拍手）

- □ a hasty decision（性急な決定）
- □ hasty words（軽率な言葉）

- □ peculiar behavior（奇妙な行動）
- □ It is peculiar that ~.（～というのは妙だ）

- □ cautious optimism（慎重な楽観論）
- □ a cautious approach（慎重な取り組み）

- □ be modest about one's success（自分の成功を誇らない）
- □ a modest amount（ささやかな量[額]）

- □ an authentic Picasso（本物のピカソの作品）
- □ authentic Italian cuisine（本格的なイタリア料理）

- □ painstaking work（骨の折れる仕事）
- □ painstaking research（入念な調査）

Check 3　Sentence

- □ The area is accessible only on foot.（その地域へは歩いてしか行けない）

- □ She is a spontaneous and selfless person.（彼女は自発的で私心のない人だ）

- □ Let's not jump to hasty conclusions.（性急な結論に飛びつくのはやめましょう）

- □ There was something peculiar in his tone.（彼の口調には奇妙なところがあった）

- □ She is a cautious driver.（彼女は慎重なドライバーだ）

- □ He is a modest and likable person.（彼は控えめで好感の持てる人物だ）

- □ If the painting is authentic, it may be worth millions of dollars.（その絵が本物ならば、何百万ドルもの価値があるかもしれない）

- □ Embroidery is painstaking work.（刺しゅうは骨の折れる仕事だ）

continued
▼

Day 47

Check 1　Listen 》CD-B12

0745 dedicated /dédikèitid/
形 **献身的な**、ひたむきな(≒committed)
名 dedication：(〜への)献身、専念(to 〜)
動 dedicate：❶(dedicate A to B で)AをBにささげる　❷(be dedicated to で)〜に専念[熱中]している

0746 lunar /lúːnər/
形 **月の**　❶「太陽の」はsolar

0747 submissive /səbmísiv/
形 **従順な**(≒obedient)
動 submit：❶〜を(…に)提出する(to …)　❷(submit to で)〜に服従する
名 submission：❶(〜の)提出(of 〜)　❷(〜への)服従(to 〜)

0748 vocational /voukéiʃənl/
形 **職業の**(≒occupational)
名 vocation：❶天職　❷職業

0749 endangered /indéindʒərd/
トビラの問題の正解はコレ！
形 (動植物が)**絶滅の危機に瀕した**、絶滅寸前の　❶「絶滅した」はextinct
動 endanger：〜を危険にさらす

0750 offensive /əfénsiv/
形 ❶(〜にとって)**不快**[不愉快]**な**(to 〜)(≒unpleasant, insulting)　❷攻撃(用)の(⇔defensive)
動 offend：❶〜の感情を害する　❷犯罪を犯す
名 offender：犯罪者
名 offense：❶違反、犯罪　❷感情を害すること

0751 charitable /tʃǽrətəbl/
形 ❶**慈善の**(≒philanthropic)　❷寛大な；慈悲深い(≒generous, merciful)
名 charity：❶慈善団体　❷慈善事業

0752 plausible /plɔ́ːzəbl/
形 ❶**もっともらしい**、まことしやかな　❷妥当な

Day 46 》CD-B11
Quick Review
答えは右ページ下

- ☐ 落胆した
- ☐ 拘束力のある
- ☐ 悪名高い
- ☐ 外来の
- ☐ 数多くの
- ☐ 保守的な
- ☐ 重大な
- ☐ あいまいな
- ☐ 印象的な
- ☐ 非常に貴重な
- ☐ 同等の
- ☐ 資格を有する
- ☐ 方向感覚を失った
- ☐ 実現可能な
- ☐ 隣接した
- ☐ 進行中の

Check 2 Phrase	Check 3 Sentence
☐ a dedicated mother（献身的な母親）	☐ Most teachers are dedicated and hard-working.（ほとんどの教師は献身的で勤勉だ）
☐ the lunar orbit（月の軌道） ☐ a lunar eclipse（月食）	☐ Apollo 11 landed on the lunar surface on July 20, 1969.（1969年7月20日にアポロ11号は月面に着陸した）
☐ submissive workers（従順な労働者）	☐ In that society, women are expected to be submissive.（その社会では、女性は従順であることが求められている）
☐ vocational training（職業訓練） ☐ a vocational school（職業訓練学校）	☐ The prime minister stressed the need for vocational education.（首相は職業教育の必要性を強調した）
☐ endangered species（絶滅危惧種）	☐ The cheetah is an endangered animal.（チーターは絶滅の危機に瀕している動物だ）
☐ an offensive smell（不快なにおい） ☐ offensive weapons（攻撃用兵器）	☐ The politician's remarks were inappropriate and offensive to women.（その政治家の発言は不適切で女性にとって不快なものだった）
☐ charitable activities（慈善活動） ☐ a charitable person（情け深い人）	☐ The company donated $10,000 to a local charitable organization.（その会社は地元の慈善団体に1万ドルを寄付した）
☐ a plausible explanation [excuse]（もっともらしい説明[言い訳]） ☐ It is plausible that ~.（～ということはありそうだ）	☐ His story sounded plausible at the time.（彼の話はその時はもっともらしく聞こえた）

CHAPTER 1
CHAPTER 2
CHAPTER 3
CHAPTER 4
CHAPTER 5
CHAPTER 6
CHAPTER 7
CHAPTER 8
CHAPTER 9
CHAPTER 10

Day 46))) CD-B11
Quick Review
答えは左ページ下

☐ dejected
☐ binding
☐ infamous
☐ exotic
☐ numerous
☐ conservative
☐ profound
☐ ambiguous
☐ impressive
☐ invaluable
☐ comparable
☐ qualified
☐ disoriented
☐ viable
☐ adjoining
☐ ongoing

Day 48　形容詞12

Check 1　Listen))) CD-B13

0753
adjacent
/ədʒéisnt/
❶発音注意

形 (〜に)**隣接した**(to 〜)(≒adjoining); 近隣の(≒neighboring)

0754
mutual
/mjúːtʃuəl/

形 ❶**相互の**、互いの(≒reciprocal)　❷共通の(≒common)
副 mutually: 互いに、相互に

0755
abandoned
/əbǽndənd/

形 **捨てられた**、放棄された(≒deserted)
動 abandon: ❶〜を断念[中止]する　❷(人・家など)を捨てる
名 abandonment: ❶(主義などの)放棄　❷断念、中止　❸遺棄

0756
irrational
/iræʃnl/
❶発音注意

形 **ばかげた**、不合理な(≒unreasonable, absurd, ridiculous)(⇔rational)

0757
demanding
/dimǽndiŋ/

形 ❶(仕事などが)**負担の大きい**、骨の折れる(≒strenuous, arduous)　❷(人が)要求の厳しい
名 demand: ❶(〜の)需要(for 〜)　❷(〜を求める)要求(for 〜)
動 demand: 〜を(…に)要求する(of [from] …)

0758
considerable
/kənsídərəbl/
❶アクセント注意

形 (数量などが)**かなりの**、相当な(≒substantial, significant)
副 considerably: かなり、相当に
動 consider: 〜をよく考える、熟慮[検討]する
名 consideration: 考慮、検討

0759
domestic
/dəméstik/

形 ❶**国内**[自国]**の**(≒internal)(⇔foreign)　❷家庭[家事]の(≒family, home, household)

0760
approximate
/əpráksəmət/

形 **おおよその**(≒rough, estimated)(⇔exact, precise: 正確な)
動 (/əpráksəmèit/)おおよそ〜になる、〜に近い
副 approximately: 約、おおよそ

continued
▼

単語がなかなか身につかないときこそ「音読」をしよう。少し遠回りのような気がしても、実はそれが英語習得の近道！

- ☐ 聞くだけモード　Check 1
- ☐ しっかりモード　Check 1 ▶ 2
- ☐ かんぺきモード　Check 1 ▶ 2 ▶ 3

Check 2　Phrase

☐ a building adjacent to the library(その図書館に隣接したビル)
☐ adjacent countries(近隣諸国)

☐ mutual trust [respect](相互信頼[尊重])
☐ a mutual friend(共通の友人)

☐ an abandoned child(捨て子)
☐ an abandoned car(乗り捨てられた車)

☐ an irrational fear [idea](ばかげた恐怖[考え])

☐ a demanding task(骨の折れる仕事)
☐ a demanding boss(厳しい上司)

☐ a considerable amount [number] of ~(かなりの量[数]の~)
☐ considerable damage(かなりの損害)

☐ domestic industries(国内産業)
☐ domestic violence(家庭内暴力)

☐ an approximate number [cost](おおよその数[費用])

Check 3　Sentence

☐ A golf course is adjacent to the hotel.(ゴルフコースがそのホテルに隣接している)

☐ Mutual understanding is the key to stabilizing the region.(相互理解がその地域の安定化の鍵だ)

☐ A newborn baby was found abandoned outside the hospital.(生まれたばかりの赤ちゃんがその病院の外に捨てられているのが発見された)

☐ I was embarrassed by his irrational behavior.(私は彼のばかげた行動に当惑した)

☐ Construction work is physically demanding.(建築作業は肉体的に負担が大きい)

☐ A considerable amount of time was spent on the construction of the dam.(かなりの時間がそのダムの建設に費やされた)

☐ The airline announced plans to reduce the number of its domestic flights.(その航空会社は国内便の数を減らす計画を発表した)

☐ The approximate population of Tokyo is 13 million.(東京のおおよその人口は1300万だ)

continued
▼

Day 48

Check 1　Listen))) CD-B13

0761 reliable /riláiəbl/
- 形 **信頼できる**、頼りになる、当てにできる(≒dependable, credible)(⇔unreliable)
- 動rely：(rely on [upon]で)～を当てにする、～に頼る
- 名reliance：(～への)依存(on [upon] ～)
- 名reliability：信頼性[度]

0762 illiterate /ilítərət/
- 形 ❶ **読み書きのできない**(⇔literate)　❷無学の(≒ignorant)
- 名illiteracy：読み書きのできないこと

0763 valid /vǽlid/
- 形 ❶(契約などが)**有効な**(≒effective)(⇔invalid, void)　❷(議論などが)妥当[正当]な(≒reasonable)
- 名validity：(～の)妥当[正当、有効]性(of ～)
- 動validate：～を証明[立証]する
- 名validation：証明、立証

0764 conceivable /kənsíːvəbl/
- 形 **考えられる**、想像できる、ありそうな(≒imaginable, possible)(⇔inconceivable)
- 動conceive：～を想像する、思い描く

0765 outstanding /àutstǽndiŋ/
- 形 **際立った**、傑出した、優れた(≒excellent, prominent)
- 動stand out：❶目立つ、際立つ　❷(～の中で)抜きん出ている、傑出している(from [among] ～)

0766 numb /nʌ́m/　❶発音注意
- 形 ❶(手・足などが)(寒さなどで)**感覚のなくなった**、麻痺した(with ～)　❷(ショックなどで)ぼう然とした(with ～)
- 動 ❶～を無感覚にする、麻痺させる　❷～をぼう然とさせる

0767 desperate /déspərət/　❶アクセント注意
- 形 ❶(～を)**欲しくてたまらない**(for ～)；(～したくて)たまらない(to do)(≒eager)　❷自暴自棄の、破れかぶれの　❸必死の、命がけの　❹絶望的な(≒hopeless)
- 副desperately：❶必死で、死に物狂いで　❷ひどく

0768 shallow /ʃǽlou/
- 形 ❶ **浅はかな**(≒superficial)　❷浅い(⇔deep)

Day 47))) CD-B12　**Quick Review**　答えは右ページ下

- □ 行きやすい
- □ 自発的な
- □ 性急な
- □ 奇妙な
- □ 慎重な
- □ 控えめな
- □ 本物の
- □ 骨の折れる
- □ 献身的な
- □ 月の
- □ 従順な
- □ 職業の
- □ 絶滅の危機に瀕した
- □ 不快な
- □ 慈善の
- □ もっともらしい

Check 2 Phrase

- a reliable source of information(信頼できる情報源)

- illiterate children(読み書きのできない子どもたち)
- economically [politically] illiterate(経済[政治]に疎い)

- a valid working visa(有効な就労ビザ)
- a valid reason(妥当な理由)

- It is conceivable that ~.(~ということが考えられる[あり得る])
- every conceivable means(ありとあらゆる手段)

- outstanding talent(際立った才能)
- an outstanding surgeon(優れた外科医)

- be numb with cold(寒さで感覚がなくなっている)
- be numb with shock(ショックでぼう然としている)

- be desperate for food(食べ物が欲しくてたまらない)
- get desperate(自暴自棄になる)

- a shallow thought(浅はかな考え)
- a shallow dish(浅い皿)

Check 3 Sentence

- In general, Japanese cars are reliable.(一般に、日本車は信頼できる)

- One in four adults in developing countries are illiterate.(発展途上国の大人の4人に1人は読み書きができない)

- A US passport is valid for 10 years.(米国のパスポートは10年間有効だ)

- It is conceivable that global warming may lead to a worldwide catastrophe.(地球温暖化は世界的な大災害につながる可能性があると考えられる)

- Her performance was satisfactory but not outstanding.(彼女の演奏は満足のいくものだったが、際立ってはいなかった)

- My fingers and toes were numb with cold.(私の手足の指は寒さで感覚がなくなっていた)

- He is desperate for a new job.(彼は新しい仕事が欲しくてたまらないでいる)

- I found him shallow and immature.(私は彼のことを浅はかで未熟だと思った)

Day 47 》CD-B12
Quick Review
答えは左ページ下

- accessible
- spontaneous
- hasty
- peculiar
- cautious
- modest
- authentic
- painstaking
- dedicated
- lunar
- submissive
- vocational
- endangered
- offensive
- charitable
- plausible

CHAPTER 1
CHAPTER 2
CHAPTER 3
CHAPTER 4
CHAPTER 5
CHAPTER 6
CHAPTER 7
CHAPTER 8
CHAPTER 9
CHAPTER 10

Day 49 形容詞13

Check 1　Listen)) CD-B14

☐ 0769
insistent
/ insístənt /

形 ❶ **しつこい**、執拗な(≒persistent)　❷(〜を)強く言い張る(on [that節] 〜)
動 insist：❶〜だと主張する　❷〜であるように要求する　❸(insist onで)〜を(強く)要求する
名 insistence：主張、強い要求

☐ 0770
strenuous
/ strénjuəs /

形 ❶(運動などが)**激しい**、骨の折れる(≒demanding, arduous)　❷猛烈[懸命]な
副 strenuously：❶猛烈[懸命]に　❷激しく

☐ 0771
primary
/ práimeri /

形 ❶ **主要な**(≒main, chief)　❷初等の、小学校の(≒elementary)
副 primarily：❶主に、主として　❷第一に

☐ 0772
thorough
/ θə́ːrou /
❶発音注意

形 **徹底的な**、完全な(≒exhaustive, in-depth, complete)　✚through(〜を通り抜けて)と混同しないように注意
副 thoroughly：徹底的に、完全に

☐ 0773
grim
/ grím /

形 ❶(状況などが)**厳しい**、暗い(≒bleak)　❷(表情などが)険しい(≒stern, severe, serious)

☐ 0774
perpetual
/ pərpétʃuəl /

形 **絶え間のない**、ひっきりなしの(≒constant, continuous, continual, incessant)
副 perpetually：絶えず

☐ 0775
classified
/ klǽsəfàid /

形 (文書などが)**機密の**、極秘扱いの(≒secret, confidential, top-secret)
動 classify：❶〜を(…に)分類する(as ...)　❷(文書など)を機密扱いにする
名 classification：分類、区分

☐ 0776
straightforward
/ strèitfɔ́ːrwərd /

形 ❶(説明などが)**分かりやすい**、簡単な(≒simple, easy)　❷率直[正直]な(≒honest, open, frank, candid)

continued
▼

Quick Reviewは使ってる? 昨日覚えた単語でも、記憶に残っているとは限らない。学習の合間に軽くチェックするだけでも効果は抜群!

☐ 聞くだけモード　Check 1
☐ しっかりモード　Check 1 ▶ 2
☐ かんぺきモード　Check 1 ▶ 2 ▶ 3

Check 2　Phrase

☐ insistent demands(しつこい要求)
☐ be insistent on going home(家に帰ると強く言い張る)

☐ strenuous exercise(激しい運動)
☐ a strenuous effort(懸命な努力)

☐ the primary purpose of the research(その研究の主要な目的)
☐ primary education(初等教育)

☐ a thorough investigation(徹底的な調査)
☐ a thorough understanding(完全な理解)

☐ a grim economic situation(厳しい経済状態)
☐ a grim face [look](険しい顔[表情])

☐ perpetual chatter(絶え間のないおしゃべり)

☐ classified documents(機密文書)

☐ a straightforward explanation(分かりやすい説明)
☐ a straightforward person(率直な人)

Check 3　Sentence

☐ I was woken up by an insistent knocking on my door.(私はドアをしつこくノックする音で目が覚めた)

☐ The doctor advised her to avoid strenuous exercise.(その医者は彼女に激しい運動を避けるように忠告した)

☐ Fossil fuels will remain the primary source of energy for decades to come.(化石燃料は今後数十年間は主要なエネルギー源であり続けるだろう)

☐ The patient underwent a thorough examination.(その患者は徹底的な検査を受けた)

☐ The country's economic outlook remains grim.(その国の経済見通しは厳しいままだ)

☐ He is sick of his mother's perpetual nagging.(彼は母親の絶え間ない小言にうんざりしている)

☐ The report contains classified information.(その報告書には機密情報が含まれている)

☐ The directions to the hotel are very straightforward.(そのホテルへの道順はとても分かりやすい)

continued
▼

Day 49

Check 1 Listen)) CD-B14

☐ 0777
mediocre
/mìːdióukər/

形 **よくも悪くもない**、平凡な、並の(≒ordinary, average)

☐ 0778
complimentary
/kàmpləméntəri/

形 ❶**無料の**(≒free) ❷称賛の ⊕complementary(補足的な)と混同しないように注意
名compliment：(〜についての)褒め言葉、賛辞；お世辞(on〜)
動compliment：〜に賛辞を述べる

☐ 0779
organic
/ɔːrɡǽnik/

形 ❶**有機栽培の**、無農薬の ❷有機(体)の(⇔inorganic) ❸有機的な
名organism：❶生物、有機体 ❷有機的組織体

☐ 0780
evasive
/ivéisiv/

形 **言い逃れの**、責任逃れの、回避的な
動evade：(追跡など)を逃れる、免れる、避ける
名evasion：(責任などの)回避；言い逃れ

☐ 0781
tangible
/tǽndʒəbl/

形 ❶(証拠などが)**明白な**、確固たる(≒clear, obvious) ❷(物が)触れられる(≒touchable)；(資産が)有形の

☐ 0782
inefficient
/ìnifíʃənt/

形 **非効率[非能率]的な**、効率[能率]の悪い(⇔efficient)
名inefficiency：非効率、非能率

☐ 0783
radioactive
/rèidiouǽktiv/

形 **放射性の**、放射能のある
名radioactivity：❶放射能 ❷放射線

☐ 0784
cozy
/kóuzi/

形 **居心地のよい**(≒comfortable, snug)

Day 48)) CD-B13
Quick Review
答えは右ページ下

☐ 隣接した ☐ 負担の大きい ☐ 信頼できる ☐ 際立った
☐ 相互の ☐ かなりの ☐ 読み書きのできない ☐ 感覚のなくなった
☐ 捨てられた ☐ 国内の ☐ 有効な ☐ 欲しくてたまらない
☐ ばかげた ☐ おおよその ☐ 考えられる ☐ 浅はかな

Check 2　Phrase

- ☐ a mediocre performance（よくも悪くもない演奏）
- ☐ a mediocre talent（平凡な才能）

- ☐ complimentary beverages（無料の飲み物）
- ☐ complimentary remarks（賛辞）

- ☐ organic farming（有機農業）
- ☐ organic matter（有機物）

- ☐ an evasive answer（言い逃れの返事）
- ☐ take evasive action（[危険を避けるため]回避行動を取る）

- ☐ tangible evidence [proof]（明白な証拠、物証）
- ☐ tangible assets（有形資産）

- ☐ an inefficient use of energy（エネルギーの非効率的な使用）

- ☐ radioactive waste（放射性廃棄物）

- ☐ a cozy living room（居心地のよい居間）

Check 3　Sentence

- ☐ I thought the movie was mediocre.（その映画はよくも悪くもないと私は思った）

- ☐ He received two complimentary tickets to the game.（彼はその試合の無料チケットを2枚もらった）

- ☐ The demand for organic vegetables has increased significantly in recent years.（有機栽培野菜の需要がこの数年で著しく増えている）

- ☐ The CEO gave evasive replies to reporters' questions.（そのCEOは記者たちの質問に対して言い逃れの返答をした）

- ☐ There was no tangible evidence that Iraq had weapons of mass destruction.（イラクが大量破壊兵器を持っているという明白な証拠はなかった）

- ☐ Some people think that the current healthcare system is inefficient.（現在の医療制度は非効率的だと考える人たちもいる）

- ☐ Large amounts of radioactive materials were released during the Chernobyl accident.（大量の放射性物質がチェルノブイリ事故の間に放出された）

- ☐ The hotel room was clean, quiet, and cozy.（そのホテルの部屋は清潔で、静かで、そして居心地がよかった）

Day 48 ◁) CD-B13
Quick Review
答えは左ページ下

- ☐ adjacent
- ☐ mutual
- ☐ abandoned
- ☐ irrational
- ☐ demanding
- ☐ considerable
- ☐ domestic
- ☐ approximate
- ☐ reliable
- ☐ illiterate
- ☐ valid
- ☐ conceivable
- ☐ outstanding
- ☐ numb
- ☐ desperate
- ☐ shallow

Day 50 形容詞14

Check 1　Listen 》CD-B15

0785 premature /prìːmətʃúər/
- 形 ❶**時期尚早の**、早過ぎる (≒ rash, hasty) ❷(通常より)早い (≒ early) ❸早産の
- 形 mature：❶(人が)大人びた、分別のある ❷(生物が)十分に成長した、成熟した ❸熟した

0786 countless /káuntləs/
- 形 **数え切れない**(ほどの)、無数の (≒ innumerable)
- 動 count：〜を数える
- 名 count：計算

0787 noticeable /nóutisəbl/
- 形 **目立つ**、際立った、著しい (≒ conspicuous, outstanding)
- 副 noticeably：目立って、著しく
- 動 notice：〜に気づく
- 名 notice：❶注目、注意 ❷通知、通達 ❸掲示、告示

0788 subjective /səbdʒéktiv/
- 形 **主観的な** (≒ personal) (⇔ objective：客観的な)
- 名 subject：❶被験者 ❷話題；主題；テーマ ❸科目、学科
- 形 subject：(be subject toで) ❶〜に左右される；〜を受けやすい ❷〜に服従している

0789 exceptional /iksépʃənl/
- 形 ❶**非常に優れた**、並外れた (≒ outstanding, extraordinary, remarkable) ❷例外的な (≒ unusual)
- 副 exceptionally：非常に、例外的に
- 名 exception：例外
- 前 except：〜を除いて、〜以外は

0790 vulgar /vʌ́lgər/
- 形 **下品な**、不作法な (≒ rude, indecent, coarse, crude)

0791 distinct /distíŋkt/
- 形 ❶**はっきりした**、明瞭な (≒ clear) ❷(〜と)(まるで)異なった、別個の (from 〜) (≒ different)
- 名 distinction：(〜の間の)違い、相違 (between 〜)
- 動 distinguish：❶〜を(…から)区別する (from …) ❷(〜を)見分ける (between 〜)

0792 pathetic /pəθétik/
- 形 ❶**情けない**(ほどの)、下手くそな (≒ feeble) ❷痛ましい、哀れな (≒ pitiful)
- 副 pathetically：❶情けないほど ❷哀れに、痛々しく

continued
▼

今日でChapter 6は最後！ 時間に余裕があったら、章末のReviewにも挑戦しておこう。忘れてしまった単語も結構あるのでは?!

☐ 聞くだけモード　Check 1
☐ しっかりモード　Check 1 ▶ 2
☐ かんぺきモード　Check 1 ▶ 2 ▶ 3

Check 2　Phrase

☐ a premature conclusion（時期尚早の結論）
☐ one's premature death（若死に、早死に）

☐ countless people（数え切れないほどの人々）
☐ countless times（[副詞的に]何度[幾度]となく）

☐ a noticeable improvement（目立った改善）
☐ It is noticeable that ~.（~ということは明らかである）

☐ a subjective point of view（主観的な考え方）

☐ his exceptional ability（彼の非常に優れた能力）
☐ in exceptional circumstances（特別な場合に限って）

☐ a vulgar joke（下品な冗談）

☐ a distinct voice（はっきりした声）
☐ two distinct groups（2つの別個の集団）

☐ a pathetic excuse（下手な言い訳）
☐ a pathetic figure（哀れな人物）

Check 3　Sentence

☐ It is premature to make a decision now.（今決断を下すのは時期尚早だ）

☐ He spent countless hours writing the novel.（彼はその小説の執筆に数え切れないほどの時間を費やした）

☐ There was no noticeable damage to the house.（その家には目立った損傷はなかった）

☐ The article was extremely subjective rather than objective.（その記事は客観的ではなく、極めて主観的だった）

☐ At the age of eight, she showed exceptional talent as a violinist.（8歳にして、彼女はバイオリニストとして非常に優れた才能を示していた）

☐ Don't use vulgar language.（下品な言葉を使わないでください）

☐ I have a very distinct memory of my first trip to Paris.（私は初めてのパリへの旅行をとてもはっきりと覚えている）

☐ Her test scores in math were pathetic.（彼女の数学のテスト成績は情けないものだった）

continued
▼

Check 1　Listen))) CD-B15

0793 stale /stéil/
形 ❶(空気が)**よどんだ**(≒stuffy)　❷(食べ物などが)古くなった、新鮮でない(⇔fresh)　❸(ジョークなどが)陳腐な

0794 long-standing /lɔ́ːŋstǽndiŋ/
形 **長年の**、古くからの

0795 protective /prətéktiv/
形 ❶**防護[保護]する**　❷(~を)かばう、守る(of [toward] ~)
動 protect：~を(…から)守る(from ...)
名 protection：(~からの)保護(from [against] ~)

0796 minimal /mínəməl/
形 **最小限の**(⇔maximal)
副 minimally：最小限に
形 minimum：最小[最低]の
名 minimum：最小[最低]限
動 minimize：❶~を最小限にする　❷~を軽視する

0797 selective /siléktiv/
形 ❶(~を)**入念に選択する**、えり好みする(about [in] ~)(≒particular, fastidious)　❷選択的な
動 select：~を(…から)選ぶ(from ...)
名 selection：❶選択　❷選び抜かれた物[人]　❸品ぞろえ

0798 abstract /ǽbstrækt/
形 **抽象的な**(⇔concrete：具体的な)
名 (/ǽbstrækt/)❶抽象芸術作品　❷(論文などの)要約、要旨
名 abstraction：❶抽象概念　❷放心(状態)

0799 opportune /ɑ̀pərtjúːn/
形 **適切[適当]な**、時宜を得た、好都合な(≒appropriate, suitable, favorable)(⇔inopportune)
名 opportunity：(~の/…する)機会、好機(for ~/to do)

0800 incredible /inkrédəbl/
形 ❶**信じられない**(ほどの)(≒unbelievable)(⇔credible)　❷驚くべき、素晴らしい(≒surprising, amazing, wonderful)
副 incredibly：❶非常に、とても　❷信じられないことに

Day 49))) CD-B14 Quick Review
答えは右ページ下

- □ しつこい
- □ 激しい
- □ 主要な
- □ 徹底的な
- □ 厳しい
- □ 絶え間のない
- □ 機密の
- □ 分かりやすい
- □ よくも悪くもない
- □ 無料の
- □ 有機栽培の
- □ 言い逃れの
- □ 明白な
- □ 非効率的な
- □ 放射性の
- □ 居心地のよい

Check 2 Phrase

- ☐ stale air（よどんだ空気）
- ☐ stale food（古くなった食べ物）

- ☐ a long-standing relationship（長年の関係）
- ☐ a long-standing custom（古くからの慣習）

- ☐ protective gloves [goggles]（防護手袋［眼鏡］）
- ☐ be too protective of one's child（子どもに過保護である）

- ☐ minimal cost（最小限の費用）

- ☐ be selective about the words（言葉を慎重に選ぶ）
- ☐ selective breeding（選択的飼育）

- ☐ abstract art（抽象芸術）

- ☐ an opportune time [moment]（適切な時）
- ☐ an opportune place [remark]（適切な場所［発言］）

- ☐ It is incredible that ~.（〜ということは信じられない）
- ☐ an incredible dancer（素晴らしいダンサー）

Check 3 Sentence

- ☐ The air in the room was stale and musty.（その部屋の空気はよどんでいて、かび臭かった）

- ☐ The long-standing border dispute between the two countries was settled last year.（両国間の長年の国境紛争は昨年、解決した）

- ☐ Employees are required to wear protective clothing while in the factory.（従業員は工場内では防護服を着用するよう求められている）

- ☐ The fire damage to the house was minimal.（火災によるその家の被害は最小限だった）

- ☐ Companies are becoming more selective in hiring new graduates.（企業は新卒者の採用の際により入念に選択するようになっている）

- ☐ "Good" and "evil" are abstract concepts.（「善」と「悪」は抽象概念だ）

- ☐ Now is the most opportune time to buy a new car.（今は新車を購入するのに最も適切な時だ）

- ☐ The judge found the witness's testimony incredible.（裁判官はその目撃者の証言を信じられないと思った）

Day 49))) CD-B14
Quick Review
答えは左ページ下

- ☐ insistent
- ☐ strenuous
- ☐ primary
- ☐ thorough
- ☐ grim
- ☐ perpetual
- ☐ classified
- ☐ straightforward
- ☐ mediocre
- ☐ complimentary
- ☐ organic
- ☐ evasive
- ☐ tangible
- ☐ inefficient
- ☐ radioactive
- ☐ cozy

CHAPTER 1
CHAPTER 2
CHAPTER 3
CHAPTER 4
CHAPTER 5
CHAPTER 6
CHAPTER 7
CHAPTER 8
CHAPTER 9
CHAPTER 10

Chapter 6 Review

左ページの(1)〜(20)の形容詞の同意・類義語（≒）、反意・反対語（⇔）を右ページのA〜Tから選び、カッコの中に答えを書き込もう。意味が分からないときは、見出し番号を参照して復習しておこう（答えは右ページ下）。

- [ ] (1) advanced (0691) ≒は? (　　)
- [ ] (2) complicated (0694) ⇔は? (　　)
- [ ] (3) questionable (0704) ≒は? (　　)
- [ ] (4) indispensable (0705) ≒は? (　　)
- [ ] (5) fertile (0709) ⇔は? (　　)
- [ ] (6) stern (0713) ≒は? (　　)
- [ ] (7) dejected (0721) ≒は? (　　)
- [ ] (8) infamous (0723) ≒は? (　　)
- [ ] (9) invaluable (0730) ⇔は? (　　)
- [ ] (10) hasty (0739) ≒は? (　　)
- [ ] (11) modest (0742) ≒は? (　　)
- [ ] (12) submissive (0747) ≒は? (　　)
- [ ] (13) adjacent (0753) ≒は? (　　)
- [ ] (14) domestic (0759) ⇔は? (　　)
- [ ] (15) shallow (0768) ≒は? (　　)
- [ ] (16) primary (0771) ≒は? (　　)
- [ ] (17) grim (0773) ≒は? (　　)
- [ ] (18) classified (0775) ≒は? (　　)
- [ ] (19) subjective (0788) ⇔は? (　　)
- [ ] (20) abstract (0798) ⇔は? (　　)

A. disappointed
B. secret
C. notorious
D. doubtful
E. superficial
F. adjoining
G. concrete
H. developed
I. humble
J. objective
K. obedient
L. essential
M. strict
N. foreign
O. main
P. simple
Q. rash
R. valueless
S. bleak
T. barren

【解答】(1) H (2) P (3) D (4) L (5) T (6) M (7) A (8) C (9) R (10) Q (11) I (12) K (13) F (14) N (15) E (16) O (17) S (18) B (19) J (20) G

CHAPTER 7

副詞：頻出32

Chapter 7では、英検準1級で頻出の副詞32をチェック。このChapterが終われば、「単語編」は終了。身につけてきた「超頻出・頻出単語」の数は832に！

Day 51【副詞1】
▶ 238
Day 52【副詞2】
▶ 242
Chapter 7 Review
▶ 246

こんなの出たよ！

A：Why did the director leave the meeting so (　　)?
B：He suddenly remembered he had to make an urgent phone call.（2008年度第3回）

1　loyally　　2　acutely
3　barely　　4　abruptly

▼
答えはDay 52でチェック！

Day 51　副詞1

Check 1　Listen 》CD-B16

☐ 0801 definitely
/défənitli/

副 間違いなく、確かに、絶対に（≒ certainly, surely, without doubt）
形 definite：❶明確[明白]な　❷（計画などが）確実な

☐ 0802 ironically
/airánikəli/

副 ❶皮肉にも　❷皮肉を込めて
形 ironic：皮肉な
名 irony：皮肉

☐ 0803 ultimately
/ʌ́ltəmətli/

副 結局（は）、最終的に、最後に（≒ finally, eventually, in the end）
形 ultimate：❶最終的な、究極[最後]の　❷最高の
名 ultimate：（the ～）（～において）最高のもの（in ～）

☐ 0804 presumably
/prizjú:məbli/

副 多分、恐らく（≒ probably）
動 presume：～ではないかと思う、～だと推測する
名 presumption：（～だろうという）推測、仮定（that節 ～）

☐ 0805 apparently
/əpǽrəntli/

副 どうやら[見たところ]（～らしい）（≒ seemingly, evidently）
形 apparent：❶明らかな　❷見かけ上の
動 appear：❶～のように見える　❷現れる
名 appearance：❶外見、外観　❷出現

☐ 0806 regularly
/régjələrli/

副 ❶定期的に（≒ periodically）　❷たびたび、よく（≒ often, frequently）
形 regular：❶定期的な　❷通常の　❸普通の
動 regulate：❶～を規制する　❷～を調節する
名 regulation：❶規則　❷規制

☐ 0807 relatively
/rélətivli/

副 比較的、割合に（≒ comparatively）
形 relative：❶比較上の、相対的な、ある程度の　❷（～に）関連した（to ～）
名 relative：親戚、親類

☐ 0808 worldwide
/wə́:rldwáid/

副 世界中に[で]、世界的に（≒ globally）　⊕「全国的に」は nationwide
形 世界的な

continued
▼

Chapter 7では、2日をかけて「頻出」副詞32をチェック。まずはCDでチャンツを聞いて、単語を「耳」からインプット！

- □ 聞くだけモード　Check 1
- □ しっかりモード　Check 1 ▶ 2
- □ かんぺきモード　Check 1 ▶ 2 ▶ 3

Check 2　Phrase

- □ **definitely** remember doing ~（~したことを確かに覚えている）
- □ **Definitely** not.（[返答として]絶対に違います）

- □ **Ironically**(,) ~.（皮肉にも~だ）
- □ smile **ironically**（皮肉を込めてほほ笑む）

- □ **ultimately** lead to ~（結局は~につながる）
- □ **Ultimately**(,) ~.（結局のところ~だ）

- □ **Presumably**(,) ~.（多分~だろう）
- □ **presumably** because ~（恐らく~なので）

- □ **Apparently**(,) ~.（どうやら~らしい）
- □ an **apparently** genuine ~（見たところ本物の~）

- □ meet **regularly**（定期的に会う）
- □ quite **regularly**（かなり頻繁に）

- □ a **relatively** inexpensive hotel（比較的安いホテル）
- □ **relatively** speaking（比較して言えば）

- □ get popular **worldwide**（世界中で人気になる）

Check 3　Sentence

- □ This song will **definitely** appeal to teenagers.（この歌は間違いなくティーンエージャーたちに気に入られるだろう）

- □ **Ironically**, the sky cleared up after the event had been called off.（皮肉にも、そのイベントが中止になった後に空が晴れ渡った）

- □ The task was difficult, but **ultimately** successful.（その仕事は難しかったが、結局はうまくいった）

- □ **Presumably**, she is coming back soon.（多分、彼女はすぐに戻ってくるだろう）

- □ **Apparently**, it's going to snow today.（どうやら今日は雪が降るようだ）

- □ Exercising **regularly** is extremely important for your health.（定期的に運動することは健康のために極めて大切だ）

- □ I thought the exam was **relatively** easy.（私はその試験は比較的簡単だと思った）

- □ The bank has over 50 branches **worldwide**.（その銀行は世界中に50以上の支店を持っている）

continued ▼

Day 51

Check 1　Listen))) CD-B16

☐ 0809
literally
/lítərəli/

副 **文字通り**(に)
形 literal：❶文字通りの　❷実際[本当]の　❸逐語[直訳]的な

☐ 0810
inevitably
/inévətəbli/

副 **必然的に**(≒naturally, necessarily)
形 inevitable：必然的な、避けられない
名 inevitable：(the ~)避けられない状況[事態]

☐ 0811
virtually
/vɚ́ːrtʃuəli/

副 **ほとんど**、事実上、実質的には(≒almost, nearly, practically)
形 virtual：❶事実[実質]上の　❷仮想の、インターネット[コンピューター]上の

☐ 0812
consequently
/kánsəkwèntli/
❶アクセント注意

副 **その結果**、従って(≒as a result, therefore, thus)
名 consequence：(通例~s) (~の)結果、影響(of ~)
形 consequent：(~の)結果として起こる(on [upon, to] ~)

☐ 0813
annually
/ǽnjuəli/

副 **毎年**、年1回(≒yearly)
形 annual：❶年1回の、毎年[年次]の　❷1年間の

☐ 0814
sparsely
/spáːrsli/

副 **まばらに**、少なく(≒thinly)
形 sparse：まばらな、少ない

☐ 0815
initially
/iníʃəli/

副 **最初**(のうち)**は**、初めに(≒at first, at the beginning)
形 initial：最初の
動 initiate：(計画など)を始める
名 initiative：❶(the ~)主導権、イニシアチブ　❷自発性

☐ 0816
unanimously
/juːnǽnəməsli/
❶発音注意

副 **満場[全員、全会]一致で**　⊕anonymously(匿名で)と混同しないように注意
形 unanimous：❶満場[全員、全会]一致の　❷(~で)意見が一致して(in ~)

| Day 50))) CD-B15
Quick Review
答えは右ページ下 | ☐ 時期尚早の
☐ 数え切れない
☐ 目立つ
☐ 主観的な | ☐ 非常に優れた
☐ 下品な
☐ はっきりした
☐ 情けない | ☐ よどんだ
☐ 長年の
☐ 防護する
☐ 最小限の | ☐ 入念に選択する
☐ 抽象的な
☐ 適切な
☐ 信じられない |

Check 2 Phrase

- ☐ take ~ literally（〜を文字通りに受け止める）
- ☐ translate literally（逐語訳する）

- ☐ inevitably lead to ~（必然的に〜につながる）

- ☐ be virtually impossible（ほとんど不可能である）
- ☐ virtually all students（ほぼ生徒全員）

- ☐ ~(,) and consequently . . .（〜そしてその結果…）

- ☐ an annually held conference（毎年開催される会議）
- ☐ renew the contract annually（年1回、その契約を更新する）

- ☐ a sparsely populated area（人口のまばらな地域）

- ☐ be lower than initially thought（当初考えられていたよりも低い）
- ☐ Initially(,) ~ .（最初は〜だ）

- ☐ approve the proposal unanimously（その提案を満場一致で承認する）

Check 3 Sentence

- ☐ The word "philosopher" literally means "lover of wisdom."（「哲学者」という言葉は文字通りには「知を愛する者」を意味する）

- ☐ The global financial crisis will inevitably have an impact on the domestic economy.（世界的な金融危機は必然的に国内経済に影響を及ぼすだろう）

- ☐ Smallpox has been virtually eradicated in the world.（天然痘は世界でほとんど根絶された）

- ☐ There was no wind, and consequently no yacht race.（無風だったので、その結果ヨットレースはなかった）

- ☐ The festival is held annually in August.（その祭りは毎年8月に開催される）

- ☐ The region is heavily forested and sparsely populated.（その地域は深い森林に覆われていて、人口はまばらだ）

- ☐ Initially, I wanted to go to art school.（最初は私は美術学校に行きたかった）

- ☐ The bill was passed unanimously.（その法案は満場一致で可決された）

Day 50))) CD-B15
Quick Review
答えは左ページ下

- ☐ premature
- ☐ countless
- ☐ noticeable
- ☐ subjective
- ☐ exceptional
- ☐ vulgar
- ☐ distinct
- ☐ pathetic
- ☐ stale
- ☐ long-standing
- ☐ protective
- ☐ minimal
- ☐ selective
- ☐ abstract
- ☐ opportune
- ☐ incredible

CHAPTER 1
CHAPTER 2
CHAPTER 3
CHAPTER 4
CHAPTER 5
CHAPTER 6
CHAPTER 7
CHAPTER 8
CHAPTER 9
CHAPTER 10

Day 52 副詞2

Check 1　Listen 》CD-B17

☐ 0817
eventually
/ivéntʃuəli/
副 **結局**(は)、最後には(≒finally, ultimately, in the end)
形 eventual：最終的な

☐ 0818
recklessly
/rékləsli/
副 **無謀に**、向こう見ずに
形 reckless：無謀な、向こう見ずな

☐ 0819
aimlessly
/éimləsli/
副 **当て[目的]もなく**
形 aimless：当て[目的]のない
名 aim：❶目標、目的　❷狙い
動 aim：❶(aim to doで)〜することを目指す　❷(aim A at Bで)AをBに向ける　❸(aim atで)〜を狙う

☐ 0820
barely
/béərli/
副 ❶**辛うじて**、何とか(≒only just, narrowly)　❷ほとんど〜ない(≒hardly, scarcely)　❸わずかに(≒only)

☐ 0821
approximately
/əpráksəmətli/
副 **約**、おおよそ(≒about, around, roughly)
形 approximate：おおよその
動 approximate：おおよそ〜になる、〜に近い

☐ 0822
frequently
/frí:kwəntli/
❶アクセント注意
副 **頻繁に**、たびたび、しばしば(≒often, a lot, regularly)
形 frequent：頻繁な、たびたびの
動 frequent：〜によく行く
名 frequency：❶頻度　❷頻発　❸周波数

☐ 0823
firsthand
/fə́:rsthǽnd/
副 **直接に**、じかに　●first-handとつづることもある(≒directly, personally, at first hand　●このatはしばしば省略される)(⇔secondhand)
形 直接の、じかの

☐ 0824
occasionally
/əkéiʒənəli/
副 **時々**、時折、たまに(≒sometimes, at times, now and then, from time to time, once in a while)
形 occasional：時折[時々]の、たまの
名 occasion：❶(特定の)時、場合　❷(〜のための/…する)機会、好機(for 〜/to do)　❸(特別な)出来事、行事

continued
▼

今日でChapter 7は最後！ 時間に余裕があったら、章末のReviewにも挑戦しておこう。もう忘れてしまった単語もあるのでは?!

☐ 聞くだけモード　Check 1
☐ しっかりモード　Check 1 ▶ 2
☐ かんぺきモード　Check 1 ▶ 2 ▶ 3

Check 2　Phrase

☐ eventually decide to do ~(結局~することに決める)

☐ drive recklessly (無謀運転をする)

☐ wander aimlessly (当てもなく歩き回る)

☐ can barely do ~(辛うじて~することができる)
☐ be barely audible [visible] (ほとんど聞こえない[見えない])

☐ arrive in approximately 10 minutes (約10分で到着する)

☐ see him quite frequently (彼にかなり頻繁に会う)

☐ experience war firsthand (戦争を実体験する)

☐ eat out occasionally (時々外食する)
☐ very occasionally (ごくたまに、めったに~ない)

Check 3　Sentence

☐ The flight eventually took off two hours late. (結局、その便は2時間遅れで離陸した)

☐ He was arrested for speeding and driving recklessly. (彼はスピード違反と無謀運転で逮捕された)

☐ She spent the day driving aimlessly around the countryside. (彼女は当てもなく田舎をドライブしてその日を過ごした)

☐ I could barely understand what he was saying. (私は彼が言っていることが辛うじて理解できた)

☐ The population of Japan is approximately half that of the US. (日本の人口は米国の約半分だ)

☐ It is important to save files frequently to avoid data loss. (データの損失を避けるために頻繁にファイルをセーブすることが大切だ)

☐ Experiencing another culture firsthand is much more exciting than just reading or hearing about it. (異文化を直接体験することは、それについて単に読んだり聞いたりするよりもはるかに刺激的だ)

☐ I see my old friends occasionally. (私は旧友たちと時々会う)

continued
▼

Day 52

Check 1　Listen))) CD-B17

0825 abruptly /əbrʌ́ptli/
トビラの問題の正解はコレ！
- 副 **突然[唐突]に**(≒ suddenly)
- 形 abrupt：突然の、唐突な

0826 invariably /invέəriəbli/
- 副 **いつも**、常に、必ず(≒ always, at all times, without fail)
- 形 invariable：いつもの、変わらない
- 動 vary：❶(～の点で)異なる、さまざまである(in ～)　❷変わる　❸～を変える

0827 drastically /drǽstikli/
- 副 **徹底[抜本]的に**、思い切って、ドラスティックに(≒ thoroughly)
- 形 drastic：(措置などが)思い切った、徹底[抜本]的な、ドラスティックな

0828 permanently /pə́ːrmənəntli/
- 副 **永久に**、ずっと(≒ forever, for good)
- 形 permanent：❶永久的な　❷(雇用が)終身の
- 名 permanent：パーマ

0829 highly /háili/
- 副 ❶**非常に**、大いに、高度に(≒ very, extremely)　❷高く(≒ favorably, well)

0830 voluntarily /vàləntέərəli/
❶アクセント注意
- 副 **自発的に**
- 形 voluntary：自発的な、ボランティアの
- 名 volunteer：志願者、ボランティア
- 動 volunteer：❶(～を)進んで申し出る(for ～)　❷(volunteer to doで)～しようと進んで申し出る

0831 largely /lάːrdʒli/
- 副 **大部分は**、主に(≒ mainly, mostly)
- 形 large：❶大きい、広い　❷多い

0832 significantly /signífikəntli/
- 副 ❶**著しく**(≒ remarkably, notably, strikingly)　❷重要なこと(に)は
- 形 significant：❶重要[重大]な　❷かなりの；著しい　❸意味ありげな
- 名 significance：❶重要[重大]性　❷意味、意義

Day 51))) CD-B16　Quick Review
答えは右ページ下

- ☐ 間違いなく
- ☐ 皮肉にも
- ☐ 結局
- ☐ 多分
- ☐ どうやら
- ☐ 定期的に
- ☐ 比較的
- ☐ 世界中に
- ☐ 文字通り
- ☐ 必然的に
- ☐ ほとんど
- ☐ その結果
- ☐ 毎年
- ☐ まばらに
- ☐ 最初は
- ☐ 満場一致で

Check 2 Phrase

- end abruptly（突然終わる）

- invariably wake up at 6 a.m.（いつも午前6時に目が覚める）

- drastically reform the pension system（年金制度を抜本的に改革する）

- settle permanently in the US（米国に永住する）

- a highly intelligent person（非常に知能の高い人）
- speak [think] highly of 〜（〜を高く評価する）

- voluntarily donate money to 〜（自発的に〜に献金する）
- voluntarily surrender to the police（警察に自首する）

- a largely male-dominated field（男性がほとんど支配している分野）
- largely because 〜（主に〜の理由で）

- significantly better [worse]（[以前よりも]かなりよい[悪い]）
- more significantly（より重要なことは）

Check 3 Sentence

- The train stopped abruptly.（その列車は突然、停止した）

- The bus is invariably late.（そのバスはいつも遅れて来る）

- The government needs to drastically reduce spending.（政府は支出を徹底的に削減する必要がある）

- Slavery was permanently abolished in the US in 1865.（奴隷制度は米国では1865年に永久に廃止された）

- Asbestos is a highly dangerous substance.（アスベストは非常に危険な物質だ）

- More than 100 people voluntarily participated in the clean-up campaign.（100人以上の人々がその清掃運動に自発的に参加した）

- The southern part of the country is largely desert.（その国の南部は、大部分は砂漠だ）

- Sales of hybrid cars have increased significantly over the year.（ハイブリッドカーの販売台数はこの1年で著しく増加している）

Day 51 》CD-B16
Quick Review
答えは左ページ下

- definitely
- ironically
- ultimately
- presumably
- apparently
- regularly
- relatively
- worldwide
- literally
- inevitably
- virtually
- consequently
- annually
- sparsely
- initially
- unanimously

CHAPTER 1
CHAPTER 2
CHAPTER 3
CHAPTER 4
CHAPTER 5
CHAPTER 6
CHAPTER 7
CHAPTER 8
CHAPTER 9
CHAPTER 10

Chapter 7 Review

左ページの(1)～(20)の副詞の同意・類義語［熟語］（≒）、反意・反対語（⇔）
を右ページのA～Tから選び、カッコの中に答えを書き込もう。意味が分から
ないときは、見出し番号を参照して復習しておこう（答えは右ページ下）。

- □ (1) definitely (0801) ≒は？（　）
- □ (2) ultimately (0803) ≒は？（　）
- □ (3) presumably (0804) ≒は？（　）
- □ (4) apparently (0805) ≒は？（　）
- □ (5) regularly (0806) ≒は？（　）
- □ (6) relatively (0807) ≒は？（　）
- □ (7) worldwide (0808) ≒は？（　）
- □ (8) inevitably (0810) ≒は？（　）
- □ (9) virtually (0811) ≒は？（　）
- □ (10) consequently (0812) ≒は？（　）
- □ (11) annually (0813) ≒は？（　）
- □ (12) sparsely (0814) ≒は？（　）
- □ (13) initially (0815) ≒は？（　）
- □ (14) barely (0820) ≒は？（　）
- □ (15) approximately (0821) ≒は？（　）
- □ (16) firsthand (0823) ⇔は？（　）
- □ (17) occasionally (0824) ≒は？（　）
- □ (18) abruptly (0825) ≒は？（　）
- □ (19) permanently (0828) ≒は？（　）
- □ (20) largely (0831) ≒は？（　）

A. about
B. comparatively
C. at first
D. eventually
E. forever
F. globally
G. yearly
H. certainly
I. seemingly
J. secondhand
K. almost
L. narrowly
M. probably
N. therefore
O. sometimes
P. periodically
Q. necessarily
R. thinly
S. mainly
T. suddenly

【解答】 (1) H (2) D (3) M (4) I (5) P (6) B (7) F (8) Q (9) K (10) N (11) G (12) R (13) C (14) L (15) A (16) J (17) O (18) T (19) E (20) S

CHAPTER 8

動詞句：頻出240

Chapter 8では、頻出の動詞表現240を見ていきましょう。本書で最も長いこのChapter。ここを乗り切れば、ゴールはすぐそこに見えてくる！

こんなの出たよ！

Sally was so nervous on her first day at kindergarten that she (   ) to her mother's leg and refused to let go.（2009年度第1回）

1　slung　　2　swapped
3　clung　　4　drooped

答えはDay 54でチェック！

Day 53 【動詞句1】「動詞＋副詞［前置詞］」型1
▶ 250
Day 54 【動詞句2】「動詞＋副詞［前置詞］」型2
▶ 254
Day 55 【動詞句3】「動詞＋副詞［前置詞］」型3
▶ 258
Day 56 【動詞句4】「動詞＋副詞［前置詞］」型4
▶ 262
Day 57 【動詞句5】「動詞＋副詞［前置詞］」型5
▶ 266
Day 58 【動詞句6】「動詞＋副詞［前置詞］」型6
▶ 270
Day 59 【動詞句7】「動詞＋副詞［前置詞］」型7
▶ 274
Day 60 【動詞句8】「動詞＋副詞［前置詞］」型8
▶ 278
Day 61 【動詞句9】「動詞＋A＋前置詞＋B」型1
▶ 282
Day 62 【動詞句10】「動詞＋A＋前置詞＋B」型2
▶ 286
Day 63 【動詞句11】「動詞＋to do」「動詞＋A＋to do」型
▶ 290
Day 64 【動詞句12】「be動詞＋形容詞＋前置詞」型1
▶ 294
Day 65 【動詞句13】「be動詞＋形容詞＋前置詞」型2
▶ 298
Day 66 【動詞句14】「be動詞＋形容詞＋to do」型
▶ 302
Day 67 【動詞句15】その他
▶ 306
Chapter 8 Review
▶ 310

Day 53 動詞句1
「動詞＋副詞［前置詞］」型1

Check 1　Listen ♪) CD-B18

0833 figure out
❶ **〜を理解する**（≒ understand, work out）　❷ (問題)を解決する、(答え)を考え出す（≒ solve）
名 figure：❶数字　❷姿　❸人物　❹図

0834 focus on
〜に集中する、重点を置く（≒ concentrate on）
名 focus：❶焦点　❷(興味などの)中心、焦点

0835 take up
❶ (趣味など)**を始める**（≒ start）　❷ (時間・場所など)を取る

0836 cope with
(問題など)**にうまく対処する**（≒ handle, manage, deal with)

0837 jot down
〜を(急いで)**書き留める**、メモする（≒ write down, note down, take down, put down）

0838 come up with
(考えなど)**を思いつく**（≒ hit on [upon]）　❶「(考えなどが)〜の心に(ふと)浮かぶ」は occur to

0839 turn out
❶ (催し物などに)**出かける**、集まる(for 〜)（≒ assemble, gather, attend）　❷ 〜であることが判明する、分かる（≒ prove）
名 turnout：❶出席者数　❷投票者数、投票率

0840 drop out
❶ (学校を)(中途)**退学する**(of 〜)　❷ (活動などを)やめる(of 〜)
名 dropout：(中途)退学者

continued
▼

Chapter 8では、頻出の動詞句240をチェック。まずは、8日をかけて「動詞＋副詞[前置詞]」型の表現を見ていこう。

☐ 聞くだけモード　Check 1
☐ しっかりモード　Check 1 ▶ 2
☐ かんぺきモード　Check 1 ▶ 2 ▶ 3

Check 2　　Phrase

☐ figure out why she did it(なぜ彼女がそうしたか理解する)
☐ figure out the issue(その問題を解決する)

☐ focus on one's study(勉強に集中する)
☐ focus on foreign policy(外交政策に重点を置く)

☐ take up golf(ゴルフを始める)
☐ take up space [room](場所を取る)

☐ cope with the situation(状況にうまく対処する)
☐ cope with stress(ストレスにうまく対処する)

☐ jot down her phone number(彼女の電話番号を書き留める)

☐ come up with a good idea(妙案を思いつく)

☐ turn out for the event(そのイベントに出かける)
☐ It turns out that ~.(~ということが判明する)

☐ drop out of high school(高校を退学する)
☐ drop out of the race(そのレースからリタイアする)

Check 3　　Sentence

☐ I can't figure out what he is thinking.(彼が何を考えているのか私には理解できない)

☐ The government should focus on solving domestic economic problems.(政府は国内の経済問題の解決に集中すべきだ)

☐ She has recently taken up yoga.(彼女は最近、ヨガを始めた)

☐ He wasn't able to cope with his increasing workload.(彼は増え続ける仕事量にうまく対処することができなかった)

☐ I jotted down his e-mail address on a scrap of paper.(私は彼の電子メールアドレスを紙の切れ端に書き留めた)

☐ She came up with a solution to the problem.(彼女はその問題の解決策を思いついた)

☐ More than 10,000 people turned out for the rally.(1万人以上の人々がその集会に出かけた)

☐ He dropped out of the university after one year.(彼は1年後にその大学を退学した)

continued ▼

Day 53

Check 1　Listen))) CD-B18

0841 stick to
❶**〜をやり通す**、最後までやり遂げる　❷(信念など)を貫く(≒keep to, adhere to)

0842 chip in
❶**金を出し合う**、寄付する　❷(金)を出し合う、寄付する(≒contribute, donate)

0843 set off
❶(装置)**を作動させる**(≒activate)　❷(〜に向けて)出発する(for 〜)(≒depart, leave, set out)

0844 contribute to
❶**〜の一因[一助]となる**　❷〜に貢献[寄与]する
图contribution：❶(〜への)貢献、寄与、助力(to [toward] 〜)　❷(〜への)寄付金、献金(to [toward] 〜)

0845 rip off
❶**〜を食い物にする**、〜に法外な値をふっかける(≒overcharge)　❷〜を盗む、かっぱらう(≒steal)
图rip-off：ぼったくり

0846 eat up
❶**〜を(どんどん)消費する**、いっぱい食う　❷〜を残さず食べる

0847 touch on [upon]
(簡単に)(問題など)**に言及する**、触れる(≒mention, refer to)

0848 sit back
❶**何もしないでいる**、(何もせずに)傍観する　❷ゆったりと座る

Day 52))) CD-B17
Quick Review
答えは右ページ下

- □ 結局
- □ 無謀に
- □ 当てもなく
- □ 辛うじて
- □ 約
- □ 頻繁に
- □ 直接に
- □ 時々
- □ 突然に
- □ いつも
- □ 徹底的に
- □ 永久に
- □ 非常に
- □ 自発的に
- □ 大部分は
- □ 著しく

Check 2 Phrase

- ☐ **stick to** one's job（仕事を最後までやり遂げる）
- ☐ **stick to** one's principles（主義を貫く）

- ☐ **chip in** to buy ～（～を買うために金を出し合う）
- ☐ **chip in** (with) $10（10ドルを寄付する）

- ☐ **set off** a burglar alarm（防犯ベルを作動させる）
- ☐ **set off** for London（ロンドンに向けて出発する）

- ☐ **contribute to** global warming（地球温暖化の一因となる）
- ☐ **contribute to** victory（勝利に貢献する）

- ☐ **rip off** tourists（観光客を食い物にする）
- ☐ **rip** money **off**（金を盗む）

- ☐ **eat up** energy（エネルギーを消費する）
- ☐ **eat up** one's vegetables（野菜を残さず食べる）

- ☐ **touch** briefly **on** ～（～に手短に言及する）

- ☐ **sit back** and let things happen（何もしないで事が起こるに任せる）
- ☐ **sit back** on one's sofa（ソファにゆったりと座る）

Check 3 Sentence

- ☐ It is not easy to **stick to** a diet.（ダイエットをやり通すことは簡単ではない）

- ☐ We **chipped in** to buy a gift for our retiring boss.（私たちは退職する上司への贈り物を買うためにお金を出し合った）

- ☐ Please note that smoking indoors will **set off** the fire alarm.（屋内でたばこを吸うと火災警報器が作動するのでご注意ください）

- ☐ Seat belt usage has **contributed to** the reduction of the death rate in traffic accidents.（シートベルトの着用は交通事故の死亡率の減少の一因となっている）

- ☐ Many elderly homeowners are being **ripped off** by home renovation contractors.（多くの年配の住宅所有者は住宅リフォーム請負業者に食い物にされている）

- ☐ This software **eats up** a lot of memory.（このソフトウエアはメモリーをたくさん消費する）

- ☐ In his speech, the prime minister **touched on** the problem of terrorism.（演説の中で、首相はテロ問題に言及した）

- ☐ Don't **sit back** and wait for a job to come to you.（何もしないで仕事が来るのを待っていてはいけません）

CHAPTER 1 / CHAPTER 2 / CHAPTER 3 / CHAPTER 4 / CHAPTER 5 / CHAPTER 6 / CHAPTER 7 / **CHAPTER 8** / CHAPTER 9 / CHAPTER 10

Day 52))) CD-B17
Quick Review
答えは左ページ下

- ☐ eventually
- ☐ recklessly
- ☐ aimlessly
- ☐ barely
- ☐ approximately
- ☐ frequently
- ☐ firsthand
- ☐ occasionally
- ☐ abruptly
- ☐ invariably
- ☐ drastically
- ☐ permanently
- ☐ highly
- ☐ voluntarily
- ☐ largely
- ☐ significantly

Day 54 動詞句2
「動詞＋副詞［前置詞］」型2

Check 1　　Listen 》CD-B19

□ 0849
work out
❶(計画など)**を考え出す**、練り上げる(≒devise)　❷(費用など)を計算[算出]する(≒calculate)　❸(事が)うまくいく　❹～を理解する(≒understand)

□ 0850
count on [upon]
～に頼る、～を当てにする(≒rely on [upon], depend on [upon], bank on [upon])

□ 0851
slip out
(発言などが)**つい口から漏れる**

□ 0852
put down
❶(…の)(頭金など)**を払う**(on . . .)(≒pay)　❷(人)をけなす、こけにする(≒criticize)　❸～を書き留める(≒write down, note down, take down, jot down)

□ 0853
cut down (on)
～を削減する(≒reduce, decrease, cut back)

□ 0854
track down
～を突き止める、やっと見つけ出す(≒discover, find, trace)
名track：❶(～s)通った跡、足跡　❷(競技場の)トラック　❸小道、道

□ 0855
push on
❶(～へ)**前進する**、先へと進む、どんどん進む(to ～)(≒advance, proceed)　❷(仕事などを)続行する(with ～)(≒continue)

□ 0856
stand out
❶**目立つ**、際立つ　❷(～の中で)抜きん出ている、傑出している(from [among] ～)
形outstanding：際立った、傑出した、優れた

continued
▼

この型の表現は準1級では、大問1の空所補充で毎回4題ほど必ず出題される。取りこぼしがないように、しっかりと押さえていこう。

☐ 聞くだけモード　Check 1
☐ しっかりモード　Check 1 ▶ 2
☐ かんぺきモード　Check 1 ▶ 2 ▶ 3

Check 2　Phrase

☐ **work out** a new plan(新しい計画を考え出す)
☐ **work out** the total cost(総費用を計算する)

☐ **count on** one's parents(両親に頼る)
☐ Don't **count on** it.(それを当てにしてはいけない)

☐ It **slipped out** that ~.(~ということがつい口から漏れた)

☐ **put down** a 5 percent deposit on ~(~の5パーセントの頭金を払う)
☐ **put** oneself **down**(卑下する)

☐ **cut down** (on) the budget(予算を削減する)

☐ **track down** the killer(その殺人犯を突き止める)

☐ **push on** to one's destination(目的地へと前進する)
☐ **push on** with one's work(仕事を続行する)

☐ **stand out** in a crowd(人々の中で目立つ)
☐ **stand out** from the rest(他のものの中で抜きん出ている)

Check 3　Sentence

☐ The government needs to **work out** ways of distributing wealth more equally.(政府はより公平に富を分配する方法を考え出す必要がある)

☐ You can **count on** me whenever you need help.(助けが必要な時はいつでも私に頼ってくれていいですよ)

☐ The secret **slipped out** of his mouth.(その秘密がつい彼の口から漏れた)

☐ He **put down** a $1,000 deposit on the car.(彼はその車の1000ドルの頭金を払った)

☐ The law is aimed at **cutting down** carbon emissions.(その法律は炭素排出量を削減することを目指している)

☐ The police **tracked down** the suspect and arrested him.(警察はその容疑者を突き止めて逮捕した)

☐ They rested for a while then **pushed on** to the summit.(彼らはしばらく休憩してから、頂上へと前進した)

☐ The tower **stood out** against the night sky.(そのタワーは夜空を背景に目立っていた)

continued
▼

Day 54

Check 1　Listen))) CD-B19

□ 0857
cling to
トビラの問題の正解はコレ！

〜にしがみつく（≒ hold on to）

□ 0858
sail through

（試験など）に楽々合格する

□ 0859
iron out

（問題など）を解決する、取り除く（≒ solve, resolve, get rid of）

□ 0860
come down with

（病気など）にかかる

□ 0861
stick with

〜を続ける（≒ continue）

□ 0862
play along

（〜に）同意したふりをする、調子を合わせる（with 〜）

□ 0863
weed out

〜を排除[除去]する、取り除く（≒ remove, get rid of）
名 weed：雑草

□ 0864
back down

非[負け]を認める、引き下がる（≒ give in）

| Day 53))) CD-B18 Quick Review 答えは右ページ下 | □ 〜を理解する
□ 〜を始める
□ 〜にうまく対処する | □ 〜を書き留める
□ 〜を思いつく
□ 出かける
□ 退学する | □ 〜をやり通す
□ 金を出し合う
□ 〜を作動させる
□ 〜の一因となる | □ 〜を食い物にする
□ 〜を消費する
□ 〜に言及する
□ 何もしないでいる |

Check 2　Phrase

- ☐ **cling to** his arm(彼の腕にしがみつく)
- ☐ **cling to** the hope that ~(~という希望にしがみつく)

- ☐ **sail through** one's driving test(運転免許試験に楽々合格する)

- ☐ **iron out** the problem(その問題を解決する)

- ☐ **come down with** a cold(風邪をひく)

- ☐ **stick with** a diet(ダイエットを続ける)

- ☐ **play along** with his idea(彼の考えに同意したふりをする)

- ☐ **weed out** unsuitable candidates(不適任の候補者を排除する)

- ☐ refuse to **back down**(非を認めることを拒む)

Check 3　Sentence

- ☐ The 10 survivors were **clinging to** life rafts.(10人の生存者たちは救命ボートにしがみついていた)

- ☐ She **sailed through** the university's entrance exam.(彼女はその大学の入試に楽々合格した)

- ☐ There are some issues we need to **iron out** first.(私たちが最初に解決する必要のある問題がいくつかある)

- ☐ I **came down with** the flu last week.(私は先週、インフルエンザにかかった)

- ☐ We should **stick with** our original plan.(私たちは最初の計画を続けるべきだ)

- ☐ I didn't like her idea, but **played along** with her.(私は彼女の考えが気に入らなかったが、彼女に同意したふりをした)

- ☐ The recession will **weed out** inefficient and unprofitable businesses.(景気後退によって非効率的で収益の少ない企業は排除されるだろう)

- ☐ He finally **backed down** and apologized.(彼はようやく非を認め、謝罪した)

Day 53))CD-B18
Quick Review
答えは左ページ下

- ☐ figure out
- ☐ focus on
- ☐ take up
- ☐ cope with
- ☐ jot down
- ☐ come up with
- ☐ turn out
- ☐ drop out
- ☐ stick to
- ☐ chip in
- ☐ set off
- ☐ contribute to
- ☐ rip off
- ☐ eat up
- ☐ touch on
- ☐ sit back

CHAPTER 1
CHAPTER 2
CHAPTER 3
CHAPTER 4
CHAPTER 5
CHAPTER 6
CHAPTER 7
CHAPTER 8
CHAPTER 9
CHAPTER 10

Day 55 動詞句3
「動詞＋副詞［前置詞］」型3

Check 1   Listen)) CD-B20

☐ 0865
die down
(風・騒音などが)**静まる**、衰える(≒ abate, subside)

☐ 0866
tone down
(言葉など)**を和らげる**
🔳 tone：❶口調　❷(文章などの)調子　❸音色

☐ 0867
brush up (on)
〜を勉強し直す、磨き直す、復習する

☐ 0868
measure up to
(水準など)**に達する**、かなう(≒ reach, match up to)
🔳 measure：❶対策、措置　❷基準　❸単位

☐ 0869
tear down
(建物など)**を取り壊す**(≒ pull down, take down, knock down, demolish)

☐ 0870
come to
意識を回復する(≒ come around)

☐ 0871
put forward
(案など)**を提出する**、出す(≒ submit, suggest)

☐ 0872
clear up
(問題・誤解など)**を解く**、解明［解決］する(≒ solve, resolve, figure out)

continued
▼

「細切れ時間」を有効活用してる？『キクタン』は2分でも学習可能。いつでもどこでもテキストとCDを持ち歩いて、単語・熟語に触れよう！

☐ 聞くだけモード　Check 1
☐ しっかりモード　Check 1 ▶ 2
☐ かんぺきモード　Check 1 ▶ 2 ▶ 3

Check 2　Phrase

☐ gradually die down（徐々に静まる）

☐ tone down one's criticism（批判を和らげる）

☐ brush up (on) one's math（数学を勉強し直す）

☐ measure up to a certain standard（一定の基準に達する）
☐ measure up to one's expectations（〜の期待にかなう）

☐ tear down the old building（その古いビルを取り壊す）

☐ come to in an ambulance（救急車の中で意識を回復する）

☐ put forward a new plan（新しい計画を提出する）

☐ clear up a misunderstanding（誤解を解く）

Check 3　Sentence

☐ The wind died down around midnight.（風は夜中の12時くらいに静まった）

☐ You should tone down your language a bit.（あなたは言葉遣いを少し和らげたほうがいい）

☐ I brushed up my English before my trip to Sydney.（私はシドニーへの旅行の前に英語を勉強し直した）

☐ His exam scores didn't measure up to the admissions standards.（彼の試験成績は合格基準に達しなかった）

☐ The city will tear down the old library and build a new one.（市はその古い図書館を取り壊して、新しい図書館を建てる予定だ）

☐ When she came to, she was in a hospital bed.（意識を回復した時、彼女は病院のベッドの中にいた）

☐ The proposal she had put forward was accepted by the board of directors.（彼女が提出した案は取締役会で承認された）

☐ There are many mysteries about the case that still haven't been cleared up.（その事件にはいまだ解かれていない多くの謎がある）

continued
▼

Day 55

Check 1　Listen 》CD-B20

0873 map out
～の計画を練る：(計画)を練る

0874 break out
(戦争などが)**勃発する**、(疫病などが)急に発生する
名outbreak：(戦争などの)勃発、(疫病などの)突発的な発生(of ～)

0875 toss out
～を捨てる(≒throw away, get rid of)

0876 cut back (on)
～を削減する(≒reduce, decrease, cut down)
名cutback：(～の)削減(in ～)

0877 adhere to
❶(規則など)**を順守する**(≒abide by, comply with)
❷(主義など)を固持する、貫く(≒stick to)
名adherence：❶(規則などの)順守(to ～)　❷(主義などの)固持(to ～)
名adherent：(～の)支持者(of ～)

0878 stick around
もうちょっと待つ[いる]

0879 excel in [at]
～に秀でている、ずば抜けている
形excellent：素晴らしい、優れた
名excellence：優秀さ

0880 give in to
～に屈する、降参する(≒yield to, surrender to)

Day 54 》CD-B19
Quick Review
答えは右ページ下

- □ ～を考え出す
- □ ～に頼る
- □ つい口から漏れる
- □ ～を払う
- □ ～を削減する
- □ ～を突き止める
- □ 前進する
- □ 目立つ
- □ ～にしがみつく
- □ ～に楽々合格する
- □ ～を解決する
- □ ～にかかる
- □ ～を続ける
- □ 同意したふりをする
- □ ～を排除する
- □ 非を認める

Check 2 Phrase

- □ **map out** one's future(将来の計画を練る)
- □ **map out** the plan for ~(~の計画を練る)

- □ prevent war from **breaking out**(戦争の勃発を防ぐ)

- □ **toss out** old clothes(古着を捨てる)

- □ **cut back** (on) spending(支出を削減する)

- □ **adhere** strictly **to** ~(~を厳格に守る、~を厳守する)
- □ **adhere to** one's ideals(理想を貫く)

- □ **stick around** for a while(もうしばらくの間待つ)

- □ **excel in** English(英語に秀でている)

- □ **give in to** the union's demands(労働組合の要求に屈する)

Check 3 Sentence

- □ The government needs to **map out** a new economic strategy.(政府は新たな経済戦略の計画を練る必要がある)

- □ World War I **broke out** in Europe in August 1914.(第1次世界大戦は1914年8月にヨーロッパで勃発した)

- □ He **tossed out** his old TV when he moved.(彼は引っ越した時に古いテレビを捨てた)

- □ The automaker announced plans to **cut back** production.(その自動車メーカーは生産量を削減する計画を発表した)

- □ All students must **adhere to** the school's dress code.(全生徒は学校の服装規定を順守しなければならない)

- □ Can you **stick around** here?(ここでもうちょっと待っていてくれますか?)

- □ The student **excels** not only **in** academics but also **in** sports.(その生徒は学業だけでなくスポーツにも秀でている)

- □ The government refused to **give in to** the terrorists' demands.(政府はテロリストの要求に屈するのを拒んだ)

Day 54))CD-B19
Quick Review
答えは左ページ下

- □ work out
- □ count on
- □ slip out
- □ put down
- □ cut down
- □ track down
- □ push on
- □ stand out
- □ cling to
- □ sail through
- □ iron out
- □ come down with
- □ stick with
- □ play along
- □ weed out
- □ back down

CHAPTER 1
CHAPTER 2
CHAPTER 3
CHAPTER 4
CHAPTER 5
CHAPTER 6
CHAPTER 7
CHAPTER 8
CHAPTER 9
CHAPTER 10

Day 56 動詞句4
「動詞＋副詞［前置詞］」型4

Check 1　Listen 》CD-B21

□ 0881
catch up on
〜の遅れ[不足]を取り戻す　◆catch up withは「〜に追いつく」

□ 0882
result in
〜という結果になる、〜に終わる(≒lead to, end in)
名result：❶(〜の)結果(of 〜)　❷(〜s)成果

□ 0883
lay off
〜を(一時)解雇する(≒fire, dismiss)
名layoff：一時解雇、レイオフ

□ 0884
wipe out
〜を全滅[絶滅]させる(≒destroy, annihilate, eradicate)
名wipeout：全滅、絶滅

□ 0885
account for
❶**(ある割合)を占める**　❷〜の理由[原因]を説明する(≒explain)
名account：❶報告　❷説明　❸口座
名accounting：会計(学)、経理
名accountant：会計士

□ 0886
run through
〜にざっと目を通す(≒look over, browse through, skim, scan)

□ 0887
draw on [upon]
(経験など)**を活用する**、生かす、よりどころとする

□ 0888
laugh off
〜を笑い飛ばす、一笑に付す

continued
▼

この型の表現は、単語ごとに区切らず、「固まり」で1つの動詞として覚えよう。「固まり」として発音されているのをチャンツでチェック！

- □ 聞くだけモード　Check 1
- □ しっかりモード　Check 1 ▶ 2
- □ かんぺきモード　Check 1 ▶ 2 ▶ 3

Check 2　Phrase	Check 3　Sentence
□ catch up on sleep（睡眠不足を取り戻す）	□ He stayed late at the office to catch up on his work.（彼は仕事の遅れを取り戻すためにオフィスに遅くまで残った）
□ result in success [failure]（成功[失敗]に終わる）	□ The economic downturn resulted in lower revenues.（景気の後退は歳入の減少という結果になった）
□ lay off employees（従業員を解雇する）	□ The manufacturer laid off more than 200 temporary workers.（そのメーカーは200人以上の臨時雇いの労働者を解雇した）
□ wipe out the enemy troops（敵軍を全滅させる）	□ The village was wiped out by the earthquake.（その村は地震で全滅した）
□ account for more than half of ~（～の半分以上を占める） □ account for one's failure（失敗の理由を説明する）	□ Christians account for about 30 percent of South Korea's population.（キリスト教徒は韓国の人口の約30パーセントを占めている）
□ run through the list（そのリストにざっと目を通す）	□ The CEO ran through the annual sales report.（CEOは年間営業報告書にざっと目を通した）
□ draw on one's experience（経験を生かす）	□ She has a wealth of teaching experience to draw on.（彼女には活用できる豊かな教師歴がある）
□ laugh off his remarks（彼の発言を笑い飛ばす）	□ The minister laughed off rumors that he would resign soon.（その大臣は近く辞任するのではとのうわさを笑い飛ばした）

continued
▼

Day 56

Check 1　Listen))) CD-B21

0889 turn to
〜に(援助などを)**求める**、頼る(for...)(≒ask)

0890 bring down
❶(政府など)**を倒す**(≒overturn, overthrow)　❷(価格など)を下げる(≒decrease, reduce, lower)

0891 glare at
〜をにらみつける(≒scowl at, glower at)
图glare：❶まぶしい[ぎらぎらした]光　❷にらみつけること

0892 get around [round] to
〜に(ようやく)手が回る、〜する余裕を見つける

0893 shoot down
❶(意見など)**をはねつける**、拒否する　❷(敵機など)を撃墜する

0894 collide with
〜と衝突する、ぶつかる(≒crash into, run into)
图collision：(〜との／…の間の)衝突(with 〜/between...)

0895 pitch in
(〜に／…するために)**協力する**(with 〜/to do)(≒co-operate, collaborate)

0896 act up
(子どもなどが)**いたずらをする**、ふざける(≒misbehave)

Day 55))) CD-B20
Quick Review
答えは右ページ下

- □ 静まる
- □ 〜を和らげる
- □ 〜を勉強し直す
- □ 〜に達する
- □ 〜を取り壊す
- □ 意識を回復する
- □ 〜を提出する
- □ 〜を解く
- □ 〜の計画を練る
- □ 勃発する
- □ 〜を捨てる
- □ 〜を削減する
- □ 〜を順守する
- □ もうちょっと待つ
- □ 〜に秀でている
- □ 〜に屈する

Check 2　Phrase

- ☐ turn to him for advice（彼に助言を求める）

- ☐ bring down the Nazi regime（ナチ政権を倒す）
- ☐ bring down the price of ~（~の価格を下げる）

- ☐ glare at him silently（彼を静かににらみつける）

- ☐ get around to visiting him（彼を訪ねる余裕を見つける）

- ☐ be shot down in flames（こき下ろされる）
- ☐ shoot down the enemy plane（敵機を撃墜する）

- ☐ collide with an oncoming car（対向車と衝突する）

- ☐ pitch in with household chores（家事に協力する）

- ☐ act up in class（授業中にいたずらをする）

Check 3　Sentence

- ☐ He still turns to his parents for financial support.（彼はいまだに金銭的な支援を親に求めている）

- ☐ The government was brought down by a military coup.（その政府は軍事クーデターによって倒された）

- ☐ He glared at me threateningly.（彼は脅すように私をにらみつけた）

- ☐ I want to fix my printer, but I haven't got around to it yet.（私はプリンターを修理したいが、まだそれに手が回らないでいる）

- ☐ My proposal was shot down at the board meeting.（私の提案は取締役会ではねつけられた）

- ☐ The car collided head-on with a bus.（その車はバスと正面衝突した）

- ☐ If everyone pitches in, the work won't take too long.（みんなが協力すれば、その仕事はそれほど長くはかからないだろう）

- ☐ All kids act up from time to time.（子どもはみんな時々いたずらをするものだ）

Day 55))) CD-B20
Quick Review
答えは左ページ下

- ☐ die down
- ☐ tone down
- ☐ brush up
- ☐ measure up to
- ☐ tear down
- ☐ come to
- ☐ put forward
- ☐ clear up
- ☐ map out
- ☐ break out
- ☐ toss out
- ☐ cut back
- ☐ adhere to
- ☐ stick around
- ☐ excel in
- ☐ give in to

CHAPTER 1
CHAPTER 2
CHAPTER 3
CHAPTER 4
CHAPTER 5
CHAPTER 6
CHAPTER 7
CHAPTER 8
CHAPTER 9
CHAPTER 10

Day 57　動詞句5
「動詞＋副詞［前置詞］」型5

Check 1　Listen)) CD-B22

□ 0897
pass out
❶ **気絶する**、気を失う（≒ faint, black out）　❷ ～を（…に）配る（to . . .）（≒ distribute, hand out, give out）

□ 0898
get away with
❶ (悪事など) **をしてもただで済む**［見つからない］、～を（罰せられずに）うまくやってのける　❷ (軽い罰) で済む

□ 0899
allow for
～を考慮に入れる、見越しておく（≒ consider）
名 allowance : ❶ 手当、支給額　❷ 小遣い　❸ 割当量

□ 0900
drag on
(会議などが) (～の間／…に至るまで) **だらだらと続く**［長引く］（for ～/into . . .）

□ 0901
pass over
～を (…の) 候補から外す (for . . .)

□ 0902
step down [aside]
(～の地位を) **辞任[辞職]する** (as ～)（≒ resign）

□ 0903
get down to
(仕事など) **に本腰を入れる**、集中する

□ 0904
wear out
❶ **～を疲れ果てさせる**（≒ exhaust, fatigue, tire out）　❷ すり減る[切れる]　❸ ～をすり減らす[切らす]
形 worn-out : 疲れ果てた

continued
▼

「声を出しながら」CDを聞いてる？ えっ、恥ずかしい?! 恥ずかしがっていては「話せる」ようにならないよ！ もっと口を動かそう！

☐ 聞くだけモード　Check 1
☐ しっかりモード　Check 1 ▶ 2
☐ かんぺきモード　Check 1 ▶ 2 ▶ 3

Check 2　　Phrase

☐ pass out for a while（しばらく気を失う）
☐ pass out leaflets（ちらしを配る）

☐ get away with wrongdoing（悪事をうまくやってのける）
☐ get away with a small fine（軽い罰金で済む）

☐ allow for traffic congestion（交通渋滞を考慮に入れる）

☐ drag on for several hours（数時間だらだらと続く）

☐ pass her over for promotion（彼女を昇進の候補から外す）

☐ step down as prime minister（首相を辞任する）

☐ get down to work [business]（仕事に本腰を入れる）

☐ wear oneself out（疲れ果てる）
☐ begin to wear out（すり減り始める）

Check 3　　Sentence

☐ It was so hot I almost passed out.（あまりに暑くて私は気絶しそうだった）

☐ You'll never get away with it.（そんなことをしたら絶対にただでは済まされないだろう）

☐ You should allow for your bank charges when sending money.（送金をする際には銀行の手数料を考慮に入れたほうがいい）

☐ The meeting dragged on into the evening.（その会議は夕方までだらだらと続いた）

☐ He was passed over for sales manager.（彼は販売部長の候補から外された）

☐ Mr. Smith has decided to step down as CEO.（スミス氏はCEOを辞任することを決心した）

☐ It's time we get down to business.（そろそろ私たちは仕事に本腰を入れる時間だ）

☐ The stress of the job has completely worn him out.（仕事のストレスで彼は完全に疲れ果ててしまった）

continued
▼

Day 57

Check 1　Listen))) CD-B22

0905 jump at
(チャンスなど)**に飛びつく**、喜んで応じる(≒ leap at)

0906 confide in
〜に秘密[私事]を打ち明ける

0907 slip away
そっと出て行く、こっそり立ち去る

0908 flip through
(本など)**をパラパラめくる**(≒ thumb through, flick through)

0909 turn away
〜に(…への)入場を断る、〜を(…から)追い払う(from ...)

0910 bounce back
(〜から)(すぐに)**回復する**、立ち直る(from 〜)(≒ recover)

0911 launch into
〜を(熱心に)始める、やり出す(≒ start, begin)
名 launch：❶(事業などの)開始　❷(ロケットなどの)発射　❸(新製品などの)発売

0912 flag down
(タクシーなど)**を手を振って[合図して]止める**(≒ hail, wave down)

Day 56))) CD-B21
Quick Review
答えは右ページ下

- □ 〜の遅れを取り戻す
- □ 〜という結果になる
- □ 〜を解雇する
- □ 〜を全滅させる
- □ 〜を占める
- □ 〜にざっと目を通す
- □ 〜を活用する
- □ 〜を笑い飛ばす
- □ 〜に求める
- □ 〜を倒す
- □ 〜をにらみつける
- □ 〜に手が回る
- □ 〜をはねつける
- □ 〜と衝突する
- □ 協力する
- □ いたずらをする

Check 2 — Phrase

- ☐ **jump at** the chance [opportunity] to do ～(～するチャンスに飛びつく)
- ☐ **confide in** him that ～(彼に～だと打ち明ける)
- ☐ **slip away** unnoticed(気づかれないでそっと出て行く)
- ☐ **flip through** a dictionary(辞書をパラパラめくる)
- ☐ be **turned away** from the stadium(スタジアムへの入場を断られる)
- ☐ **bounce back** from illness(病気から回復する)
- ☐ **launch into** an explanation(説明を始める)
- ☐ **flag down** a passing car(通り過ぎようとする車を手を振って止める)

Check 3 — Sentence

- ☐ She **jumped at** the chance to go to Rome.(彼女はローマに行くチャンスに飛びついた)
- ☐ It is good to have someone to **confide in**.(秘密を打ち明けられる人がいることはいいことだ)
- ☐ He **slipped away** without us being aware of it.(彼は私たちが気づかないうちにそっと出て行った)
- ☐ She sat on the sofa **flipping through** a magazine.(彼女はソファに座って雑誌をパラパラめくっていた)
- ☐ He was **turned away** at the entrance because his ticket was fake.(チケットが偽物だったため、彼は入り口で入場を断られた)
- ☐ The global economy is **bouncing back** from the recession.(世界経済は景気後退から回復しつつある)
- ☐ He **launched into** a lengthy story about his life experiences.(彼は自分の人生経験について長ったらしい話を始めた)
- ☐ I **flagged down** a taxi to take me to the office.(職場へ送ってもらうために私はタクシーを手を振って止めた)

CHAPTER 8

Day 56))CD-B21
Quick Review
答えは左ページ下

- ☐ catch up on
- ☐ result in
- ☐ lay off
- ☐ wipe out
- ☐ account for
- ☐ run through
- ☐ draw on
- ☐ laugh off
- ☐ turn to
- ☐ bring down
- ☐ glare at
- ☐ get around to
- ☐ shoot down
- ☐ collide with
- ☐ pitch in
- ☐ act up

Day 58 動詞句6
「動詞＋副詞［前置詞］」型6

Check 1　Listen ») CD-B23

□ 0913
settle down
❶**落ち着く**　❷～を落ち着かせる（≒calm down）　❸（結婚して）身を固める
图settlement：❶解決、和解　❷集落　❸決済　❹入植

□ 0914
hand out
～を（…に）配る、分配する（to . . .）（≒distribute, pass out, give out）
图handout：配付資料、ハンドアウト

□ 0915
show up
姿を現す、（やって）来る（≒appear, arrive, come, turn up）

□ 0916
grow into
❶**成長して～になる**　❷（成長して）（服など）が着られるようになる
图growth：❶増加　❷成長　❸発達

□ 0917
take over
❶（職務など）**を（…から）引き継ぐ**（from . . .）（≒succeed）　❷（会社など）を買収する、乗っ取る
图takeover：（会社などの）買収、乗っ取り

□ 0918
pay off
（借金など）**を完済する**（≒settle, clear）

□ 0919
bump into
～に偶然出会う（≒encounter, run across, come across）

□ 0920
spell out
❶**～を詳しく説明する**　❷（名前など）のつづりを1文字ずつ言う［書く］
图spelling：❶語のつづり方　❷（単語の）つづり、スペル（of ～）

continued
▼

表現を「固まり」として覚えるように心がけてる?! 読むだけではなかなか「固まり」で身につかない。積極的に音読していこう。

☐ 聞くだけモード　Check 1
☐ しっかりモード　Check 1 ▶ 2
☐ かんぺきモード　Check 1 ▶ 2 ▶ 3

Check 2　Phrase

☐ settle down gradually(次第に落ち着く)
☐ settle him down(彼を落ち着かせる)

☐ hand out fliers to pedestrians(ちらしを歩行者に配る)

☐ show up unexpectedly(不意に姿を現す)

☐ grow into a fine young man(成長して立派な若者になる)
☐ grow into one's father's jacket(父親のジャケットが着られるようになる)

☐ take over ~ from one's predecessor(前任者から~を引き継ぐ)
☐ take over a competitor(競合企業を買収する)

☐ pay off one's debt [mortgage](借金[住宅ローン]を完済する)

☐ bump into one's ex-boyfriend(元カレに偶然出会う)

☐ spell out the plan(その計画を詳しく説明する)
☐ spell out one's name(名前のつづりを1文字ずつ言う)

Check 3　Sentence

☐ Things are settling down a bit.(状況は少し落ち着きつつある)

☐ The teacher handed out worksheets to the class.(その先生は問題プリントを生徒たちに配った)

☐ Only half of the 100 invited guests showed up.(100人の招待客のうち半分しか姿を現さなかった)

☐ The firm grew into one of the nation's largest manufacturers.(その会社は成長して国内最大のメーカーの1つになった)

☐ Everyone wants him to take over the family business.(誰もが彼に家業を引き継いでもらいたいと思っている)

☐ I paid off my car loan in two years.(私は自動車ローンを2年で完済した)

☐ I bumped into an old friend at the mall yesterday.(私は昨日、ショッピングセンターで旧友に偶然出会った)

☐ Can you spell out what happened there?(そこで何が起きたか詳しく説明してくれますか?)

continued
▼

Check 1　Listen)) CD-B23

0921 turn in
❶ ~を(…に)**提出する**(to . . .)(≒ submit, hand in)
❷ 寝る

0922 pick on
~をいじめる、からかう(≒ bully)

0923 embark on [upon]
~に着手する、乗り出す、~を開始する(≒ start, begin)

0924 single out
~を(…のために)**選び出す**、取り上げる(for . . .)(≒ select, choose)

0925 stir up
❶(騒動など)**を引き起こす**、巻き起こす(≒ cause, trigger)　❷(感情など)をかき立てる(≒ provoke)

0926 indulge in
(快楽など)**にふける**
名 indulgence：❶楽しみ、道楽　❷(~に)ふけること(in ~)
❸甘やかし
形 indulgent：(~に)甘い、寛大過ぎる(with ~)

0927 rule out
~を除外[排除]する(≒ exclude, eliminate)

0928 bank on [upon]
~を当てにする(≒ rely on [upon], depend on [upon], count on [upon])

Day 57)) CD-B22
Quick Review
答えは右ページ下

- □ 気絶する
- □ ~をしてもただで済む
- □ ~を考慮に入れる
- □ だらだらと続く
- □ ~を候補から外す
- □ 辞任する
- □ ~に本腰を入れる
- □ ~を疲れ果てさせる
- □ ~に飛びつく
- □ ~に秘密を打ち明ける
- □ そっと出て行く
- □ ~をパラパラめくる
- □ ~に入場を断る
- □ 回復する
- □ ~を始める
- □ ~を手を振って止める

Check 2　Phrase

- ☐ turn in one's resignation(辞表を提出する)
- ☐ turn in before 10 p.m.(午後10時前に寝る)

- ☐ pick on a particular child(特定の子どもをいじめる)

- ☐ embark on a new career(新しい仕事を始める)

- ☐ single out ~ for special praise(~を特別に称賛するために選び出す)

- ☐ stir up a debate(論争を巻き起こす)
- ☐ stir up hatred(憎悪をかき立てる)

- ☐ indulge in nostalgia(郷愁にふける)

- ☐ rule out the possibility of ~(~の可能性を排除する)

- ☐ bank on his support(彼の支援を当てにする)

Check 3　Sentence

- ☐ They turned in a petition with more than 10,000 signatures to the city council.(彼らは1万人以上の署名が入った請願書を市議会に提出した)

- ☐ Don't pick on people because of their looks.(容ぼうで人をいじめてはいけない)

- ☐ We will embark on a new project this year.(私たちは今年、新しい事業に着手する予定だ)

- ☐ He was singled out as the MVP of the game.(彼はその試合のMVPに選び出された)

- ☐ He always stirs up trouble.(彼はいつも面倒を引き起こす)

- ☐ In her free time, she likes to indulge in music.(暇な時には、彼女は音楽にふけるのが好きだ)

- ☐ The police ruled the man out as a suspect.(警察はその男性を容疑者としては除外した)

- ☐ "Do you think he'll come on time?" "I wouldn't bank on it."(「彼は時間通りに来るでしょうか?」「それは当てにはならないですね」)

Day 57 》CD-B22
Quick Review
答えは左ページ下

- ☐ pass out
- ☐ get away with
- ☐ allow for
- ☐ drag on
- ☐ pass over
- ☐ step down
- ☐ get down to
- ☐ wear out
- ☐ jump at
- ☐ confide in
- ☐ slip away
- ☐ flip through
- ☐ turn away
- ☐ bounce back
- ☐ launch into
- ☐ flag down

CHAPTER 1
CHAPTER 2
CHAPTER 3
CHAPTER 4
CHAPTER 5
CHAPTER 6
CHAPTER 7
CHAPTER 8
CHAPTER 9
CHAPTER 10

Day 59 動詞句7
「動詞＋副詞［前置詞］」型7

Check 1　Listen)) CD-B24

☐ 0929
size up
(状況など)**を見極める**、判断［評価］する(≒weigh up, assess, appraise, evaluate, judge)

☐ 0930
make for [toward]
～に向かう、行く、進む(≒head for)

☐ 0931
adapt to
(環境など)**に順応［適応］する**(≒adjust to, accommodate to, get used to)
名adaptation：(～への)順応、適応(to ～)
形adaptable：(be adaptable toで)～に順応［適応］できる

☐ 0932
stem from
(問題などが)**～から生じる**、～に由来［起因］する(≒arise from, originate from)
名stem：(草の)茎、(木の)幹

☐ 0933
crash into
～に衝突する(≒collide with)

☐ 0934
play down
～を軽視する、軽く扱う(≒make light of, make little of)(⇔play up：～を誇張［強調］する)

☐ 0935
bid for
～に入札する(≒tender for)
名bid：❶(工事などの)入札(for ～)　❷(～のための)試み(for ～)
名bidder：入札者

☐ 0936
hand down
❶(判決など)**を言い渡す**　❷(伝統など)を(…に)伝える(to . . .)(≒pass down, pass on)

continued
▼

チャンツを聞く際には、「英語→日本語→英語」の2回目の「英語」の部分で声に出して読んでみよう。定着度が倍増するはず！

- □ 聞くだけモード　Check 1
- □ しっかりモード　Check 1 ▶ 2
- □ かんぺきモード　Check 1 ▶ 2 ▶ 3

Check 2　　Phrase

□ size up the political climate（政治情勢を見極める）

□ make for the door（ドアに向かう）

□ adapt to one's new life（新しい生活に順応する）
□ adapt to change（変化に適応する）

□ stem from a misunderstanding（[不和などが]誤解から生じる）

□ crash into the back of a car（車の後部に衝突する）

□ play down the importance [significance] of ~（〜の重要性を軽視する）

□ bid for the bridge-building project（その橋の建設プロジェクトに入札する）

□ hand down a verdict（評決を言い渡す）
□ a tradition handed down through generations（何世代にもわたって伝えられた慣習）

Check 3　　Sentence

□ We need to size up the situation carefully.（私たちは状況を慎重に見極める必要がある）

□ We made for the center of town after breakfast.（朝食後、私たちは町の中心部に向かった）

□ It took her a while to adapt to her new surroundings.（彼女が新しい環境に順応するのに少し時間がかかった）

□ The global financial crisis stemmed from the sharp decline of the American real estate market.（世界的な金融危機は米国の不動産市場の急落から生じた）

□ His car crashed into a tree.（彼の車は木に衝突した）

□ The government is trying to play down the severity of the problem.（政府はその問題の深刻さを軽視しようとしている）

□ Eight companies bid for the contract.（8社がその契約に入札した）

□ The court handed down a 10-year sentence to the defendant.（法廷はその被告に10年の刑を言い渡した）

continued
▼

Day 59

Check 1　Listen))) CD-B24

0937 turn up
❶(人が)**現れる**、到着する(≒appear, arrive, show up)　❷〜を探し出す、発見する(≒find, discover)　❸(ガスの火など)を強める、(テレビなど)の音を大きくする(⇔turn down)

0938 carry over [forward]
〜を繰り越す、持ち越す
图carryover：繰り越し(額)

0939 abstain from
〜を控える、慎む(≒refrain from)
图abstinence：節制、禁酒、禁欲

0940 mark down
❶**〜を値下げする**(≒reduce, decrease, lower)(⇔mark up)　❷〜を書き留める、記録する(≒write down)
图markdown：値下げ

0941 go through
❶(苦しさなど)**を経験[体験]する**(≒experience, undergo)　❷(段階など)を経る　❸〜を詳しく調べる(≒examine, search)

0942 reach out to
〜に援助の手を差し伸べる

0943 enroll in [for]
〜に入学[入会]する(≒register for, sign up for)
图enrollment：❶入学、入会　❷入学[入会]者数

0944 wrap up
〜を終える、仕上げる、締めくくる(≒finish, end, conclude)

Day 58))) CD-B23
Quick Review
答えは右ページ下

□ 落ち着く　□ 〜を引き継ぐ　□ 〜を提出する　□ 〜を引き起こす
□ 〜を配る　□ 〜を完済する　□ 〜をいじめる　□ 〜にふける
□ 姿を現す　□ 〜に偶然出会う　□ 〜に着手する　□ 〜を除外する
□ 成長して〜になる　□ 〜を詳しく説明する　□ 〜を選び出す　□ 〜を当てにする

Check 2 Phrase

- □ turn up late(遅れて現れる)
- □ turn up the missing person(行方不明者を探し出す)

- □ carry over the balance to the next year(残高を翌年に繰り越す)

- □ abstain from alcohol(酒を控える)

- □ mark down merchandise(商品を値下げする)
- □ mark down his name(彼の名前を書き留める)

- □ go through a lot of difficulties(多くの困難を経験する)
- □ go through a phase(段階を経る)

- □ reach out to the poor(貧しい人々に援助の手を差し伸べる)

- □ enroll in Harvard University(ハーバード大学に入学する)

- □ wrap up the meeting(会議を終える)
- □ Let's wrap it up.([仕事などを]終わりにしましょう)

Check 3 Sentence

- □ We arranged to meet at 7 p.m. and he turned up on time.(私たちは午後7時に会う約束をして、彼は時間通りに現れた)

- □ A maximum of one week paid vacation can be carried over to the next year.(最長1週間の有給休暇を翌年に繰り越すことができる)

- □ The doctor advised me to abstain from smoking.(その医者はたばこを控えるように私に忠告した)

- □ All goods have been marked down by 50 percent.(全商品が50パーセント値下げされている)

- □ The global economy is going through one of its worst crises since the 1930s.(世界経済は1930年代以降で最悪の危機の1つを経験しているところだ)

- □ The charity was set up to reach out to homeless people.(その慈善団体はホームレスの人々に援助の手を差し伸べるために設立された)

- □ He enrolled in a vocational school to learn web design.(彼はウェブデザインを学ぶために職業訓練校に入学した)

- □ She wrapped up her speech by expressing her gratitude.(彼女は感謝の意を述べてスピーチを終えた)

Day 58))) CD-B23
Quick Review
答えは左ページ下

- □ settle down
- □ hand out
- □ show up
- □ grow into
- □ take over
- □ pay off
- □ bump into
- □ spell out
- □ turn in
- □ pick on
- □ embark on
- □ single out
- □ stir up
- □ indulge in
- □ rule out
- □ bank on

CHAPTER 1
CHAPTER 2
CHAPTER 3
CHAPTER 4
CHAPTER 5
CHAPTER 6
CHAPTER 7
CHAPTER 8
CHAPTER 9
CHAPTER 10

Day 60 動詞句8
「動詞＋副詞［前置詞］」型8

Check 1　Listen 》CD-B25

□ 0945 **pass up**
(機会など)**を(あえて)見送る**、断る、辞退する(≒turn down, reject, refuse, decline)

□ 0946 **burst into**
突然[急に]〜しだす(≒break out in)

□ 0947 **show off**
❶**いいところを見せようとする**、見えを張る(≒put on airs)　❷〜を見せびらかす
图showoff：見せびらかす人、自慢屋

□ 0948 **hold off** (on)
〜を延期する、延ばす、遅らせる(≒delay, postpone)

□ 0949 **rest on** [upon]
(決定などが)**〜にかかっている**、左右される、〜次第である(≒depend on [upon])
图rest：❶(the 〜)残り(の物)　❷休息、休み

□ 0950 **live off**
〜で生計を立てる、〜を頼りに暮らす

□ 0951 **deal in**
〜を扱う、商う、売買する(≒trade in)
图deal：商取引、契約
图dealer：業者、ディーラー

□ 0952 **put off**
❶**〜を不快にする**　❷〜を(…まで)延期する(till [until] ...)(≒postpone, delay)

continued
▼

今日が終われば、本書も残すところあと10日。マラソンに例えるなら、ゴールはわずか6キロほど先。ここからラストスパートをかけよう！

- □ 聞くだけモード　Check 1
- □ しっかりモード　Check 1 ▶ 2
- □ かんぺきモード　Check 1 ▶ 2 ▶ 3

Check 2　Phrase

- □ pass up a chance [an opportunity]（チャンスを見送る）
- □ pass up an offer（申し出を断る）

- □ burst into song [laughter]（突然歌いだす[笑いだす]）

- □ show off to one's friends（友達にいいところを見せようとする）
- □ show off one's talent（才能を見せびらかす）

- □ hold off (on) buying a new car（新しい車を買うのを延期する）

- □ rest on his shoulders（[責任などが]彼の双肩にかかっている）

- □ live off welfare（生活保護で生計を立てる）
- □ live off the land（自給自足の生活をする）

- □ deal in old cars（中古車を売買する）

- □ put other people off（他の人たちを不快にする）
- □ put off the game until tomorrow（その試合を明日まで延期する）

Check 3　Sentence

- □ He passed up the opportunity to go to Rome.（彼はローマに行くチャンスを見送った）

- □ She burst into tears when she received the award.（彼女はその賞を受け取ると突然泣きだした）

- □ He is always showing off to his girlfriend.（彼はいつもガールフレンドに対していいところを見せようとしている）

- □ Many companies are holding off hiring new employees.（多くの企業は新入社員の採用を延期している）

- □ The future of our country rests on new energy technologies.（私たちの国の将来は新しいエネルギー技術にかかっている）

- □ He lives off his pension.（彼は年金で生計を立てている）

- □ The store deals in a variety of home appliances.（その店はさまざまな家電製品を扱っている）

- □ The smell of cigarette smoke always puts me off.（たばこの煙のにおいはいつも私を不快にする）

continued
▼

Day 60

Check 1　Listen))) CD-B25

0953 struggle for
〜のために奮闘[努力]する(≒strive for)
名struggle：❶奮闘　❷(〜を求める)闘争(for 〜)

0954 fill in [out]
〜に必要事項を記入する

0955 yield to
〜に応じる、屈する、譲歩する(≒give in to, give way to, submit to)
名yield：❶利潤、収益、利回り　❷産出[収穫]高

0956 put in
(時間など)を費やす、つぎ込む(≒spend)

0957 sign up for
(署名して)〜に申し込む、参加する
名sign：❶兆候　❷標識
名signature：署名、サイン

0958 drop by [in]
(ちょっと)立ち寄る、ひょっこり訪ねる(≒stop by)

0959 set out
(〜に向けて)出発する(for 〜)(≒depart, leave, set off)

0960 cover up
(事実など)を隠す、秘密にしておく(≒conceal, hide)
名cover-up：隠蔽

Day 59))) CD-B24
Quick Review
答えは右ページ下

- □ 〜を見極める
- □ 〜に向かう
- □ 〜に順応する
- □ 〜から生じる
- □ 〜に衝突する
- □ 〜を軽視する
- □ 〜に入札する
- □ 〜を言い渡す
- □ 現れる
- □ 〜を繰り越す
- □ 〜を控える
- □ 〜を値下げする
- □ 〜を経験する
- □ 〜に援助の手を差し伸べる
- □ 〜に入学する
- □ 〜を終える

Check 2 Phrase	Check 3 Sentence
☐ struggle for market share（市場占有率を求めて奮闘する）	☐ Many airlines are struggling for survival.（多くの航空会社は生き残りのために奮闘している）
☐ fill in an application form（申込用紙に必要事項を記入する） ☐ fill in the blanks（空所に必要事項を記入する）	☐ Please fill in the questionnaire and click the "submit" button.（アンケートに必要事項を記入して、「提出」ボタンをクリックしてください）
☐ yield to requests [demands]（要求に応じる） ☐ yield to temptation（誘惑に屈する）	☐ The management finally yielded to the union's demands.（経営陣は最後には労働組合の要求に応じた）
☐ put in a lot of time and effort（多くの時間と労力を費やす）	☐ We have put in countless hours preparing for the event.（私たちはそのイベントの準備のために数え切れないほどの時間を費やしてきた）
☐ sign up for a workshop（講習会に申し込む）	☐ So far, 33 players have signed up for the tournament.（これまでのところ、33人の選手がそのトーナメントに申し込んでいる）
☐ drop by on one's way home（帰宅途中に立ち寄る）	☐ Please drop by anytime you want.（お好きな時にいつでもお立ち寄りください）
☐ set out for San Francisco（サンフランシスコに向けて出発する）	☐ He set out for Athens yesterday morning.（彼は昨日の朝、アテネに向けて出発した）
☐ cover up one's mistake（失敗を隠す）	☐ The politician tried to cover up the scandal.（その政治家はスキャンダルを隠そうとした）

Day 59 》CD-B24
Quick Review
答えは左ページ下

☐ size up　☐ crash into　☐ turn up　☐ go through
☐ make for　☐ play down　☐ carry over　☐ reach out to
☐ adapt to　☐ bid for　☐ abstain from　☐ enroll in
☐ stem from　☐ hand down　☐ mark down　☐ wrap up

Day 61 動詞句9 「動詞＋A＋前置詞＋B」型1

Check 1 Listen)) CD-B26

0961
donate A **to** B
AをBに寄付[寄贈]する(≒contribute A to B)
图donation：❶(〜への)寄付、寄贈(to 〜)　❷(〜への)寄付金、寄贈品(to 〜)
图donor：❶寄贈者　❷(臓器などの)提供者、ドナー

0962
impose A **on** B
❶**A(税・罰など)をBに課す**、科す、負わす(≒levy A on B)　❷A(意見など)をBに押しつける(≒force A on B)
图imposition：(税などを)課すこと
形imposing：荘厳[壮大]な、堂々とした

0963
accuse A **of** B
❶**AをB(の罪)で訴える**[告発する、告訴する](≒charge A with B, sue A for B)　❷AをB(の理由)で非難する(≒blame A for B, criticize A for B, condemn A for B)(⇔praise A for B：AをBのことで褒める)
图accusation：❶告発、告訴　❷非難

0964
drag A **into** B
AをB(争いなど)に巻き込む、引きずり込む

0965
aim A **at** B
Bを対象にAを行う、A(言葉・行為など)をBに向ける(≒target A at [on] B)
图aim：❶目標、目的　❷狙い
形aimless：当て[目的]のない
副aimlessly：当て[目的]もなく

0966
divert A (away) **from** B
A(注意・批判など)をBからそらす(≒distract A from B)
图diversion：❶注意をそらすもの　❷気分転換、気晴らし

0967
abbreviate A **to** [as] B
AをBに短縮[省略]する(≒shorten A to B)
图abbreviation：(〜の)略語(of [for] 〜)

0968
lure A **into** [to] B
AをBに誘い込む、誘惑する(≒tempt A into B, entice A into B)
图lure：❶(通例the 〜)(〜の)魅力、誘惑(of 〜)　❷おとり；(釣りの)ルアー

continued ▼

今日と明日は、「動詞＋A＋前置詞＋B」型の表現をチェック！　まずはCDでチャンツを聞いて、表現を「耳」からインプットしよう。

☐ 聞くだけモード　Check 1
☐ しっかりモード　Check 1 ▶ 2
☐ かんぺきモード　Check 1 ▶ 2 ▶ 3

Check 2　Phrase

☐ donate $10,000 to the Red Cross(1万ドルを赤十字社へ寄付する)

☐ impose economic sanctions on ~(~に経済制裁を科す)
☐ impose one's ideas on others(自分の考えを他人に押しつける)

☐ accuse the man of theft(その男を窃盗で訴える)
☐ accuse him of lying(うそをついたことで彼を非難する)

☐ drag the country into war(その国を戦争に巻き込む)

☐ aim one's promotion at children(子どもを対象に宣伝活動を行う)
☐ aim one's criticism at ~(~に非難を向ける)

☐ divert attention [suspicion] from ~(~から注意[疑惑の目]をそらす)

☐ be abbreviated to "ASAP"([as soon as possibleは]「ASAP」に短縮される)

☐ lure customers into one's store(客を店に誘い込む)
☐ lure ~ into a trap(~をわなに誘い込む)

Check 3　Sentence

☐ He donated $2,000 to a local charity.(彼は2000ドルを地元の慈善団体に寄付した)

☐ A consumption tax is imposed on almost all goods and services in Japan.(日本ではほぼすべての商品とサービスに消費税が課されている)

☐ The professor was accused of sexual harassment by a female student.(その教授はセクハラで女子学生に訴えられた)

☐ I don't want to be dragged into such an unnecessary debate.(私はそんな無用な議論に巻き込まれたくない)

☐ This advertisement is aimed at young women.(この広告は若い女性を対象にしている)

☐ The government is trying to divert public attention from economic problems.(政府は国民の注目を経済問題からそらそうとしている)

☐ "Electronic mail" is usually abbreviated to "e-mail."(「電子メール」は普通、「Eメール」に短縮される)

☐ The woman was lured into a car, but managed to escape.(その女性は車の中に誘い込まれたが、何とか逃げることができた)

continued ▼

Day 61

Check 1 　Listen 》CD-B26

0969 see A as B
AをBと見なす、考える(≒regard A as B, view A as B, think of A as B, look on A as B)

0970 devote A to B
A(時間など)をB(仕事・目的など)にささげる、充てる(≒dedicate A to B)
名devotion：(〜への)献身、専念(to 〜)
形devoted：献身的な

0971 sue A for B
AをBで訴える、告訴する(≒accuse A of B, charge A with B)
名suit：訴訟

0972 expose A to B
AをB(危険など)にさらす
名exposure：(危険などに)(身を)さらす[さらされる]こと(to 〜)

0973 endear A to B
(性格などが)AをBに好かれるようにする、慕われるようにする
形endearing：かわいらしい

0974 transform A into B
AをBに変ぼう[様変わり、一変]させる(≒change A into B, convert A into B)
名transformation：(〜から／…への)変ぼう、様変わり(from 〜/to ...)

0975 assign A to B
❶AをB(部署など)に配属[任命]する(≒appoint A as [to] B) ❷AをBに割り当てる(≒allocate A to B, allot A to B)
名assignment：❶宿題、研究課題 ❷任務；割り当て

0976 put A through to B
Aの電話をBにつなぐ：A(電話)をBにつなぐ(≒connect A to B)

Day 60 》CD-B25
Quick Review
答えは右ページ下

- □ 〜を見送る
- □ 突然〜しだす
- □ いいところを見せようとする
- □ 〜を延期する
- □ 〜にかかっている
- □ 〜で生計を立てる
- □ 〜を扱う
- □ 〜を不快にする
- □ 〜のために奮闘する
- □ 〜に必要事項を記入する
- □ 〜に応じる
- □ 〜を費やす
- □ 〜に申し込む
- □ 立ち寄る
- □ 出発する
- □ 〜を隠す

Check 2　Phrase

- ☐ see life as a journey(人生を旅と見なす)

- ☐ devote one's energies to ~(〜に精力をささげる)
- ☐ devote more time to one's family(より多くの時間を家族にささげる)

- ☐ sue him for breach of contract(彼を契約違反で訴える)

- ☐ expose one's skin to sunlight(肌を日光にさらす)
- ☐ expose oneself to danger(危険に身をさらす)

- ☐ endear him to his colleagues([性格などが]彼を同僚たちに好かれるようにする)
- ☐ endear oneself to ~(〜に好かれる、慕われる)

- ☐ transform ~ into a different person(〜を別人に変ぼうさせる)

- ☐ be assigned to the sales department(販売部に配属される)
- ☐ assign different roles to each student(異なる役割を各生徒に割り当てる)

- ☐ put the call through to her(その電話を彼女につなぐ)

Check 3　Sentence

- ☐ About 35 percent of Americans see global warming as a very serious problem.(米国人の約35パーセントは地球温暖化を非常に深刻な問題と見なしている)

- ☐ Mother Teresa devoted her life to helping the poor.(マザー・テレサは一生を貧しい人々の救済にささげた)

- ☐ The doctor was sued for medical negligence.(その医者は医療過失で訴えられた)

- ☐ It is estimated that about five million people were exposed to radiation from Chernobyl.(約500万人がチェルノブイリからの放射線にさらされたと推測されている)

- ☐ Her easygoing nature endears her to everyone.(彼女はそののんびりした性格でみんなに好かれている)

- ☐ China's rapid economic growth has transformed China into an economic power.(中国の急速な経済成長は中国を経済大国に変ぼうさせた)

- ☐ She was assigned to the Paris branch.(彼女はパリ支店に配属された)

- ☐ Could you put me through to extension 531, please?(この電話を内線531につないでいただけますか？)

Day 60)) CD-B25
Quick Review
答えは左ページ下

- ☐ pass up
- ☐ burst into
- ☐ show off
- ☐ hold off
- ☐ rest on
- ☐ live off
- ☐ deal in
- ☐ put off
- ☐ struggle for
- ☐ fill in
- ☐ yield to
- ☐ put in
- ☐ sign up for
- ☐ drop by
- ☐ set out
- ☐ cover up

CHAPTER 1
CHAPTER 2
CHAPTER 3
CHAPTER 4
CHAPTER 5
CHAPTER 6
CHAPTER 7
CHAPTER 8
CHAPTER 9
CHAPTER 10

Day 62 動詞句10
「動詞＋A＋前置詞＋B」型2

Check 1　Listen)) CD-B27

□ 0977
view A as B
- **AをBと見なす**、考える(≒regard A as B, see A as B, think of A as B, look on A as B)
- 名view：❶意見、考え　❷考え方、見方　❸眺め、景色

□ 0978
fill A in on B
- **AにBの最新情報を与える**

□ 0979
confine A to B
- ❶**AをB(の範囲)に制限[限定]する**(≒limit A to B, restrict A to B)　❷AをBに閉じ込める、監禁する
- 名confinement：監禁
- 形confined：(場所が)限られた、狭い

□ 0980
trace A (back) to B
- **A(事柄など)をBまでたどる**
- 名trace：痕跡、形跡

□ 0981
adapt A to B
- **AをBに適応[適合、順応]させる**(≒adjust A to B)
- 名adaptation：(〜への)順応、適応(to 〜)
- 形adaptable：(be adaptable to で)〜に順応[適応]できる

□ 0982
prescribe A for B
- **A(薬)をB(病気・人)に処方する**
- 名prescription：処方箋

□ 0983
enroll A in [for] B
- **AをBに入学[入会]させる**
- 名enrollment：❶入学、入会　❷入学[入会]者数

□ 0984
charge A with B
- **AをBで告発する**(≒accuse A of B, sue A for B)
- 名charge：❶料金　❷責任　❸(〜に対する)告発(against 〜)

continued
▼

この型の表現は、Aが主語になって受動態で使われることも多い。今日は9つの表現が受動態で使われている。Check 3でチェック！

- □ 聞くだけモード　Check 1
- □ しっかりモード　Check 1 ▶ 2
- □ かんぺきモード　Check 1 ▶ 2 ▶ 3

Check 2　Phrase

□ view the situation as an emergency（状況を緊急事態と見なす）

□ fill him in on the current situation（彼に現在の状況の最新情報を与える）

□ confine the discussion to one issue（討議を1つの問題に制限する）
□ confine oneself to ～（～に閉じこもる）

□ trace one's family tree (back) to ～（家系図を～までたどる）

□ adapt a product to a specific market（製品を特定の市場に適応させる）
□ adapt oneself to ～（～に順応する）

□ prescribe antibiotics for a sore throat（抗生物質をのどの痛みに処方する）

□ enroll one's child in a private school（子どもを私立学校に入学させる）

□ charge him with murder（彼を殺人罪で告発する）

Check 3　Sentence

□ India is now viewed as a market with a huge potential.（インドは現在では巨大な可能性を持つ市場と見なされている）

□ Can you fill me in on what's going on there?（そこで何が起きているのか私に最新情報を与えてくれますか？）

□ Smoking is confined to designated areas.（喫煙は指定された区域に制限されている）

□ His ancestry can be traced to the 17th century.（彼の祖先は17世紀までたどることができる）

□ Desert plants are adapted to their arid environment.（砂漠の植物は乾燥した環境に適応している）

□ The drug is often prescribed for patients with asthma.（その薬はぜんそくの患者に処方されることが多い）

□ Many parents want to enroll their children in the best universities.（多くの親は子どもを最良の大学に入学させたいと思っている）

□ The mayor was charged with accepting bribes.（その市長は収賄で告発された）

continued
▼

Day 62

Check 1　Listen)) CD-B27

0985 leave A (up) to B
AをBに任せる、委ねる (≒ entrust A to B)

0986 distract A from B
Aの注意をBからそらす、A(注意など)をBからそらす (≒ divert A from B)
名distraction：❶注意をそらすもの　❷集中できないこと　❸気晴らし、娯楽
形distracting：気を散らせる、集中を妨げる

0987 insert A in [into] B
AをBに挿入する、差し込む
名insert：❶折り込み広告　❷挿入物
名insertion：❶挿入　❷書き込み

0988 evict A from B
AをBから立ち退かせる (≒ expel A from B)
名eviction：立ち退き

0989 apologize to A for B
AにBを謝罪する、謝る、わびる
名apology：(〜に対する)謝罪 (for 〜)

0990 put A before B
❶AをBに提出する (≒ submit A to B)　**❷AをBより優先する**

0991 convert A into [to] B
AをBに変える、AをBに変換[転換、改造、改装]する (≒ change A into B, turn A into B)
名conversion：(〜から/…への)変換、転換、改造、改装 (from 〜/to [into] …)

0992 portray A as B
AをBとして描く、描写する (≒ depict A as B, represent A as B)
名portrait：肖像画
名portrayal：描写、記述

Day 61)) CD-B26
Quick Review
答えは右ページ下

□ AをBに寄付する　□ Bを対象にAを行う　□ AをBと見なす　□ AをBに好かれるようにする
□ AをBに課す　□ AをBからそらす　□ AをBにささげる　□ AをBに変ぼうさせる
□ AをBで訴える　□ AをBに短縮する　□ AをBで訴える　□ AをBに配属する
□ AをBに巻き込む　□ AをBに誘い込む　□ AをBにさらす　□ Aの電話をBにつなぐ

Check 2 Phrase

- leave the final decision (up) to him(最終決定を彼に任せる)

- distract him from his studies(彼の注意を勉強からそらす)
- distract attention from ~(~から注意をそらす)

- insert a DVD in one's DVD player(DVDプレーヤーにDVDを挿入する)
- insert the key into the lock(錠に鍵を差し込む)

- evict tenants from ~(テナントを~から立ち退かせる)

- apologize to him for one's lateness(彼に遅れたことを謝る)

- put the report before the council(その報告書を議会に提出する)
- put profit before safety(利益を安全性より優先する)

- convert an attic into a bedroom(屋根裏部屋を寝室に変える)
- convert dollars into euros(ドルをユーロに変える)

- portray women as victims(女性を犠牲者として描く)

Check 3 Sentence

- He leaves all the housework to his wife.(彼はすべての家事を妻に任せている)

- Stop distracting me from my work.(私の注意を仕事からそらすのはやめてください)

- Insert your card in the ATM and enter your four-digit PIN.(ATMにカードを挿入して、4けたの暗証番号を入力してください)

- He was evicted from his apartment for not paying the rent.(彼は家賃を払わなかったためアパートから立ち退かされた)

- You should apologize to her for your thoughtless remarks.(あなたは心ない発言をしたことを彼女に謝罪したほうがいい)

- He put the proposal before the board of directors.(彼はその案を取締役会に提出した)

- The building is going to be converted into a hotel.(その建物はホテルに変えられることになっている)

- The main character in the film is portrayed as a tragic hero.(その映画の主人公は悲劇のヒーローとして描かれている)

CHAPTER 1
CHAPTER 2
CHAPTER 3
CHAPTER 4
CHAPTER 5
CHAPTER 6
CHAPTER 7
CHAPTER 8
CHAPTER 9
CHAPTER 10

Day 61))CD-B26
Quick Review
答えは左ページ下

- donate A to B
- impose A on B
- accuse A of B
- drag A into B
- aim A at B
- divert A from B
- abbreviate A to B
- lure A into B
- see A as B
- devote A to B
- sue A for B
- expose A to B
- endear A to B
- transform A into B
- assign A to B
- put A through to B

Day 63 動詞句11
「動詞＋to do」「動詞＋A＋to do」型

Check 1　Listen 》CD-B28

□ 0993
struggle to do
〜しようと奮闘[努力]する(≒ strive to do)
名struggle：❶奮闘　❷(〜を求める)闘争(for 〜)

□ 0994
yearn to do
〜することを切望する、しきりに〜したがる(≒ long to do, desire to do, aspire to do)
名yearning：(〜に対する)切望(for 〜)

□ 0995
refuse to do
〜することを拒む(≒ decline to do)
名refusal：(〜することの)拒絶、拒否(to do)

□ 0996
choose to do
〜することにする、決める(≒ decide to do)
名choice：❶選択の権利[自由]　❷選択

□ 0997
afford to do
(canを伴って)**〜する**(金銭的な)**余裕がある**
形affordable：(価格などが)手ごろな

□ 0998
strive to do
〜しようと努力する(≒ struggle to do)

□ 0999
aspire to do
〜することを熱望[切望]する(≒ long to do, desire to do, yearn to do)
名aspiration：(〜に対する/…したいという)熱望、切望(to 〜/to do)

□ 1000
vow to do
〜することを誓う(≒ pledge to do, swear to do, promise to do)
名vow：(〜の/…する)誓い、誓約(of 〜/to do)

continued
▼

今日は「動詞＋to do」、「動詞＋A＋to do」型の表現をチェック。後者では、「A」がto doの意味上の主語になることをしっかり押さえよう。

- ☐ 聞くだけモード　Check 1
- ☐ しっかりモード　Check 1 ▶ 2
- ☐ かんぺきモード　Check 1 ▶ 2 ▶ 3

Check 2　Phrase

☐ struggle to succeed（成功を収めようと奮闘する）

☐ yearn to get married（結婚することを切望する）
☐ yearn to be an actor（俳優になることを切望する）

☐ refuse to discuss the matter（その件について話し合うことを拒む）

☐ choose to study abroad（留学することにする）

☐ can't afford to buy a new car（新車を買う余裕がない）

☐ strive to win the prize（その賞を得ようと努力する）
☐ strive to be honest（正直であろうと努力する）

☐ aspire to contribute to world peace（世界平和に貢献することを熱望する）
☐ aspire to be a professional singer（プロの歌手になることを熱望する）

☐ vow to marry her（彼女と結婚することを誓う）
☐ vow never to see him again（彼に二度と会わないことを誓う）

Check 3　Sentence

☐ Many companies are struggling to survive in a fiercely competitive market.（多くの企業は非常に競争の激しい市場で生き残ろうと奮闘している）

☐ He yearns to go back home and be reunited with his family.（彼は家に戻って家族と再会することを切望している）

☐ The prime minister refused to step down.（首相は辞任することを拒んだ）

☐ More and more people are choosing to do their shopping online.（インターネット上で買い物をすることにしている人が増えている）

☐ The number of Chinese people who can afford to travel abroad is growing rapidly.（海外旅行をする余裕のある中国人の数が急速に増えている）

☐ Manufacturers are striving to remain competitive in the global market.（製造業者は世界市場の中で競争力を持ち続けようと努力している）

☐ He aspires to set up his own company.（彼は自分の会社を設立することを熱望している）

☐ He vowed never to drink alcohol again.（彼は二度と酒を飲まないことを誓った）

continued

Day 63

Check 1　Listen)) CD-B28

1001 urge A to do
Aに〜するよう強く勧める、強く促す、説得する(≒persuade A to do, push A to do)
- 名urge：(〜したいという)衝動(to do)
- 形urgent：緊急の、急を要する
- 名urgency：緊急(性)

1002 force A to do
Aに〜するよう強いる(≒compel A to do) ◎force A to do＝force A into doing

1003 encourage A to do
Aに〜するよう勧める、励ます(⇔discourage A from doing：Aに〜するのをやめさせる)
- 名encouragement：激励、奨励、励まし
- 形encouraging：激励の、励みになる

1004 lead A to do
Aに〜させる、〜するよう仕向ける(≒cause A to do, induce A to do, prompt A to do)

1005 motivate A to do
Aを〜する気にさせる、Aに〜する動機を与える(≒stimulate A to do, inspire A to do)
- 名motivation：❶やる気、意欲 ❷動機、動機づけ
- 名motive：動機

1006 authorize A to do
Aに〜する権限[許可]を与える(≒empower A to do)
- 名authority：❶(〜に対する／…する)権力、権限、権威(over 〜/to do) ❷(the 〜ies)当局

1007 tempt A to do
Aの気を引いて〜させる、Aをそそのかして〜する気にさせる(≒entice A to do, induce A to do) ◎tempt A to do＝tempt A into doing
- 名temptation：誘惑、衝動
- 形tempting：心をそそる

1008 push A to do
Aに〜するよう強く求める、強要する(≒urge A to do, press A to do) ◎push A to do＝push A into doing

---

Day 62)) CD-B27
Quick Review
答えは右ページ下

- □ AをBと見なす
- □ AにBの最新情報を与える
- □ AをBに制限する
- □ AをBまでたどる
- □ AをBに適応させる
- □ AをBに処方する
- □ AをBに入学させる
- □ AをBで告発する
- □ AをBに任せる
- □ Aの注意をBからそらす
- □ AをBに挿入する
- □ AをBから立ち退かせる
- □ AにBを謝罪する
- □ AをBに提出する
- □ AをBに変える
- □ AをBとして描く

Check 2 Phrase

- urge him to reconsider his decision（彼に決心を考え直すよう強く勧める）
- force the CEO to resign（そのCEOに辞職するよう強いる）
- encourage children to study English（子どもたちに英語を勉強するよう勧める）
- lead him to believe [understand] ～（彼に～を信じさせる[理解させる]）
- motivate students to study harder（生徒たちをより熱心に勉強する気にさせる）
- authorize the chairperson to make a decision（議長に決定権を与える）
- tempt him to buy a new car（彼の気を引いて新しい車を買わせる）
- push a suspect to confess（容疑者に自白するよう強要する）

Check 3 Sentence

- Her parents urged her to go to the hospital again.（彼女の両親は彼女にもう1度病院に行くよう強く勧めた）
- The company forced its employees to work overtime without pay.（その会社は従業員に無給で残業するよう強いた）
- The government program encourages homeowners to install solar panels.（その政府計画は住宅所有者たちにソーラーパネルを設置するよう勧めている）
- He led her to believe that he was going to marry her.（彼は自分が彼女と結婚するつもりだということを彼女に信じさせた）
- Performance-related pay may motivate employees to work harder.（業績に基づく賃金は従業員たちをより熱心に働く気にさせるかもしれない）
- Police officers are authorized to carry firearms.（警官は銃器を携帯する権限を与えられている）
- TV commercials tempt us to buy and consume things that we don't really need.（テレビコマーシャルは私たちの気を引いてそれほど必要でない物を買わせたり消費させたりする）
- His parents pushed him to take the job.（彼の両親は彼にその仕事に就くよう強く求めた）

Day 62 》CD-B27
Quick Review
答えは左ページ下

- [ ] view A as B
- [ ] fill A in on B
- [ ] confine A to B
- [ ] trace A to B
- [ ] adapt A to B
- [ ] prescribe A for B
- [ ] enroll A in B
- [ ] charge A with B
- [ ] leave A to B
- [ ] distract A from B
- [ ] insert A in B
- [ ] evict A from B
- [ ] apologize to A for B
- [ ] put A before B
- [ ] convert A into B
- [ ] portray A as B

CHAPTER 1
CHAPTER 2
CHAPTER 3
CHAPTER 4
CHAPTER 5
CHAPTER 6
CHAPTER 7
CHAPTER 8
CHAPTER 9
CHAPTER 10

Day 64　動詞句12
「be動詞＋形容詞＋前置詞」型1

Check 1　Listen 》CD-B29

□ 1009
be obsessed with [by]
(考えなど)**にとりつかれている**
名 obsession：強迫観念、異常な執着

□ 1010
be overwhelmed by [with]
～に圧倒される
形 overwhelming：圧倒的な

□ 1011
be vulnerable to
～に弱い、傷つきやすい
名 vulnerability：弱さ、傷つきやすさ

□ 1012
be fascinated by [with]
～に魅了される(≒ be captivated by)
形 fascinating：魅力[魅惑]的な
名 fascination：魅了

□ 1013
be deprived of
～を奪われている
名 deprivation：欠乏、欠如

□ 1014
be compatible with
～と互換性がある
名 compatibility：互換性

□ 1015
be geared to [toward]
～をターゲットにしている、対象としている、～向きである(≒ be targeted at)
名 gear：❶(車などの)(変速)ギア　❷道具、用具　❸装備

□ 1016
be crammed with
～でいっぱい[満杯]である(≒ be filled with, be packed with)

continued
▼

今日と明日は、「be動詞＋形容詞＋前置詞」型の表現をチェック！ まずはCDでチャンツを聞いて、表現を「耳」からインプット！

- ☐ 聞くだけモード　Check 1
- ☐ しっかりモード　Check 1 ▶ 2
- ☐ かんぺきモード　Check 1 ▶ 2 ▶ 3

Check 2　Phrase

☐ be obsessed with money（金にとりつかれている、金の亡者である）

☐ be overwhelmed by the forces of nature（自然の力に圧倒される）

☐ be vulnerable to disease（病気に弱い）
☐ be vulnerable to attack（攻撃を受けやすい）

☐ be fascinated by her beauty（彼女の美しさに魅了される）

☐ be deprived of one's civil rights（公民権を奪われている）

☐ be compatible with a Macintosh computer（[ソフトウエアなどが]マッキントッシュのコンピューターと互換性がある）

☐ books geared to children（子ども向けの本）

☐ a closet crammed with clothes（服でいっぱいのクローゼット）

Check 3　Sentence

☐ He is obsessed with the idea of becoming rich.（彼は金持ちになるという考えにとりつかれている）

☐ We were completely overwhelmed by the beauty of the landscape.（私たちはその景色の美しさに完全に圧倒された）

☐ People are vulnerable to temptation.（人は誘惑に弱い）

☐ As a boy, he was fascinated by astronomy.（少年のころ、彼は天文学に魅了された）

☐ People in that country are deprived of their freedom of speech and expression.（その国の人々は言論と表現の自由を奪われている）

☐ This software is compatible with my new computer.（このソフトウエアは私の新しいコンピューターと互換性がある）

☐ This magazine is geared to women around 40 years of age.（この雑誌は40歳前後の女性をターゲットにしている）

☐ Her bookshelves are crammed with art books.（彼女の本棚は美術書でいっぱいである）

continued
▼

Day 64

Check 1　Listen)) CD-B29

1017 be essential to [for]
〜にとって不可欠である（≒be indispensable to [for], be vital to [for]）
▶ 名essential：（通例〜s）不可欠な物

1018 be skeptical about [of]
〜を疑っている、〜に懐疑的である（≒be dubious about, be suspicious about [of]）
▶ 名skeptic：懐疑論者、疑い深い人
名skepticism：懐疑的な態度

1019 be instrumental in
〜に重要な役割を果たす
▶ 名instrument：❶楽器　❷道具、器具

1020 be preoccupied with
〜のことで頭がいっぱいである、〜に夢中になっている、心を奪われている（≒be absorbed in）
▶ 名preoccupation：（〜への）没頭、夢中（with 〜）

1021 be grateful to
（…のことで）〜に感謝している（for . . .）（≒be thankful to）
▶ 副gratefully：感謝して、喜んで

1022 be susceptible to
❶〜に感染しやすい　❷〜の影響を受けやすい
▶ 名susceptibility：❶感染しやすいこと　❷影響を受けやすいこと

1023 be committed to
〜に打ち込んでいる、傾倒している（≒be dedicated to）
▶ 名commitment：❶（〜の／…するという）約束（to 〜/to do）　❷（〜への）献身（to 〜）

1024 be resistant to
❶〜に抵抗［耐性］がある　❷〜に抵抗する
▶ 動resist：❶〜に抵抗［反抗］する　❷（通例否定文で）〜を我慢する、こらえる
名resistance：❶（〜に対する）抵抗、反抗（to 〜）　❷（〜に対する）抵抗力（to 〜）

Day 63)) CD-B28
Quick Review
答えは右ページ下

- □ 〜しようと奮闘する
- □ 〜することを切望する
- □ 〜することを拒む
- □ 〜することにする
- □ 〜する余裕がある
- □ 〜しようと努力する
- □ 〜することを熱望する
- □ 〜することを誓う
- □ Aに〜するよう強く勧める
- □ Aに〜するよう強いる
- □ Aに〜するよう勧める
- □ Aに〜させる
- □ Aを〜する気にさせる
- □ Aに〜する権限を与える
- □ Aの気を引いて〜させる
- □ Aに〜するよう強く求める

Check 2 Phrase

- ☐ factors essential to success（成功に不可欠な要素）

- ☐ be skeptical about the feasibility of ~（~の実現性を疑っている）

- ☐ be instrumental in founding the organization（その団体の創設に重要な役割を果たす）

- ☐ be preoccupied with one's new boyfriend（新しい彼氏のことで頭がいっぱいである）

- ☐ be grateful to him for his help（彼の助けに感謝している）

- ☐ be susceptible to colds（風邪をひきやすい）
- ☐ be susceptible to flattery（お世辞に弱い）

- ☐ be committed to voluntary work（ボランティア活動に打ち込んでいる）

- ☐ flu virus resistant to drugs（薬に抵抗力のあるインフルエンザ・ウイルス）
- ☐ be resistant to change（変化に抵抗する）

Check 3 Sentence

- ☐ Moderate exercise is essential to good health.（適度な運動は健康に不可欠である）

- ☐ Some analysts were skeptical about Obama's chances of winning the presidency.（オバマが大統領選に勝利する可能性を疑っていたアナリストもいた）

- ☐ Bill Clinton was instrumental in freeing two imprisoned American journalists.（ビル・クリントンは拘束された2人の米国人ジャーナリストの解放に重要な役割を果たした）

- ☐ He was too preoccupied with his own problems to focus on his work.（彼は自分の問題であまりに頭がいっぱいになっていて、仕事に集中できなかった）

- ☐ I am deeply grateful to my parents for their support and encouragement.（私は両親の支援と励ましに深く感謝している）

- ☐ People with diabetes are more susceptible to influenza than people who do not have diabetes.（糖尿病の人は糖尿病でない人よりもインフルエンザに感染しやすい）

- ☐ The charity is committed to improving the quality of life for the poor.（その慈善団体は貧しい人々の生活の質の向上に打ち込んでいる）

- ☐ Some bacteria are resistant to antibiotics.（抗生物質に抵抗力のあるバクテリアもいる）

Day 63 》CD-B28
Quick Review
答えは左ページ下

- ☐ struggle to do
- ☐ yearn to do
- ☐ refuse to do
- ☐ choose to do
- ☐ afford to do
- ☐ strive to do
- ☐ aspire to do
- ☐ vow to do
- ☐ urge A to do
- ☐ force A to do
- ☐ encourage A to do
- ☐ lead A to do
- ☐ motivate A to do
- ☐ authorize A to do
- ☐ tempt A to do
- ☐ push A to do

Day 65 動詞句13 「be動詞＋形容詞＋前置詞」型2

Check 1 Listen)) CD-B30

1025 be ignorant of [about]
〜を知らない
名 ignorance：❶(〜を)知らないこと(of [about] 〜) ❷無知、無学
動 ignore：〜を無視する

1026 be weary of
〜にうんざりしている(≒ be tired of, be sick of, be bored with, be fed up with)

1027 be cluttered with
〜で散らかっている(≒ be littered with)

1028 be oblivious to [of]
〜に気づいていない(≒ be unaware of, be unconscious of)

1029 be acquainted with
❶〜と知り合いである、面識がある ❷〜の知識がある
名 acquaintance：❶知人、知り合い ❷(〜の)知識、心得(with 〜)

1030 be stranded in [on, at]
〜で立ち往生している、〜に取り残されている

1031 be endowed with
(才能など)に恵まれている、〜を生まれながらに持っている(≒ be blessed with)
名 endowment：❶寄付(金) ❷才能、資質

1032 be indifferent to
〜に無関心である(≒ be unconcerned with, be uninterested in)
名 indifference：(〜に対する)無関心(to 〜)

continued
▼

Quick Reviewは使ってる？ 昨日覚えた表現でも、記憶に残っているとは限らない。学習の合間に軽くチェックするだけでも効果は抜群！

- □ 聞くだけモード　Check 1
- □ しっかりモード　Check 1 ▶ 2
- □ かんぺきモード　Check 1 ▶ 2 ▶ 3

Check 2　　Phrase

□ be ignorant of history(歴史を知らない)

□ be weary of one's job(仕事にうんざりしている)

□ be cluttered with toys([部屋などが]おもちゃで散らかっている)

□ be oblivious to danger(危険に気づいていない)

□ get better acquainted with ~(~と親しくなる)
□ be acquainted with classical music(クラシック音楽の知識がある)

□ passengers stranded in the airport(空港に取り残された乗客たち)

□ be endowed with intelligence [beauty](知性[美ぼう]に恵まれている)

□ be indifferent to environmental issues(環境問題に無関心である)

Check 3　　Sentence

□ It is often said that many Americans are ignorant of the world outside of their own country.(多くの米国人は自国以外の世界のことを知らないとよく言われる)

□ She is growing weary of her monotonous life.(彼女は単調な生活にうんざりし始めている)

□ His room was cluttered with dirty clothes.(彼の部屋は汚れた服で散らかっていた)

□ She seemed completely oblivious to my presence.(彼女は私がいることに全く気づいていないようだった)

□ How did you get acquainted with him?(あなたはどのようにして彼と知り合いになったのですか?)

□ More than 100 cars were stranded in two locations due to the blizzard.(猛吹雪のため100台以上の車が2カ所で立ち往生した)

□ She is endowed with musical talent.(彼女は音楽の才能に恵まれている)

□ The majority of young people are indifferent to politics.(若者の大半は政治に無関心だ)

continued
▼

Check 1　Listen))) CD-B30

1033
be concerned about [for]

~を心配している、気にしている(≒be worried about, be anxious about)
▶ 名concern：❶(~についての)心配、懸念、関心(about [over] ~)　❷心配[関心]事
　前concerning：~について、関して

1034
be responsive to

(要求など)にすぐに対応する
▶ 動respond：❶(~に)対応[反応]する(to ~)　❷(~に)応答[返答]する(to ~)
　名response：❶(~に対する)反応、対応(to ~)　❷(~への)返答、回答(to ~)

1035
be credited with

~の功績を認められている
▶ 名credit：❶信用貸し、クレジット　❷(~に対する)称賛、名誉(for ~)　❸履修単位　❹信用、信頼

1036
be prone to

(望ましくないことなど)をしがちである、しやすい、~になりやすい

1037
be engaged in [on]

~に従事している、携わっている(≒be involved in)
▶ 名engagement：❶(~との)婚約(to ~)　❷(会合などの)約束

1038
be comprised of

~で構成されている(≒consist of, be made up of, be composed of)

1039
be intrigued by

~に興味を持つ、好奇心をかき立てられる
▶ 名intrigue：陰謀、策略
　形intriguing：興味[好奇心]をそそる、面白い

1040
be scheduled for

(日時)に予定されている(≒be arranged for)
▶ 名schedule：予定、スケジュール

Day 64))) CD-B29
Quick Review
答えは右ページ下

- □ ~にとりつかれている
- □ ~に圧倒される
- □ ~に弱い
- □ ~に魅了される
- □ ~を奪われている
- □ ~と互換性がある
- □ ~をターゲットにしている
- □ ~でいっぱいである
- □ ~にとって不可欠である
- □ ~を疑っている
- □ ~に重要な役割を果たす
- □ ~のことで頭がいっぱいである
- □ ~に感謝している
- □ ~に打ち込んでいる
- □ ~に感染しやすい
- □ ~に抵抗力がある

Check 2　Phrase

- ☐ be **concerned about** his safety（彼の安否を心配している）
- ☐ be **concerned about** one's appearance（容姿を気にしている）

- ☐ be **responsive to** customers' needs（顧客のニーズにすぐに対応する）

- ☐ be **credited with** the project's success（その事業の成功の功績を認められている）

- ☐ be **prone to** colds（風邪をひきやすい）

- ☐ be **engaged in** cancer research（がんの研究に従事している）

- ☐ be **comprised of** 50 members（[委員会などが]50人の委員で構成されている）

- ☐ be **intrigued by** the article（その記事に興味を持つ）

- ☐ be **scheduled for** Friday morning（[会議などが]金曜日の午前に予定されている）

Check 3　Sentence

- ☐ The survey shows that 60 percent of consumers are **concerned about** the safety of the food they purchase.（その調査によると、消費者の60パーセントは購入する食品の安全性を心配している）

- ☐ Firms must be **responsive to** changes in the market.（企業は市場の変化にすぐに対応しなければならない）

- ☐ Gorbachev is widely **credited with** ending the Cold War.（ゴルバチョフは冷戦を終結させた功績を広く認められている）

- ☐ Human beings are **prone to** error.（人間は間違いを犯しがちだ）

- ☐ Presently, she is **engaged in** volunteer activities.（現在、彼女はボランティア活動に従事している）

- ☐ Australia is **comprised of** six states and two territories.（オーストラリアは6つの州と2つの準州で構成されている）

- ☐ I was **intrigued by** his story.（私は彼の話に興味を持った）

- ☐ The next meeting is **scheduled for** 1 p.m. on September 22.（次の会議は9月22日の午後1時に予定されている）

CHAPTER 1
CHAPTER 2
CHAPTER 3
CHAPTER 4
CHAPTER 5
CHAPTER 6
CHAPTER 7
CHAPTER 8
CHAPTER 9
CHAPTER 10

Day 64　CD-B29
Quick Review
答えは左ページ下

- ☐ be obsessed with
- ☐ be overwhelmed by
- ☐ be vulnerable to
- ☐ be fascinated by
- ☐ be deprived of
- ☐ be compatible with
- ☐ be geared to
- ☐ be crammed with
- ☐ be essential to
- ☐ be skeptical about
- ☐ be instrumental in
- ☐ be preoccupied with
- ☐ be grateful to
- ☐ be susceptible to
- ☐ be committed to
- ☐ be resistant to

Day 66 動詞句14
「be動詞＋形容詞＋to do」型

Check 1　Listen ») CD-B31

□ 1041
be **expected** to do
～すると思われている、予想されている
名expectation：予想、期待

□ 1042
be **reluctant** to do
～したくない、～することに気が進まない(≒ be unwilling to do)
副reluctantly：嫌々ながら、渋々

□ 1043
be **forced** to do
～せざるを得ない、～しなければならない(≒ be compelled to do, be obliged to do)

□ 1044
be **keen** to do
(非常に)**～したがっている**、～することを熱望している(≒ be eager to do, be anxious to do)
副keenly：強く、大いに、熱心に

□ 1045
be **destined** to do
～する運命にある(≒ be fated to do)
名destiny：運命、宿命
名destination：目的地、行き先

□ 1046
be **obliged** to do
～する義務がある、～せざるを得ない、～しなければならない(≒ be forced to do, be compelled to do)
名obligation：(～に対する／…する)義務、責任(to ～/to do)
形obligatory：義務[強制]的な

□ 1047
be **due** to do
～する予定である、～することになっている(≒ be scheduled to do)

□ 1048
be **apt** to do
～しがちである、～しやすい(≒ be likely to do, be liable to do, be inclined to do, tend to do)

continued
▼

今日は、「be動詞＋形容詞＋to do」型の表現をチェック！ まずはCDを聞いて、表現を「耳」からインプット！

- ☐ 聞くだけモード　Check 1
- ☐ しっかりモード　Check 1 ▶ 2
- ☐ かんぺきモード　Check 1 ▶ 2 ▶ 3

Check 2　Phrase

☐ be expected to announce one's resignation（辞任を発表すると思われている）

☐ be reluctant to leave（帰りたくない）

☐ be forced to call off the search due to bad weather（悪天候のため捜索を中止せざるを得ない）

☐ be keen to see her again（もう一度彼女に会いたがっている）

☐ be destined to marry him（彼と結婚する運命にある）

☐ be obliged to do military service（兵役に就く義務がある）
☐ be obliged to apologize to him（彼に謝らなければならない）

☐ be due to be published next week（来週、出版される予定だ）

☐ be apt to be forgetful（忘れっぽい）
☐ be apt to make mistakes（間違いを犯しやすい）

Check 3　Sentence

☐ The world's population is expected to reach nine billion by 2050.（世界の人口は2050年までに90億に達すると思われている）

☐ She seemed reluctant to talk about it.（彼女はそのことについて話したくないようだった）

☐ I was forced to take a taxi because the last train had left.（終電が出てしまったので、私はタクシーに乗らざるを得なかった）

☐ He is keen to start work as soon as possible.（彼はできるだけ早く仕事を始めたがっている）

☐ Barack Obama was destined to be president of the United States.（バラク・オバマは米国大統領になる運命にあった）

☐ Citizens are obliged to pay taxes.（国民は納税する義務がある）

☐ The mall is due to open next month.（そのショッピングセンターは来月オープンする予定だ）

☐ When we fail, we are apt to blame others.（失敗をした時、私たちは他人のせいにしがちだ）

continued
▼

Day 66

Check 1　Listen))) CD-B31

□ 1049
be unlikely to do
〜しそうもない（⇔ be likely to do）
圃unlike：〜と違って

□ 1050
be anxious to do
〜したがっている、〜することを切望している（≒ be eager to do, be keen to do）
名anxiety：❶（〜についての）心配、不安、懸念（about [over] 〜）　❷心配事　❸（〜したいという）熱望、切望（to do）

□ 1051
be hesitant to do
〜するのをためらっている
動hesitate：❶ためらう　❷（hesitate to do で）〜するのをためらう
名hesitation：（〜することの）ためらい、ちゅうちょ（in doing）

□ 1052
be timed to do
〜するようタイミングが合わされている

□ 1053
be entitled to do
〜する権利[資格]がある（≒ be qualified to do）
名entitlement：（受給）資格[権利]

□ 1054
be inclined to do
❶〜したいと思っている（≒ want to do）　❷〜しがちである（≒ be likely to do, be apt to do, be liable to do, tend to do）

□ 1055
be unwilling to do
〜する気がしない、〜したがらない（≒ be reluctant to do）（⇔ be willing to do）
圃unwillingly：嫌々ながら

□ 1056
be projected to do
〜すると予測されている（≒ be predicted to do, be forecast to do）
名project：（大規模な）事業、計画、プロジェクト
名projection：（将来の）見通し、予測

Day 65))) CD-B30　Quick Review　答えは右ページ下

- □ 〜を知らない
- □ 〜にうんざりしている
- □ 〜で散らかっている
- □ 〜に気づいていない
- □ 〜と知り合いである
- □ 〜で立ち往生している
- □ 〜に恵まれている
- □ 〜に無関心である
- □ 〜を心配している
- □ 〜にすぐに対応する
- □ 〜の功績を認められている
- □ 〜をしがちである
- □ 〜に従事している
- □ 〜で構成されている
- □ 〜に興味を持つ
- □ 〜に予定されている

Check 2 Phrase

☐ be unlikely to succeed (成功しそうもない)

☐ be anxious to get a job (就職したがっている)

☐ be hesitant to sign the contract (その契約書にサインするのをためらっている)

☐ be timed to coincide with 〜 (〜と同時になるようタイミングが合わされている)

☐ be entitled to take paid leave (有給休暇を取る権利がある)

☐ be inclined to study abroad (留学したいと思っている)
☐ be inclined to be lazy (怠けがちである)

☐ be unwilling to study (勉強する気がしない)

☐ be projected to fall [decrease, drop] ([売り上げなどが] 下がると予測されている)

Check 3 Sentence

☐ The train is unlikely to arrive on time. (その列車は時間通りに到着しそうもない)

☐ Some employees are not anxious to be promoted to a job with more responsibility. (責任が増える仕事には昇進したがらない従業員もいる)

☐ She is still hesitant to accept his marriage proposal. (彼女は彼のプロポーズを受け入れるのをまだためらっている)

☐ This event was timed to coincide with the play's debut. (このイベントはその劇の初演と同時になるようタイミングが合わされていた)

☐ Every child is entitled to receive education. (すべての子どもは教育を受ける権利がある)

☐ I'm inclined to trust his judgment on this. (私はこの件に関する彼の判断を信頼したいと思っている)

☐ He seemed unwilling to discuss the matter further. (彼はその件についてそれ以上は話し合う気がないようだった)

☐ Unemployment is projected to increase to 6 percent later this year. (失業率は今年中に6パーセントまで上がると予測されている)

CHAPTER 1
CHAPTER 2
CHAPTER 3
CHAPTER 4
CHAPTER 5
CHAPTER 6
CHAPTER 7
CHAPTER 8
CHAPTER 9
CHAPTER 10

Day 65 》CD-B30
Quick Review
答えは左ページ下

☐ be ignorant of
☐ be weary of
☐ be cluttered with
☐ be oblivious to

☐ be acquainted with
☐ be stranded in
☐ be endowed with
☐ be indifferent to

☐ be concerned about
☐ be responsive to
☐ be credited with
☐ be prone to

☐ be engaged in
☐ be comprised of
☐ be intrigued by
☐ be scheduled for

Day 67 動詞句15 その他

Check 1   Listen ») CD-B32

1057 make it
❶(〜に)**到着する**、間に合う(to 〜)(≒arrive) ❷成功する、うまくやる(≒succeed)

1058 catch [get] a glimpse of
〜をちらりと見かける、一目見る(≒catch sight of)
名glimpse：一瞬見る[見える]こと

1059 play a role [part] in
〜で役割を果たす
名role/part：役目

1060 have trouble doing
〜するのに苦労する(≒have a hard time doing)
名trouble：困難

1061 familiarize oneself with
〜に精通する、慣れ親しむ(≒acquaint oneself with)
形familiar：❶(〜に)聞き[見]覚えのある、よく知られた(to 〜) ❷(be familiar withで)〜に精通している
名familiarity：❶(〜に)精通していること(with 〜) ❷親しさ、親密さ

1062 have yet to do
まだ〜していない

1063 give oneself up to
〜に自首する(≒surrender to)

1064 lose sight of
〜を見失う
名sight：見ること、見えること

continued
▼

今日はその他の動詞句をチェック！ そして今日でChapter 8は最後。時間に余裕があったら、章末のReviewにも挑戦しておこう。

- □ 聞くだけモード　Check 1
- □ しっかりモード　Check 1 ▶ 2
- □ かんぺきモード　Check 1 ▶ 2 ▶ 3

Check 2　Phrase

□ make it to the next appointment（次の約束に間に合う）
□ make it big（大成功する）

□ catch a fleeting glimpse of ～（～をほんのちらりと見かける）

□ play a major [key] role in ～（～で大きな[重要な]役割を果たす）

□ have trouble getting up early（早起きするのに苦労する）
□ have no trouble doing ～（～するのに苦労しない）

□ familiarize oneself with the computer system（コンピューターシステムに精通する）

□ have yet to finish one's work（仕事をまだ終えていない）

□ give oneself up to the police（警察に自首する）

□ lose sight of him in the dark（暗闇の中で彼を見失う）

Check 3　Sentence

□ If you hurry, you can make it there on time.（急げば、時間通りにそこに到着できますよ）

□ I caught a glimpse of her in the crowd.（私は人込みの中で彼女をちらりと見かけた）

□ Norway has played a central role in maintaining peace in troubled areas.（ノルウェーは紛争地域での平和の維持において中心的な役割を果たしてきた）

□ He was laid off and had trouble finding a new job.（彼は解雇されて、新しい仕事を見つけるのに苦労した）

□ It took me a while to familiarize myself with the software.（そのソフトウエアに精通するのに私は少し時間がかかった）

□ Congress has yet to pass the budget.（議会は予算案をまだ可決していない）

□ After a few days on the run, the suspect gave himself up to the police.（数日間逃亡した後、その容疑者は警察に自首した）

□ I lost sight of her in the crowd.（私は人込みの中で彼女を見失った）

continued
▼

Day 67

Check 1　Listen))) CD-B32

1065 get on one's nerves
〜をいらいらさせる、〜の神経に障る (≒ irritate, annoy)
名nerve：神経

1066 make ends meet
収入内でやりくりする、収支を合わせる

1067 foot the bill
(〜の)費用を負担する、経費[支払い]を持つ (for 〜)
名bill：請求書

1068 immerse oneself in
〜に没頭[熱中]する
名immersion：(〜への)没頭、熱中 (in 〜)

1069 have had enough of
〜にはもううんざりだ、〜はもうたくさんだ

1070 give rise to
〜を引き起こす、生じさせる (≒ cause)

1071 make way for
(新たなものなど)に場所を明け渡す (≒ give way to)

1072 have a hard time doing
〜するのに苦労する、〜するのは大変である (≒ have trouble doing)

Day 66))) CD-B31 Quick Review　答えは右ページ下

- □ 〜すると思われている
- □ 〜したくない
- □ 〜せざるを得ない
- □ 〜したがっている
- □ 〜する運命にある
- □ 〜する義務がある
- □ 〜する予定である
- □ 〜しがちである
- □ 〜しそうもない
- □ 〜したがっている
- □ 〜するのをためらっている
- □ 〜するようタイミングが合わされている
- □ 〜する権利がある
- □ 〜したいと思っている
- □ 〜する気がしない
- □ 〜すると予測されている

Check 2 Phrase

- ☐ **get on his [her] nerves**（彼[彼女]をいらいらさせる）

- ☐ **make ends meet** on one's salary（給料の範囲内でやりくりする）

- ☐ agree to **foot the bill**（費用を負担することに同意する）

- ☐ **immerse oneself in** one's work（仕事に没頭する）
- ☐ **immerse oneself in** conversation（会話に夢中になる）

- ☐ **have had enough of** her complaints（彼女の愚痴にはもううんざりだ）

- ☐ **give rise to** anxiety（不安を引き起こす）

- ☐ be demolished to **make way for** a new road（[建物などが]新しい道に場所を明け渡すために壊される）

- ☐ **have a hard time** getting to sleep（寝つくのに苦労する）

Check 3 Sentence

- ☐ His incessant chatter really **gets on my nerves.**（彼の絶え間のないおしゃべりは私を本当にいらいらさせる）

- ☐ Many families find it difficult to **make ends meet.**（多くの家庭は収入内でやりくりするのが難しいと思っている）

- ☐ Taxpayers will have to **foot the bill** for the bank's bailout.（納税者はその銀行の救済措置の費用を負担しなければならなくなるだろう）

- ☐ He has **immersed himself in** the study of international politics.（彼は国際政治の研究に没頭している）

- ☐ I've **had enough of** this hot weather.（この暑い天気にはもううんざりだ）

- ☐ Cloning has **given rise to** numerous ethical problems.（クローン技術は多くの倫理的問題を引き起こしている）

- ☐ The old building was pulled down to **make way for** a new 30-story building.（その古いビルは30階建ての新しいビルに場所を明け渡すために解体された）

- ☐ She **had a hard time** adjusting to her new environment.（彼女は新しい環境に慣れるのに苦労した）

Day 66))CD-B31
Quick Review
答えは左ページ下

- ☐ be expected to do
- ☐ be reluctant to do
- ☐ be forced to do
- ☐ be keen to do
- ☐ be destined to do
- ☐ be obliged to do
- ☐ be due to do
- ☐ be apt to do
- ☐ be unlikely to do
- ☐ be anxious to do
- ☐ be hesitant to do
- ☐ be timed to do
- ☐ be entitled to do
- ☐ be inclined to do
- ☐ be unwilling to do
- ☐ be projected to do

CHAPTER 1
CHAPTER 2
CHAPTER 3
CHAPTER 4
CHAPTER 5
CHAPTER 6
CHAPTER 7
CHAPTER 8
CHAPTER 9
CHAPTER 10

Chapter 8 Review

左ページの(1)～(20)の動詞句の同意熟語・類義熟語（または同意語・類義語）（≒）、反意熟語（⇔）を右ページのA～Tから選び、カッコの中に答えを書き込もう。意味が分からないときは、見出し番号を参照して復習しておこう（答えは右ページ下）。

- [ ] (1) figure out (0833) ≒は? (　　)
- [ ] (2) touch on (0847) ≒は? (　　)
- [ ] (3) cut down (0853) ≒は? (　　)
- [ ] (4) put forward (0871) ≒は? (　　)
- [ ] (5) bring down (0890) ≒は? (　　)
- [ ] (6) act up (0896) ≒は? (　　)
- [ ] (7) pass out (0897) ≒は? (　　)
- [ ] (8) bounce back (0910) ≒は? (　　)
- [ ] (9) show up (0915) ≒は? (　　)
- [ ] (10) wrap up (0944) ≒は? (　　)
- [ ] (11) show off (0947) ≒は? (　　)
- [ ] (12) accuse A of B (0963) ≒は? (　　)
- [ ] (13) put A through to B (0976) ≒は? (　　)
- [ ] (14) confine A to B (0979) ≒は? (　　)
- [ ] (15) distract A from B (0986) ≒は? (　　)
- [ ] (16) encourage A to do (1003) ⇔は? (　　)
- [ ] (17) be geared to (1015) ≒は? (　　)
- [ ] (18) be oblivious to (1028) ≒は? (　　)
- [ ] (19) be destined to do (1045) ≒は? (　　)
- [ ] (20) give rise to (1070) ≒は? (　　)

A. misbehave
B. cause
C. reduce
D. connect A to B
E. overturn
F. be unaware of
G. finish
H. mention
I. divert A from B
J. faint
K. appear
L. limit A to B
M. submit
N. be fated to do
O. discourage A from doing
P. put on airs
Q. understand
R. be targeted at
S. charge A with B
T. recover

【解答】 (1) Q (2) H (3) C (4) M (5) E (6) A (7) J (8) T (9) K (10) G
(11) P (12) S (13) D (14) L (15) I (16) O (17) R (18) F (19) N (20) B

CHAPTER 9

形容詞句・副詞句：
頻出32

Chapter 9では、数語で1つの形容詞・副詞の働きをする熟語をチェック。どれも「固まり」で覚えるのがポイントです。本書も残りわずか3日。ゴールを目指して、ラストスパートをかけましょう！

Day 68【形容詞句・副詞句1】
▶ 314
Day 69【形容詞句・副詞句2】
▶ 318
Chapter 9 Review
▶ 322

こんなの出るかも

In that country there are hundreds of species (　　　) of extinction, many of which are marine species.

1　at risk　2　at large
4　at most　4　at best

▼

答えはDay 68でチェック！

Day 68　形容詞句・副詞句1

Check 1　Listen 》CD-B33

□ 1073　in [by] contrast
(〜とは)**対照的に**(to [with] 〜)
名contrast：対照、相違

□ 1074　at risk
トビラの問題の正解はコレ！
(〜の)**危険にさらされて**(of [from] 〜)(≒in danger, in peril, in jeopardy, at stake)
名risk：危険

□ 1075　for the time being
当分の間、差し当たり、ここしばらく(≒for the meantime)

□ 1076　in the meantime
その間(に)、それまで(の間)、一方で(≒meanwhile, in the meanwhile)　❶for the meantimeは「差し当たり」

□ 1077　in jeopardy
危険にさらされて(≒in danger, at risk, in peril, at stake)
名jeopardy：危険
動jeopardize：〜を危険にさらす

□ 1078　in turn
❶**今度は**、次には、それが原因で　❷順番に(≒one after the other, one by one)
名turn：順番

□ 1079　in retrospect
今になって思えば、振り返ってみると(≒looking back)
名retrospection：回顧、追想
形retrospective：回顧的な
名retrospective：(画家などの)回顧展

□ 1080　around the clock
24時間[昼夜]ぶっ通しで
形around-the-clock：24時間連続[営業、態勢]の

continued
▼

Chapter 9では、2日をかけて頻出の形容詞句・副詞句32をチェック！ まずはCDでチャンツを聞いて、表現を「耳」からインプットしよう。

☐ 聞くだけモード　Check 1
☐ しっかりモード　Check 1 ▶ 2
☐ かんぺきモード　Check 1 ▶ 2 ▶ 3

Check 2　Phrase

☐ in marked [stark] contrast to ~(~とは全く対照的に)

☐ put ~ at risk(~を危険にさらす)
☐ be at risk of bankruptcy(倒産の危機にさらされている)

☐ stay in Canada for the time being(当分の間、カナダに滞在する)

☐ ~, and in the meantime . . .(~で、その間に…)
☐ In the meantime, take care of yourself.(それまで、お元気で)

☐ put ~ in jeopardy(~を危険にさらす)

☐ in turn lead to ~(今度は~につながる)
☐ call out students' names in turn(生徒の名前を順番に呼ぶ)

☐ ~, but in retrospect . . .(~だが、今になって思えば…だ)

☐ work around the clock(24時間ぶっ通しで働く)

Check 3　Sentence

☐ He is introverted, but in contrast, his younger brother is extroverted.(彼は内向的だが、対照的に彼の弟は外向的だ)

☐ Thousands of lives are at risk because of serious medicine shortages.(深刻な医薬品不足のため数千人の命が危険にさらされている)

☐ The global economy will remain unstable for the time being.(世界経済は当分の間、不安定なままだろう)

☐ I lost contact with him for years, and in the meantime he had got married.(私は彼と数年間、音信不通だったが、その間に彼は結婚していた)

☐ The current economic crisis has put the company's survival in jeopardy.(現在の経済危機がその会社の存続を危険にさらしている)

☐ Higher prices in turn lead to lower consumption.(価格の高騰は今度は消費の低迷につながる)

☐ In retrospect, his decision was the right one.(今になって思えば、彼の決断は正しいものだった)

☐ Most convenience stores are open around the clock.(ほとんどのコンビニエンスストアは24時間営業だ)

continued
▼

Check 1　Listen))) CD-B33

1081 on the spot
❶ **すぐに** (≒immediately, at once, right away)　❷ その場[現場]に[で]
- 名 spot：場所
- 動 spot：〜を見つけ出す

1082 as follows
次[以下]**の通り**
- 形 following：(the 〜)次の
- 前 following：〜の後で[に]、〜に引き続いて

1083 the other way around
(順序などが)**逆で**、反対で

1084 all but
ほとんど (≒almost)

1085 in unison
❶ **一斉**[同時]**に** (≒simultaneously, at the same time, at once, together)　❷ 一致して、調和して
- 名 unison：斉唱、斉奏

1086 at one's disposal
(人)**が自由に使える**、〜の思いのままの
- 名 disposal：処分、処理

1087 nothing more than
〜にすぎない (≒only, no more than)

1088 as such
❶ **厳密な意味で**(の)、真の意味における　❷ それ自体

Day 67))) CD-B32
Quick Review
答えは右ページ下

- □ 到着する
- □ 〜をちらりと見かける
- □ 〜で役割を果たす
- □ 〜するのに苦労する
- □ 〜に精通する
- □ まだ〜していない
- □ 〜に自首する
- □ 〜を見失う
- □ 〜をいらいらさせる
- □ 収入内でやりくりする
- □ 費用を負担する
- □ 〜に没頭する
- □ 〜にはもううんざりだ
- □ 〜を引き起こす
- □ 〜に場所を明け渡す
- □ 〜するのに苦労する

Check 2　Phrase

- ☐ **make a decision on the spot**（すぐに決定する）
- ☐ **arrest ~ on the spot**（~を現行犯逮捕する）

- ☐ **The results are as follows:** ~.（結果は次の通り。~）

- ☐ **~, not the other way around.**（~であって、その逆ではない）

- ☐ **be all but impossible**（ほとんど不可能である）

- ☐ **sing the national anthem in unison**（国歌を斉唱する）
- ☐ **work in unison**（一致協力して働く）

- ☐ **money at his disposal**（彼が自由に使える金）

- ☐ **be nothing more than a fool**（愚か者にすぎない）

- ☐ **not mean ~ as such**（厳密な意味で~を意味するものではない）
- ☐ **be not afraid of death as such**（死それ自体を恐れているのではない）

Check 3　Sentence

- ☐ **A witness to the accident called an ambulance on the spot.**（その事故の目撃者はすぐに救急車を呼んだ）

- ☐ **The winners are as follows: Smith, Walker, and Brown.**（受賞者は次の通りです。スミス、ウォーカー、そしてブラウン）

- ☐ **She proposed to me, not the other way around.**（彼女が私にプロポーズしたのであって、その逆ではない）

- ☐ **The game was all but over when we arrived.**（私たちが到着したころには、その試合はほとんど終わっていた）

- ☐ **The demonstrators shouted slogans in unison as they marched down the streets.**（デモ参加者たちは通りを練り歩きながらスローガンを一斉に叫んだ）

- ☐ **She has sufficient time at her disposal.**（彼女には自由に使える時間が十分にある）

- ☐ **The movie is nothing more than an average comedy.**（その映画は並の喜劇にすぎない）

- ☐ **The company does not have an environmental strategy as such.**（その会社には厳密な意味での環境戦略はない）

Day 67 》CD-B32
Quick Review
答えは左ページ下

- ☐ make it
- ☐ catch a glimpse of
- ☐ play a role in
- ☐ have trouble doing
- ☐ familiarize oneself with
- ☐ have yet to do
- ☐ give oneself up to
- ☐ lose sight of
- ☐ get on one's nerves
- ☐ make ends meet
- ☐ foot the bill
- ☐ immerse oneself in
- ☐ have had enough of
- ☐ give rise to
- ☐ make way for
- ☐ have a hard time doing

Day 69　形容詞句・副詞句2

Check 1　Listen ») CD-B34

1089 in a row
❶連続して (≒ consecutively, successively, in succession)　❷(横)1列に
图 row：(横に並んだ)列

1090 on display
展示[陳列]されて (≒ on show)
图 display：展示、陳列

1091 at all costs [any cost]
どんな犠牲を払っても、どんなことがあっても
图 cost：犠牲

1092 in shape
体調がよくて、好調で (⇔ out of shape)
图 shape：状態、調子

1093 for sure
はっきりと、確実に、ちゃんと (≒ definitely, surely, certainly)
形 sure：確実な、はっきりしている

1094 on paper
❶理論上は (≒ in theory, theoretically)　❷紙に書いて、書面で

1095 in short
手短に言うと、要するに (≒ briefly, in brief, in a word)

1096 out of date
❶時代遅れの、古い (≒ old-fashioned, outdated) (⇔ up to date)　❷賞味期限の切れた、期限切れの　➕限定用法の場合は通例out-of-dateとハイフンつきでつづられる

continued
▼

今日でChapter 9は最後！ 時間に余裕があったら、章末のReviewにも挑戦しておこう。もう忘れてしまった表現もあるのでは?!

- ☐ 聞くだけモード　Check 1
- ☐ しっかりモード　Check 1 ▶ 2
- ☐ かんぺきモード　Check 1 ▶ 2 ▶ 3

Check 2　Phrase

- ☐ win [lose] five times in a row (5連勝[連敗]する)
- ☐ stand in a row (横1列に並ぶ)

- ☐ put ~ on display (~を展示する)
- ☐ go on display (展示される)

- ☐ avoid war at all costs (どんな犠牲を払っても戦争を回避する)

- ☐ get in shape (体調がよくなる)
- ☐ keep [stay] in shape (体調を維持する)

- ☐ One thing is for sure: ~. (1つだけはっきりしているのは~ということだ)

- ☐ be possible on paper (理論上は可能である)
- ☐ put ~ (down) on paper (~を書き留める)

- ☐ In short, the situation is ~. (手短に言うと、状況は~だ)

- ☐ out-of-date technology (時代遅れの技術)
- ☐ out-of-date food (賞味期限の切れた食品)

Check 3　Sentence

- ☐ It has been sunny for five days in a row. (5日間連続して晴天が続いている)

- ☐ Please do not touch the objects on display. (展示品には手を触れないでください)

- ☐ He was determined to succeed at all costs. (彼はどんな犠牲を払っても成功しようと決意していた)

- ☐ She has been in great shape recently. (彼女は最近、体調がとてもいい)

- ☐ Nobody knows for sure what is causing global warming. (何が地球温暖化を引き起こしているのか誰もはっきりとは分かっていない)

- ☐ The idea certainly looks good on paper. (その考えは理論上は確かによさそうだ)

- ☐ In short, the movie was mediocre. (手短に言うと、その映画はよくも悪くもなかった)

- ☐ His views are hopelessly out of date. (彼の考え方はどうしようもないほど時代遅れだ)

continued ▼

Day 69

Check 1 Listen)) CD-B34

1097 at stake
危険にさらされて(≒in danger, at risk, in peril, in jeopardy)
名stake：賭け

1098 on the blink
(機械などが)故障して、調子が悪い(≒broken, out of order)
名blink：まばたき

1099 far from
〜には程遠い、決して〜でない
形far：遠い

1100 in person
(代理人でなく)自分で、自ら、本人が(直接に)(≒personally)
名person：人

1101 on the rise
(物価などが)増加傾向で、上昇中で(≒on the increase)
名rise：増加、上昇

1102 down [along] the line
この先、いつか、そのうち

1103 on the market
売りに出されて、市販されて(≒on sale)
名market：(通例the 〜)市場

1104 from scratch
ゼロ[最初]から
名scratch：引っかき傷

Day 68)) CD-B33
Quick Review
答えは右ページ下

- □ 対照的に
- □ 危険にさらされて
- □ 当分の間
- □ その間
- □ 危険にさらされて
- □ 今度は
- □ 今になって思えば
- □ 24時間ぶっ通しで
- □ すぐに
- □ 次の通り
- □ 逆で
- □ ほとんど
- □ 一斉に
- □ 〜が自由に使える
- □ 〜にすぎない
- □ 厳密な意味で

Check 2　Phrase	Check 3　Sentence
☐ put hundreds of lives at stake（何百人もの命を危険にさらす）	☐ The future of the company is at stake.（その会社の将来が危険にさらされている）
☐ go on the blink（故障する）	☐ My computer went on the blink again.（私のコンピューターがまた故障した）
☐ be far from over（終わりには程遠い） ☐ Far from it!（[返答として]とんでもない！）	☐ The results were far from satisfactory.（その結果は満足には程遠かった）
☐ go there in person（自分でそこに行く） ☐ apply in person（本人が直接申し込む）	☐ You should apologize to her in person.（あなたは自分で彼女に謝ったほうがいい）
☐ be steadily on the rise（徐々に増加している）	☐ Global food prices are on the rise.（世界の食糧価格は増加傾向にある）
☐ somewhere down the line（この先いつか、いつかある時点で）	☐ Somewhere down the line, you'll have to decide what is best for you.（この先いつか、あなたは自分にとって何が最適かを決めなければならないだろう）
☐ put ~ on the market（~を売りに出す） ☐ come on the market（売りに出される）	☐ The hotel came on the market last month.（そのホテルは先月、売りに出された）
☐ build the firm from scratch（ゼロから会社を築く） ☐ start again from scratch（最初からやり直す）	☐ I started to learn Spanish from scratch.（私はスペイン語をゼロから習い始めた）

Day 68))) CD-B33
Quick Review
答えは左ページ下

☐ in contrast　☐ in jeopardy　☐ on the spot　☐ in unison
☐ at risk　☐ in turn　☐ as follows　☐ at one's disposal
☐ for the time being　☐ in retrospect　☐ the other way around　☐ nothing more than
☐ in the meantime　☐ around the clock　☐ all but　☐ as such

CHAPTER 1
CHAPTER 2
CHAPTER 3
CHAPTER 4
CHAPTER 5
CHAPTER 6
CHAPTER 7
CHAPTER 8
CHAPTER 9
CHAPTER 10

Chapter 9 Review

左ページの(1)〜(16)の形容詞句・副詞句の同意熟語・類義熟語（または同意語・類義語）(≒)、反意熟語（⇔）を右ページのA〜Pから選び、カッコの中に答えを書き込もう。意味が分からないときは、見出し番号を参照して復習しておこう（答えは右ページ下）。

- ☐ (1) at risk (1074) ≒は? (　　)
- ☐ (2) for the time being (1075) ≒は? (　　)
- ☐ (3) in retrospect (1079) ≒は? (　　)
- ☐ (4) all but (1084) ≒は? (　　)
- ☐ (5) in unison (1085) ≒は? (　　)
- ☐ (6) nothing more than (1087) ≒は? (　　)
- ☐ (7) in a row (1089) ≒は? (　　)
- ☐ (8) on display (1090) ≒は? (　　)
- ☐ (9) for sure (1093) ≒は? (　　)
- ☐ (10) on paper (1094) ≒は? (　　)
- ☐ (11) in short (1095) ≒は? (　　)
- ☐ (12) out of date (1096) ⇔は? (　　)
- ☐ (13) on the blink (1098) ≒は? (　　)
- ☐ (14) in person (1100) ≒は? (　　)
- ☐ (15) on the rise (1101) ≒は? (　　)
- ☐ (16) on the market (1103) ≒は? (　　)

A. in theory
B. on show
C. looking back
D. personally
E. in danger
F. only
G. briefly
H. almost
I. out of order
J. for the meantime
K. up to date
L. consecutively
M. definitely
N. simultaneously
O. on sale
P. on the increase

【解答】(1) E (2) J (3) C (4) H (5) N (6) F (7) L (8) B (9) M (10) A (11) G (12) K (13) I (14) D (15) P (16) O

CHAPTER 10

群前置詞：頻出16

Chapter 10では、群前置詞をマスター。ここでも、「数語で1つの前置詞」といった具合に「固まり」で覚えることが大切です。残りはたった1日。英検準1級合格は、目前です！

Day 70【群前置詞】
▶ 326
Chapter 10 Review
▶ 330

こんなの出るかも

At the time, the cost of the project was calculated at $33 million (　　　) the current projected cost of $56 million.

1　in terms of　　2　apart from
3　with regard to　4　compared to

▼
答えはDay 70でチェック！

Day 70　群前置詞

Check 1　Listen 》CD-B35

1105 as a token of
〜の印として
名token：印、証し

1106 in favor of
〜を支持して、〜に賛成で（≒ on the side of）
名favor：支持、賛成

1107 due to
〜が原因で、〜のために（≒ because of, owing to, on account of）

1108 in terms of
〜の点で[から]、〜に関して
名term：用語、表現

1109 up to
（数量などを示して）〜まで

1110 in the vicinity of
〜の近く[付近]に[で]
名vicinity：付近、近辺

1111 compared to [with]
トビラの問題の正解はコレ！
〜と比べると、比較すると（≒ in comparison to [with]）
動compare：〜を（…と）比較する（with [to] …）
名comparison：（〜との）比較（with 〜）
副comparatively：比較的

1112 on the verge of
〜の寸前[間際]で、今にも〜しようとして（≒ on the brink of）
名verge：寸前、間際

continued
▼

Chapter 10では、頻出の群前置詞をチェック。
そして、本書も今日で最終！ ここまで学習を
続けてくれて、本当にありがとう！

- □ 聞くだけモード　Check 1
- □ しっかりモード　Check 1 ▶ 2
- □ かんぺきモード　Check 1 ▶ 2 ▶ 3

Check 2　　Phrase

□ as a token of one's appreciation [friendship]（感謝［友情］の印として）

□ be in favor of the Democratic Party（［米国の］民主党を支持している）
□ be all in favor of ～（～を強く支持している）

□ be postponed due to snow（雪のため延期される）
□ due largely to ～（主に～が原因で）

□ in terms of money（お金の点で）
□ explain ～ in terms of ...（…の点から～を説明する）

□ can carry up to 40 passengers（［バスなどが］40人まで乗客を乗せることができる）
□ up to now（今まで）

□ in the vicinity of the station（駅の近くに）
□ in the immediate vicinity of ～（～のすぐ近くに）

□ compared to the previous year（前年と比べると）

□ be on the verge of bankruptcy（倒産寸前である）
□ be on the verge of tears（今にも泣きだしそうである）

Check 3　　Sentence

□ Please accept this wine as a small token of my appreciation.（ささやかな感謝の印として、このワインをお受け取りください）

□ According to the poll, approximately 50 percent are in favor of constitutional revision.（その世論調査によると、約50パーセントが憲法改正を支持している）

□ The project was canceled due to lack of funding.（そのプロジェクトは資金不足が原因で中止になった）

□ He is satisfied with his current job in terms of salary.（彼は給与の点では現在の仕事に満足している）

□ The temperature will go up to 38 degrees Celsius today.（今日は気温が摂氏38度まで上がるだろう）

□ Over 100 demonstrators gathered in the vicinity of the US Embassy.（100人を超えるデモ参加者たちが米国大使館の近くに集まった）

□ The crime rate in Japan is low compared to other industrialized countries.（日本の犯罪率は他の先進工業国と比べると低い）

□ Polar bears are on the verge of extinction.（ホッキョクグマは絶滅寸前である）

continued ▼

Day 70

Check 1　Listen)) CD-B35

1113 in response to
〜に応えて、応じて
名 response：応答

1114 as opposed to
〜とは対照的に、違って（≒ in contrast to [with]）
動 oppose：〜に反対する
名 opposition：（〜に対する）反対（to 〜）
副 opposite：〜の向かいに
形 opposite：❶ 正反対の、逆の　❷ 反対側の

1115 on behalf of
〜に代わって、〜の代理として、〜を代表して（≒ in place of, instead of）

1116 in the event of
〜の場合には（≒ in case of）
名 event：出来事

1117 for all
〜にもかかわらず（≒ despite, in spite of）

1118 in the face of
（困難など）に直面して

1119 regardless of
〜に関係なく、かかわらず（≒ irrespective of）
副 regardless：ともかく、何があっても

1120 in need of
〜を必要として
名 need：必要（性）

Day 69)) CD-B34
Quick Review
答えは右ページ下

- □ 連続して
- □ 展示されて
- □ どんな犠牲を払っても
- □ 体調がよくて
- □ はっきりと
- □ 理論上は
- □ 手短に言うと
- □ 時代遅れの
- □ 危険にさらされて
- □ 故障して
- □ 〜には程遠い
- □ 自分で
- □ 増加傾向で
- □ この先
- □ 売りに出されて
- □ ゼロから

Check 2 — Phrase

- ☐ **in response to** public opinion(世論に応えて)

- ☐ favor the rich **as opposed to** the poor(貧困層とは対照的に富裕層を優遇する)
- ☐ **as opposed to** ~ (in) the previous year(前年の~とは対照的に)

- ☐ **on behalf of** one's client(依頼人に代わって)
- ☐ **on behalf of** the company(会社を代表して)

- ☐ **in the event of** an emergency(緊急の場合には)

- ☐ **for all** the advances in science(科学の進歩にもかかわらず)

- ☐ **in the face of** danger [adversity](危険[逆境]に直面して)

- ☐ **regardless of** race, religion, or gender(人種、宗教、性別に関係なく)
- ☐ **regardless of** the weather(天候に関係なく)

- ☐ patients **in need of** urgent medical care(緊急の治療を必要としている患者たち)

Check 3 — Sentence

- ☐ The product was developed **in response to** customer feedback.(その製品は顧客の意見に応えて開発された)

- ☐ The annual net profit grew only 1.2 percent, **as opposed to** 5.7 percent the previous year.(年間の純利益は、前年の5.7パーセントとは対照的に、1.2パーセントしか伸びなかった)

- ☐ He attended the meeting **on behalf of** his boss.(彼は上司に代わってその会議に出席した)

- ☐ **In the event of** fire, call 911 immediately.(火事の場合には、すぐに911に電話してください)❶911は米国で警察・消防署・救急車を呼び出すための緊急電話番号

- ☐ **For all** his faults, she still loves him.(彼の欠点にもかかわらず、彼女はいまだに彼を愛している)

- ☐ He showed courage **in the face of** fear.(彼は恐怖に直面しても勇気を見せた)

- ☐ The tennis club welcomes new members **regardless of** age or experience.(そのテニスクラブでは年齢や経験に関係なく新規会員を歓迎している)

- ☐ My car is **in need of** repair.(私の車は修理が必要だ)

Day 69 》CD-B34
Quick Review
答えは左ページ下

- ☐ in a row
- ☐ on display
- ☐ at all costs
- ☐ in shape
- ☐ for sure
- ☐ on paper
- ☐ in short
- ☐ out of date
- ☐ at stake
- ☐ on the blink
- ☐ far from
- ☐ in person
- ☐ on the rise
- ☐ down the line
- ☐ on the market
- ☐ from scratch

CHAPTER 10

Chapter 10 Review

左ページの(1)～(9)の群前置詞の同意熟語・類義熟語（≒）を右ページのA～Iから選び、カッコの中に答えを書き込もう。意味が分からないときは、見出し番号を参照して復習しておこう（答えは右ページ下）。

- □ (1) in favor of (1106) ≒は? (   )
- □ (2) due to (1107) ≒は? (   )
- □ (3) compared to (1111) ≒は? (   )
- □ (4) on the verge of (1112) ≒は? (   )
- □ (5) as opposed to (1114) ≒は? (   )
- □ (6) on behalf of (1115) ≒は? (   )
- □ (7) in the event of (1116) ≒は? (   )
- □ (8) for all (1117) ≒は? (   )
- □ (9) regardless of (1119) ≒は? (   )

Day 70))) CD-B35
Quick Review
答えは右ページ下

- □ ～の印として
- □ ～を支持して
- □ ～が原因で
- □ ～の点で
- □ ～まで
- □ ～の近くに
- □ ～と比べると
- □ ～の寸前で
- □ ～に応えて
- □ ～とは対照的に
- □ ～に代わって
- □ ～の場合には
- □ ～にもかかわらず
- □ ～に直面して
- □ ～に関係なく
- □ ～を必要として

A. in comparison to
B. in case of
C. in contrast to
D. on the side of
E. in spite of
F. on the brink of
G. irrespective of
H. on account of
I. in place of

【解答】(1) D (2) H (3) A (4) F (5) C (6) I (7) B (8) E (9) G

Day 70)) CD-B35
Quick Review
答えは左ページ下

- as a token of
- in favor of
- due to
- in terms of
- up to
- in the vicinity of
- compared to
- on the verge of
- in response to
- as opposed to
- on behalf of
- in the event of
- for all
- in the face of
- regardless of
- in need of

ねぇねぇ、どれくらい覚えてる？
Hey, how many do you remember?

Index

*見出しとして掲載されている単語・熟語は赤字、それ以外のものは黒字で示されています。それぞれの語の右側にある数字は、見出し番号を表しています。赤字の番号は、見出しとなっている番号を示します。意味が分かった単語・熟語を2回に分けて数え、各ページ下のチェックボックスにその数を書き込みましょう。

Index

A

- [ ] a diversity of 0368
- [ ] a lot 0822
- [ ] a lot of 0725
- [ ] a mass of 0316
- [ ] abandon 0650, 0755
- [ ] **abandoned** 0755
- [ ] abandonment 0755
- [ ] abate 0865
- [ ] abbreviate A as B 0967
- [ ] **abbreviate A to B** 0967
- [ ] abbreviated 0550
- [ ] abbreviation 0967
- [ ] abide by 0877
- [ ] ability 0039, 0090
- [ ] abolish 0555, 0650
- [ ] **abolition** 0555
- [ ] about 0821
- [ ] abridged 0550
- [ ] abrupt 0825
- [ ] **abruptly** 0825
- [ ] **absorb** 0232
- [ ] absorbing 0232
- [ ] absorption 0232
- [ ] **abstain from** 0939
- [ ] abstinence 0939
- [ ] **abstract** 0798, 0550
- [ ] abstraction 0798
- [ ] absurd 0756
- [ ] **abuse** 0419
- [ ] **accelerate** 0284
- [ ] acceleration 0284
- [ ] accelerator 0284
- [ ] accept 0172, 0191, 0210, 0594, 0659
- [ ] acceptance 0172
- [ ] access 0737
- [ ] **accessible** 0737
- [ ] accident 0439, 0466, 0567
- [ ] **accommodate** 0210
- [ ] accommodate to 0931
- [ ] accommodating 0210
- [ ] accommodation 0210
- [ ] **accompany** 0598, 0536, 0611
- [ ] accomplished 0348
- [ ] accomplishment 0449, 0551
- [ ] accord 0466
- [ ] account 0885
- [ ] **account for** 0885
- [ ] accountant 0885
- [ ] accounting 0885
- [ ] **accumulate** 0212
- [ ] accumulation 0212
- [ ] accusation 0963
- [ ] **accuse A of B** 0963, 0971, 0984
- [ ] achieve 0449
- [ ] **achievement** 0449
- [ ] **acknowledge** 0594
- [ ] acknowledgment 0112, 0517, 0594
- [ ] acquaint oneself with 1061
- [ ] acquaintance 1029
- [ ] acquire 0205, 0696
- [ ] acquittal 0143
- [ ] **act up** 0896
- [ ] **activate** 0668, 0843
- [ ] active 0326, 0668, 0710
- [ ] **activist** 0576
- [ ] activity 0576, 0668
- [ ] acumen 0457
- [ ] **acute** 0333, 0296
- [ ] **adapt A to B** 0981
- [ ] **adapt to** 0931
- [ ] adaptable 0699, 0931, 0981
- [ ] adaptation 0489, 0931, 0981
- [ ] addict 0041
- [ ] addicted 0041
- [ ] **addiction** 0041
- [ ] addictive 0041
- [ ] **additive** 0539
- [ ] address 0584
- [ ] **adhere to** 0877, 0841
- [ ] adherence 0877
- [ ] adherent 0877
- [ ] **adjacent** 0753, 0735
- [ ] **adjoin** 0735
- [ ] **adjoining** 0735, 0753
- [ ] adjourn 0140
- [ ] adjournment 0140
- [ ] adjust A to B 0981
- [ ] adjust to 0931
- [ ] **administer** 0684, 0031, 0670
- [ ] **administration** 0031, 0516, 0684
- [ ] administrative 0031, 0684
- [ ] admirable 0717
- [ ] **admiration** 0425, 0520
- [ ] admire 0425, 0520
- [ ] admired 0385
- [ ] admirer 0425
- [ ] admission 0517
- [ ] admit 0590, 0594
- [ ] adolescence 0528
- [ ] **adolescent** 0528
- [ ] adopt 0191, 0628
- [ ] adult 0175
- [ ] advance 0443, 0691, 0855
- [ ] **advanced** 0691
- [ ] advantage 0061
- [ ] advantageous 0697
- [ ] adversary 0158, 0365
- [ ] **adverse** 0365, 0320
- [ ] advertise 0121
- [ ] advertisement 0121
- [ ] **advertising** 0121, 0037
- [ ] advocacy 0189
- [ ] **advocate** 0189
- [ ] **afford to do** 0997
- [ ] affordable 0997
- [ ] aggravate 0636
- [ ] agree to 0172
- [ ] agreement 0033, 0172, 0466, 0562
- [ ] **agricultural** 0328

どれだけチェックできた？ 1 ☐ 2 ☐

☐ agriculture 0328	☐ analysis 0583	☐ approval 0112, 0114, 0172
☐ aim 0122, 0524, 0819, 0965	☐ analyst 0583	☐ approve 0114, 0172, 0236
☐ **aim A at B** 0965, 0819	☐ analytical 0583	☐ **approximate** 0760, 0821
☐ aim at 0819	☐ **analyze** 0583	☐ **approximately** 0821, 0760
☐ aim to do 0819	☐ **anatomy** 0070	☐ approximation 0021
☐ aimless 0819, 0965	☐ anguish 0410	☐ **aptitude** 0453
☐ **aimlessly** 0819, 0965	☐ annihilate 0884	☐ arbitrary 0327
☐ air 0085, 0633	☐ annoy 1065	☐ archaeological 0152
☐ **alert** 0064	☐ annoyance 0166	☐ **archaeologist** 0152
☐ **all but** 1084	☐ annual 0813	☐ archaeology 0152
☐ all-around 0698	☐ **annually** 0813	☐ **architect** 0564
☐ alleviate 0264	☐ annul 0660	☐ architectural 0564
☐ **alliance** 0507	☐ anonymously 0816	☐ architecture 0564
☐ allocate A to B 0975	☐ answer 0054	☐ **archive** 0126
☐ allocation 0164, 0485	☐ **anticipate** 0221	☐ arduous 0757, 0770
☐ allot A to B 0975	☐ anticipation 0221	☐ arguable 0389
☐ allotment 0485	☐ anxiety 1050	☐ argue 0025
☐ allow 0019, 0285, 0659	☐ anxious 0366	☐ **argument** 0025, 0009, 0095
☐ **allow for** 0899	☐ **apologize to A for B** 0989	☐ arise from 0932
☐ allowance 0899	☐ apology 0989	☐ around 0821
☐ all-purpose 0698	☐ apparatus 0584	☐ **around the clock** 1080
☐ ally 0507	☐ apparent 0805	☐ around-the-clock 1080
☐ ally oneself to 0507	☐ **apparently** 0805	☐ arouse 0239
☐ ally oneself with 0507	☐ appeal 0020	☐ arrange 0608
☐ almost 0811, 1084	☐ appear 0249, 0805, 0915, 0937	☐ arrest 0205
☐ along the line 1102	☐ appearance 0805	☐ arrive 0915, 0937, 1057
☐ **alter** 0203, 0220, 0441	☐ appease 0193	☐ artefact 0402
☐ alteration 0203, 0441, 0489	☐ appendix 0468	☐ **articulate** 0297
☐ alternate 0007	☐ applause 0422, 0425	☐ articulation 0297
☐ **alternative** 0007	☐ **applicant** 0445, 0110, 0141	☐ **artifact** 0402
☐ altogether 0308	☐ **application** 0110, 0445	☐ as a result 0812
☐ always 0826	☐ apply 0110, 0445	☐ **as a token of** 1105
☐ amalgamate 0259	☐ apply A to B 0110, 0445	☐ **as follows** 1082
☐ amass 0212	☐ apply for 0110, 0445	☐ **as opposed to** 1114
☐ amazing 0344, 0800	☐ apply to 0110, 0445	☐ **as such** 1088
☐ ambience 0085	☐ appoint 0218	☐ ask 0020, 0889
☐ ambiguity 0728	☐ appoint A as B 0975	☐ aspect 0165
☐ **ambiguous** 0728	☐ appoint A to B 0975	☐ aspiration 0999
☐ ambiguously 0728	☐ appraisal 0174	☐ **aspire to do** 0999, 0994
☐ **amenity** 0173	☐ appraise 0288, 0635, 0929	☐ **assemble** 0663, 0548, 0585, 0839
☐ **amicable** 0319	☐ **appropriate** 0340, 0799	☐ **assembly** 0548, 0553, 0663
☐ amplifier 0653	☐ appropriately 0340	
☐ **amplify** 0653		

どれだけチェックできた？ 1 ☐ 2 ☐

☐ assent to	0172	
☐ assert	0621	
☐ **assess**	**0635**, 0288, 0929	
☐ assessment	0174, 0635	
☐ asset	0008, 0559	
☐ assign	0164	
☐ **assign A to B**	**0975**, 0164	
☐ assign A to do	0164	
☐ **assignment**	0157, **0975**	
☐ associate	0157, 0407	
☐ associate A with B	0157	
☐ **association**	0157, 0420, 0507	
☐ astonish	0641	
☐ astonishing	0344	
☐ **at all costs**	**1091**	
☐ at all times	0826	
☐ at any cost	1091	
☐ at first	0815	
☐ at first hand	0823	
☐ at once	1081, 1085	
☐ **at one's disposal**	**1086**	
☐ **at risk**	**1074**, 1077, 1097	
☐ **at stake**	**1097**, 1074, 1077	
☐ at the beginning	0815	
☐ at the same time	1085	
☐ at times	0824	
☐ **atmosphere**	**0085**	
☐ atmospheric	0085	
☐ atom	0149	
☐ attainment	0449	
☐ attend	0839	
☐ attendant	0536	
☐ attitude	0119	
☐ austerity	0547	
☐ **authentic**	0743, 0313, 0370	
☐ authenticity	0743	
☐ author	0499	
☐ authority	1006	
☐ authorization	0114	
☐ authorize	0114	
☐ **authorize A to do**	**1006**	
☐ authorized	0700	

☐ available	0737	
☐ average	0361, 0777	
☐ avert	0612	
☐ avoid	0646	
☐ award	0590	
☐ aware	0448	
☐ **awareness**	**0448**	

B

☐ baby	0505	
☐ back	0189, 0236	
☐ **back down**	**0864**	
☐ **backbone**	**0099**	
☐ backer	0189	
☐ background	0471	
☐ **balance**	0490, **0515**	
☐ balanced	0490	
☐ **ballot**	**0169**	
☐ **ban**	**0019**, 0285	
☐ ban A from doing	0019, 0285	
☐ banish	0100	
☐ banishment	0100	
☐ **bank on**	**0928**, 0850	
☐ bank upon	0850, 0928	
☐ **bankrupt**	**0712**	
☐ bankruptcy	0712	
☐ bare	0294	
☐ **barely**	**0820**	
☐ bargain	0608	
☐ **barren**	**0391**, 0709	
☐ barrier	0003, 0525	
☐ basket	0607	
☐ be absorbed in	0232, 1020	
☐ **be acquainted with**	**1029**	
☐ be adaptable to	0931, 0981	
☐ be anxious about	1033	
☐ **be anxious to do**	**1050**, 1044	
☐ **be apt to do**	**1048**, 1054	
☐ be arranged for	1040	
☐ be associated with	0157	
☐ be aware of	0448	

☐ be blessed with	1031	
☐ be bored with	1026	
☐ be captivated by	1012	
☐ **be cluttered with**	**1027**	
☐ **be committed to**	**1023**	
☐ **be compatible with**	**1014**	
☐ be compelled to do	1043, 1046	
☐ be composed of	1038	
☐ **be comprised of**	**1038**	
☐ **be concerned about**	**1033**	
☐ be concerned for	1033	
☐ be consistent with	0014	
☐ **be crammed with**	**1016**	
☐ **be credited with**	**1035**	
☐ be dedicated to	0745, 1023	
☐ be depressed about	0146	
☐ be depressed over	0146	
☐ **be deprived of**	**1013**	
☐ **be destined to do**	**1045**	
☐ be dubious about	1018	
☐ **be due to do**	**1047**	
☐ be eager to do	1044, 1050	
☐ **be endowed with**	**1031**	
☐ **be engaged in**	**1037**	
☐ be engaged on	1037	
☐ **be entitled to do**	**1053**	
☐ be envious of	0379	
☐ be equal to	0088	
☐ be essential for	1017	
☐ **be essential to**	**1017**	
☐ **be expected to do**	**1041**	
☐ be familiar with	1061	
☐ **be fascinated by**	**1012**	
☐ be fascinated with	1012	
☐ be fated to do	1045	
☐ be fed up with	1026	
☐ be filled with	1016	
☐ **be forced to do**	**1043**, 1046	
☐ be forecast to do	1056	
☐ **be geared to**	**1015**	

☐ be geared toward 1015	☐ be relieved to do 0264	☐ **beneficial** 0697
☐ **be grateful to** 1021	☐ **be reluctant to do**	☐ benefit 0089, 0697
☐ **be hesitant to do** 1051	1042, 1055	☐ benefit by 0697
☐ be ignorant about	☐ **be resistant to** 1024	☐ benefit from 0697
0549, 1025	☐ **be responsive to** 1034	☐ **betray** 0596
☐ **be ignorant of**	☐ **be scheduled for** 1040	☐ betrayal 0596
1025, 0549	☐ be scheduled to do 1047	☐ betrayer 0596
☐ be impressed by 0729	☐ be sick of 1026	☐ bid 0935
☐ be impressed with 0729	☐ be sited in 0029	☐ **bid for** 0935
☐ **be inclined to do**	☐ **be skeptical about**	☐ bidder 0935
1054, 1048	1018	☐ bill 1067
☐ **be indifferent to** 1032	☐ be skeptical of 1018	☐ bind 0722
☐ be indispensable for 1017	☐ be stranded at 1030	☐ bind A to do 0722
☐ be indispensable to 1017	☐ **be stranded in** 1030	☐ **binding** 0722
☐ **be instrumental in**	☐ be stranded on 1030	☐ bitter 0393
1019	☐ be subject to 0404, 0788	☐ **bizarre** 0349, 0740
☐ **be intrigued by** 1039	☐ **be susceptible to** 1022	☐ black out 0897
☐ be involved in 1037	☐ be suspicious about 1018	☐ blame 0197
☐ **be keen to do**	☐ be suspicious of 1018	☐ blame A for B 0963
1044, 1050	☐ be targeted at 1015	☐ blameless 0358
☐ be liable to do 1048, 1054	☐ be thankful to 1021	☐ blaze 0260
☐ be likely to do	☐ **be timed to do** 1052	☐ **bleak** 0294, 0773
0065, 1048, 1049, 1054	☐ be tired of 1026	☐ blend 0254
☐ be littered with 1027	☐ be unaware of 1028	☐ blink 1098
☐ be located in 0029	☐ be unconcerned with	☐ **blunder** 0145
☐ be made up of 1038	1032	☐ **boast** 0269
☐ **be obliged to do**	☐ be unconscious of 1028	☐ boastful 0742
1046, 1043	☐ be uninterested in 1032	☐ book 0069
☐ be oblivious of 1028	☐ **be unlikely to do** 1049	☐ booklet 0561
☐ **be oblivious to** 1028	☐ **be unwilling to do**	☐ **boost** 0177
☐ be obsessed by 1009	1055, 1042	☐ border 0534
☐ **be obsessed with** 1009	☐ be vital for 1017	☐ boss 0542
☐ **be overwhelmed by**	☐ be vital to 1017	☐ **bounce back** 0910
1010	☐ **be vulnerable to** 1011	☐ **boundary** 0534
☐ be overwhelmed with	☐ **be weary of** 1026	☐ brag 0269
1010	☐ be willing to do 1055	☐ breach 0463
☐ be packed with 1016	☐ be worried about 1033	☐ break 0140
☐ be predicted to do 1056	☐ bear 0275, 0659	☐ **break out** 0874, 0032
☐ **be preoccupied with**	☐ because of 1107	☐ break out in 0946
1020	☐ beg for 0266	☐ break up 0535, 0630
☐ be privileged to do 0089	☐ begin 0287, 0911, 0923	☐ **breakthrough** 0443
☐ **be projected to do** 1056	☐ being 0132	☐ breathtaking 0399
☐ **be prone to** 1036	☐ belief 0143	☐ **breed** 0079
☐ be qualified to do 1053	☐ believable 0400	☐ breeder 0079
☐ be reconciled with 0586	☐ belonging 0559	☐ breeding 0079

どれだけチェックできた？ 1 ☐ 2 ☐

☐ bribery	0506	
☐ briefly	1095	
☐ bright	0710	
☐ **bring down**	**0890**	
☐ bring up	0628	
☐ **brisk**	**0299**	
☐ broad	0298	
☐ broadcast	0633	
☐ **brochure**	**0561**	
☐ broke	0712	
☐ broken	1098	
☐ **browse**	**0183**	
☐ browse through	0886	
☐ browser	0183	
☐ brush	0687	
☐ **brush up**	**0867**	
☐ brush up on	0867	
☐ brutal	0346, 0364	
☐ **budget**	**0035**	
☐ budgetary	0035	
☐ bully	0922	
☐ **bump into**	**0919**	
☐ burglary	0444	
☐ burst	0260	
☐ **burst into**	**0946**	
☐ business	0494, 0560	
☐ busy	0299	
☐ butcher	0666	
☐ by contrast	1073	

C

☐ calamity	0483	
☐ calculate	0849	
☐ calm	0130, 0351	
☐ calm down	0193, 0913	
☐ cancel	0625	
☐ candid	0776	
☐ candidacy	0141	
☐ **candidate**	**0141**, 0445	
☐ capability	0039, 0090	
☐ capacious	0298	
☐ **capacity**	**0090**	
☐ **capital**	**0046**, 0008	
☐ capitalism	0046	
☐ capitalist	0046	

☐ **capsize**	**0274**
☐ captive	0106, 0205
☐ **captivity**	**0106**
☐ **capture**	**0205**
☐ carbon	0462
☐ **carbon dioxide**	**0462**
☐ careful	0300, 0690, 0741
☐ carefulness	0118
☐ carry	0667
☐ carry forward	0938
☐ carry out	0238
☐ **carry over**	**0938**
☐ carryover	0938
☐ **catastrophe**	**0483**
☐ catastrophic	0483
☐ catch	0205
☐ **catch a glimpse of**	1058
☐ catch sight of	1058
☐ **catch up on**	**0881**
☐ catch up with	0881
☐ categorize	0615
☐ cause	
0079, 0148, 0184, 0239,	
0454, 0589, 0925, 1070	
☐ cause A to do	1004
☐ caution	0508, 0741
☐ caution A about B	0741
☐ caution A against B	0741
☐ caution A to do	0741
☐ **cautious**	**0741**
☐ **cease**	**0688**, 0323
☐ **ceaseless**	**0323**, 0688
☐ ceaselessly	0323, 0688
☐ **celebrity**	**0417**, 0571
☐ **cell phone**	**0115**
☐ cellphone	0115
☐ cellular phone	0115
☐ censure	0197
☐ center	0127
☐ century	0159
☐ certain	0360
☐ certainly	0801, 1093
☐ certificate	0578
☐ certified	0578, 0732

☐ **certify**	**0578**
☐ chance	0065, 0466
☐ change	
0203, 0220, 0441, 0489	
☐ change A into B	
0974, 0991	
☐ changeable	0382
☐ chaos	0352
☐ **chaotic**	**0352**
☐ characteristic	0049
☐ charge	0681, 0984
☐ **charge A with B**	
0984, 0963, 0971	
☐ **charitable**	**0751**
☐ charity	0751
☐ chase	0500
☐ check	0230
☐ **cherish**	**0267**
☐ chief	0771
☐ child	0566
☐ **chip in**	**0842**
☐ choice	0007, 0996
☐ choose	0924
☐ **choose to do**	**0996**
☐ **chronic** **0296**, 0303, 0333
☐ chronically	0296
☐ **chronological**	**0292**
☐ chronologically	0292
☐ circulate	0012, 0254
☐ **circulation**	**0012**
☐ circumspection	0118
☐ **circumstance**	
0459, 0471	
☐ citation	0053, 0643
☐ **cite**	**0643**, 0053
☐ citizen	0027
☐ civil	0331
☐ claim	0621
☐ **clarify**	**0228**
☐ clarity	0228
☐ clash	0059, 0415
☐ clasp	0252
☐ classification	0615, 0775
☐ **classified**	
0775, 0388, 0615	

☐ **classify**	0615, 0775
☐ **clause**	0057
☐ clean	0687
☐ clear	0297, 0693, 0781, 0791, 0918
☐ **clear up**	0872
☐ **cling to**	0857
☐ closeness	0437
☐ **clue**	0428
☐ clutch	0252
☐ clutter up	0675
☐ coarse	0790
☐ **coauthor**	0499
☐ co-author	0499
☐ cohere	0708
☐ coherence	0708
☐ **coherent**	0708
☐ coherently	0708
☐ coincide	0466
☐ coincide with	0466
☐ **coincidence**	0466
☐ coincidental	0466
☐ cold	0294
☐ **collaborate**	0658, 0895
☐ collaboration	0658
☐ collaborator	0658
☐ **colleague**	0407
☐ collect	0212, 0663
☐ collide	0059
☐ **collide with**	0894, 0059, 0933
☐ **collision**	0059, 0894
☐ come	0915
☐ come across	0182, 0919
☐ come around	0870
☐ **come down with**	0860
☐ **come to**	0870, 0610
☐ **come up with**	0838
☐ comfort	0530
☐ comfortable	0784
☐ command	0656
☐ **commemorate**	0605
☐ commemoration	0605
☐ commemorative	0605
☐ **commence**	0287
☐ commencement	0287
☐ commend	0717
☐ **commendable**	0717
☐ commendation	0010, 0717
☐ commitment	1023
☐ committed	0745
☐ **commodity**	0478
☐ common	0361, 0754
☐ commotion	0117
☐ communicate	0667
☐ communication	0113
☐ **commute**	0026
☐ commuter	0026
☐ company	0494, 0560
☐ **comparable**	0731
☐ comparatively	0731, 0807, 1111
☐ compare	0731, 1111
☐ **compared to**	1111
☐ compared with	1111
☐ comparison	0731, 1111
☐ **compassion**	0452
☐ compatibility	1014
☐ compatible	0341
☐ compel	0338
☐ compel A to do	0338, 1002
☐ compensate	0018
☐ compensate A for B	0018
☐ compensate for	0018
☐ **compensation**	0018
☐ compete	0398
☐ **competence**	0039
☐ competent	0039
☐ competition	0080, 0398
☐ **competitive**	0398
☐ competitor	0158, 0398
☐ compilation	0187
☐ **compile**	0187
☐ complain	0280, 0580
☐ complaint	0280
☐ complement	0051
☐ complementary	0778
☐ complete	0551, 0772
☐ completely	0551
☐ **completion**	0551
☐ **complex**	0156, 0537, 0694
☐ **complexity**	0537, 0156
☐ compliant	0397
☐ complicate	0694
☐ **complicated**	0694, 0156
☐ complication	0694
☐ **compliment**	0051, 0778
☐ **complimentary**	0778, 0051
☐ comply with	0877
☐ **component**	0436, 0098
☐ composition	0153
☐ **composure**	0130
☐ comprehend	0252, 0304
☐ comprehensible	0297, 0304
☐ comprehension	0252, 0304
☐ **comprehensive**	0304, 0295, 0308, 0347
☐ **compromise**	0216, 0155
☐ **compulsory**	0338, 0334
☐ **conceal**	0671, 0200, 0277, 0279, 0960
☐ concealment	0671
☐ concede	0155
☐ **conceivable**	0764
☐ conceive	0185, 0613, 0764
☐ concentrate on	0834
☐ concern	1033
☐ concerning	1033
☐ **concession**	0155
☐ conclude	0944
☐ conclusive	0695
☐ concrete	0798
☐ **condemn**	0197
☐ condemn A for B	0963
☐ condition	0103, 0343, 0459, 0471

☐ **conditional** 0343	0726, 0068, 0247, 0314	☐ contract 0195
☐ **condolence** 0066	☐ **conserve**	☐ contract out 0685
☐ confederation 0507	0247, 0068, 0726	☐ contraction 0503
☐ confess 0517	☐ consider 0300, 0758, 0899	☐ **contradict** 0600
☐ confess to 0517	☐ **considerable**	☐ contradiction 0600
☐ **confession** 0517	0758, 0371	☐ contradictory 0600
☐ **confide in** 0906	☐ considerably 0758	☐ contrast 1073
☐ confidence 0143	☐ considerate 0386	☐ contribute 0401, 0842
☐ **confidential** 0388, 0775	☐ consideration 0758	☐ contribute A to B
☐ confidentiality 0388	☐ consist of 1038	0401, 0961
☐ confidentially 0388	☐ **consistency** 0014	☐ **contribute to** 0844, 0401
☐ **confine A to B** 0979	☐ consistent 0014	☐ **contribution** 0401, 0844
☐ confined 0979	☐ **consolation** 0530	☐ control 0096, 0601, 0657
☐ confinement 0106, 0979	☐ console 0530	☐ controversial
☐ confirm 0230, 0578	☐ conspicuous 0787	0095, 0389, 0704
☐ confiscate 0225, 0579	☐ conspiracy 0071, 0084	☐ **controversy** 0095, 0009
☐ **conflict**	☐ constant 0323, 0774	☐ **convene** 0585
0030, 0009, 0144, 0415	☐ constituent 0436	☐ convention 0394, 0585
☐ conflicting 0341	☐ constitution 0153	☐ **conventional** 0394
☐ **confront**	☐ construct 0663	☐ **conversion** 0489, 0991
0609, 0182, 0415	☐ construction 0548	☐ convert 0489
☐ **confrontation**	☐ consume 0495	☐ **convert A into B**
0415, 0609	☐ consumer 0495	0991, 0489, 0974
☐ confused 0733	☐ **consumption** 0495	☐ convert A to B 0489, 0991
☐ confusion 0017	☐ contagion 0001, 0701	☐ **convey** 0667, 0633
☐ congested 0024	☐ **contagious** 0701, 0716	☐ conveyance 0067, 0667
☐ **congestion** 0024	☐ contaminant 0226, 0513	☐ convict 0143
☐ congress 0548	☐ **contaminate**	☐ convict A of B 0143
☐ connect A to B 0976	0226, 0513, 0680	☐ **conviction** 0143
☐ connection 0420	☐ **contamination**	☐ convoy 0611
☐ conquest 0047	0513, 0076, 0226	☐ cooperate 0658, 0895
☐ consciousness 0448	☐ **contend** 0621	☐ **cope with** 0836, 0621
☐ **consecutive** 0374	☐ contend for 0621	☐ copy 0215, 0235, 0258
☐ consecutively 0374, 1089	☐ contend with 0621	☐ core 0127
☐ **consensus** 0033, 0172	☐ contender 0621	☐ cornerstone 0099
☐ **consent** 0172, 0033	☐ content 0480	☐ corporation 0494, 0560
☐ consent to 0033, 0172	☐ content oneself 0480	☐ correlate 0420
☐ **consequence**	☐ contention 0621	☐ **correlation** 0420
0148, 0161, 0812	☐ **contentment** 0480	☐ correspond 0113
☐ consequent 0148, 0812	☐ **context** 0471	☐ correspond to 0113
☐ **consequently**	☐ contingent 0343	☐ correspond with 0113
0812, 0148	☐ continual 0323, 0774	☐ **correspondence** 0113
☐ **conservation**	☐ continue	☐ correspondent 0113
0068, 0247, 0726	0206, 0275, 0855, 0861	☐ **corrupt** 0706, 0506
☐ **conservative**	☐ continuous 0323, 0774	☐ **corruption** 0506, 0706

☐ cosmetic	0153	
☐ **cosmopolitan**	0315	
☐ cosset	0257	
☐ cost		
0035, 0055, 0689, 1091		
☐ **costly**	0689, 0487	
☐ count	0786	
☐ **count on**	0850, 0928	
☐ count upon	0850, 0928	
☐ counterfeit	0370	
☐ **counterpart**	0120, 0357	
☐ **countless**	0786	
☐ coupon	0469	
☐ **courteous**	0331	
☐ courteously	0331	
☐ courtesy	0331	
☐ cover	0074	
☐ **cover up**	0960	
☐ **coverage**	0074	
☐ cover-up	0960	
☐ co-worker	0407	
☐ **cozy**	0784	
☐ crack	0048	
☐ crafty	0375	
☐ crash	0059	
☐ **crash into**	0933, 0894	
☐ crave	0442	
☐ **craving**	0442	
☐ create	0184	
☐ **credibility**	0167, 0400	
☐ **credible**		
0400, 0167, 0761, 0800		
☐ credit	1035	
☐ credulous	0345	
☐ **crisis**	0569	
☐ **critic**	0043	
☐ critical	0043, 0569, 0702	
☐ criticism	0043	
☐ criticize	0043, 0197, 0852	
☐ criticize A for B	0963	
☐ **crucial** 0702, 0291, 0695		
☐ crucially	0702	
☐ crude	0790	
☐ cuddle	0191	
☐ **cultivate**	0192	
☐ cultivated	0192	
☐ cultivation	0192	
☐ cunning	0375	
☐ **curator**	0543	
☐ **curb**	0603, 0657	
☐ cure	0087, 0137	
☐ **currency**	0522	
☐ current	0522	
☐ currently	0522	
☐ cut	0599	
☐ **cut back**	0876, 0853	
☐ cut back on	0876	
☐ **cut down**	0853, 0876	
☐ cut down on	0853	
☐ cutback	0135, 0876	

D

☐ damage 0216, 0591, 0655		
☐ danger	0563	
☐ dangerous	0336, 0692	
☐ deal	0951	
☐ **deal in**	0951	
☐ deal with		
0584, 0621, 0836		
☐ dealer	0951	
☐ dearth	0541	
☐ **debatable**	0389	
☐ debate		
0009, 0025, 0095, 0389		
☐ debris	0567	
☐ **debt**	0101	
☐ debtor	0101	
☐ **decade**	0159	
☐ decadence	0506	
☐ **decay**	0199, 0669	
☐ deceit	0432, 0574	
☐ deceive	0384, 0432	
☐ decelerate	0284	
☐ decency	0362	
☐ **decent**	0362	
☐ decently	0362	
☐ **deception**		
0432, 0384, 0574		
☐ **deceptive**	0384, 0432	
☐ decide	0695	

☐ decide to do	0996	
☐ deciding	0695	
☐ decision	0695	
☐ **decisive**		
0695, 0356, 0702		
☐ decline	0945	
☐ decline to do	0995	
☐ decompose	0199, 0669	
☐ decomposition		
0199, 0669		
☐ decrease		
0135, 0195, 0639, 0853,		
0876, 0890, 0940		
☐ dedicate	0745	
☐ dedicate A to B		
0745, 0970		
☐ **dedicated**	0745	
☐ dedication	0745	
☐ deep	0727, 0768	
☐ defeat	0047	
☐ defect	0107, 0131	
☐ defendant	0111	
☐ defensive	0750	
☐ **deficiency**	0541, 0042	
☐ deficient	0541	
☐ **deficit**	0136, 0042	
☐ **define**	0592	
☐ definite	0801	
☐ **definitely**	0801, 1093	
☐ definition	0592	
☐ **deflect**	0612	
☐ deflection	0612	
☐ **deforestation**	0568	
☐ degradation	0506	
☐ **dejected**	0721	
☐ dejection	0721	
☐ delay		
0179, 0231, 0948, 0952		
☐ delegate	0509	
☐ **delete**	0676	
☐ deletion	0676	
☐ **deliberate**	0300	
☐ deliberate about	0300	
☐ deliberate on	0300	
☐ deliberate over	0300	

どれだけチェックできた？ 1 ☐ 2 ☐

☐ deliberately	0300	☐ **desperate**	0767	☐ **diminish**	0639
☐ delicate	0321	☐ desperately	0767	☐ direct	0255, 0684
☐ demand	0757	☐ despite	1117	☐ directly	0823
☐ **demanding**	0757, 0770	☐ destination	1045	☐ director	0036
☐ **demolish**	0234, 0869	☐ destiny	1045	☐ dirty	0383
☐ demolition	0234	☐ destroy	0214, 0234, 0884	☐ disadvantage	0430
☐ **demonstrate**	0261	☐ detach	0665	☐ disadvantageous	0365
☐ demonstration	0261	☐ **detect**	0181	☐ disagree	0030
☐ demonstrator	0261	☐ detection	0181	☐ disagreeable	0325
☐ **demote**	0582	☐ detective	0181	☐ disagreement	
☐ demotion	0062, 0582	☐ detector	0181		0030, 0033, 0144
☐ denial	0360	☐ deteriorate	0636	☐ disappear	0620
☐ deny	0360, 0594	☐ determine	0656	☐ disappoint	0134
☐ depart	0843, 0959	☐ **detour**	0176	☐ disappointed	0721
☐ depend	0526	☐ **devastate**	0214	☐ disappointment	0134
☐ depend on		☐ devastating	0214	☐ disaster	0483
0526, 0850, 0928, 0949		☐ devastation	0214	☐ disband	0660
☐ depend upon		☐ develop	0192, 0616	☐ **discard**	0618
0526, 0850, 0928, 0949		☐ developed	0691	☐ **discharge**	
☐ dependable	0526, 0761	☐ development	0443, 0523		0237, 0011, 0083
☐ dependence	0041, 0526	☐ deviate	0224	☐ **discipline**	0473
☐ **dependency**	0526	☐ device	0185	☐ **disclose**	
☐ dependent	0343	☐ **devise**	0185, 0613, 0849		0277, 0200, 0219
☐ **depict**	0624	☐ **devote A to B**	0970	☐ disclosure	0277
☐ depict A as B	0992	☐ devoted	0970	☐ discontent	0480
☐ depiction	0624	☐ devotion	0970	☐ discontinue	0179
☐ **deploy**	0651	☐ diagnose	0004	☐ discord	0144
☐ deployment	0651	☐ diagnose A as B	0004	☐ discourage A from doing
☐ **deposit**	0558, 0606	☐ diagnose A with B	0004		1003
☐ depot	0573	☐ diagnoses	0004	☐ discourteous	0331
☐ deprave	0706	☐ **diagnosis**	0004	☐ discover	
☐ depress	0146	☐ diagnostic	0004	0181, 0219, 0854, 0937	
☐ depressed	0146	☐ **dialect**	0109	☐ discovery	0545
☐ **depression**	0146	☐ **dictate**	0656	☐ discreet	0118
☐ deprivation	1013	☐ dictation	0656	☐ **discretion**	0118
☐ deride	0645	☐ **die down**	0865	☐ disease	0017
☐ derision	0645	☐ different	0791	☐ **disengage**	0665
☐ descendant	0566	☐ difficulty	0547	☐ disengagement	0665
☐ describe	0624	☐ dig up	0219	☐ **disguise**	0279
☐ deserted	0755	☐ digest	0550	☐ disgusting	0325
☐ **designate**	0218	☐ dignified	0554, 0711	☐ dishonest	0706
☐ designation	0218	☐ dignify	0554	☐ **dismay**	0134
☐ desire	0442	☐ **dignity**	0554	☐ dismiss	
☐ desire to do	0994, 0999	☐ digress	0224	0083, 0237, 0686, 0883	
☐ desolate	0294	☐ **dimension**	0165	☐ dismiss A as B	0083

☐ **dismissal**	0083	
☐ disobedient	0397	
☐ **disorder**	0017	
☐ disordered	0017	
☐ disorderly	0017, 0352	
☐ **disoriented**	0733	
☐ **dispatch**	0271	
☐ **disperse**	0630, 0272	
☐ **displace**	0686	
☐ displacement	0083, 0686	
☐ display	1090	
☐ disposal	1086	
☐ dispose of	0618, 0650	
☐ disputable	0389	
☐ **dispute**	0009, 0025, 0095	
☐ **disregard**	0674	
☐ **disrupt**	0194	
☐ disruption	0194	
☐ disruptive	0194	
☐ dissent	0172	
☐ dissolution	0660	
☐ **dissolve**	0660	
☐ **distinct**	0791	
☐ distinction	0335, 0791	
☐ distinguish	0335, 0791	
☐ **distinguished**	0335, 0381	
☐ **distort**	0282	
☐ distorted	0282	
☐ distortion	0282	
☐ **distract A from B**	0986, 0966	
☐ distracting	0986	
☐ distraction	0986	
☐ **distress**	0410	
☐ distressed	0410	
☐ distribute	0897, 0914	
☐ distribution	0012	
☐ disturb	0577	
☐ disturbance	0017	
☐ dive	0245	
☐ **diverse**	0368	
☐ diversify	0368	
☐ diversion	0176, 0966	

☐ diversity	0368	
☐ divert	0612	
☐ divert A away from B	0966	
☐ **divert A from B**	0966, 0986	
☐ **divorce**	0470	
☐ docile	0397	
☐ **domestic**	0759	
☐ dominant	0601	
☐ **dominate**	0601	
☐ domination	0601	
☐ donate	0842	
☐ **donate A to B**	0961	
☐ donation	0401, 0961	
☐ donor	0961	
☐ **dormant**	0326	
☐ **dosage**	0151	
☐ dose	0151	
☐ doubtful	0704, 0714	
☐ down payment	0558	
☐ **down the line**	1102	
☐ downcast	0721	
☐ downgrade	0582	
☐ downswing	0532	
☐ **downturn**	0532	
☐ **drag A into B**	0964	
☐ **drag on**	0900	
☐ **drastic**	0311, 0827	
☐ **drastically**	0827, 0311	
☐ **draw on**	0887	
☐ draw upon	0887	
☐ **drawback**	0430	
☐ **dread**	0263	
☐ dread doing	0263	
☐ dreadful	0263	
☐ dreadfully	0263	
☐ droop	0661	
☐ drop	0245	
☐ **drop by**	0958	
☐ drop in	0958	
☐ **drop out**	0840	
☐ dropout	0840	
☐ **dubious**	0714	
☐ **due to**	1107	
☐ **duplicate**	0258	

☐ **durability**	0396	
☐ **durable**	0396	
☐ dweller	0027, 0412	

E

☐ eager	0767	
☐ early	0785	
☐ ease	0264	
☐ easy	0776	
☐ **eat up**	0846	
☐ eccentric	0349, 0740	
☐ ecology	0094	
☐ **ecosystem**	0094	
☐ **edge**	0061	
☐ edit	0187	
☐ effect	0148, 0161	
☐ effective	0763	
☐ **efficiency**	0129	
☐ efficient	0129, 0782	
☐ efficiently	0129	
☐ **elaborate**	0690	
☐ elaborate on	0653	
☐ elaborately	0690	
☐ elaboration	0690	
☐ election	0169	
☐ element	0098, 0436	
☐ elementary	0691, 0771	
☐ **elevate**	0678	
☐ elevation	0678	
☐ **eliminate**	0201, 0927	
☐ elimination	0201, 0481	
☐ eloquent	0297	
☐ **elude**	0646	
☐ elusive	0646	
☐ emancipate	0644	
☐ **embark on**	0923, 0188, 0587	
☐ embark upon	0923	
☐ embarrass	0270	
☐ **embrace**	0191	
☐ **emerge**	0249, 0421	
☐ emergence	0249, 0421	
☐ **emergency**	0421, 0249	
☐ emergent	0249, 0421	
☐ emigrant	0514	

どれだけチェックできた？ 1 ☐ 2 ☐

☐ emigrate 0286	☐ **enroll A in B** 0983	☐ **estimate**
☐ eminent 0335, 0373, 0381	☐ enroll for 0248, 0943	0021, 0243, 0635
☐ **emission** 0011	☐ **enroll in** 0943, 0248	☐ estimated 0021, 0760
☐ emit 0011, 0237	☐ enrollment 0943, 0983	☐ estimation 0021
☐ empathy 0472	☐ **ensure** 0207, 0265	☐ ethical 0484
☐ emphasis 0632	☐ **enterprise**	☐ **ethics** 0484
☐ **emphasize** 0632	0494, 0409, 0560	☐ **evacuate** 0223
☐ emphatic 0632	☐ entice A into B 0968	☐ evacuation 0223
☐ employ 0191, 0617	☐ entice A to do 1007	☐ evade 0646, 0780
☐ empower A to do 1006	☐ entire 0308	☐ **evaluate**
☐ **encounter** 0182, 0919	☐ entitlement 1053	0288, 0174, 0635, 0929
☐ encourage	☐ entrust A to B 0985	☐ **evaluation** 0174, 0288
0178, 0628, 0634	☐ **enviable** 0379	☐ **evaporate** 0620
☐ **encourage A to do**	☐ envious 0379	☐ evaporation 0620
1003, 0634	☐ environment 0307, 0527	☐ evasion 0780
☐ encouragement	☐ **environmental** 0307	☐ **evasive** 0780
0062, 1003	☐ environmentalist 0307	☐ event 0439, 1116
☐ encouraging 1003	☐ environmentally 0307	☐ eventual 0817
☐ end	☐ environmentally-friendly	☐ **eventually** 0817, 0803
0097, 0190, 0688, 0944	0307	☐ **evict A from B** 0988
☐ end in 0882	☐ envisage 0268	☐ eviction 0988
☐ endanger 0749	☐ **envision** 0268	☐ evidence 0492
☐ **endangered** 0749	☐ envy 0379	☐ evidently 0805
☐ **endear A to B** 0973	☐ **epidemic** 0001	☐ evoke 0239
☐ endearing 0973	☐ equal 0088, 0357, 0731	☐ **evolution** 0523, 0616
☐ endemic 0001	☐ **equality** 0088	☐ evolutionary 0523, 0616
☐ **endorse** 0236	☐ equalize 0088	☐ **evolve** 0616, 0523
☐ endorsement 0236	☐ equilibrium 0490	☐ exact 0760
☐ endowment 1031	☐ equipment 0584	☐ **exaggerate** 0204
☐ endurable 0275	☐ **equivalent** 0357, 0120	☐ exaggerated 0204
☐ endurance 0275	☐ equivocal 0728	☐ exaggeration 0204
☐ **endure** 0275, 0659	☐ eradicate 0186, 0884	☐ examination 0073, 0556
☐ energetic 0299	☐ erase 0676	☐ examine 0233, 0941
☐ **enforce** 0670, 0516	☐ erode 0125	☐ excavate 0219
☐ **enforcement**	☐ **erosion** 0125	☐ **exceed** 0246, 0213, 0354
0516, 0670	☐ error 0145, 0504	☐ excel 0213
☐ engagement 1037	☐ erupt 0162, 0260	☐ excel at 0879
☐ engulf 0687	☐ **eruption** 0162, 0044	☐ **excel in** 0879
☐ **enhance** 0196	☐ **escalate** 0202	☐ excellence 0879
☐ enhancement 0196	☐ escalation 0202	☐ excellent 0765, 0879
☐ enlarge 0649	☐ escalator 0202	☐ except 0789
☐ enlargement 0503	☐ **escort** 0611, 0536	☐ exception 0789
☐ **enormous** 0387, 0316	☐ essential 0334, 0705, 1017	☐ **exceptional** 0789
☐ enormously 0387	☐ estate 0413	☐ exceptionally 0789
☐ enroll A for B 0983	☐ **esteem** 0520, 0531	☐ **excerpt** 0053, 0602

☐ excess 0042, 0246, 0354	☐ **expose A to B** 0972	☐ fascinating 1012
☐ **excessive** 0354, 0246, 0361	☐ exposure 0972	☐ fascination 1012
☐ exclude 0201, 0927	☐ expulsion 0626	☐ fashion 0092
☐ execute 0036, 0238	☐ **extend** 0649, 0347, 0460	☐ fastidious 0797
☐ execution 0036	☐ extended 0342	☐ **fatigue** 0077, 0904
☐ **executive** 0036	☐ **extension** 0460, 0347, 0649	☐ fatigued 0077
☐ exercise 0683	☐ **extensive** 0347, 0295, 0460, 0649	☐ fault 0107, 0131
☐ **exert** 0683	☐ extensively 0347, 0460, 0649	☐ favor 1106
☐ exert oneself 0683	☐ **exterminate** 0186	☐ favorable 0697, 0799
☐ exertion 0683	☐ extermination 0072, 0186	☐ favorably 0829
☐ exhaust 0337, 0904	☐ exterminator 0186	☐ fear 0263
☐ **exhausted** 0337	☐ extinct 0072, 0211, 0749	☐ feasibility 0317
☐ exhaustion 0077, 0337	☐ **extinction** 0072, 0211	☐ **feasible** 0317, 0734
☐ exhaustive 0772	☐ **extinguish** 0211, 0072	☐ feature 0049
☐ **exile** 0100	☐ extinguisher 0072, 0211	☐ **federal** 0310
☐ exist 0132	☐ extra 0353	☐ federalism 0310
☐ **existence** 0132	☐ **extract** 0602, 0053	☐ federalist 0310
☐ existing 0132	☐ extraordinary 0344, 0789	☐ federation 0310
☐ exorbitant 0354	☐ extravagant 0354	☐ feeble 0792
☐ **exotic** 0724, 0380	☐ extreme 0314, 0354, 0361	☐ feeling 0050, 0116, 0418
☐ expand 0503, 0649	☐ extremely 0829	☐ feign 0370
☐ expanse 0503		☐ fellow worker 0407
☐ **expansion** 0503, 0460	**F**	☐ ferocious 0346, 0364
☐ expect 0221	☐ face 0182	☐ **fertile** 0709, 0391
☐ expectation 1041	☐ face up to 0609	☐ fertilize 0709
☐ expedite 0284	☐ facilitate 0002, 0284	☐ fertilizer 0709
☐ **expel** 0626	☐ **facility** 0002, 0173	☐ **fierce** 0364, 0346, 0369
☐ expel A from B 0988	☐ faint 0720, 0897	☐ fiercely 0364
☐ expenditure 0055	☐ fair 0362	☐ fight 0030
☐ **expense** 0055, 0035	☐ **fake** 0370, 0313, 0743	☐ figure 0833
☐ expensive 0055, 0487, 0689	☐ fall 0245	☐ **figure out** 0833, 0872
☐ experience 0673, 0941	☐ **fame** 0571, 0417	☐ **fill A in on B** 0978
☐ experiment 0376	☐ familiar 1061	☐ **fill in** 0954
☐ **experimental** 0376	☐ familiarity 1061	☐ fill out 0954
☐ expert 0045	☐ **familiarize oneself with** 1061	☐ finally 0803, 0817
☐ **expertise** 0045	☐ family 0759	☐ finance 0028, 0046
☐ expiration 0190	☐ **famine** 0479	☐ find 0181, 0545, 0854, 0937
☐ **expire** 0190	☐ famous 0335, 0381, 0571	☐ **finding** 0545
☐ explain 0885	☐ far 1099	☐ **fine** 0565, 0720
☐ **exploit** 0180	☐ **far from** 1099	☐ fine A for B 0565
☐ exploitation 0180	☐ farm 0192	☐ finish 0944
☐ explosion 0044		☐ fire 0883
☐ expose 0200, 0219, 0277		☐ **firm** 0560, 0318, 0339, 0494

☐ **firsthand**	0823	
☐ first-hand	0823	
☐ fix	0597	
☐ **flag down**	0912	
☐ **flare**	0260	
☐ flash	0260	
☐ flattery	0051	
☐ **flaw**	0107, 0131	
☐ flawed	0107	
☐ flawless	0107, 0358	
☐ flexibility	0699	
☐ **flexible**	0699	
☐ flick through	0908	
☐ **flip through**	0908	
☐ **flourish**	0642, 0209, 0227	
☐ flourishing	0642	
☐ fluctuating	0382	
☐ **fluid**	0382	
☐ focus	0127, 0834	
☐ **focus on**	0834	
☐ follow	0662	
☐ following	0324, 1082	
☐ **foot the bill**	1067	
☐ **for all**	1117	
☐ for good	0828	
☐ **for sure**	1093	
☐ for the meantime	1075, 1076	
☐ **for the time being**	1075	
☐ **forbid**	0285, 0019	
☐ forbid A from doing	0019, 0285	
☐ forbid A to do	0019, 0285	
☐ forbidden	0285	
☐ force A into doing	1002	
☐ force A on B	0962	
☐ **force A to do**	1002	
☐ **forecast**	0498, 0496	
☐ foreign	0724, 0759	
☐ foresee	0221	
☐ forever	0828	
☐ **forfeit**	0225	
☐ forge	0370	
☐ forged	0370	
☐ forgery	0370	
☐ formula	0613	
☐ **formulate**	0613, 0185	
☐ fortify	0281	
☐ fortune	0008	
☐ **fossil**	0081	
☐ **foster**	0628	
☐ foundation	0099	
☐ **fracture**	0048	
☐ **fragile**	0321, 0302	
☐ fragility	0321	
☐ **fragment**	0535, 0650	
☐ **frail**	0302, 0321	
☐ frailty	0302	
☐ frank	0776	
☐ **fraud**	0574, 0432	
☐ fraudulence	0432, 0574	
☐ fraudulent	0574	
☐ free	0237, 0644, 0665, 0778	
☐ freedom	0106	
☐ frequency	0822	
☐ frequent	0822	
☐ **frequently**	0822, 0806	
☐ fresh	0793	
☐ **friction**	0144	
☐ friendly	0319, 0320	
☐ frighten	0641	
☐ **from scratch**	1104	
☐ from time to time	0824	
☐ fulfill	0238	
☐ **fund**	0028, 0046	
☐ fundamental	0314	
☐ funding	0028	

G

☐ gain	0696	
☐ garbage	0675	
☐ gash	0599	
☐ gather	0212, 0585, 0663, 0839	
☐ gathering	0548, 0553	
☐ gear	0584, 1015	
☐ **gender**	0058	
☐ **gene**	0521, 0309	
☐ general	0308	
☐ generally	0308	
☐ **generate**	0184	
☐ generation	0184	
☐ generator	0184	
☐ generous	0332, 0751	
☐ **genetic**	0309, 0521	
☐ genetically	0309, 0521	
☐ genetics	0309, 0521	
☐ **genuine**	0313, 0370, 0743	
☐ genuinely	0313	
☐ get	0205	
☐ get a glimpse of	1058	
☐ **get around to**	0892	
☐ **get away with**	0898	
☐ **get down to**	0903	
☐ get lost	0224	
☐ **get on one's nerves**	1065	
☐ get rid of	0201, 0618, 0650, 0859, 0863, 0875	
☐ get round to	0892	
☐ get used to	0931	
☐ gigantic	0387	
☐ give	0590	
☐ give in	0864	
☐ **give in to**	0880, 0652, 0955	
☐ **give oneself up to**	1063	
☐ give out	0897, 0914	
☐ **give rise to**	1070, 0184	
☐ give way to	0955, 1071	
☐ glare	0891	
☐ **glare at**	0891	
☐ **gleam**	0273	
☐ glimmer	0273	
☐ glimpse	1058	
☐ glint	0273	
☐ glitter	0273	
☐ global	0139	
☐ **global warming**	0139	
☐ globally	0808	
☐ gloomy	0294	

☐ glower at	0891	☐ handout	0914	☐ hit upon	0838
☐ go bad	0199, 0669	☐ hang	0179	☐ hold	0210, 0252
☐ **go through**	0941, 0673	☐ hard	0318, 0393, 0560	☐ hold back	0240
☐ goal	0122, 0524	☐ hardly	0820	☐ **hold off**	0948
☐ good point	0063	☐ **hardship**	0547	☐ hold off on	0948
☐ goodness	0063	☐ harm	0655	☐ hold on to	0857
☐ government	0031	☐ harmonize	0586	☐ home	0040, 0759
☐ governor	0427	☐ **harsh**	0393	☐ homework	0164
☐ grab	0579	☐ harshly	0393	☐ honest	0313, 0776
☐ grand	0711	☐ haste	0739	☐ honor	0089
☐ **grant**	0590, 0078, 0458	☐ hasten	0284, 0739	☐ hopeless	0767
☐ **grasp**	0252, 0579	☐ **hasty**	0739, 0785	☐ hospitable	0093
☐ gratefully	1021	☐ **have a hard time doing**	1072, 1060	☐ **hospitality**	0093
☐ gratuity	0097	☐ **have had enough of**	1069	☐ **hostage**	0446, 0168
☐ gravitation	0718	☐ **have trouble doing**	1060, 1072	☐ **hostile**	0320
☐ **gravitational**	0718	☐ **have yet to do**	1062	☐ hostility	0320
☐ gravity	0718	☐ **hazard**	0563, 0692	☐ household	0759
☐ greatest	0367	☐ **hazardous**	0692, 0336, 0563	☐ **hub**	0127
☐ grief	0104	☐ head for	0930	☐ hug	0191
☐ **grim**	0773, 0294	☐ healthy	0715	☐ huge	0316, 0387
☐ grip	0252	☐ heart	0127	☐ humble	0742
☐ group	0615	☐ heighten	0196	☐ **humiliate**	0270
☐ grow	0192	☐ helpful	0487	☐ humiliating	0270
☐ **grow into**	0916	☐ helping	0447	☐ humiliation	0270
☐ grow up	0703	☐ **heritage**	0005, 0123	☐ **hunch**	0050, 0116
☐ grown-up	0703	☐ hesitant	0356	☐ hurdle	0003
☐ growth	0523, 0916	☐ hesitate	0251, 1051	☐ hurt	0128, 0591
☐ grudge	0253	☐ hesitate to do	1051	☐ **hypnosis**	0552
☐ **grumble**	0280, 0580	☐ hesitation	1051	☐ hypnotism	0552
☐ **guarantee**	0265, 0207, 0578	☐ hide	0200, 0277, 0279, 0671, 0960	☐ hypnotist	0552
☐ guard	0611	☐ highlight	0632	☐ hypnotize	0552
☐ guide	0536, 0611	☐ **highly**	0829		
☐ **guideline**	0405	☐ **hilarious**	0322	**I**	
☐ **gullible**	0345	☐ **hinder**	0231, 0525, 0607	☐ ID	0472
H		☐ **hindrance**	0525, 0003, 0231	☐ **identification**	0472
☐ **habitat**	0040	☐ hint	0428, 0637	☐ identify	0472
☐ hail	0912	☐ hire	0617	☐ identity	0472
☐ **halt**	0283	☐ hit on	0838	☐ **ignorance**	0549, 1025
☐ **hamper**	0607, 0231			☐ ignorant	0549, 0762
☐ **hand down**	0936			☐ ignore	0549, 0674, 1025
☐ hand in	0652, 0921			☐ illegal	0355
☐ **hand out**	0914, 0897			☐ illegible	0350
☐ handle	0584, 0836			☐ illegitimate	0355
				☐ **illicit**	0355
				☐ illiteracy	0015, 0762

☐ **illiterate**	0762	
☐ illness	0017	
☐ **illogical**	0359	
☐ imaginable	0764	
☐ imagine	0268	
☐ imitate	0215, 0235	
☐ immaculate	0358	
☐ immature	0703	
☐ immediate	0550	
☐ immediately	1081	
☐ immense	0316, 0387	
☐ **immerse oneself in**	1068	
☐ immersion	1068	
☐ **immigrant**	0514	
☐ immigrate	0286, 0514	
☐ immigration	0514	
☐ imminence	0373	
☐ **imminent**	0373	
☐ immodest	0742	
☐ **impair**	0655	
☐ impaired	0655	
☐ impediment	0525	
☐ impending	0373	
☐ **impersonate**	0215, 0235	
☐ implant	0614	
☐ **implement**	0238	
☐ implementation	0238	
☐ implication	0637	
☐ **imply**	0637	
☐ importance	0165	
☐ important	0291	
☐ **impose A on B**	0962	
☐ imposing	0962	
☐ imposition	0962	
☐ impress	0729	
☐ impression	0729	
☐ **impressive**	0729, 0399	
☐ imprisonment	0106	
☐ improve	0177	
☐ **in a row**	1089	
☐ in a word	1095	
☐ in brief	1095	
☐ in case of	1116	
☐ in comparison to	1111	
☐ in comparison with	1111	
☐ **in contrast**	1073	
☐ in contrast to	1114	
☐ in contrast with	1114	
☐ in danger	1074, 1077, 1097	
☐ **in favor of**	1106	
☐ **in jeopardy**	1077, 1074, 1097	
☐ **in need of**	1120	
☐ in peril	1074, 1077, 1097	
☐ **in person**	1100	
☐ in place of	1115	
☐ in progress	0736	
☐ **in response to**	1113	
☐ **in retrospect**	1079	
☐ **in shape**	1092	
☐ **in short**	1095	
☐ in spite of	1117	
☐ in succession	1089	
☐ **in terms of**	1108	
☐ in the end	0803, 0817	
☐ **in the event of**	1116	
☐ **in the face of**	1118	
☐ **in the meantime**	1076	
☐ in the meanwhile	1076	
☐ **in the vicinity of**	1110	
☐ in theory	1094	
☐ **in turn**	1078	
☐ **in unison**	1085	
☐ inaccessible	0737	
☐ inactive	0326	
☐ inadequate	0390	
☐ inappropriate	0340	
☐ inarticulate	0297	
☐ **incentive**	0052, 0572	
☐ incessant	0774	
☐ incidence	0439	
☐ **incident**	0439	
☐ incidental	0439	
☐ inclusive	0304	
☐ incoherent	0708	
☐ **incompatible**	0341	
☐ incompetence	0039	
☐ inconceivable	0764	
☐ **inconsiderate**	0386	
☐ inconsistency	0014	
☐ **increase**	0177, 0196	
☐ **incredible**	0800	
☐ incredibly	0800	
☐ indecent	0362, 0790	
☐ **indecisive**	0356, 0695	
☐ in-depth	0772	
☐ indict	0681	
☐ indifference	1032	
☐ **indigenous**	0380, 0724	
☐ **indispensable**	0705	
☐ indisputable	0360	
☐ induce A to do	1004, 1007	
☐ inducement	0052, 0572	
☐ indulge	0257	
☐ **indulge in**	0926	
☐ indulgence	0926	
☐ indulgent	0926	
☐ inefficiency	0782	
☐ **inefficient**	0782	
☐ inequality	0088	
☐ inevitable	0810	
☐ **inevitably**	0810	
☐ **infamous**	0723	
☐ infant	0505	
☐ infect	0680, 0716	
☐ infection	0001, 0680, 0716	
☐ **infectious**	0716, 0680, 0701	
☐ inferior	0542	
☐ inflexible	0318, 0699	
☐ **infrastructure**	0023	
☐ infringement	0463, 0477	
☐ **ingredient**	0098, 0436	
☐ inhabit	0040, 0412, 0595	
☐ **inhabitant**	0412, 0027, 0040	
☐ inherit	0123	
☐ **inheritance**	0123, 0005	
☐ initial	0038, 0815	
☐ **initially**	0815, 0038	
☐ initiate	0038, 0815	
☐ **initiative**	0038, 0815	

☐ injure	0128, 0591	☐ integrated	0424	☐ **ironically**	0802
☐ innovate	0301, 0434	☐ **integration**	0424	☐ irony	0802
☐ **innovation**	0434, 0301	☐ **intense** 0369, 0342, 0364		☐ **irrational**	0756, 0359
☐ **innovative**	0301, 0434	☐ intensify 0196, 0342, 0369		☐ irreconcilable	0341
☐ innumerable	0786	☐ intensity	0342, 0369	☐ **irrelevant**	0329, 0290
☐ inopportune	0799	☐ **intensive**	0342, 0369	☐ irresolute	0356
☐ inorganic	0779	☐ intentional	0300	☐ irrespective of	1119
☐ inquire	0073	☐ interact	0486	☐ irrigate	0464
☐ inquire about	0073	☐ **interaction**	0486	☐ **irrigation**	0464
☐ inquire into	0073	☐ interactive	0486	☐ irritate	1065
☐ **inquiry**	0073, 0556	☐ interfere	0529, 0577	☐ isolate	0414, 0570
☐ insanitary	0383	☐ interfere in	0529	☐ isolated	0414
☐ insecure	0321, 0336	☐ interfere with	0529	☐ **isolation**	
☐ insert	0987	☐ **interference** 0529, 0160			0414, 0060, 0570
☐ **insert A in B**	0987	☐ internal	0759	☐ issue	0012
☐ insert A into B	0987	☐ international	0315	☐ item	0478
☐ insertion	0987	☐ interrupt	0194, 0577	☐ **itinerary**	0501
☐ **insight**	0457	☐ intervene	0160		
☐ insignificant	0378	☐ intervene in	0160	**J**	
☐ insinuate	0637	☐ **intervention** 0160, 0529			
☐ insist	0769	☐ intricate	0156, 0694	☐ jam	0024
☐ insist on	0769	☐ intrigue 0071, 0084, 1039		☐ jeopardize	1077
☐ insistence	0769	☐ intriguing	1039	☐ jeopardy	1077
☐ **insistent**	0769	☐ **intrude**	0577	☐ joint author	0499
☐ insolvent	0712	☐ intruder	0577	☐ **jot down**	0837, 0852
☐ inspect	0233	☐ intrusion	0529, 0577	☐ judge	0929
☐ inspection	0556	☐ **intuition**	0518, 0457	☐ jump	0245
☐ inspiration	0634	☐ intuitive	0518	☐ **jump at**	0905
☐ **inspire**	0634	☐ invade	0477	☐ junior	0542
☐ inspire A to do 0634, 1005		☐ invader	0477	☐ justifiable	0377
☐ **install**	0276	☐ invalid	0763	☐ justification	0244
☐ installation	0276	☐ **invaluable**	0730	☐ **justify**	0244
☐ instant	0550	☐ invariable	0826		
☐ instead of	1115	☐ **invariably**	0826	**K**	
☐ instinct	0518	☐ **invasion**	0477, 0463	☐ keen	0333
☐ institution	0002	☐ **invest**	0256, 0091	☐ keenly	1044
☐ instruction	0456	☐ invest A in B	0091, 0256	☐ keep	0581
☐ instrument	0238, 1019	☐ investigate	0233, 0556	☐ keep back	0240
☐ insufficient	0390	☐ **investigation**		☐ keep to	0841
☐ insulting	0750		0556, 0073	☐ kidnapping	0168, 0446
☐ insurance	0074	☐ investigator	0556	☐ kill	0666
☐ insure	0207	☐ **investment**	0091, 0256	☐ kind	0022
☐ **intact**	0293	☐ investor	0091, 0256	☐ kit	0584
☐ **intake**	0575	☐ **iron out**	0859	☐ knock down	0234, 0869
☐ integrate	0424	☐ ironic	0802	☐ know-how	0045
				☐ knowledge	0458

L

- [ ] labor force 0438
- [ ] lack 0541
- [ ] large 0831
- [ ] **largely** 0831
- [ ] large-scale 0347
- [ ] last 0275
- [ ] laugh at 0645
- [ ] **laugh off** 0888
- [ ] **launch** 0188, 0911
- [ ] **launch into** 0911, 0188
- [ ] law 0408
- [ ] lawful 0355, 0377
- [ ] lawmaking 0408
- [ ] **lawsuit** 0540
- [ ] **lay off** 0883
- [ ] layoff 0883
- [ ] **lead A to do** 1004
- [ ] lead to 0882
- [ ] league 0507
- [ ] leap at 0905
- [ ] learning 0458
- [ ] leave 0223, 0677, 0843, 0959
- [ ] **leave A to B** 0985
- [ ] leave A up to B 0985
- [ ] **leftover** 0170
- [ ] legacy 0123
- [ ] legal 0355, 0377
- [ ] **legible** 0350
- [ ] **legislation** 0408
- [ ] legislative 0408
- [ ] legislator 0408
- [ ] legislature 0408
- [ ] legitimacy 0377
- [ ] **legitimate** 0377
- [ ] lengthen 0649
- [ ] leniency 0332
- [ ] **lenient** 0332
- [ ] lessen 0639
- [ ] levy A on B 0962
- [ ] liberal 0644
- [ ] **liberate** 0644, 0665
- [ ] liberty 0644

- [ ] license 0578
- [ ] licensed 0732
- [ ] life 0132
- [ ] lift 0678
- [ ] light 0211
- [ ] **likelihood** 0065
- [ ] likely 0065
- [ ] liking 0491
- [ ] limit 0367, 0455, 0603, 0657
- [ ] limit A to B 0979
- [ ] **limitation** 0455, 0502
- [ ] limited 0455
- [ ] **linger** 0622
- [ ] lingering 0622
- [ ] liquid 0382
- [ ] **literacy** 0015
- [ ] literal 0809
- [ ] **literally** 0809
- [ ] literate 0015, 0762
- [ ] **litter** 0675
- [ ] **live off** 0950
- [ ] **livelihood** 0510
- [ ] lively 0299, 0710
- [ ] living 0027, 0510
- [ ] location 0029
- [ ] logic 0359
- [ ] logical 0359, 0708
- [ ] **loiter** 0229, 0241
- [ ] loneliness 0060
- [ ] long to do 0994, 0999
- [ ] longing 0442
- [ ] long-lasting 0396
- [ ] **long-standing** 0794
- [ ] look on A as B 0969, 0977
- [ ] look over 0886
- [ ] looking back 1079
- [ ] lose 0225
- [ ] **lose sight of** 1064
- [ ] lost 0733
- [ ] lower 0542, 0599, 0890, 0940
- [ ] **lunar** 0746
- [ ] lure 0968
- [ ] **lure A into B** 0968

- [ ] lure A to B 0968

M

- [ ] **magnificent** 0399, 0711
- [ ] mail 0271
- [ ] main 0771
- [ ] mainly 0831
- [ ] mainstay 0099
- [ ] **mainstream** 0392
- [ ] maintain 0206, 0493, 0581, 0621
- [ ] maintenance 0493
- [ ] **majestic** 0711
- [ ] majesty 0554, 0711
- [ ] major 0056, 0175
- [ ] major in 0056
- [ ] **majority** 0056
- [ ] make 0262
- [ ] make an effort 0683
- [ ] **make ends meet** 1066
- [ ] **make for** 0930
- [ ] **make it** 1057
- [ ] make light of 0934
- [ ] make little of 0934
- [ ] make sure 0207
- [ ] make toward 0930
- [ ] make up 0153
- [ ] make use of 0648
- [ ] **make way for** 1071
- [ ] **makeup** 0153
- [ ] malevolent 0346
- [ ] malicious 0346
- [ ] manage 0255, 0684, 0836
- [ ] management 0031
- [ ] mandate 0334
- [ ] **mandatory** 0334, 0338
- [ ] manifestation 0433
- [ ] **manipulate** 0664
- [ ] manipulation 0664
- [ ] manipulative 0664
- [ ] manpower 0438
- [ ] **manufacture** 0262
- [ ] manufacturer 0262
- [ ] **manuscript** 0142
- [ ] many 0725

☐ **map out**	0873	
☐ mark	0122	
☐ **mark down**	0940	
☐ mark up	0940	
☐ markdown	0940	
☐ market	1103	
☐ marriage	0470	
☐ mass	0316	
☐ massacre	0666	
☐ **massive**	0316, 0387	
☐ match up to	0868	
☐ **mature**	0703, 0785	
☐ maturity	0703	
☐ maximal	0796	
☐ maximum	0367	
☐ **mayor**	0427	
☐ meaningful	0291	
☐ meanwhile	1076	
☐ measure	0868	
☐ **measure up to**	0868	
☐ measurement	0165	
☐ mediation	0160	
☐ medication	0087	
☐ medicine	0087	
☐ **mediocre**	0777	
☐ meeting	0548, 0553	
☐ melt	0660	
☐ **memento**	0488	
☐ **menace**	0475	
☐ mend	0597	
☐ mental	0363	
☐ mention	0643, 0847	
☐ merciful	0332, 0751	
☐ **merge**	0259	
☐ merger	0259	
☐ mess up	0675	
☐ meticulous	0744	
☐ migrant	0286	
☐ **migrate**	0286	
☐ migration	0286	
☐ millennium	0159	
☐ **mimic**	0235, 0215	
☐ mimicry	0235	
☐ **mingle**	0254	
☐ **minimal**	0796	

☐ minimally	0796	
☐ minimize	0796	
☐ minimum	0796	
☐ **minor**	0175	
☐ minority	0056, 0175	
☐ misbehave	0896	
☐ misleading	0384	
☐ miss	0242	
☐ mistake	0145, 0504	
☐ mistreat	0419	
☐ mistreatment	0419	
☐ misuse	0419	
☐ mitigate	0264	
☐ mix	0254	
☐ mobile	0115	
☐ mobile phone	0115	
☐ mock	0645	
☐ mockery	0645	
☐ **moderate** 0361, 0354, 0742		
☐ moderately	0361	
☐ **modest** 0742, 0361, 0362, 0726		
☐ modestly	0742	
☐ modesty	0742	
☐ modification	0220	
☐ **modify**	0220, 0203	
☐ molecular	0149	
☐ **molecule**	0149	
☐ money	0522	
☐ monopolization	0250	
☐ **monopolize**	0250	
☐ monopoly	0250	
☐ mood	0085	
☐ moon	0150	
☐ moral	0484	
☐ mortify	0270	
☐ mostly	0831	
☐ motivate	0572, 0634	
☐ **motivate A to do** 1005, 0572, 0634		
☐ motivation 0052, 0572, 1005		
☐ **motive** 0572, 0052, 1005		
☐ mourn	0104	

☐ **mourning**	0104	
☐ move	0441	
☐ **mutual**	0754	
☐ mutually	0754	

N

☐ naive	0345	
☐ narrowly	0820	
☐ nationwide	0808	
☐ native	0380, 0724	
☐ naturally	0810	
☐ nearly	0811	
☐ nearness	0437	
☐ necessarily	0810	
☐ necessary	0705	
☐ need	1120	
☐ neglect	0504, 0674	
☐ **negligence**	0504	
☐ negligent	0504	
☐ negotiable	0608	
☐ **negotiate**	0608	
☐ negotiation	0608	
☐ neighboring	0753	
☐ nerve	1065	
☐ nervous	0366	
☐ newborn	0505	
☐ no more than	1087	
☐ nobility	0554	
☐ nominate	0218	
☐ notable	0291	
☐ notably	0832	
☐ note down	0837, 0852	
☐ **nothing more than** 1087		
☐ notice	0181, 0787	
☐ **noticeable**	0787	
☐ noticeably	0787	
☐ notorious	0723	
☐ now and then	0824	
☐ **nuisance**	0166	
☐ **numb**	0766	
☐ **numerous**	0725	
☐ nutrient	0719	
☐ nutrition	0719	
☐ **nutritious**	0719	

O

- obedience 0397
- **obedient** 0397, 0747
- obediently 0397
- obey 0397
- object 0524
- object to 0524
- objection 0524
- **objective** 0524, 0122, 0788
- obligation 1046
- obligatory 0334, 0338, 1046
- **obnoxious** 0325
- **obscure** 0693, 0728
- obscurity 0693
- obsession 1009
- **obsolete** 0306
- **obstacle** 0003, 0430, 0525
- obstruct 0231
- obtain 0696
- obvious 0781
- occasion 0824
- occasional 0824
- **occasionally** 0824
- occupational 0748
- occupy 0205
- occur to 0838
- odd 0349, 0740
- offend 0750
- offender 0750
- offense 0463, 0750
- **offensive** 0750
- **offspring** 0566
- often 0806, 0822
- old-fashioned 1096
- on account of 1107
- **on behalf of** 1115
- **on display** 1090
- **on paper** 1094
- on sale 1103
- on show 1090
- **on the blink** 1098

- on the brink of 1112
- on the increase 1101
- **on the market** 1103
- **on the rise** 1101
- on the side of 1106
- **on the spot** 1081
- **on the verge of** 1112
- once in a while 0824
- one after the other 1078
- one by one 1078
- **ongoing** 0736
- only 0820, 1087
- only just 0820
- open 0776
- operation 0516
- **opponent** 0158
- **opportune** 0799
- opportunity 0799
- oppose 0158, 1114
- opposite 0158, 1114
- opposition 0158, 1114
- option 0007
- **orbit** 0467
- order 0473, 0497, 0656
- ordinary 0361, 0777
- **organic** 0779
- organism 0779
- organization 0002, 0157
- origin 0454
- originate from 0932
- orthodox 0394
- **out of date** 1096
- out of order 1098
- out of shape 1092
- **outbreak** 0032, 0001, 0874
- **outburst** 0044
- **outcome** 0161, 0148
- outdated 0306, 1096
- outline 0550
- out-of-date 0306, 1096
- outrage 0395
- outraged 0395
- **outrageous** 0395
- **outsource** 0685

- outsourcing 0685
- **outstanding** 0765, 0344, 0787, 0789, 0856
- **outweigh** 0619
- **ovation** 0422
- **overall** 0308
- overcharge 0845
- overestimate 0243
- **overhaul** 0493
- **overlap** 0623
- **overlook** 0242
- oversee 0255
- overstate 0204
- **overtake** 0198
- overthrow 0890
- overturn 0274, 0890
- overwhelming 1010
- owing to 1107
- ownership 0559
- oxygen 0462

P

- pacific 0193
- **pacify** 0193
- pact 0562
- **painstaking** 0744
- **pamper** 0257
- pamphlet 0561
- pandemic 0001
- paralysis 0640
- **paralyze** 0640
- parliament 0548
- part 0436, 0447, 0515, 0557, 1059
- **participant** 0163
- participate 0163
- participate in 0163
- participation 0163
- particular 0797
- pass 0198
- pass down 0936
- pass on 0667, 0936
- **pass out** 0897, 0914

☐ **pass over**	0901	☐ placid	0351	☐ postpone	
☐ **pass up**	0945	☐ plague	0001		0179, 0948, 0952
☐ **pathetic**	0792	☐ plan	0084	☐ postponement	0460
☐ pathetically	0792	☐ plant	0086	☐ **potential**	0289
☐ pay	0222, 0852	☐ **plantation**	0086	☐ potentiality	0289
☐ pay back	0450	☐ **plausible**	0752	☐ potentially	0289
☐ **pay off**	0918	☐ play a part in	1059	☐ **powerhouse**	0482
☐ peaceful	0351	☐ **play a role in**	1059	☐ practicable	0317, 0734
☐ **peculiar**	0740, 0349	☐ **play along**	0862	☐ practically	0811
☐ peculiarity	0740	☐ **play down**	0934	☐ praise	0010, 0051, 0425
☐ peculiarly	0740	☐ play up	0934	☐ praise A for B	0963
☐ penalty	0451, 0565	☐ plea	0020	☐ praiseworthy	0717
☐ penetration	0457	☐ **plead**	0266	☐ **precarious**	0336
☐ perfection	0551	☐ plead for	0266	☐ **precaution**	0508
☐ peril	0563	☐ pledge to do	1000	☐ **precede**	0662
☐ perilous	0692	☐ plentiful	0390	☐ precedence	0082, 0662
☐ periodically	0806	☐ **plot**	0071, 0084	☐ precedent	0662
☐ permanent	0828	☐ plot to do	0071	☐ preceding	0662
☐ **permanently**	0828	☐ plummet	0245	☐ precious	0487, 0730
☐ permission	0114, 0612	☐ **plunge**	0245	☐ precise	0760
☐ permit		☐ point	0097	☐ precursor	0403
0019, 0114, 0285, 0659		☐ point of view	0006	☐ **predecessor**	0403
☐ **perpetual**	0774	☐ polite	0331, 0362	☐ predict	0221, 0496, 0498
☐ perpetually	0774	☐ **poll**	0519, 0169	☐ predictable	0496
☐ persist	0303	☐ pollutant	0076	☐ **prediction**	0496, 0498
☐ persist in	0303	☐ pollute	0076, 0226, 0680	☐ prefer	0491
☐ persist with	0303	☐ **pollution**	0076, 0513	☐ preferable	0491
☐ persistence	0303	☐ popular	0092	☐ preferably	0491
☐ **persistent**	0303, 0769	☐ **popularity**	0092, 0037	☐ **preference**	0491, 0082
☐ person	1100	☐ **populate**	0595	☐ **preliminary**	0372
☐ personal	0788	☐ population	0595	☐ **premature**	0785
☐ personally	0823, 1100	☐ populous	0595	☐ **premonition**	0116, 0050
☐ personnel	0438	☐ **portion**		☐ preoccupation	1020
☐ **perspective**	0006	0447, 0515, 0557		☐ preparatory	0372
☐ persuade A to do	1001	☐ portrait	0992	☐ prerequisite	0461
☐ pertinent	0290	☐ portray	0624	☐ prerogative	0089
☐ **petition**	0020	☐ **portray A as B**	0992	☐ prescribe	0102
☐ philanthropic	0751	☐ portrayal	0992	☐ **prescribe A for B**	
☐ physical	0363	☐ position	0103, 0119		0982, 0102
☐ **pick on**	0922	☐ **possess**	0559	☐ **prescription**	0102, 0982
☐ **pitch in**	0895	☐ **possession**	0559	☐ preservation	0068, 0147
☐ pitiful	0792	☐ possessive	0559	☐ **preservative**	0147
☐ pity	0452	☐ possibility	0065, 0289	☐ preserve	
☐ placate	0193	☐ possible	0289, 0764		0147, 0247, 0581
☐ place	0029	☐ post	0271	☐ press A to do	1008

☐ pressure	0128	
☐ prestige	0385	
☐ **prestigious**	**0385**	
☐ **presumably**	**0804**	
☐ presume	0804	
☐ presumption	0804	
☐ pretend	0370	
☐ **prevail**	**0631**, **0707**	
☐ **prevailing**		
	0707, 0295, 0631	
☐ prevalent	0631, 0707	
☐ prevent	0231, 0607	
☐ previous	0324	
☐ priceless	0487	
☐ pride	0269, 0531	
☐ primarily	0771	
☐ **primary**	**0771**	
☐ prior	0082	
☐ prior to	0082	
☐ **priority**	**0082**	
☐ privacy	0037, 0060	
☐ private	0388	
☐ privation	0547	
☐ **privilege**	**0089**	
☐ privileged	0089	
☐ probability	0065	
☐ probably	0804	
☐ probe	0073	
☐ **procedure**	**0034**	
☐ proceed	0034, 0855	
☐ proceed to	0034	
☐ proceed with	0034	
☐ proceeding	0034	
☐ process	0034	
☐ produce	0184, 0262, 0474	
☐ product	0262, 0474, 0478	
☐ production	0262, 0474	
☐ productive	0474	
☐ **productivity**	**0474**	
☐ proficiency	0348	
☐ **proficient**	**0348**	
☐ **profile**	**0465**	
☐ **profound**	**0727**	
☐ profoundly	0727	
☐ progress	0523	
☐ prohibit	0019, 0285
☐ prohibit A from doing	
	0019, 0285
☐ prohibition	0019
☐ project	0084, 0164, 1056
☐ projection	1056
☐ prolong	0649
☐ prolongation	0460
☐ prominent	0335, 0765
☐ promise to do	0587, 1000
☐ promote	
	0062, 0582, 0628, 0678
☐ promote A to B	0062
☐ **promotion**	**0062**, 0037
☐ promotional	0062
☐ prompt	0589
☐ prompt A to do	1004
☐ proper	0340
☐ **property**	
	0049, 0008, 0559
☐ proponent	0158
☐ **proportion**	**0515**
☐ **prosecute**	**0681**
☐ prosecution	0681
☐ prosecutor	0681
☐ prospect	0065
☐ **prosper**	
	0227, 0209, 0538, 0642
☐ **prosperity**	**0538**, 0227
☐ prosperous	0227, 0538
☐ protect	0247, 0696, 0795
☐ protection	0068, 0795
☐ **protective**	**0795**
☐ protest	0261
☐ prove	
	0230, 0261, 0578, 0839
☐ provocation	0239
☐ provocative	0239
☐ **provoke**	**0239**, 0925
☐ **proximity**	**0437**
☐ **psychological**	**0363**
☐ psychologically	0363
☐ psychologist	0363
☐ psychology	0363
☐ **publicity**	**0037**, 0092
☐ publicize	0037
☐ pull down	0234, 0869
☐ pull out	0602
☐ punctual	0075
☐ **punctuality**	**0075**
☐ punctually	0075
☐ punish	0473
☐ punishment	0451
☐ pursue	0500
☐ **pursuit**	**0500**
☐ push A into doing	1008
☐ **push A to do**	**1008**, 1001
☐ push on	0855
☐ **put A before B**	**0990**
☐ **put A through to B**	
	0976
☐ **put down**	**0852**, 0837
☐ **put forward**	**0871**
☐ put in	0956, 0276
☐ **put off**	**0952**
☐ put on airs	0947
☐ put out	0211
☐ put up with	0275, 0659

Q

☐ qualification	0732
☐ **qualified**	**0732**
☐ qualify	0732
☐ qualify as	0732
☐ quality	0049
☐ **quarantine**	**0570**
☐ quarrel	0025
☐ queer	0349, 0740
☐ query	0073
☐ quest	0500
☐ question	0073, 0704
☐ **questionable**	
	0704, 0389
☐ quick	0299
☐ quit	0677
☐ **quota**	**0485**
☐ quotation	0053, 0602
☐ quote	0053, 0602, 0643

R

☐ radical	0314	0135, 0195, 0599, 0639, 0853, 0876, 0890, 0940
☐ radicalism	0314	
☐ radioactive	0783	☐ reduction 0135
☐ radioactivity	0783	☐ redundancy 0353
☐ rain forest	0440	☐ redundant 0353
☐ rainforest	0440	☐ re-establish 0610
☐ raise		☐ refer to 0643, 0847
0079, 0177, 0628, 0678		☐ refrain from 0939
☐ rally	0261	☐ refuge 0544
☐ random	0327	☐ refugee 0544
☐ ransom	0168, 0446	☐ refund 0450
☐ rash	0739, 0785	☐ refusal 0995
☐ ratio	0515	☐ refuse 0945
☐ rational	0756	☐ refuse to do 0995
☐ reach	0868	☐ regard A as B 0969, 0977
☐ reach out to	0942	☐ regardless 1119
☐ readable	0350	☐ regardless of 1119
☐ real 0313, 0370, 0743		☐ register 0248, 0511
☐ real estate 0413, 0049		☐ register for
☐ realization	0112, 0448	0248, 0511, 0943
☐ rear	0079, 0628	☐ registered 0248, 0511
☐ reasonable		☐ registration 0511, 0248
0362, 0377, 0708, 0763		☐ regular 0806
☐ reasoned	0708	☐ regularly 0806, 0822
☐ reassurance	0604	☐ regulate 0096, 0806
☐ reassure	0604	☐ regulation 0096, 0806
☐ rebuke	0197	☐ reimburse 0450
☐ recess	0140, 0154	☐ reimbursement 0450
☐ recession	0154, 0140	☐ reinforce 0281
☐ reciprocal	0754	☐ reinforcement 0281
☐ reciprocate	0222	☐ reject 0945
☐ reciprocation	0222	☐ related 0290
☐ reciprocity	0222	☐ relation 0420
☐ reckless	0818	☐ relative 0807
☐ recklessly	0818	☐ relatively 0807
☐ recognition	0112, 0448	☐ relaxing 0305
☐ recognize	0112	☐ release 0011, 0237, 0644
☐ recognize A as B	0112	☐ relegate 0582
☐ recompense	0018	☐ relevant 0290, 0329
☐ reconcile	0586	☐ reliability 0167, 0761
☐ reconciliation	0586	☐ reliable 0761, 0400
☐ record	0248	☐ reliance 0526, 0761
☐ recover 0588, 0597, 0910		☐ relic 0402
☐ recruit	0617	☐ relief 0264
☐ reduce		☐ relieve 0264

☐ relieved	0264
☐ relinquish	0225
☐ relocate	0672
☐ relocation	0672
☐ reluctantly	1042
☐ rely	0761
☐ rely on 0761, 0850, 0928	
☐ rely upon	
0761, 0850, 0928	
☐ remainder	0042, 0171
☐ remark	0344
☐ remarkable	
0344, 0291, 0789	
☐ remarkably	0344, 0832
☐ remedy	0087, 0137
☐ remind	0171
☐ remind A about B	0171
☐ remind A of B	0171
☐ reminder	0171
☐ removal	0481
☐ remove	
0124, 0201, 0223, 0481, 0627, 0665, 0863	
☐ renew	0278, 0217
☐ renewable	0278
☐ renewal	0278
☐ renown	0381, 0571
☐ renowned	0381, 0335
☐ reopen	0217, 0278
☐ repair	0493, 0597
☐ repay	0222, 0450
☐ repayment	0450
☐ repeal	0625
☐ replace	0686
☐ represent	0509, 0624
☐ represent A as B	0992
☐ representation	0509
☐ representative	0509
☐ reprimand	0197
☐ reproduce	0079
☐ reputable	0435
☐ reputation	0435
☐ request	0020
☐ require	0461
☐ requirement	0461

どれだけチェックできた？ 1 ☐ 2 ☐

☐ **reschedule** 0654	☐ resuscitate 0610	☐ **rot** 0669, 0199
☐ **resent** 0253	☐ retail 0411	☐ rotten 0669
☐ resentful 0253	☐ **retailer** 0411	☐ rough 0760
☐ resentment 0253	☐ **retain** 0581	☐ roughly 0821
☐ reservation 0069	☐ retention 0581	☐ **routine** 0431
☐ **reserve** 0069	☐ retire 0476, 0677	☐ row 1089
☐ reserve A for B 0069	☐ retired 0476	☐ rubbish 0675
☐ residence 0027	☐ retiree 0476	☐ rude 0331, 0790
☐ **resident** 0027, 0412	☐ **retirement** 0476	☐ ruin 0214, 0483, 0567
☐ residential 0027	☐ **retreat** 0647, 0606, 0665	☐ rule 0096
☐ **resign** 0677, 0902	☐ retrieval 0588	☐ **rule out** 0927
☐ resignation 0476, 0677	☐ **retrieve** 0588	☐ run across 0182, 0919
☐ resist 1024	☐ retrospection 1079	☐ run into 0894
☐ resistance 1024	☐ retrospective 1079	☐ run out 0190
☐ resolute 0695	☐ return 0597	☐ **run through** 0886
☐ resolution 0054	☐ **reveal** 0200, 0219, 0277, 0671	
☐ resolve 0859, 0872	☐ revelation 0200	**S**
☐ resonant 0710	☐ reviewer 0043	☐ **sacrifice** 0629, 0055
☐ **resource** 0008	☐ revival 0610	☐ safe 0696
☐ resourceful 0008	☐ **revive** 0610	☐ safeguard 0508
☐ respect 0425, 0520	☐ revocation 0625	☐ **sail through** 0858
☐ respected 0385	☐ **revoke** 0625	☐ **sanction** 0114
☐ respond 1034	☐ reward 0222	☐ sanitary 0383
☐ response 1034, 1113	☐ rich 0709	☐ sanitation 0383
☐ rest 0042, 0140, 0949	☐ **ridicule** 0645	☐ **satellite** 0150
☐ **rest on** 0949	☐ ridiculous 0645, 0756	☐ satisfaction 0480
☐ rest upon 0949	☐ right away 1081	☐ satisfactory 0362
☐ restart 0217, 0278	☐ **rigid** 0318, 0699, 0713	☐ save 0212, 0247
☐ restful 0305	☐ rigidly 0318	☐ scale 0165
☐ restoration 0597	☐ rigorous 0318	☐ **scan** 0593, 0183, 0627, 0886
☐ **restore** 0597	☐ **rip off** 0845	☐ scandal 0506
☐ **restrain** 0657, 0603	☐ ripe 0703	☐ scandalous 0395
☐ restrain oneself from doing 0657	☐ rip-off 0845	☐ scanner 0593
☐ restrained 0657	☐ rise 0177, 1101	☐ **scarce** 0390
☐ restraint 0603, 0657	☐ risk 0563, 1074	☐ scarcely 0390, 0820
☐ restrict 0502, 0603	☐ risky 0336, 0692	☐ **scatter** 0272, 0630
☐ restrict A to B 0979	☐ rival 0080, 0158	☐ scene 0029
☐ restricted 0502	☐ **rivalry** 0080	☐ schedule 1040
☐ **restriction** 0502, 0455, 0603	☐ **roam** 0241, 0229	☐ **scheme** 0084, 0071
☐ result 0148, 0161, 0882	☐ robbery 0444	☐ scholar 0458
☐ **result in** 0882	☐ robust 0715	☐ scholarly 0458
☐ **resume** 0217, 0278	☐ role 1059	☐ **scholarship** 0458, 0590
☐ resumption 0217	☐ rookie 0617	☐ scowl at 0891
	☐ roomy 0298	☐ **scrap** 0650

☐ scratch	1104	☐ setback	0108	☐ simplicity	0537
☐ scrutinize	0233	☐ setting	0527	☐ simulate	0638
☐ scrutiny	0233	☐ settle	0918	☐ simulation	0638
☐ search	0500, 0941	☐ settle down	0913	☐ simultaneously	1085
☐ seclusion	0060	☐ settlement	0913	☐ sincere	0313
☐ secondary	0542	☐ settler	0514	☐ single out	0924
☐ secondhand	0823	☐ severe		☐ sit back	0848
☐ secret	0388, 0775		0333, 0393, 0713, 0773	☐ site	0029
☐ section	0057	☐ sex	0058	☐ situation	0103, 0459, 0471
☐ sector	0133	☐ shallow	0768, 0312	☐ size	0165
☐ secure	0696, 0207, 0339	☐ shame	0270	☐ size up	0929
☐ security	0696	☐ shape	1092	☐ skeptic	1018
☐ see A as B	0969, 0977	☐ sharp	0333	☐ skeptical	0714
☐ seemingly	0805	☐ shatter	0208	☐ skepticism	1018
☐ segment	0557, 0447	☐ shift	0441	☐ skilled	0348
☐ segmentation	0557	☐ shine	0273	☐ skim	
☐ seize	0579, 0205	☐ shock	0214		0627, 0183, 0593, 0886
☐ seizure	0205, 0579	☐ shocking	0395	☐ slash	0599
☐ select	0797, 0924	☐ shoot down	0893	☐ slaughter	0666
☐ selection	0797	☐ shoplift	0679	☐ slip away	0907
☐ selective	0797	☐ shoplifter	0679	☐ slip out	0851
☐ self-esteem	0531, 0520	☐ shoplifting	0679	☐ slit	0599
☐ self-respect	0531	☐ short	0390	☐ slow down	0284
☐ self-worth	0531	☐ shortage	0541	☐ slump	0245
☐ semester	0553	☐ shortcoming	0131, 0107	☐ sly	0375
☐ senator	0509	☐ shorten A to B	0967	☐ smash	0208
☐ send	0271	☐ show	0261	☐ smooth	0382
☐ sensation	0418	☐ show off	0947	☐ snug	0784
☐ sensational	0418	☐ show up	0915, 0937	☐ social security	0533
☐ sense	0181, 0418	☐ showoff	0947	☐ socialize	0254
☐ sensible	0703	☐ shrink	0195	☐ solace	0530
☐ sentence	0451, 0143	☐ shrinkage	0195	☐ solar	0746
☐ separate	0470	☐ shrivel	0661	☐ solitary	0060
☐ separation	0470	☐ sickness	0017	☐ solitude	0060
☐ sequence	0497	☐ sight	1064	☐ solution	0054, 0087
☐ sequential	0497	☐ sign	0433, 0957	☐ solve	
☐ serene	0351	☐ sign up for	0957, 0943		0054, 0833, 0859, 0872
☐ series	0497	☐ signature	0957	☐ somber	0294
☐ serious	0713, 0773	☐ significance		☐ sometimes	0824
☐ service	0493		0165, 0291, 0832	☐ soothe	0305
☐ serving	0447	☐ significant		☐ soothing	0305
☐ session	0553		0291, 0371, 0758, 0832	☐ soothingly	0305
☐ set back	0108	☐ significantly	0832, 0291	☐ sort	0022
☐ set off	0843, 0668, 0959	☐ similar	0731	☐ sound	0377
☐ set out	0959, 0843	☐ simple	0156, 0694, 0776	☐ source	0454

どれだけチェックできた？ 1 ☐ 2 ☐

☐ souvenir	0488	
☐ space	0298	
☐ spacious	0298	
☐ spare A for B	0069	
☐ sparkle	0273	
☐ sparse	0814	
☐ sparsely	0814	
☐ species	0022	
☐ spectacle	0399	
☐ spectacular	0399	
☐ speed up	0284	
☐ spell out	0920	
☐ spelling	0920	
☐ spend	0423, 0956	
☐ spending	0423	
☐ spine	0099	
☐ splendid	0711	
☐ spoil	0199, 0257, 0567, 0669	
☐ spontaneous	0738	
☐ spontaneously	0738	
☐ spot	0029, 0358, 1081	
☐ spotless	0358	
☐ spread	0272, 0295	
☐ sprinkle	0272	
☐ stability	0339	
☐ stabilize	0339	
☐ stable	0339, 0696	
☐ staff	0438	
☐ stake	1097	
☐ stale	0793	
☐ stance	0119	
☐ stand out	0856, 0765	
☐ standing	0103	
☐ standpoint	0006	
☐ start	0287, 0835, 0911, 0923	
☐ startle	0641	
☐ startling	0641	
☐ state	0103	
☐ stately	0711	
☐ state-of-the-art	0691	
☐ statistical	0013	
☐ statistician	0013	
☐ statistics	0013	
☐ status	0103
☐ staying	0027
☐ steady	0339
☐ steal	0845
☐ stealing	0444
☐ stem	0932
☐ stem from	0932
☐ step aside	0902
☐ step down	0902
☐ stern	0713, 0318, 0773
☐ stick around	0878
☐ stick to	0841, 0877
☐ stick with	0861
☐ stiff	0318
☐ stimulant	0178
☐ stimulate	0178, 0634
☐ stimulate A to do	0634, 1005
☐ stimulating	0178
☐ stimulation	0178
☐ stimulus	0052, 0178
☐ stir up	0925
☐ stock	0069
☐ stop	0179, 0283, 0688
☐ stop by	0958
☐ storage	0416
☐ store	0069, 0416
☐ story line	0071
☐ straight	0374
☐ straightforward	0776
☐ strain	0128
☐ strained	0128
☐ strange	0349, 0740
☐ strategic	0016
☐ strategically	0016
☐ strategist	0016
☐ strategy	0016
☐ stray	0224
☐ strengthen	0281
☐ strenuous	0770, 0715, 0757
☐ strenuously	0770
☐ stress	0128, 0632
☐ strew	0272
☐ strict	0318, 0713
☐ strikingly	0832
☐ stringent	0318
☐ strive for	0953
☐ strive to do	0998, 0993
☐ stroll	0229, 0241
☐ strong	0715
☐ strong point	0063
☐ structure	0153
☐ struggle	0030, 0953, 0993
☐ struggle for	0953
☐ struggle to do	0993, 0998
☐ stuffy	0793
☐ stun	0214
☐ subject	0404, 0788
☐ subjective	0788, 0404, 0524
☐ submission	0652, 0747
☐ submissive	0747, 0652
☐ submit	0652, 0747, 0871, 0921
☐ submit A to B	0990
☐ submit to	0652, 0747, 0955
☐ subordinate	0542
☐ subsequent	0324
☐ subsequently	0324
☐ subside	0865
☐ subsidize	0078
☐ subsidy	0078, 0590
☐ substance	0371
☐ substantial	0371, 0758
☐ substantially	0371
☐ subtle	0720
☐ subtlety	0720
☐ subtly	0720
☐ succeed	0209, 0227, 0642, 0917, 1057
☐ succession	0497
☐ successive	0374
☐ successively	1089
☐ successor	0403
☐ suddenly	0825
☐ sue A for B	

	0971, 0963, 0984	☐ swear to do	1000	☐ theoretically	1094
☐ suffer	0206	☐ **sweep**	0687	☐ therapeutic	0137
☐ suffering	0410	☐ sympathy	0066, 0452	☐ therapist	0137
☐ suggest	0637, 0871	☐ **symptom**	0433	☐ **therapy**	0137, 0087
☐ suggestive	0291	☐ synopsis	0550	☐ therefore	0812
☐ suit	0540, 0971	**T**		☐ thickness	0014
☐ suitable	0340, 0799			☐ thief	0444
☐ summarize	0550	☐ **tackle**	0584	☐ thieve	0444
☐ **summary**	0550	☐ tactics	0016	☐ think of A as B	0969, 0977
☐ summon	0585	☐ take back	0606	☐ think up	0185, 0613
☐ **superficial**	0312, 0768	☐ take down		☐ thinly	0814
☐ superfluous	0353		0234, 0837, 0852, 0869	☐ **thorough**	
☐ superior	0542	☐ take on	0587		0772, 0311, 0314, 0342
☐ superpower	0482	☐ take out	0602	☐ thoroughly	0772, 0827
☐ **supervise**	0255	☐ **take over**	0917	☐ thoughtless	0386
☐ supervision	0255	☐ **take up**	0835	☐ threat	0475
☐ supervisor	0255, 0542	☐ takeover	0917	☐ threaten	0475, 0591
☐ **supplement**	0468	☐ **tangible**	0781	☐ **thrive**	0209, 0227, 0642
☐ supplementary	0468	☐ **target**	0122, 0524	☐ thriving	0209
☐ support	0189, 0236	☐ target A at B	0965	☐ through	0772
☐ supporter	0189	☐ target A on B	0965	☐ throw away	
☐ sure	1093	☐ task	0164		0618, 0650, 0875
☐ surely	0801, 1093	☐ taut	0366	☐ thumb through	0908
☐ surface	0312	☐ teaching	0456	☐ thus	0812
☐ **surpass**	0213, 0246	☐ **tear down**	0869	☐ tight	0366
☐ **surplus**	0042, 0136	☐ teenager	0528	☐ tiny	0316
☐ surprise	0641	☐ temporary	0296	☐ **tip**	0097
☐ surprising	0800	☐ tempt A into B	0968	☐ tire out	0904
☐ surrender	0225	☐ tempt A into doing	1007	☐ tired	0337
☐ surrender to	0880, 1063	☐ **tempt A to do**	1007	☐ tiredness	0077
☐ surround	0527	☐ temptation	1007	☐ together	1085
☐ **surrounding**	0527	☐ tempting	1007	☐ token	0469, 1105
☐ survey	0233	☐ tenacious	0303	☐ tolerance	0659
☐ susceptibility	1022	☐ tend to do	1048, 1054	☐ tolerant	0332, 0659
☐ **suspect**	0111	☐ tender for	0935	☐ **tolerate**	0659, 0275
☐ suspect A of B	0111	☐ **tense**	0366	☐ tone	0866
☐ **suspend**	0179	☐ tension	0128, 0144, 0366	☐ **tone down**	0866
☐ suspension	0179	☐ term	0553, 1108	☐ tool	0238
☐ suspicion	0111	☐ testify	0492	☐ topic	0404
☐ suspicious		☐ **testimony**	0492	☐ top-secret	0775
	0111, 0704, 0714	☐ thaw	0660	☐ torment	0410
☐ **sustain**	0206	☐ **the other way around**		☐ **toss out**	0875
☐ sustainability	0206		1083	☐ total	0308
☐ sustainable	0206	☐ **theft**	0444	☐ **touch on**	0847
☐ sustenance	0206	☐ theme	0404	☐ touch upon	0847

☐ touchable	0781	
☐ trace	0854, 0980	
☐ trace A back to B	0980	
☐ **trace A to B**	**0980**	
☐ track	0854	
☐ **track down**	**0854**	
☐ trade in	0951	
☐ tradition	0005	
☐ traditional	0394	
☐ train	0473	
☐ training	0473	
☐ **tranquil**	**0351**	
☐ tranquilizer	0351	
☐ tranquillity	0351	
☐ **transfer**	**0124**, 0633	
☐ **transform A into B**	**0974**	
☐ transformation	0489, 0974	
☐ transmission	0633	
☐ **transmit**	**0633**	
☐ transpire	0249	
☐ **transplant**	**0614**	
☐ transplantation	0614	
☐ transplanted	0614	
☐ transport	0067, 0667	
☐ **transportation**	**0067**	
☐ trash	0675	
☐ trauma	0330	
☐ **traumatic**	**0330**	
☐ travel	0286	
☐ travel plan	0501	
☐ treasure	0267	
☐ treatment	0087, 0137	
☐ **treaty**	**0562**	
☐ trend	0092	
☐ **tribute**	**0010**	
☐ trifling	0378	
☐ **trigger**	**0589**, 0925	
☐ **triumph**	**0047**, 0631	
☐ triumphant	0047	
☐ trivia	0378	
☐ **trivial**	**0378**	
☐ trouble	0166, 1060	
☐ true	0360	
☐ **tuition**	**0456**	

☐ tuition fee	0456	
☐ tumult	0429	
☐ **turbulence**	**0117**	
☐ turbulent	0117	
☐ turmoil	0429	
☐ turn	1078	
☐ turn A into B	0991	
☐ **turn away**	**0909**	
☐ turn down	0937, 0945	
☐ **turn in**	**0921**, 0652	
☐ **turn out**	**0839**	
☐ turn over	0274	
☐ **turn to**	**0889**	
☐ **turn up**	**0937**, 0915	
☐ turnout	0839	
☐ twinkle	0273	
☐ typical	0509	

U

☐ ultimate	0803	
☐ **ultimately**	**0803**, 0817	
☐ unanimous	0816	
☐ **unanimously**	**0816**	
☐ **unauthorized**	**0700**	
☐ unbelievable	0800	
☐ uncertain	0336	
☐ unclean	0383	
☐ unclear	0693, 0728	
☐ unconditional	0343	
☐ unconventional	0394	
☐ uncover	0200, 0219, 0277	
☐ undamaged	0293	
☐ **undeniable**	**0360**	
☐ under way	0736	
☐ **underestimate**	**0243**	
☐ **undergo**	**0673**, 0941	
☐ underline	0632	
☐ **undermine**	**0591**, 0216	
☐ underrate	0243	
☐ understand	0252, 0833, 0849	
☐ understandable	0297	
☐ understanding	0252	
☐ **undertake**	**0587**	
☐ undertake to do	0587	

☐ undertaking	0409, 0494, 0587	
☐ undervalue	0243	
☐ **unearth**	**0219**, 0200, 0277	
☐ unfavorable	0320, 0365	
☐ unhygienic	0383	
☐ unification	0424	
☐ unimportant	0175, 0378	
☐ union	0507	
☐ unison	1085	
☐ unkind	0386	
☐ unknown	0693	
☐ unlawful	0355	
☐ unlike	1049	
☐ unnecessary	0353	
☐ unpleasant	0325, 0750	
☐ unquestionable	0360	
☐ unreasonable	0354, 0359, 0395, 0756	
☐ unrelated	0329	
☐ unreliable	0761	
☐ unrest	0017	
☐ **unsanitary**	**0383**	
☐ unsmiling	0713	
☐ unstable	0336, 0339	
☐ unsuited	0341	
☐ untidiness	0017	
☐ unusual	0789	
☐ unwillingly	1055	
☐ **up to**	**1109**	
☐ up to date	1096	
☐ **update**	**0682**	
☐ upheaval	0117	
☐ uplift	0177	
☐ **uproar**	**0429**	
☐ upshot	0148, 0161	
☐ up-to-date	0682	
☐ upturn	0532	
☐ urge	1001	
☐ **urge A to do**	**1001**, 1008	
☐ urgency	1001	
☐ urgent	1001	
☐ use	0180, 0648	
☐ useful	0487, 0697	

☐ usefulness	0546	
☐ **usher**	0536, 0611	
☐ utensil	0238	
☐ **utility**	0546, 0648	
☐ utilization	0546, 0648	
☐ **utilize**	0648, 0180, 0546	
☐ **utmost**	0367	

V

☐ vague	0693
☐ **valid**	0763, 0377, 0406
☐ validate	0406, 0763
☐ validation	0406, 0763
☐ **validity**	0406, 0763
☐ **valuable**	0487, 0730
☐ value	0487, 0635, 0730
☐ valueless	0730
☐ vapor	0620
☐ variety	0079, 0128
☐ various	0368
☐ vary	0826
☐ vast	0316, 0387
☐ **vault**	0512
☐ ventilate	0138
☐ **ventilation**	0138
☐ **venture**	0409, 0494
☐ verge	1112
☐ verification	0230
☐ **verify**	0230, 0578
☐ vernacular	0109
☐ **versatile**	0698
☐ versatility	0698
☐ very	0829
☐ viability	0734
☐ **viable**	0734, 0317
☐ **vibrant**	0710
☐ vice	0063, 0346
☐ vicinity	0437, 1110
☐ **vicious**	0346, 0364
☐ victory	0047
☐ view	0977
☐ **view A as B**	0977, 0969
☐ viewpoint	0006
☐ vigor	0715
☐ **vigorous**	0715, 0299

☐ vigorously	0715
☐ violate	0463
☐ **violation**	0463, 0477
☐ violent	0346, 0364
☐ virtual	0811
☐ **virtually**	0811
☐ **virtue**	0063
☐ virtuous	0063
☐ **virus**	0105
☐ visitor	0027
☐ visualize	0268
☐ vital	0291, 0702
☐ vivid	0710
☐ vocation	0748
☐ **vocational**	0748
☐ void	0763
☐ volume	0090
☐ **voluntarily**	0830
☐ voluntary	0334, 0338, 0738, 0830
☐ volunteer	0830
☐ volunteer to do	0830
☐ vote	0169
☐ **voucher**	0469
☐ vow	1000
☐ **vow to do**	1000
☐ **vulgar**	0790
☐ vulnerability	1011

W

☐ waiver	0251
☐ wander	0224, 0229, 0241
☐ want	0541
☐ want to do	1054
☐ **warehouse**	0573
☐ warning	0064
☐ warranty	0265
☐ wave down	0912
☐ **waver**	0251
☐ weak	0302
☐ **wear out**	0904
☐ weariness	0077
☐ weed	0863
☐ **weed out**	0863
☐ weigh up	0929

☐ weird	0349, 0740
☐ **welfare**	0533
☐ well	0829
☐ well-being	0533
☐ well-mannered	0331
☐ **whine**	0580, 0280
☐ wholesaler	0411
☐ **widespread**	0295, 0347, 0707
☐ wilt	0661
☐ win	0047, 0631
☐ **wipe out**	0884, 0186
☐ wipeout	0884
☐ **withdraw**	0606, 0558, 0647, 0665
☐ withdrawal	0558, 0606, 0647
☐ **wither**	0661
☐ **withhold**	0240
☐ without doubt	0801
☐ without fail	0826
☐ wonderful	0800
☐ **work out**	0849, 0833
☐ work together	0658
☐ **workforce**	0438
☐ **workplace**	0426
☐ **worldwide**	0808
☐ worn-out	0337, 0904
☐ worse	0636
☐ **worsen**	0636
☐ **wrap up**	0944
☐ **wreck**	0567
☐ wreckage	0567
☐ write down	0837, 0852, 0940

Y

☐ yearly	0813
☐ **yearn to do**	0994, 0999
☐ yearning	0442, 0994
☐ yield	0955
☐ **yield to**	0955, 0652, 0880

どれだけチェックできた？ 1 ☐ 2 ☐

聞いて覚えるコーパス単熟語

キクタン
英検準1級

発行日	2010年3月31日（初版） 2016年1月22日（第10刷）
編著	一杉武史
編集	英語出版編集部
英文校正	Peter Branscombe、Joel Weinberg、Owen Schaefer
アートディレクション	細山田光宣
デザイン	奥山志乃（株式会社細山田デザイン事務所）
イラスト	shimizu masashi（gaimgraphics）
ナレーション	Chris Koprowski、Julia Yermakov、河原木志穂
音楽制作	東海林敏行（onetrap）
録音・編集	千野幸男（有限会社ログスタジオ）
CDプレス	株式会社学研教育アイ・シー・ティー
DTP	株式会社秀文社
印刷・製本	広研印刷株式会社
発行者	平本照麿
発行所	株式会社アルク 〒168-8611　東京都杉並区永福2-54-12 TEL：03-3327-1101　FAX：03-3327-1300 Email：csss@alc.co.jp Website http://www.alc.co.jp/

・落丁本、乱丁本は弊社にてお取り替えいたしております。
　アルクお客様センター（電話：03-3327-1101　受付時間：
　平日9時～17時）までご相談ください。
・本書の全部または一部の無断転載を禁じます。
・著作権法上で認められた場合を除いて、本書からのコピー
　を禁じます。
・定価はカバーに表示してあります。

©2010 Takeshi Hitosugi/ALC PRESS INC.
shimizu masashi（gaimgraphics）/Toshiyuki Shoji（onetrap）
Printed in Japan.
PC：7010004
ISBN：978-4-7574-1846-2

地球人ネットワークを創る

アルクのシンボル
「地球人マーク」です。

アルクは個人、企業、学校に
語学教育の総合サービスを提供しています。

英語

通信講座
- 1000 HOUR HEARING MARATHON
- TOEIC®対策
- 『イングリッシュ・クイックマスター』シリーズ
- ほか

書籍
- キクタン　ユメタン
- 『起きてから寝るまで』シリーズ
- TOEIC®／TOEFL®／児童英検
- ほか

月刊誌
- ENGLISH JOURNAL

辞書データ検索サービス
- 英辞郎 on the WEB Pro

オンライン英会話
- アルクオンライン英会話

アプリ
- 英会話ペラペラビジネス100
- ほか

会員組織
- CLUB ALC

セミナー
- TOEIC®対策セミナー
- ほか

子ども英語教室
- Kiddy CAT 英語教室

留学支援
- アルク留学センター

学校

e-learning
- ALC NetAcademy 2

学習アドバイス
- ESAC

書籍
- 高校・大学向け副教材

企業

団体向けレッスン
- クリエイティブスピーキング
- ほか

スピーキングテスト
- TSST

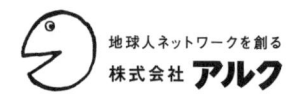

地球人ネットワークを創る
株式会社 **アルク**

▼ サービスの詳細はこちら ▼

website **http://www.alc.co.jp/**

日本語

通信講座	書籍	スピーキングテスト	セミナー
NAFL日本語教師 養成プログラム	**できる 日本語** ほか	**JSST**	**日本語教育 能力検定 試験対策**